Modern
FRENCH
Grammar

Second Edition

Routledge Modern Grammars

Series concept and development – Sarah Butler

Other books in series:

Modern German Grammar, Second Edition
Modern German Grammar Workbook, Second Edition

Modern Italian Grammar
Modern Italian Grammar Workbook

Modern Spanish Grammar, Second Edition
Modern Spanish Grammar Workbook, Second Edition

Modern FRENCH Grammar

A practical guide

Second Edition

Margaret Lang
and Isabelle Perez

Routledge
Taylor & Francis Group

LONDON AND NEW YORK

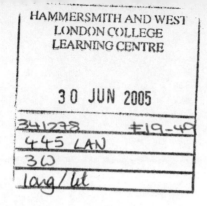
First published 1996
by Routledge

Reprinted 1997, 2000, 2002 (twice), 2003

Second edition published 2004
by Routledge
11 New Fetter Lane, London EC4P 4EE

Simultaneously published in the USA and Canada
by Routledge
29 West 35th Street, New York, NY 10001

Routledge is an imprint of the Taylor & Francis Group

© 1996, 2004 Margaret Lang and Isabelle Perez

Typeset in ITC Stone Serif/Sans by RefineCatch Limited, Bungay, Suffolk
Printed and bound in Great Britain by TJ International Ltd, Padstow, Cornwall

British Library Cataloguing in Publication Data
A catalogue record for this book is available from the British Library

Library of Congress Cataloging in Publication Data
Lang, Margaret, 1940-
    Modern French grammar : a practicle guide/Margaret Lang and Isabelle Perez.—2nd ed.
        p. cm.—(Routledge modern grammars)
Includes index.
    1. French language—Grammar.   2. French language—Textbook for foreign speakers—English.
I. Perez, Isabelle, 1962-.   II. Title.   III. Series.

PC2112.L35 2004
448.2′421—dc22   2003026062

ISBN 0–415–33482–9 (hbk)
        0–415–33162–5 (pbk)

Contents

SECTION A Structures

SECTION B Functions

Contents

Acknowledgements

The authors would like to thank the following for their permission to reproduce extracts from copyright material: Grasset, Paris, Roger Vailland, *Un Jeune Homme Seul*, 1951 (p. 77) *Le Monde* 23.3.95 and 17.9.03 (pp. 83, 88); Plon, Paris, for H. Troyat, *Grandeur Nature*, 1936 (p. 86); *The Guardian* 16.2.95 (p. 104); M. Noailles for G. Moustaki, 'Le Métèque' (p. 134); Editions La Découverte, collection Repères, Paris, for J. Vallin, *La Population française*, 1989 (p. 139); Documentation européenne for P. Fontaine, 'Les Grandes Phases historiques' in *Dix Leçons sur l'Europe*, 1992 (p. 164); *Journal Officiel des Communarités Européennes* for Débats du Parlement européen 15.2.90 (p. 205); *Capital*, August 1994 (p. 245).

Introduction

This book is designed to provide the essential elements of French grammar, for students in the final year of school and in the first and later years of higher education. Advanced learners will find much that is useful for extending their knowledge of French, and for revision. The book is organized in two major sections: a reference section containing the structures of grammar and a section containing functional grammar. Each section includes cross-references to the other.

The reference grammar, which is as comprehensive as possible, has been structured around the noun phrase – dealing with all the elements related to the noun: articles, pronouns, adjectives and numbers – and the verb phrase – dealing with all the elements related to the verb: tenses, mood, participles and adverbs.

The functional grammar is composed of three parts, each demonstrating how to do things with language in order to communicate. The three principal functions identified are exposition, attitude and argumentation. Each of these is divided into smaller function areas related to the principal function.

The functions

Exposition

Communication involves both giving and obtaining information: we make statements and we ask questions about someone or something. This involves

(a) referring to people, things and places
(b) narrating events in some sort of sequence
(c) reporting what we or other people say or think.

In other words, we are giving or obtaining information about who, what, when, how, where and why. Exposition includes three groups of functions identified, very broadly, as *referring, narrating* and *reporting*.

Referring to people, things and places involves giving and obtaining information about physical characteristics, personality, relationships, age, ownership dimensions, quantity and number, quality or distinguishing characteristics, comparison, direction, location and manner.

Narrating involves talking about events or actions in terms of present, past and future time, dates and time, and sequence.

Introduction

Reporting describes what we or other people say and write. Reporting is usually clearly indicated by the presence of an introductory verb. There are many verbs which can introduce reported speech of which the commonest is 'say'. Some of the others are 'think, remind, ask, hope, believe, want, suggest, answer, admit, forget'. Interrogative structures are included in this section because we need to know how to obtain information, and to do this we ask questions, and negation is included because, of course, sometimes we need to say that something is not the case.

Attitude

Expressing an attitude towards someone or something usually means that we are introducing a personal, subjective element into communication: we are indicating our reaction to someone or something, we are evaluating, and making judgements – in a non-detached way. And we may do so spontaneously or intentionally.

Closely related to attitudes are the emotions and feelings which most of us experience and express from time to time. These, too, are personal and subjective, and, on occasion, they may in fact be attitudes. The focus of this section is, then, on the communication of attitudes, emotions and feelings and how we express them. We look first at the ways in which we *greet* or *take leave of* people when we are speaking or writing to them. Then we turn to the ways in which we express *congratulations* and *appreciation, apologies* and *sympathy*, and *surprise* and *disgust*. Finally, we consider ways in which we express contrasting attitudes, emotions and feelings: *likes, dislikes* and *preference, love* and *hate, enthusiasm* and *indifference, hopes* and *fears, approval* and *disapproval*.

Argumentation

Effective communication usually requires a certain amount of planning, and this involves the need to

(a) structure what we want to say or write
(b) determine the best strategies to employ
(c) select the means of expression most suited to the structure, to the strategies, and, above all, to a specific context or situation.

The structure is the *plan* in what we are saying or writing, the strategy is the *function* we are employing, and the means of expression is the *grammatical* or *lexical* structure (for example, verb construction, noun phrase) which is most appropriate for the plan and the function.

It may be that a single word is enough to achieve what we want, but more frequently we are involved in a discussion or explaining something or arguing a case and so on. Often, there is simply not enough time to plan carefully what we want to say – though there is more time when we are writing. Also, it would be virtually impossible to try to learn every function and every means of expression. However, if we are familiar with some kinds of plan, with various types of function, and with some of the means for expressing them, then we can not only use them ourselves, but recognize them when we are listening to or reading what other people are saying or writing.

There are many kinds of plan in what is said and written, and these plans vary in complexity. Examples of plans, or planning, are the following:

(a) creating a clear overall structure with an introduction, middle section and conclusion
(b) listing a series of points
(c) putting another point of view and defending it
(d) proceeding from cause to effect, or vice versa.

In some situations, parts of plans may be enough and indeed appropriate for achieving what we want, for example, only part of (c). At other times we may need to put into action a fully developed plan, for example, a combination of (a)–(d). Finally, we must remember that there is no single, perfect plan suitable for every situation or context.

The functions available to us when we want to achieve something in argumentation are many. We may, for example, want to agree, indicate doubt, reject, criticize. We may wish to emphasize, persuade, influence, express obligation. Whatever it may be, whether we are initiating a discussion, making a speech, contributing to a conversation, reacting to a comment, broadcast or report, we have at our disposal a wide range of possible moves. We cannot, of course, know how someone is going to react to what we are saying or writing, so we need to have access to a range of responses in order to adapt to an unforeseen reaction, and respond appropriately.

The section on argumentation provides a comprehensive range of functions – and the means of expressing them – which are in fairly common use. You will recognize them when people are speaking and writing. It is recommended that you try to put them into practice in speech and writing whenever appropriate. The functions are presented as follows – *agreeing* and *disagreeing, asserting* and *confirming, admitting* and *conceding, correcting* and *protesting, contradicting* and *criticizing, suggesting* and *persuading,* expressing *volition, permission* and *obligation, doubt* and *certainty, logical relations, opposition,* and *structuring.*

The examples

The examples in the reference section are simple illustrations of the grammar structure in question. In the functional section the examples are selected from contemporary spoken and written French to demonstrate the function in question. They are actual examples which have been used in our own experience, and they are quoted within as much context as possible to illustrate the function and the related grammar structure.

The translations

The examples in both the reference and the functional sections are translated into English. In the reference section, translations are kept as close as possible to the French, in the functional section, on the other hand, where there is usually a substantial amount of context, the English equivalent is provided, rather than a direct and possibly, therefore, stilted version of the original.

Forms and functions

The forms in any living language are flexible and changing. At any one time they can vary according to the individual speaker or writer, to the part of the country he/she comes from or lives in, and indeed to fashion. There is seldom only one way of saying or writing something, and not very often a one-to-one equivalence of form and function.

This is clearly illustrated in the section on the imperative (A.44) where this one grammar structure is shown to have a variety of functions: the imperative form can be used to express an order, an instruction, an invitation, etc. It is also illustrated in the many functions of each of the tenses. Similarly, in the functional section, many forms are suggested for expressing one function: giving directions (B.49.10), for example, can be expressed through the imperative, the future tense, a combination of the two, etc.

Just as there is a network of relations between forms and functions, so there is a network of functions related to each single function. Agreeing (B.63.1), for example, is naturally associated with its opposite – disagreeing (B.63.2), and then also with a combination of the two – agreeing to differ (B.63.3)

Register

Register refers by and large to the different vocabulary and grammar structures we use when we are talking or writing to different people, and the levels of formality and informality we use. For example, we would be more formal with a teacher, a doctor, a policeman, at an interview . . ., but fairly informal with members of our family, friends or when simply chatting. We usually take into account the status, age, and the relationship we have with other people, and the situation we are in, and we automatically adjust our language to them.

At times, we switch from formality to informality, when, for example, we begin to feel more comfortable with a person, or from informality to formality if, for example, a conversation with our bank manager switches from friendly conversation to a request for an increase in a loan.

What we are doing is quite normal and acceptable and is simply adapting to a situation.

In the grammar it is not possible to cover the wide range of levels that exist between formality and informality, but we have indicated in the examples where the register is formal or informal. Otherwise, examples should be taken as standard register – the register used by an average, educated speaker or writer.

> Don't you want to take them round all the museums?
> **Tu veux pas les balader dans tous les musées?** (informal)
> **Voulez-vous leur faire visiter tous les musées?** (formal)

How to use this book

This book brings together two sets of guidelines on the French language:

> A – A reference grammar covering the major points which need to be mastered so that you get things right.
> B – A functional grammar covering the major types of communication you may want or need to carry out.

At your disposal, then, you have the essentials of grammar (section A) and applications of the grammar in a wide selection of functions (section B). When we were preparing this book, we kept in mind the frequent changes which any living language undergoes, and we have, therefore, included comments on exceptions to the guidelines. And, wherever appropriate, we have included informal ways of saying or writing something. The majority of examples have cross-references to information concerning one or more grammar points or concerning additional details on the function.

How, then, will you use the book? If, for example, you want to greet someone you look up B.54.1. In this section you will find a number of suggestions on different ways of saying 'Hi!' or 'Good morning!', for example. It's not very difficult to know how to say hello, of course, but, are you aware of the difference between **Bonjour!** and **Bonsoir!**? On the other hand, you might want to persuade someone to do something. To find a suitable way of doing this you look up B.68.3 and you will again find a number of suggestions for persuading, and cross-references to the appropriate grammar guideline. When you are looking at the functions, we suggest that you also consider the much longer context that is provided to see what happens to a grammatical form when it is in use.

There are other ways of saying and writing the same things – the examples given here are only suggestions, and you are bound to come across other means of expression the more you come into contact with French either at university or in your professional life. We recommend that you consider the suggestions provided here, select the form, or forms, that suit you best and learn them; when you meet alternative ways of saying or writing something, add them to your repertoire.

Before the verb tables we have included a section with the sounds of French, and several words for you to practise the sounds. Your teacher will be able to help you with them.

Glossary

Many of the terms used in this grammar are explained at the beginning of the section in which they are used, but there are some terms which are not explained in a specific section because they occur in several sections, and there are some which may cause difficulty for students. The short list which follows includes the terms which we think need special attention. We have assumed that most students using this grammar are familiar with most of the traditional grammar terms such as noun, verb, adjective.

Adverb
A word or phrase which gives information about how, where and/or when something occurs. There are adverbs of manner, place, time, degree, duration and frequency. Adverbs can modify a verb (**faire *avec soin***), an adjective (***très* difficile**), or another adverb (***beaucoup* trop**). Adverbs are always invariable, unlike some other parts of speech, that is, they never change their spelling to agree with another part of speech.

Antecedent
A word or group of words which precedes another word or group of words. Relative pronouns, or words such as **ce**, have antecedents to which they refer back (***L'homme* qui a donné un pourboire n'a pas beaucoup d'argent**).

Apposition
The placing of a word or phrase directly beside another word or phrase in order to provide more information about the other one (***Jacques Chirac, Président* de la République**). There is no article between the words in apposition.

Cohesion
The linking of words, phrases, sentences and paragraphs by means of **cohesive devices**, which may be clauses, adverbs, pronouns, negatives, etc. (the adverbs include **et, mais, par contre, d'abord**).

Complement
A word or phrase which completes the meaning of, or gives more information about, something. The complement may be a word in apposition (see above), a direct object (**Elle a mangé *la pomme***), an indirect object (**Il le *leur* a vendu**), the agent in a passive sentence (**La tarte a été volée *par le petit garçon***). . . .

Conjugation
This refers to all the endings of a verb. Verbs are usually classified according to one of four main conjugations in French: **-er, -ir, -re, -oir**. Each of the conjugations has its own set of six endings for each tense. Regular verbs have the set of endings which belong to a

particular conjugation, so grammar books are able to give a model verb for each conjugation which all the regular verbs of that conjugation will follow (regular -er verbs follow **donner**, for example). Irregular verbs are those which do not follow either the stem or the endings of a conjugation. The most useful irregular verbs are included in verb tables in grammar books.

Determiners
These are words which are part of the noun group. There are many of them in French – all the articles (**le, un, du** . . .); the possessive adjectives (**mon, ton, son** . . .); the demonstrative adjectives (**ce, cet, cette** . . .); the interrogative and exclamatory adjective **quel** (as in *Quelle* **maison?/!**); indefinite adjectives (**certain, chaque, différents, divers, maint, plusieurs, quelque, tout**); **aucun**, normally in the singular (**Elle n'a aucun talent**); the cardinal numbers used as adjectives (as in **deux journaux**).

Direct and indirect objects
The direct object is a noun or pronoun referring to a person or thing directly affected in some way by an action. The direct object is never introduced by a preposition (**Il a lu** *le livre*) The object is indirect when it is introduced by a preposition, usually à or de (**Nous le donnons** *à nos parents*. **Ça dépend** *de nos parents*). Indirect object pronouns are **me, te, lui, nous, vous, leur.** These pronouns are not preceded by à – it is built into the pronoun (**Nous le** *leur* **donnons**). Following **de**, and other prepositions, the emphatic pronouns are used (**Ça dépend de** *toi*).

Finite
Refers to the many parts of verbs which have endings. These endings indicate whether the subject is singular or plural, the tense and the mood. The **infinitive** is the part of the verb which ends in **-er, -ir, -re, -oir**, and in this case there is no finite ending giving information about whether the subject is singular or plural, or the tense.

Gender and number
These are very important grammar concepts in French. If you forget to make adjectives agree with nouns or verbs with subjects, then you have simply made mistakes, and that can cost you marks! Gender in French is either masculine (**le, il** . . .), or feminine (**la, elle** . . .), and all nouns are masculine or feminine, and adjectives have to agree with their noun. Number refers to whether a noun or pronoun is singular (just one person, thing or action), or plural (two or more people, things or actions). Verbs have to agree with their noun or pronoun subject.

Impersonal verb
A verb of which the subject is **il** 'it' (**il faut** 'it is necessary'). The impersonal verb can sometimes become personal by the addition of a personal pronoun (**il me faut** 'I must').

To modulate
To change or influence the meaning of a word or phrase in some way. There are various ways of doing this, using nouns, adjectives, verbs or adverbs which have specific nuances. You can also, for example, in greeting and leave-taking – merely by altering the intonation you use – make what you say courteous or discourteous, friendly or aggressive. A slight change of meaning is called a *nuance* (of meaning). You can achieve a different nuance simply by adding, or changing, the intonation you use.

Mood

This refers to the different forms in the conjugation of a verb which indicate the functions for which the verb is used. So, you have the indicative mood (fact), the subjunctive mood (non-fact), the interrogative mood (questions), the conditional mood (conditions and hypotheses), the imperative mood (orders). The mood of the verb can be changed according to what you want to express; for example, fact, non-fact, questions.

Transitive and intransitive verbs

Verbs can be transitive or intransitive. A transitive verb is a verb with a direct object (**Il a lu le livre**). An intransitive verb does not have an object (**Il travaille bien**). Verbs may be directly transitive (**Il a lu le livre. Mange ta soupe**) or indirectly transitive (**Pense à nous**).

Almost all normally transitive verbs can be used intransitively (**Il boit un verre. Il ne boit pas**). And some normally intransitive verbs can be used transitively (**Il sort. Il sort sa voiture**).

Abbreviations used in the grammar

f – feminine, m – masculine, s – singular, pl – plural
qn – quelqu'un, qch – quelque chose

Section A

Structures

I

The noun group

1 Articles

French has three articles: the definite article, the indefinite article and the partitive article. They agree with nouns in gender and number. In general, they are used in a similar way to English articles, but there are several important differences.

1.1 Forms

	Definite	Indefinite	Partitive
Masculine singular	**le** (**l'**)	**un**	**du** (**de l'**)
Feminine singular	**la** (**l'**)	**une**	**de la** (**de l'**)
Plural	**les**	**des**	**des**
		+ de/d'	**+ de/d'**

2 The definite article

The definite articles are **le, la, les** 'the'. Contracted forms are used when the prepositions **de** 'of, from' or **à** 'to' (and sometimes 'from': **emprunter à** 'to borrow from') precede the articles **le, les**: **de + le > du, de + les > des, à + le > au, à + les > aux**.

C'est le livre *du* professeur.	It's the teacher's book.
Ce sont les copies *des* étudiants.	They are the students' papers.

English frequently uses 's (singular) or s' (plural) to indicate possession, rather than 'of the'. It would sound odd to say: 'It is the book of the teacher'.

Elle parle *au* président.	She is speaking to the president/ chairman.
Nous avons donné les billets *aux* enfants.	We have given the tickets to the children.

But there is no change when **de** or **à** precede **la** or **l'**:

La porte *de l'*école est fermée.	The school door is shut.
Elle va *à la* maison.	She is going home.

2.1　**Contracted forms**

When they precede words beginning with a vowel or a mute **h**, **le** and **la** are shortened to **l'** (see **81.1**):

*l'*issue	the exit	*l'*accident	the accident
*l'*histoire	history, the story	*l'*homme	man, the man

NOTE　The articles are not necessarily translated into English.

2.2　**Place of the article**

The article precedes nouns, and adjectives which precede nouns:

la petite table	the little table	*le grand* garçon	the big boy

but note that they *follow* **tout, tous, toute(s)** 'all, every, the whole' (see **11.1**):

tout le vin	all the wine	*toute la* famille	the whole family
*tout l'*argent	all the money	*toutes les* filles	all the girls
tous les mois	every month		

2.3　**How the definite articles are used**

The definite article refers to specific people or things:

Le livre est sur *la* table.　　The book is on the table.

In lists of nouns, the article is usually repeated before each noun:

Il aime *les* chats, *les* chiens et *les* chevaux.　　He likes cats, dogs and horses.

but increasingly today, in written French, the article is omitted from lists:

Chats, chiens, chevaux, il les aime tous.　　Cats, dogs and horses – he loves them all.

2.4　**Differences between French and English articles**

In certain contexts French and English articles are used differently.

(a)　where the noun is used in a general sense:

*L'*herbe est verte.	Grass is green.
Aime-t-il *le* vin?	Does he like wine?
Elle aime *la* musique.	She loves music.
Les ordinateurs deviennent de moins en moins chers.	Computers are becoming less and less expensive.

(b)　with parts of the body, or mind, where English uses the possessive adjective ('my, your . . .') French uses the definite article (see **49.1**):

Il secoua *la* tête.	He shook his head.
Ouvre *les* yeux.	Open your eyes.
Il a froid *aux* pieds.	He has cold feet.
Elle a mal *à la* tête.	She has a headache.
Elle a perdu *la* mémoire.	She has lost her memory.
Il souffre *du* dos.	He has back problems.

and with reflexive verbs (see **42.3** for agreement of participle, **49.5e**) referring to the owner:

Elle s'est lavé *les* cheveux.	She washed her hair.

When something is done to someone else, that other person is indicated by including an indirect object pronoun (see **49.5e**):

Elle *lui* a saisi la main.	She took his/her hand.
Elle *lui* a lavé les cheveux.	She washed his/her hair.

The definite article is also used with parts of the body in description following **avoir** (see **49.1**):

Le bébé *a les* mains dodues.	The baby has chubby hands.
Elle *a les* cheveux longs.	She has long hair.

Note the use of the possessive adjective **mon, ton** . . . 'my, your . . .' with verbs other than **avoir**:

Il *caressa sa* longue barbe noire.	He stroked his long black beard.

And note the following descriptive phrases where English uses 'with' (see **49.1**):

la femme *aux* yeux verts	the woman with the green eyes
la maison *aux* fenêtres ouvertes	the house with the open windows
Il marchait *les* mains derrière *le* dos.	He was walking with his hands behind his back.

French normally uses the singular form of nouns if they refer to something of which we have only one, e.g. **la** *vie* 'life', **la** *tête* 'head/face', **le** *cou* 'neck':

Elle leur a sauvé *la* vie.	She saved their lives.

(c) in many expressions of time, and with seasons, dates and festivals (see **50.4**):

à trois heures *du* matin/*de l'*après-midi	at three in the morning/ afternoon
Il arrivera vers *les* sept heures.	He'll arrive about seven o'clock.
Elle le fera pendant *la* semaine.	She will do it during the week.

Note the English equivalent with the use or omission of the articles:

la semaine dernière/prochaine	last/next week
au jour *le* jour	from day to day
Elle travaille *le* matin.	She works in the morning(s).
Ils viennent *le* jour.	They come during the day.
tous *les* vendredis	every Friday
toutes *les* semaines	every week
tous *les* deux jours	every second/other day

but

Elle le rencontre trois fois par semaine.	She meets him three times a week.

Some examples with the seasons:

L'hiver est merveilleux.	Winter is wonderful.
On y va l'été prochain.	We are going there next summer.

The article is omitted with en: *en* **hiver**, *en* **été**, *en* **automne** 'in winter, summer, autumn', but not in *au* **printemps** 'in spring'.

Some examples with dates and use of the article:

Nous sommes *le* mardi 11 décembre.	It's Tuesday, 11th December.
le **26 mai 1968**	26th May 1968
Le **jeudi on va au marché.**	On Thursdays we go to (the) market. (every Thursday)
On se voit *le* 7.	See you on the 7th.

but no article

Nous sommes mardi.	It's Tuesday.
Il me le donnera jeudi.	He'll give it to me on Thursday.
lundi dernier	last Monday

Some examples with festivals, which are usually feminine:

à *la* Toussaint	at Hallowe'en/on All Saints' Day
à *la* Pentecôte	at Whitsun

but

à **Noël**	at Christmas
à **Pâques**	at Easter

(d) in certain expressions of price, pay, quantity and speed:

Cela se vend à 30 euros *le* kilo.	That costs 30 euros a kilo.
Cela se vend à 2 euros cinquante *les*100 grammes.	That costs 2 euros fifty (for) a hundred grammes.
Ce tissu coûte 500 euros *le* mètre.	This material is 500 euros a metre.

but

Il est payé à *l'*heure.	He is paid by the hour.
La voiture roulait à 100 km/h. (you would *say* **100 kilomètres heure**)	The car was travelling at 60 mph.

or

Elle roulait à 80 à *l'*heure.	It was going at 50 mph.

(e) with names of towns and cities 'from, to/in' are expressed by **de**, **à**: 'from Paris' *de* **Paris**, 'to/in Paris' *à* **Paris**. But if the town or city is qualified by an adjective, the article is used: *le* **vieux Paris** 'the old part(s) of Paris' (see **49.10, 49.11**). The names of some towns and cities include the article as part of the name. In such cases the rules for **de**, **à** and the article (see **2**) are followed:

Il revient *du* Mans, *de La* Rochelle, *des* Echelles.	He is just back from Le Mans, La Rochelle, Les Echelles.
Elle habite *Le* Havre.	She lives in Le Havre.
Elle va *au* Havre.	She is going to Le Havre.
Il est *à La* Rochelle.	He is in La Rochelle.

With countries and regions the article is usually included if the name of the country is masculine singular, or masculine or feminine plural:

Il revient *des* Philippines.	He is just back from the Philippines.
Elle va *au* Portugal.	She is going to Portugal.

But when names of countries and regions are feminine and singular – and most of them are – **en** is used for 'to/in' and there is no article: **aller/demeurer** *en* **Allemagne**, *en* **Ecosse**, *en* **Charente** 'to go to/live in Germany, Scotland, the Charente'. **De** is used for 'from' and there is no article: **revenir** *de* **Russie**, *d'***Espagne**, *de* **Provence**, 'to return from Russia, Spain, Provence'.

NOTE   If the town or country is qualified by an adjective, the article is used: *la* **Chine moderne** 'modern China'. The article is also used when expressing north, south, east and west: *le* **nord** *de la* **France** 'the north of France', *le* **sud** *de l'***Angleterre** 'the south of England'.

There is no precise pattern in some expressions. They simply have to be learned. Some examples:

les vins *de* **France**	the wines of France/French wines
l'histoire *de* **France**	the history of France/French history

(Many phrases have the pattern **de** + noun which is very similar to an adjective: **une écharpe** *de* **soie blanche** 'a white silk scarf', **une maison** *de* **campagne** 'a house in the country'.)

but

la géographie *de la* **France**	the geography of France/French geography
la capitale *de la* **France**	the capital of France/the French capital

and

le président *de la* **République**	the president of France/the French president

There is a rule of thumb for a few phrases: feminine countries – *no* article, masculine countries – *include* an article:

la reine *d'***Angleterre**	the Queen of England
l'ambassade *d'***Autriche**	the Austrian embassy

but

l'empereur *du* Japon	the Emperor of Japan
l'ambassade *du* Sénégal	the Senegalese embassy

(f) in titles, forms of address, and qualified proper nouns:

le général de Gaulle	General de Gaulle
As-tu connu *le* Président Mitterrand?	Did you know President Mitterrand?
Voilà *le* docteur Knock.	Here/there is Doctor Knock.
M. *le* Président . . .	(Mr) President, . . .
Messieurs *les* délégués . . .	Delegates, . . .
le vieux M. Guiat	old Mr Guiat
la petite Isabelle	little Isabelle

But the article is normally omitted before a noun in apposition:

le général de Gaulle, Président de la république	General de Gaulle, (the) President of France
Paris, capitale de la France	Paris, the capital of France

Articles are not used in titles such as **Elizabeth II** 'Elizabeth the Second', **Henri IV** 'Henry the Fourth': in French you would *say* **Elizabeth deux, Henri quatre**.

(g) with names of languages, use of the article is also variable, but it is normally omitted after **parler**:

Parlez-vous italien?	Do you speak Italian?
Il ne parle pas français.	He doesn't speak French.
Il est difficile de trouver un équivalent en anglais.	It is difficult to find an equivalent in English/an English equivalent.

but

Apprenez-vous *l'*espagnol à l'école?	Are you learning Spanish at school?
***L'*allemand est une langue compliquée.**	German is a complicated language.

Note the use of capital letters in English, but not in French, for names of languages. Capitals are used in French *only* if referring to a human being – whatever his/her nationality:

le Français, la Française	the Frenchman, the Frenchwoman
le français	(the) French (language)
français, française(s)	French (adjective)

(h) with meals, games and musical instruments:

pendant *le* dîner	during dinner
jouer *au* tennis	to play tennis
jouer *du* violon	to play the violin

(i) with other parts of speech to form nouns:

les pauvres	the poor (people)
le manger et *le* boire	food and drink

les blessés	the injured
les dires	statements, sayings
le savoir	knowledge
le rouge	red (colour), red wine
le primaire, *le* secondaire	the primary, secondary level of education

(j) note that if the nouns are qualified, by a relative clause for example, **de** + the definite article are used:

Il a bu une carafe *du* vin *qu'on a acheté en Australie.*
He drank a carafe of the wine we bought in Australia.

Un ciel couvert *des* nuages *qui annoncent une tempête.*
A sky full of storm clouds.

3   The indefinite article

The indefinite articles are **un(e)**, **des**, **de/d'** 'a, an, some, any'. Indefinite articles are repeated in lists; their English equivalents are often omitted.

J'ai *un* hérisson et *un* chat à la maison.
I have a hedgehog and a cat at home.

Il y a *des* livres intéressants dans ce magasin.
There are some interesting books in this shop.

***Une* femme m'a téléphoné ce soir.**
A woman telephoned me this evening.

Ya-t-il *des* voitures devant la mairie?
Are there (any) cars in front of the town hall?

3.1   Differences between French and English indefinite articles

In certain contexts French and English articles are used differently.

(a) the article is used with abstract nouns qualified by an adjective:

un équilibre parfait	perfect balance/equilibrium
avec *une* grande émotion	full of emotion

(b) the article is not used when talking about occupations, religions, nationality:

Il est professeur.	He is a teacher.
J'ai été nommé ministre.	I've been appointed minister.
Son fils est protestant.	His/her son is a Protestant.
Sa femme est écossaise.	His wife is Scottish.

but when the noun is qualified, the article *is* used:

Son cousin est *un* peintre célèbre.	His/her cousin is a famous painter.

Note the alternative possibilities:

Il est député./C'est *un* député.	He is a member of the National Assembly.
Elle est italienne./C'est *une* Italienne.	She's (an) Italian.

(c) the article is also omitted when two nouns are in apposition:

Le gouvernement, représentant du peuple, n'a pas le droit de lui refuser un référendum.
The government, the representative of the people, does not have the right to refuse them a referendum.

(d) the article is used for emphasis:

Elle a *des* pieds!	What feet she's got!
Il fait *un* temps!	What amazing weather!

(e) the singular forms **un** and **une** are the same as the number 'one' – as opposed to another number:

Il a bu *un* verre de vin.	He drank a/one glass of wine.

(f) there is no article after the exclamatory **quel!** 'what (a/an)!':

***Quel* imbécile!**	What an idiot!
***Quelle* coïncidence!**	What a coincidence!
***Quelles* drôles d'histoires!**	What strange tales!
***Quels* hommes distingués!**	What distinguished men!

4   The partitive article

The partitive articles are **du, de la, des, de/d'** 'some, any'. Before a word beginning with a vowel or a mute **h, du** and **de la > de l':** *de l'*honneur 'honour', *de l'*ail 'garlic', *de l'*herbe 'grass', *de l'*eau 'water'. The article may be omitted in English, but not in French. The article is repeated in lists.

Il a demandé *du* sucre et *du* lait.	He asked for (some) sugar and milk.
Tu veux *de la* moutarde et *du* sel?	You want (some, any) mustard and salt?

4.1   How the indefinite and partitive articles are used

(a) in a negative context **un, une, du, de la, des > de/d'** when the noun they precede is made negative, and their meaning is 'no, not a, not any':

pas *de* monnaie, plus *d'*eau	no change, no more water
Il n'a pas *d'*argent.	He hasn't any money.
Elle n'a plus *de* patience, *d'*humour, *de* tendresse.	She has no patience, humour or affection left.

But if the speaker or writer intends the negative to focus on something in the sentence other than the noun, the articles remain unchanged:

Il ne m'a pas donné *de* conseils.	He didn't give me any *advice*.
Il ne m'a pas donné *des* **conseils, il me les a vendus!**	He didn't *give* me any advice, he *sold* it to me!

(b) the articles also remain unchanged when expressing a contrast:

Elle n'achète pas *du* vin mais *de la* bière.
She doesn't buy wine, she buys beer.

Elle n'a pas donné *des* livres mais *des* CD pour l'anniversaire de son neveu.
She didn't give books to her nephew for his birthday, she gave him CDs.

(c) when the article **un**(**e**) expresses a number, there is no change:

Le gouvernement n'avait pas *un* député honnête.
The government did not have one honest member.

Il n'y avait pas *une* femme au gouvernement.
There was not a single woman in the government.

Note the meanings in the following examples:

Elle n'a pas *une* paire de chaussures. Elle en a trente.
She doesn't have one pair of shoes. She has thirty.

Elle n'a pas *de* chaussures. Elle n'a que des pantoufles.
She hasn't any shoes. She only has slippers.

(d) the articles are not changed when the negative form used is **ne . . . que** 'only':

Elle *n'*a *qu'un* mouchoir.	She has only one handkerchief.
Elle *ne* vend *que des* chapeaux.	She only sells hats.
Il *ne* boit *que du* vin.	He only drinks wine.

(e) after **ni . . . ni** 'neither . . . nor' or **sans** 'without' the partitive articles are omitted (see **53a**):

Elle ne prend *ni* sel, *ni* poivre, *ni* moutarde.	She doesn't take salt, pepper or mustard.
Il boit du thé *sans* lait.	He drinks tea without milk./He doesn't take milk in his tea.
Il est sorti *sans* chapeau.	He has gone out without a hat.

But if the noun is qualified in some way the articles are included:

Elle est sortie *sans un* chapeau *qui pourrait la protéger*.
She has gone out without a hat which could give her some protection.

Nous n'avons *ni le* temps *ni l'* argent *pour le faire*.
We have neither the time nor the money to do it.

If the verb is **être**, the articles remain unchanged:

Ce n'*est* pas *un* désastre.	It's not a disaster.
Ce ne *sont* pas *des* chaussures.	They're not shoes.

Note that when the definite articles **le, la, les** are preceded by **de** in verb constructions such as **se souvenir de** 'to remember', **parler de** 'to speak about', they are changed to **du, de la, de l', des**. They remain in these forms in a negative context:

Nous *ne* parlions *pas des* victimes de la guerre.
We were not speaking about the victims of the war.

Elle *n'a pas* peur *des* chiens.
She is not afraid of dogs.

4.2 Forms of the indefinite and partitive articles when an adjective precedes a noun

The indefinite and partitive articles **des > de/d'** when an adjective precedes a noun:

Elle a *de grands* yeux bleus.	She has big blue eyes.
Il nous raconte toujours *d'intéressantes* histoires.	He always tells us interesting stories.
J'ai eu *de ses* nouvelles.	I've had some news about him/her.

Note that there are some exceptions to this rule when the adjective and noun form a unit:

C'est *du* bon café!	It's good coffee!
des petits pains	rolls

If the adjective follows the noun, or is virtually part of it, **des** remains unchanged.

Il nous raconte toujours *des* histoires *incroyables*.	He always tells us unbelievable stories.

and **des** always > **d'** before **autre(s)**:

On a *d'autres* devoirs à faire.	We have (more) other homework.
Il en a *d'autres*.	He has others/more of them.

4.3 Forms of the partitive articles in expressions of quantity

The partitive articles > **de/d'** in expressions of quantity (see **21, 49.7**).

(a) with adverbs such as **assez de** 'enough', **autant de** 'as much, as many', **beaucoup de** 'a lot of, many', **combien de?** 'how much, how many?', **moins de** 'less', **(un) peu de** '(a) little', **plus de** 'more', **tant de** 'as much/many, so much/many', **trop de** 'too much/many':

Combien de gens?	How many people?
peu de gens	few people

Note that **bien** 'a lot of, many' is followed by the full partitive:

Il a *bien du* mal à suivre les cours d'allemand.
He is having a lot of difficulty following the German classes.

(b) with adjectives which express an amount, or lack, of something, such as **entouré de** 'surrounded by', **couvert de** 'covered in/with', **vide de** 'empty of, lacking in':

vide de sens	meaningless
rempli de livres	full of books

(c) with nouns such as **une bouteille de** 'a bottle of', **un manque de** 'a lack of':

une bouteille de (**vin**) **rouge**	a bottle of red wine
un manque de **ressources**	a lack of resources

Forms of the partitive articles after indefinite, neuter and negative pronouns

De/d' is also used after indefinite, neuter and negative pronouns: **quelqu'un** 'someone', **quelque chose** 'something', **ceci/cela** 'this/that', **ce qui/ce que** 'what', **que** 'what', **quoi?** 'what?', **personne** 'nobody', **rien** 'nothing':

*quelqu'un d'*intéressant	someone interesting
*quelque chose d'*acceptable	something acceptable
*rien d'*urgent	nothing urgent
Quoi de neuf?	What's new?
*Tout ce qu'*il avait *de* valable a été volé.	Everything valuable he had has been stolen.

Note the expression **la plupart de** 'most of' which is followed by the full partitive (the verb is plural) (see **22.3.1**):

La plupart des **étudiants** *ont* **réussi dans les trois matières.**
Most of the students have passed in the three subjects.

And note the preposition **d'après** 'according to':

D'après **la météo il va pleuvoir.**
According to the weather forecast it's going to rain.

Articles are omitted from many expressions in French, of which the following represent a very small selection:

rendre service à	to help	**tomber par terre**	to fall down
faire signe de	to indicate	**avoir envie de**	to want to
mettre fin à	to end	**en auto**	by car
en vélo/à bicyclette	by bicycle	**sous prétexte de**	on the pretext of
par hasard	by chance	**sans gêne**	without embarrassment

soit indifférence, *soit* ressentiment	either indifference or resentment
Plus il crie, *moins* elle écoute.	The more he shouts, the less she listens.
Plus elle travaille, *plus* elle gagne.	The more she works, the more she earns.

5 Demonstrative adjectives

There are three singular forms but only one plural form of the demonstrative adjective. They agree in gender and number with the noun, and the English equivalent is 'this, these, that, those', or simply 'the'.

Forms

	Singular	Plural
Masculine	ce (cet)	ces
Feminine	cette	ces

The form **cet** is used before masculine singular nouns beginning with a vowel or a mute **h**: **cet enfant** 'this child', **cet hommage** 'this tribute', **cette addition** 'this addition', **cette habitation** 'this house', **ces amis** 'these friends', **ces activités** 'these activities', **ces hommes** 'these men', **ces histoires** 'these stories'.

> **Il a lu** *ce livre.*
> He has read this book.

> **Elle n'aime pas** *cet homme.*
> She does not like the man.

> *Cette jeune étudiante* **n'a pas travaillé** *cette année.*
> That young student has not done any work this year.

> **On a vu trop de** *ces films* **dont vous avez parlé.**
> We've seen too many of those films you spoke about.

Adding *-ci* and *-là* to nouns

By adding **-ci** to the noun it is possible to emphasize *proximity* in space or time, and by adding **-là** to the noun it is possible to emphasize *distance* in space or time. Addition of **-ci** or **-là** also helps to distinguish between two or more people or things.

> **Il est entré par** *cette fenêtre-ci.*
> He entered by this window.

> **Elle est venue** *ce matin-là.*
> She came that morning.

> **Laquelle préfères-tu?** *Cette robe-ci* **ou** *cette robe-là?*
> Which do you prefer? This dress or that one?

The demonstrative adjective, or the demonstrative adjective + noun + **-là** often carry a pejorative, obsequious or contemptuous overtone.

> *Ce* **Jean est un peu insolent, n'est-ce pas?** | That John is a bit rude, isn't he?
>
> *Ces dames* **sont servies?** | You are being served, ladies?
>
> **Elle ne pouvait tolérer** *cet homme-là.* | She couldn't stand that man.

-ci and **-là** are present in **voici, voilà, ici, là** 'here, there' denoting proximity or distance. But increasingly today the forms **voilà** and **là** are used in preference to **voici** and **ici**:

> *Voilà* **ton livre.**
> Here/there is your book.

Je ne sais pas quand il va arriver. Il est *là* maintenant.
I don't know when he'll arrive. He's here now.

Repetition of the demonstrative adjective in lists

Like the definite article (see **2.3**) the demonstrative adjective is usually repeated in lists.

Cette maison et *ce beau jardin* me plaisent beaucoup.
I like this house and the lovely garden very much.

6 Demonstrative pronouns

Demonstrative pronouns are simple or compound. Unlike demonstrative adjectives there are separate forms for the masculine and feminine plurals (see **5.1**). They agree in gender and number with the noun, and the English equivalent is 'this one, these, that one, those'. There is also a small group of neuter demonstrative pronouns meaning 'this, it, that'.

Simple forms

	Singular	Plural
Masculine	**celui**	**ceux**
Feminine	**celle**	**celles**

The simple forms are always followed by a relative pronoun **qui, que, dont** . . . (see **15**) or by a preposition **de, pour** . . .:

On a visité beaucoup d'appartements dans cet immeuble mais on préfère *ceux qui* ne donnent pas sur la rue.
We have seen a lot of flats in that building but we prefer those/the ones which don't overlook the street.

Il y a deux écoles. *Celle des* filles et *celle des* garçons.
There are two schools. The girls' (one) and the boys' (one).

Note that there is no need to translate 'one(s)' into French.

Compound forms

	Singular	Plural
Masculine	**celui-ci/-là**	**ceux-ci/-là**
Feminine	**celle-ci/-là**	**celles-ci/-là**

The compound forms usually express a contrast or distinguish between two people or things 'this (one), these/that (one), those'.

J'ai apporté deux romans policiers. Veux-tu *celui-ci* ou *celui-là?*
I've brought two detective novels. Do you want this one or that one?

> Le frère ou la sœur? *Celle-ci* est charmante, *celui-là* pas du tout!
> The brother or the sister? She's delightful, he's just awful!

Celui-là/-ci may mean 'the former, the latter'. In sentences where only 'the latter' is used, **ce dernier** sometimes replaces **celui-ci**.

6.3 **The neuter pronouns *ce/c'*; *ceci, cela*; *ça***

(a) ce/c'

Ce/c' is normally combined with **être** to form **c'est** or **ce sont**, which are often followed by a relative pronoun (**ce qui, ce que, ce dont**) or by an emphatic pronoun (see **14.2c**).

C'est une belle maison!	It's a lovely house!
C'était ce que tu voulais.	It was what you wanted.
C'est moi. C'est nous.	It's me. It's us.

With a third person plural pronoun **ce/c'** is normally followed by a third person plural verb:

Ce sont eux. C'étaient elles.	It's them. It was them.

and note:

C'est à moi. *C'était* à elles.	It's mine. It was theirs.

Ce/c' also occurs in a few set phrases:

Ce me semble . . .	It seems to me . . .
Sur *ce* . . .	And at that point . . .
Ce disant . . .	And saying this/that . . .
Ce faisant . . .	And as he/she did this/that . . .

(b) **c'est** and **il** (impersonal) **est** 'it is, that is'

C'est usually refers *back* to a previously mentioned idea or matter.

Il parle bien français.
He speaks French well.

Oui, *c'est* **vrai.**
Yes, that's true.

Note that there are many expressions of the type **c'est** + adjective – all referring back to something:

C'est possible.	It's possible.
C'est difficile.	That's difficult.

If **être** + adjective are followed by an infinitive, the preposition **à** links the adjective and the infinitive.

C'était facile à faire.	It was easy to do.

Il est usually refers *forward* to a new idea. The preposition linking **être** + adjective to an infinitive is **de**.

> *Il sera* intéressant *de* le faire. It will be interesting to do it.
> *Il n'est pas* facile *de* parler grec. It's not easy to speak Greek.

NOTE   These are only guidelines. When they are speaking, French people do not always observe the differences between the two types of expression.

(c) **ceci, cela**

Ceci, like **-ci**, refers to something near in time or space, and **cela**, like **-là**, refers to something more distant in time or space.

> **Regardez** *ceci*! Look at this!
> *Cela* ne m'appartient pas. That does not belong to me.

Note the spelling of **cela**: there is *no* accent. And note also that **ceci** refers forward to something about to be said, whereas **cela** refers back to something which has been said:

> Ecoutez *ceci* . . . Listen to this . . .
> Avez-vous entendu *cela*? Did you hear that?

(d) **ça**

Ça (= **cela**) is used informally, mainly when speaking. It may have a pejorative meaning.

> *Ça* ne se dit pas. You don't say that kind of thing.
> *Ça* va? Comment *ça* va? You OK? How're things?
> *Ça* c'est impossible! That's impossible!
> Pourquoi *ça*? Why's that?
> *Ça* sent mauvais! That smells awful!

and in very informal use:

> *Ça* se croit capable de le faire! And he/she thinks he/she can do it!

7 Possessive adjectives

These adjectives denote ownership or relationship. They are always placed before the noun they qualify, and they always agree with that noun. They also indicate the number (singular or plural) of the owner. The English equivalents are 'my, your, his, her, its, our, your, their'.

7.1 Forms and functions

(a) When there is only *one* owner the forms are:

mon, ton, son	before a masculine singular noun
ma, ta, sa	before a feminine singular noun
mes, tes, ses	before a plural noun (masculine or feminine)

mon livre	my book	*ma* voiture	my car	*mes* gants	my gloves
ton billet	your ticket	*ta* main	your hand	*tes* frères	your brothers
son dos	his/her/its back	*sa* nourriture	his/her/its food	*ses* fleurs	his/her/its flowers

When the possessive adjective is followed by a feminine noun or adjective, beginning with a vowel or a mute **h, ma, ta, sa** are replaced by **mon, ton, son**.

mon (*ton, son*) amie	my (your, his, her, its) friend
mon (*ton, son*) horloge	my (your, his, her) clock
mon (*ton, son*) ancienne institutrice	my (your, his, her) old teacher
mon (*ton, son*) horrible maison	my (your, his, her) horrible house

Ton, ta, tes are the familiar forms of the adjective and correspond to the personal pronoun **tu**.

(b) When there is *more than one* owner the forms are:

notre, votre, leur	before a singular noun (masculine or feminine)
nos, vos, leurs	before a plural noun (masculine or feminine)

notre cousin(e)	our cousin	*votre* père	your father	*leur* oncle	their uncle
nos voitures	our cars	*vos* livres	your books	*leurs* amies	their friends

Votre, vos are the polite and plural forms and correspond to the personal pronoun **vous**. They can therefore refer to *one* owner (politely) or to *several* owners.

(c) Like the articles (see **2.3**), possessive adjectives are usually repeated before nouns in lists, unless the nouns refer to almost identical people and things.

son oncle et *sa* tante	his/her uncle and aunt
mon auto et *ma* bicyclette	my car and my bicycle
leur table et *leurs* chaises	their table and chairs

In a few expressions the possessive adjective covers both nouns:

leurs allées et venues	their comings and goings
vos nom et prénoms	your surname and first names/your full name

(d) Some points to remember:

In French, possessive adjectives agree with the noun qualified, whereas in English they agree with the owner:

Il a trouvé *sa montre*.	He has found his watch.
Elles ont perdu *leur clé*.	They have lost their key.

Each of the third persons singular (**son, sa, ses**) has three English equivalents: **son** 'his, her, its'; **sa** 'his, her, its'; **ses** 'his, her, its'.

son bol	his/her/its bowl
sa mère	his/her/its mother
ses jouets	his/her/its toys

If it is felt necessary to identify exactly who or what the owner is, a French speaker will add à and the appropriate emphatic pronoun (see **14.2b**):

son bol *à elle*	*her/its* bowl
ses jouets *à lui*	*his/its* toys

Note the use of possessive adjectives in forms of address:

madame, Madam	Mrs, Ms
mesdames	Ladies
mademoiselle	Miss, Ms
mesdemoiselles	Ladies
monsieur	Sir, Mr
messieurs	Gentlemen
mesdames, mesdemoiselles, messieurs	Ladies and Gentlemen

Remember the French equivalent of phrases such as 'with his hands behind his back' *les* **mains derrière** *le* **dos** (see **2.4b**), and certain other phrases in which French and English do not correspond:

Que sait-elle à *mon* **sujet?**	What does she know about me?
Il a reçu de *leurs* **nouvelles.**	He has had news of them.
Non, *mon* **vieux.**	No, mate/old chap.
Peut-être, *mon* **colonel.**	Perhaps, Colonel.

In the last two examples, the first person possessives express affection and/or respect and are used when talking directly to someone.

Finally, note the two possible English translations of the following:

un de *mes* **amis**	a friend of mine/one of my friends
un de *leurs* **amis**	a friend of theirs/one of their friends
un médecin de *leurs* **amis**	a doctor friend of theirs/one of their doctor friends

8   Possessive pronouns

Like the possessive adjectives, the possessive pronouns indicate who the owner is, but they must agree with the gender and number of the object owned (see **7**). The English equivalents are 'mine, yours, his, hers, its, ours, yours, theirs'.

8.1   Forms

(a) When there is only *one* owner the forms are:

le mien, la mienne, les miens, les miennes	mine
le tien, la tienne, les tiens, les tiennes	yours
le sien, la sienne, les siens, les siennes	his/hers/its

Le tien . . . corresponds to the personal pronoun **tu**.

(b) When there is *more than one* owner the forms are:

le nôtre, la nôtre, les nôtres	ours
le vôtre, la vôtre, les vôtres	yours
le leur, la leur, les leurs	theirs

Le vôtre . . . corresponds to the personal pronoun **vous**. Note the accents on the pronouns **nôtre(s)**, **vôtre(s)**, but not on the adjectives **notre**, **votre**.

> **Voilà ma voiture. Où est *la tienne*?**
> Here is my car. Where is yours (your one)?

> **Il adore son petit frère. Je déteste *le mien*.**
> He loves his little brother. I hate mine.

> **Elle a réussi son examen, mais nos amis ont raté *les leurs*.**
> She has passed her exam, but our friends have failed theirs.

NOTE | There is no need to translate the English 'one'.

(c) The possessive pronouns may follow **à** or **de**, in which case the contracted forms **au/aux**, **du/des** must be used.

> **Nous pensons souvent à nos amis. Pensent-ils *aux leurs*?**
> We often think of our friends. Do they think of theirs?

> **Elle ne craint pas son chien, mais elle a peur *des vôtres*.**
> She is not frightened of his/her dog, but she is of yours (your dogs).

8.2 ### *Etre* + *à* expressing ownership

Usually, following **être**, ownership or possession is expressed by **à** + emphatic pronoun or **à** + article + noun. For other ways of expressing ownership see **49.5**.

> **C'est *à elle*.**   It's hers.
> **Les journaux *sont à eux*.**   The papers are theirs.
> **Le livre *est au professeur*.**   It's the teacher's book.

9 # Nouns

French nouns are masculine or feminine in gender. There are guidelines which help to identify the gender of the majority of nouns, but there are many exceptions and therefore, unless you are absolutely sure, it is always better to check genders and to learn a noun and its definite article (see **9.1–9.13**) together.

9.1 ### How to identify masculine nouns according to meaning

(a) nouns referring to the male sex:

> **le père** 'father', **le garçon** 'boy', **le facteur** 'postman'

but **la victime** 'victim', **la sentinelle** 'sentry', **la personne** 'person', **la recrue** 'recruit' – all of which can refer to men or women (see **9.3**).

(b) male animals:

> **le chien** 'dog', **l'âne** 'donkey', **le veau** 'calf'

(c) days, months, seasons, points of the compass, parts of the world:

> **jeudi** 'Thursday', **octobre** 'October', **automne** 'autumn', **le sud** 'south', **l'orient** 'the East(ern world)'

(d) metals, languages, trees and shrubs, weights, measures, currencies, letters, numbers:

> **l'or** 'gold', **le français** 'French', **le cerisier** 'cherry-tree', **le kilo** 'kilo', **le millimètre** 'millimetre', **l'euro**, 'euro', **le b** 'b', **le 10** '10'

but **la vigne** 'vine', **la tonne** 'ton', **la moitié** 'half', **la livre** 'pound sterling/pound in weight' . . .

(e) other parts of speech used as nouns:

> **le noir** 'black', **le pour et le contre** 'pros and cons', **le savoir-faire** 'know-how', **le déjeuner** 'lunch', **le pourboire** 'tip'

9.2 How to identify masculine nouns according to ending

(a) most nouns ending in a consonant:

> **le bec** 'beak', **le mot** 'word', **le canard** 'duck', **le bras** 'arm', **l'étang** 'pond', **le foin** 'hay', **le nez** 'nose', **le choix** 'choice', **le billet** 'ticket', **le procès** 'trial', **le coup** 'blow', **le changement** 'change', **le reporter** 'reporter'

but **la faim** 'hunger', **la boisson** 'drink', **la largeur** 'width', **la mer** 'sea'. see also **9.3**.

(b) most nouns ending in **-age, -au, -é, -ède, -ège, -ème, -eu, -i, -il, -isme, -ou**:

> **le courage** 'courage', **le bureau** 'office', **le comité** 'committee', **le remède** 'remedy', **le collège** 'college', **le problème** 'problem', **le feu** 'fire', **le parti** '(political) party', **le détail** 'detail', **le socialisme** 'socialism', **le hibou** 'owl'

but **la plage** 'beach', **la cage** 'cage', **la page** 'page', **l'image** 'picture', **la rage** 'anger', **la peau** 'skin', **l'eau** 'water', **la crème** 'cream', **la clé** 'key', **la fourmi** 'ant' . . .

9.3 How to identify feminine nouns according to meaning

(a) nouns referring to the feminine sex:

> **la mère** 'mother', **la fille** 'girl/daughter', **la grand-mère** 'grandmother'

(b) female animals:

> **la chèvre** 'goat', **la lionne** 'lioness', **la vache** 'cow', **la jument** 'mare'

(c) names of festivals:

> **la Pentecôte** 'Whitsun', **la Toussaint** 'All Saints' Day', **la Noël** 'Christmas', **Pâques** (f pl) 'Easter'

but **Noël** is masculine in **Joyeux Noël!** 'Merry Christmas', as is **Pâques** in **Pâques est tombé au mois de mars** 'Easter was in March this year'.

(d) academic subjects at school or university:

> **l'histoire** 'history', **les sciences naturelles** 'biology', **les mathématiques** 'maths', **la lecture** 'reading'

but **le calcul** 'arithmetic', **le dessin** 'drawing', **le droit** 'law' . . .

9.4 How to identify feminine nouns according to ending

(a) most nouns ending in **-on** are masculine:

> **le camion** 'lorry', **le crayon** 'pencil'

but nouns ending in **-aison**, **-ssion**, **-sion**, **-tion**, **-xion** are normally feminine:

> **la combinaison** 'combination', **la commission** 'commission', **la décision** 'decision', **la nation** 'nation', **la réflexion** 'thought' . . .

(b) many nouns ending in a silent **e**:

> **la parole** 'the (spoken) word', **la mémoire** 'memory/dissertation', **la rivière** 'the river/necklace', **la tasse** 'the cup', **la visite** 'the visit', **la rentrée** 'return to school/university', **la mine** 'expression/mine', **la défense** 'defence', **la monnaie** 'change'

but **le manque** 'lack', **l'incendie** 'fire', **le lycée** 'secondary school/lycée', **le musée** 'museum', **le légume** 'vegetable', **le silence** 'silence', **le fleuve** '(big) river', **le territoire** 'the country/France', **le genre** 'kind', **le groupe** 'group', **le service** 'service', **le contrôle** 'control' . . .

This group is perhaps the most difficult to classify since there are many exceptions which are masculine and they are words which are used frequently. Extra care must, therefore, be taken with all nouns ending in a silent **e**.

(c) geographical names ending in a silent **e**:

> **la France** 'France', **l'Angleterre** 'England', **la Bretagne** 'Brittany', **la Loire** 'the Loire', **la Tamise** 'the Thames'

but **le Mexique** 'Mexico', **le Cambodge** 'Cambodia', **le Rhône** 'the Rhone', **le Danube** 'the Danube' . . .

Those which do not end in **e** are usually masculine:

> **le Canada** 'Canada', **le Danemark** 'Denmark', **le Japon** 'Japan', **le Hainaut** 'Hainaut', **le Var** 'Var'

Towns are often masculine: **le vieux Paris**, but the preferred form is *la ville de* **Bruxelles** 'Brussels', for example.

9.5 **Guidelines on gender and forms**

Some nouns which can refer to either sex are masculine:

> **un ange** 'angel', **un auteur** 'author', **le professeur** 'teacher', **le témoin** 'witness', **le médecin** 'doctor'

but sometimes **une femme médecin** 'a woman doctor', and usually **un écrivain** 'writer' but also **une écrivaine**, and **la prof** 'the (female) teacher' . . .

9.5.1 Some nouns have a feminine form and, therefore, feminine gender for referring to the female counterpart:

> **un acteur/une actrice** 'actor', **un époux/une épouse** 'husband/wife', **un Français/une Française** 'Frenchman/Frenchwoman', **un écolier/une écolière** 'schoolboy/schoolgirl'

9.5.2 Note the formation of feminine nouns from masculine nouns:

-en -enne	un Italien/une Italien*ne*	an Italian
-an -anne	un paysan/une pays*anne*	a small farmer
-on -onne	le patron/la patr*onne*	manager, boss
-eur -euse	le vendeur/la vend*euse*	shop assistant
-teur -trice	le lecteur/la lec*trice*	language assistant
-ier -ière	le pâtissier/la pâtiss*ière*	pastry-cook

9.5.3 Some nouns add **-sse** to the masculine noun to form the feminine counterpart:

> **un hôte/une hôtesse** 'host/hostess', **le maître/la maîtresse** 'master/mistress'

9.5.4 Some nouns have a different form for the opposite sex:

> **le fils, la fille**   son, daughter
> **l'homme, la femme**   man, woman
> **le monsieur, la dame**   gentleman, lady
> **l'oncle, la tante**   uncle, aunt
> **le speaker, la speakerine**   announcer/broadcaster
> **le compagnon, la compagne**   companion

9.5.5 Some nouns may have either gender, whichever is appropriate:

> **un/une enfant** 'child', **un/une propriétaire** 'owner', **un/une élève** 'pupil'

9.5.6 There are a few nouns which may be masculine or feminine, but today they are usually given masculine gender:

> **un/une après-midi** 'an afternoon'

9.6 **Change of gender and a change of meaning**

Some nouns may be either masculine or feminine, but the meaning changes according to the gender:

le livre	the book	*la* livre	the pound
le mode	the method	*la* mode	fashion
le tour	the turn	*la* tour	the tower
le critique	the critic	*la* critique	criticism
le poste	the radio/job	*la* poste	the post office
le physique	physique	*la* physique	physics

9.7 *Gens*

Special care should be taken with the plural noun **gens** 'people', which may be accompanied by masculine *or* feminine adjectives:

(a) when adjectives *follow* **gens** they are masculine:

les *gens* bons et courageux   good, courageous people

(b) when adjectives *precede* **gens** they are feminine:

toutes ces bonnes *gens*   all these good people

(c) if adjectives *precede* and *follow* **gens** they are feminine and masculine:

les vieilles *gens* peu intéressants old, boring people

9.8 Gender of compound nouns

(a) If one element is equivalent to an adjective, the compound noun takes the gender of the main noun: **le *chef*-d'œuvre** 'work of art', **la *main*-d'œuvre** 'workforce', **le *timbre*-poste** 'postage stamp'.

(b) If one element is an adjective or an adverb, the compound noun takes the gender of the noun: **la belle-*fille*** 'daughter-in-law' (but note **le rouge-*gorge*** 'robin'), **le non-*paiement*** 'non-payment', **la non-*agression*** 'non-aggression'.

(c) If one element is a preposition, the compound noun is normally masculine: **l'*en*-tête** 'heading'.

(d) If the first element is verbal, the compound noun is masculine: **le *para*pluie** 'umbrella', **le *tire*-bouchon** 'corkscrew'.

9.9 Plural forms of nouns and adjectives

The plural forms in most cases simply add **s** to the singular noun or adjective. The final s is rarely heard – unless liaison is required, but it *must* be used in writing: **des trous** 'holes', **des hommes** 'men', **les ennemis** 'enemies', **bons/bonnes** 'good', **fous/folles** 'mad'. Special attention should be given to the following groups:

(a) a small group of nouns ending in -ou add x: **bijoux** 'jewels', **cailloux** 'pebbles', **choux** 'cabbages', **genoux** 'knees', **hiboux** 'owls', **joujoux** 'toys', **poux** 'lice'.

(b) nouns and adjectives ending in -au, -eu, -eau add x: **des tuyaux** 'pipes/tips', **des cheveux** 'hair', **nouveaux** 'new'. (But note **pneus** 'tyres', **bleus** 'blue/bruises'.)

(c) if nouns and adjectives end in **s, x, z** there is no change in the plural: **souris** 'mouse/mice', **prix** 'price(s)', **nez** 'nose(s)', **gris** 'grey', **heureux** 'happy'.

(d) the majority of nouns and adjectives ending in **-al** change to **-aux**:

> **cheval/chev*aux*** 'horse(s)', **moral/mor*aux*** 'moral', **légal/lég*aux*** 'legal', **international/internation*aux*** 'international'

but there are a few exceptions to this important rule, such as:

> **bal/bals** 'ball(s)', **festival/festivals** 'festival(s)', **naval/navals** 'naval', **fatal/fatals** 'fatal', **final/finals** *or* finaux 'final' . . .

The *only* way to be sure is to check in a dictionary.

(e) nouns ending in **-ail** add **s**:

> **chandail(s)** 'sweater(s)'

but a few change to **-aux**:

> **travail/trav*aux*** 'work, roadworks', **vitrail/vitr*aux*** 'stained-glass window/s' . . .

and adjectives ending in **-eil** add **s**:

> **pareil(s)** 'alike, similar'

(f) note **l'œil/les yeux** 'eye(s)', and **le ciel/les ciels** 'sky, skies', **les cieux** 'skies – firmament, climate, paradise'.

(g) some nouns are used only in the singular:

> **l'électricité** 'electricity', **le Moyen Age** 'the Middle Ages'

and some nouns are used only in the plural:

> **les mœurs** 'customs, behaviour', **les environs** 'outskirts, vicinity', **les frais** 'expenses', **les vivres** 'foodstuffs', **les alentours** 'surrounding areas'

(h) family names do not normally change:

Les Dupont n'aiment pas les Régnier.	The Duponts don't like the Régnier family.

Names important in history or art can be used in the plural:

J'ai plusieurs Monets.	I have several paintings by Monet.

(i) and some special cases:

monsieur/messieurs	Sir, Mr/Gentlemen
madame/mesdames	Madam, Mrs/Ladies
mademoiselle/mesdemoiselles	Miss, Ms/Misses, Young Ladies
bonhomme/bonshommes	fellow/fellows

9.10   The plural of compound nouns

(a) If the noun is written as a single word, the plural is formed according to the rules above:

les **portefeuilles** 'wallets', les **portemanteaux** 'coat pegs/coat stands', les **passeports** 'passports'

(b) Some guidelines for compound nouns formed with a hyphen:

noun + noun (both + s): **les chefs-lieux** 'administrative centres'
noun + adjective (both + s): **les coffres-forts** 'safes'
adjective + noun (both + s): **les rouges-gorges** 'robins'
adjective + adjective (both + s): **les sourds-muets** 'deaf-mutes'
noun + preposition + noun (main noun + s): **les chefs-d'œuvre** 'works of art'
verb + noun (noun + s): **les bouche-trous** 'stand-ins' (*but* see **9.10e**)
verb + verb (no change): **les laissez-passer** 'passes'
verb + adverb (no change): **les passe-partout** 'master keys'
adverb + noun (noun + s): **les haut-parleurs** 'loudspeakers'

NOTE 1 Only nouns and adjectives used to form compound nouns can be made plural.

NOTE 2 Where both nouns are of equal value, both become plural (see above) but if the second noun is equivalent to a prepositional phrase, the *first noun only* is made plural: **les timbres-poste** 'stamps' (= **de poste**).

(c) some compound nouns are variable: e.g., **les après-midi/les après-midis** 'afternoons', **les grand-mères/les grands-mères** 'grandmothers'.

(d) some have an **s** even in the singular: e.g., **le porte-clés, les porte-clés** 'keyring(s)', **le pare-chocs, les pare-chocs** 'bumper(s)'.

(e) for some there is no change in the plural: e.g., **les abat-jour** 'lightshades', **les pare-brise** 'windscreens', **les pour et les contre** 'the pros and cons'.

9.11 Plural forms of imported words

(a) generally imported words form their plural by adding **s**: **les référendums, les meetings, les biftecks, les panoramas, les médias**.

(b) some do not change: e.g. **les veto, les post-scriptum**.

(c) some keep the plural form of their language of origin: e.g. **les sportsmen, les graffiti**.

(d) some words of Latin origin have both French and Latin plurals: e.g. **les maximums/maxima, les minimums/minima**.

(e) and the English word **baby** becomes **babies** or **babys**, **whisky** becomes **whiskies** or **whiskys**, **sandwich** become **sandwiches** or **sandwichs** . . .

Plural forms and a change of meaning

Certain nouns may have a change of meaning in the plural form: **les lettres** 'letters, arts subjects, literature', **les affaires** 'business, affairs' . . .

9.13 **Singular nouns in French with a plural English equivalent**

Un pantalon 'trousers', **un maillot** 'swimming trunks', **un collant** 'tights/panty hose', **un pyjama** 'pyjamas' . . . and, conversely, some singular English nouns have a plural French equivalent: 'funeral' **les funérailles**, 'darkness' **les ténèbres**, 'the Treasury' **les Finances**, 'information' **les informations** . . .

10   Adjectives

Adjectives normally follow the noun if they express a distinguishing feature of the person or thing referred to, although some very common adjectives precede the noun. But, for stylistic reasons or for emphasis, they may be located in a place that is different from their normal one. Adjectives must agree with their noun in gender and number.

10.1 **Adjectives which normally *follow* the noun**

(a) adjectives of nationality, religion, politics:

> **La langue espagnole n'est pas difficile.**
> Spanish isn't difficult.

> **Ils se sont mariés à l'église protestante.**
> They got married in the Protestant church.

> **Elle a la carte du parti socialiste.**
> She's a card-carrying member of the Socialist Party.

(b) adjectives expressing a physical characteristic, form, colour:

> **C'est un enfant très maigre.**
> He/She is a very thin child.

> **C'est une maison blanche.**
> It's a white house.

(c) participles used as adjectives:

> **un ouvrier fatigué**   a tired worker
> **une histoire connue**   a well-known story
> **l'eau courante**   running water

(d) adjectives qualified by an adverb ending in **-ment**:

> **un homme extrêmement laid**   an extremely ugly man
> **un enfant incroyablement**   an unbelievably stupid child
> **stupide**

10.2   **Some adjectives are usually placed *before* the noun**

(a) **beau** 'handsome', **bon** 'good', **bref** 'short', **dernier** 'last', **gentil** 'nice', **grand** 'great', **gros** 'big', **haut** 'high', **jeune** 'young', **joli** 'pretty', **long** 'long', **mauvais** 'bad', **meilleur** 'better', **moindre** 'lesser', **nombreux** 'many', **nouveau** 'new', **petit** 'little', **premier** 'first', **vaste** 'huge', **vieux** 'old', **vrai** 'real', **vilain** 'ugly' . . .

une belle femme	a lovely woman
de gros pieds	big feet
un long voyage	a long journey
la première page	the first page

(b) some of these, in certain contexts, follow the noun:

la marée haute	high tide
d'un ton bref	curtly

and with days of the week, seasons, parts of the year:

l'été prochain	next summer
la semaine dernière	last week

otherwise, they precede the noun:

le prochain arrêt	the next stop
la première/dernière semaine des vacances	the first/last week of the holidays

10.3   **Some adjectives change their meaning according to their position**

ancien:	une maison *ancienne*/une *ancienne* maison
	a (very) old house/a former house
cher:	un livre *cher*/mes *chers* amis
	an expensive book/my dear friends
dernier:	lundi *dernier*/la *dernière* page
	last Monday/the last (of a series) page
nouveau:	un mot *nouveau*/une *nouvelle* voiture
	a new (original) word/a new (could be second-hand) car
pauvre:	une fille *pauvre*/une *pauvre* fille
	a poor (not rich) girl/a poor girl (pity her)
propre:	les mains *propres*/tes *propres* paroles
	clean hands/your own words
seul:	une femme *seule*/le *seul* candidat
	a lonely woman/the only candidate

10.4   **When there is more than one adjective add *et***

If more than one adjective follows the noun, and each refers to a distinct and equal characteristic, they are linked by **et**. But if they form a unit of meaning *with* the noun there is no need for **et**. Usually, the longest adjective is placed last:

| une vue triste et sans intérêt | a sad, boring view |

but

| la scène politique anglaise | the British political scene |
| le parti démocrate américain | the American democratic party |

Note the different order in French and English when a number is used with an adjective preceding a noun:

Les trois premiers étudiants recevront les bourses.
The first three students will receive the grants.

10.5 Feminine forms of adjectives

For demonstrative (see **5**), possessive (see **7**), indefinite (see **11**), interrogative (see **16**), numeral (**17**), verbal (see **42.1**, **43.1**) and exclamatory (see **3.1d**) adjectives – see the section references in brackets.

10.5.1 There are usually some exceptions to the feminine forms of adjectives, so it is always advisable to check in a dictionary.

(a) feminine adjectives are mostly formed by adding **e** to the masculine form:

fort/forte 'strong', **écossais/écossaise** 'Scottish', **direct/directe** 'direct', **noir/noire** 'black'

If the masculine form ends in an **e**, there is no need for change in the feminine form:

jeune (m and f) 'young', **aimable** (m and f) 'pleasant'

But if the masculine form ends in **é** an **e** *must* be added to make the adjective feminine:

nominé/nominée 'nominated, shortlisted', **énervé/énervée** 'excited, irritated'

(b) if the masculine adjective ends in **-as, -el-, -eil, -en, -et, -on** double the last consonant and add **e**:

bas/basse 'low', **traditionnel/traditionnelle** 'traditional', **pareil/pareille** 'like', **italien/italienne** 'Italian', **cadet/cadette** 'younger (brother/sister)', **bon/bonne** 'good'

NOTE   Exceptions **-et** > **-ète**: **complet/complète** 'full, complete', **inquiet/inquiète** 'worried', **concret/concrète** 'concrete' . . .

(c) some feminine adjectives require specific changes:

-er > -ère	premier/première	first
-f > -ve	attentif/attentive	attentive
-eux > -euse	heureux/heureuse	happy
-teur > -trice	consolateur/consolatrice	comforting
-eur > -euse	menteur/menteuse	deceitful

Note that a small group of comparative adjectives ending in **-eur** form the feminine by adding **e**:

> **meilleur(e)** 'better', **supérieur(e)** 'superior, upper', **inférieur(e)** 'inferior, lower', **extérieur(e)** 'exterior, external', **intérieur(e)** 'interior', **antérieur(e)** 'prior, previous', **postérieur(e)** 'later, subsequent', **ultérieur(e)** 'further', **majeur(e)** 'major', **mineur(e)** 'minor'

(d) adjectives ending in **-at**, **-ot** add **e** to form the feminine: **délicat(e)** 'delicate'. Note the exceptions: **sot/sotte** 'stupid', **vieillot/vieillotte** 'quaint', **boulot/boulotte** 'tubby', **pâlot/pâlotte** 'rather pale'.

(e) adjectives ending in **-in**, **-ain**, **-ein**, **-un** add **e** (they do *not* double the last consonant): **voisin/voisine** 'neighbouring', **hautain/hautaine** 'haughty', **plein/pleine** 'full', **commun/commune** 'common' . . .

(f) adjectives ending in **-gu** > **-guë**: **aigu/aiguë** 'sharp'. (see also **79.6**)

(g) some special forms:

> **blanc/blanche** 'white', **doux/douce** 'soft, gentle', **favori/favorite** 'favourite', **frais/fraîche** 'fresh, cool', **franc/franche** 'frank, open', **long/longue** 'long', **public/publique** 'public', **sec/sèche** 'dry' . . .

| 10.5.2 | There are five adjectives which have two masculine singular forms – the second is used before a masculine singular noun beginning with a vowel or a mute **h**. It is from the second form that the feminine adjective is formed by doubling the last consonant and adding **e**: |

un *beau* garçon a handsome boy	un *bel* arbre a fine tree	une *belle* dame a beautiful lady
un homme *fou* a crazy man	un *fol* espoir a silly hope	une *folle* amie a foolish friend
un coussin *mou* a soft cushion	un *mol* abandon listlessness	une *molle* résistance feeble resistance
un *nouveau* directeur a new manager	un *nouvel* habit a new coat	une *nouvelle* robe a new dress
un *vieux* soulier an old shoe	un *vieil* homme an old man	une *vieille* femme an old woman

The two masculine singular forms have only *one* plural form: **beaux, fous, mous, nouveaux, vieux**.

10.6 *Grand, demi, nu*

The adjectives **grand, demi, nu** do not always follow the above guidelines:

(a) **grand** does not add an **e** in feminine compound nouns: **grand-mère** 'grandmother', **grand-route** 'main road/highway', **grand-rue** 'main street',

grand-place 'main square', **grand-faim** 'very hungry', **grand-soif** 'very thirsty', **ne . . . grand-chose** 'not very much'.

J'ai grand-faim.	I'm very hungry.
C'est où la grand-place?	Where is the main square?
Il n'a pas dit grand-chose.	He didn't say much.

The plural forms of the first three in the list can be written with or without an **s**: **grand(s)-mères, grand(s)-routes, grand(s)-rues**.

(b) The adjectives **grand, large, frais, premier, dernier** followed by a past participle agree with their noun:

une fenêtre *grande* ouverte	a wide open window
les fleurs *fraîches* cueillies	freshly cut flowers

Note that in the case of **mort** 'dead', **nouveau** 'new', **court** 'short', **haut** 'high' followed by a past participle there is *no* agreement, whatever the gender and number of the noun:

une enfant *mort*-née	a still-born child
leurs fils *nouveau*-nés	their new-born sons

(c) **demi** 'half', preceding and linked to a noun by a hyphen, does not agree with its noun, but when it follows a noun and is linked to it by **et**, it agrees in gender only:

une *demi*-heure	a half hour
trois *demi*-kilos	three half kilos
une heure et *demie*	an hour and a half/1.30
dix litres et *demi*	ten and a half litres

(d) **nu** 'bare', preceding and linked to a noun by a hyphen, does not agree with its noun, but when it follows a noun it agrees with it in gender and number:

nu-tête	bareheaded	*nu*-pieds	barefoot

Elles sont tête *nue*, pieds *nus*.	They are bareheaded, barefoot.

Agreement of adjectives of colour

(a) adjectives of colour normally agree in gender and number with their noun

une fleur *blanche*	a white flower
des fleurs *blanches*	white flowers

(b) compound adjectives do not agree with their noun:

une jupe *bleu foncé*	a dark blue skirt
des jupes *bleu foncé*	dark blue skirts

(c) if the adjective of colour is also a noun, there is no agreement:

une robe *citron*	a lemon dress
des robes *citron*	lemon dresses

Note the exceptions: **des nuages *roses*** 'pink clouds' and also **mauve, fauve, écarlate**:

fleurs *mauves* et blanches	mauve and white flowers

(d) if two or more colours are involved, the adjectives may agree, or not, with the noun:

une chemise *blanc(he)* et *vert(e)*	a white and green shirt
des chemises *blanc(hes)* et *vert(es)*	white and green shirts

10.8 Adjectives used as adverbs

Sometimes adjectives may be used as adverbs and in such cases there is no agreement:

Il parle *haut*.	He is speaking loudly.
Elle verra *clair* désormais.	She will see clearly from now on.
On travaille *dur* en ce moment.	We are working hard just now.

Other adjectives which do not agree when they are used as adverbs include: **bon/mauvais** 'good/bad', **fort** 'loud', **juste** 'exactly right', **droit** 'straight ahead'.

10.9 Plural adjectives and agreement

For plural forms of adjectives see **9.9**. Note the following rules for plural agreement:

(a) an adjective qualifying two or more nouns is in the plural after the last noun. If one of the nouns is masculine the adjective is in the masculine plural:

Il a un oncle et une tante *généreux*.	He has a generous uncle and aunt.
une revue et un journal *mensuels*	a monthly magazine and newspaper

(b) when compound adjectives are used with a plural noun, both adjectives are plural:

une pomme aigre-douce/des pommes aigres-douces
a bittersweet apple/bittersweet apples

10.10 Comparison of adjectives (see **49.9**)

(a) to compare people, or things, English adds '-er' to the adjective: 'bigger than, prettier than'. With longer adjectives English uses 'more/less . . . than': 'more difficult than'. In French, comparatives are usually formed by using **plus . . . que** 'more . . . than', **moins . . . que** 'less . . . than', **aussi . . . que** 'as . . . as', **d'autant plus . . . que** 'all the more . . . as/because' and in a negative comparison **ne . . . pas aussi** (*or* si) **. . . que** 'not as . . . as':

Elle est *plus* grande *que* vous.
She is bigger than you.

Elles *ne* sont *pas aussi* (*or si*) petites *que* leur mère.
They are not as small as their mother.

> Ce vin est *d'autant plus* recherché *qu'*il est rare.
> This wine is all the more sought after because it is rare.

NOTE	In comparisons **ne** may be added when **que** is followed by a verb.

> Il est *moins* stupide *qu'*on *ne* (le) pensait.
> He is less stupid than (not as stupid as) we thought.

(b) the adverbs **plus**, **moins** may be qualified by **beaucoup, un peu**:

> Elle est *un peu plus* intelligente *que* son frère.
> She is a little more intelligent than her brother.

> Ce livre-ci est *beaucoup moins* cher *que* celui-là.
> This book is much cheaper than that one.

(c) the expressions **de plus en plus/de moins en moins** 'increasingly/less and less' may modify an adjective, often with **devenir**:

> Les négociations sont devenues *de plus en plus* compliquées.
> The negotiations have become more and more complicated.

(d) **comme** 'like' is used in similes:

> **blanc(he)** *comme* **neige**   as white as snow
> **lisse** *comme* **de la soie**   as smooth as silk
> **fort** *comme* **un bœuf**   as strong as an ox

NOTE	Small changes in each phrase – the use of an article in some. They have to be learned individually.

10.11   Superlative forms of adjectives

To form the superlative in English '-est' is added to the adjective, which is preceded by 'the': 'the longest, the commonest'. With longer adjectives English uses 'most/least': 'the most/least spectacular'. In French, the structure is as follows:

> **le (la, les)** + **plus/moins** + adjective (+ noun) (+ **de**)

or

> **le (la, les)** + noun + **le (la, les)** + **plus/moins** + adjective (+ **de**)

> Sa maison est *la plus belle de la* ville.
> His house is the most beautiful (one) in the town.

> Elle a mis son chapeau *le plus chic.*
> She put on her smartest hat.

> C'est un *des plus intéressants* bâtiments *de la* ville médiévale.
> It's one of the most interesting buildings in the medieval city.

NOTE	The possessive adjective (**mon, ma, mes** . . .) can replace the definite article, and **de** (**du, de la, de l', des**) is used where English uses 'in, of'.

10.12	**Comparative and superlative forms of *bon, mauvais, petit***

(a) The comparative and superlative forms of **bon** are **meilleur(e)(s)** 'better' and **le, la, les** (or **mon, ma, mes . . .**) **meilleur(e)(s)** 'best'.

> Ses résultats sont *meilleurs que* les miens.
> Her/His results are better than mine.

> Elles sont *nos meilleures* amies.
> They are our best friends.

> C'est *la meilleure* qualité *qu'*on puisse acheter.
> It's the best you can buy.

(b) **mauvais** has two different comparative and superlative forms – with different meanings:

- **plus mauvais(e)(s)** 'worse' and **le, la, les** (or **mon, ma, mes . . .**) **plus mauvais(e)(s)** 'worst' (in terms of quality)
- **pire(s)** 'worse' and **le, la, les** (or **mon, ma, mes . . .**) **pire(s)** 'worst' (in a moral sense)

> Le vin était *plus mauvais que* le repas.
> The wine was worse than the meal.

> C'est *le plus mauvais* restaurant *du* quartier.
> It's the worst restaurant in the area.

> Un escroc *de la pire* espèce!
> The worst kind of cheat!

> Ça sera *ton pire* ennemi.
> He'll be your worst enemy.

(c) **petit** has two different comparative and superlative forms – with different meanings:

- **plus petit(e)(s)** 'smaller' and **le, la, les** (or **mon, ma, mes . . .**) **plus petit(e)(s)** 'smallest' (in terms of size)
- **moindre(s)** 'less, smaller' and **le, la, les** (or **mon, ma, mes . . .**) **moindre(s)** 'least, smallest' (in a moral sense)

> Elles sont *plus petites* que les autres.
> They are smaller than the others.

> Il est *le plus petit des* enfants.
> He is the smallest of the children.

> Je le considère comme *un moindre* mal.
> I consider it to be a lesser evil.

> Elle n'a pas *le moindre* doute.
> She hasn't the least doubt about it.

and note:

> Dernier point à souligner et non *des moindres*.
> Last but not least.

Indefinite adjectives, pronouns and adverbs

This section includes a large group of words and phrases which function as adjectives, or pronouns, or both. Some also function as adverbs. For negative adjectives and pronouns see **47.7, 47.13**.

11.1 *Tout*

(a) adjective: **tout, tous** (ms/pl); **toute, toutes** (fs/pl) 'all, every, whole, any' followed by:

● an article **le . . ., un . . .**
● a possessive adjective **mon, ton, son . . .**
● a demonstrative adjective **ce . . .**
● the adjective **autre**

> **Elle a posé** *toute une* **série de questions.**
> She asked a whole series of questions.

> **J'ai fait** *tout mon* **possible.**
> I've done all I could.

> **Tu dois ramasser** *tous ces* **livres.**
> You must pick up all these books.

> *Toute autre* **solution me paraît impossible.**
> Any other solution seems impossible to me.

Tout, toute can precede the noun directly:

> *Toute* **femme est belle à mon avis.**
> Every woman is beautiful in my opinion.

In some expressions the article is omitted:

à *tout* prix	at any price
à *toute* heure	at any time
de *tous* côtés	on (from) all sides

(b) pronoun: **tous, toutes, tout le monde, tout ce qui/que, tous/toutes les deux** 'all (of you), everyone, everything, both (of you)':

> *Tous* **sont arrivés à temps.**
> They all arrived on/in time.

> **Vous pouvez les manger** *toutes.*
> You can eat all of them.

> *Tout le monde* **connaît ses défauts.**
> Everyone is aware of his/her faults.

> **Je t'ai raconté** *tout ce que* **je sais.**
> I've told you all I know.

The pronoun **tout** (ms only) often precedes past participles and infinitives:

> **Nous vous avons** *tout* **raconté.**
> We have told you everything.

> On veut *tout* préparer avant son arrivée.
> We want everything ready before he/she arrives.

Tout may also be the subject of the verb:

> *Tout* est prêt.
> Everything is ready.

(c) **Tout** followed by **autre** may be either an adjective or an adverb. When **tout autre** = 'any other', **tout** is an adjective and agrees with the following noun:

> *Toute autre réaction* m'aurait étonné(e).
> Any other reaction (other than this) would have surprised me.

When **tout autre** = 'quite different', **tout** is an adverb and modifies the adjective **autre**. It is normally invariable.

> Elle a eu une *tout autre* réaction.
> She had quite a different reaction.

(d) The adverb **tout** 'completely, quite' adopts the feminine gender and number when it precedes a feminine adjective beginning with a consonant or an aspirate **h** (see **80.3**).

> C'est une voiture *tout* extraordinaire.
> It's quite an extraordinary car.

> Elle est arrivé *toute* seule.
> She arrived by herself.

> Leurs chaussures étaient *toutes* mouillées.
> Their shoes were soaking wet.

> Elles sont *tout* heureuses d'entendre vos nouvelles.
> They are quite delighted to hear your news.

> Elle est *toute* honteuse.
> She's completely ashamed.

11.2   *Différent(e)s, divers(es)* 'several/various, different'

When these adjectives *precede* a noun they mean 'several, various' and when they *follow* a noun they mean 'different'. They do not require an article.

> Elles achètent *différentes* choses.
> They are buying several things.

> Il a *divers* livres à ce sujet.
> He has various books on the subject.

> On a goûté des vins *différents*.
> We tried different wines.

> Elles ont des opinions très *diverses* à son sujet.
> They have very different opinions about him.

11.3   *Plusieurs* (pl invariable) 'several, a number of, some'

Plusieurs does not require an article. It may be followed by **autres**.

(a) adjective

> *Plusieurs* **étudiantes manifestaient devant l'ambassade.**
> Several students were demonstrating in front of the embassy.

> **Il y a** *plusieurs autres* **raisons à la crise.**
> There are several other reasons for the (economic) crisis.

(b) pronoun

> *Plusieurs* **décidèrent de partir.**
> A number of them decided to leave.

> **J'en ai vu** *plusieurs.*
> I saw several (of them).

11.4 *Chaque; chacun(e)*

(a) adjective: **chaque** (invariable) 'each, every'

> *Chaque* **enfant portait un chapeau.**
> Each child was wearing a hat.

> **A** *chaque* **fenêtre il y avait des rideaux.**
> At every window there were curtains.

(b) pronoun: **chacun(e)** 'each (one), every (one)'

> **Il a répondu à** *chacune* **des femmes.**
> He answered each of the women.

> *Chacun* **te l'expliquera.**
> Each one will explain it to you.

11.5 *Certain(e)(s)* 'certain, some, definite, sure'

(a) adjective

When **certain** *precedes* the noun it means 'certain, a certain, some', and when it *follows* the noun it means 'definite, sure'. **Certain(e)** may be preceded by **un(e)**.

> **C'est une dame d'***un certain* **âge.**
> She's a lady of advanced years.

> *Certains* **étudiants n'ont pas remis leurs mémoires.**
> Some students have not submitted their dissertations.

> **Elles ont sur les jeunes élèves une influence** *certaine.*
> They have a definite influence on young pupils.

(b) pronoun

certains, certaines 'certain, some (people)'

> *Certains* **sont toujours prêts à la croire.**
> Some people are always ready to believe her.

> *Certaines* **des amies de votre mère sont capables de le dire.**
> Some of your mother's friends are capable of saying it.

11.6   *Autre(s)* 'other, new, another, different'

(a) adjective

> **Elle a donné le cadeau à son *autre* tante.**
> She gave the present to her other aunt.

> **Nous avons vu d'*autres* films.**
> We have seen (some) other films.

> **Elle a trouvé un *autre* ami.**
> She has found a new/another friend.

> **Son opinion est tout *autre*.**
> His/her opinion is quite different.

(b) pronoun

The pronoun **autre(s)** 'someone else, others' may be preceded by the indefinite or definite articles **un(e), d', l', les.**

> **Une *autre* aurait accepté.**
> Someone else would have accepted.

> **Elle n'en a pas *d'autres*.**
> She hasn't any others/more.

> **Où sont *les autres* ?**
> Where are the others?

(c) **autre chose** 'something else'

> **Il n'aime pas ce cadeau. Il veut *autre chose*.**
> He doesn't like this present. He wants something else.

(d) **d'autrui** 'of others, other people, someone else' – used only in formal written French.

> **Sans l'aide *d'autrui* on n'aurait pas su le faire.**
> Without someone else's help we could not have done it.

> **Ne prenez jamais les biens *d'autrui*.**
> Never take other people's property.

11.7   *l'un(e) . . . l'autre, les un(e)s . . . les autres* 'the one . . . the other, some . . . (the) others, both, each other'

These pronouns are used to link, contrast or compare people or things. If a preposition is required to link, contrast or compare, it is inserted before the second pronoun.

> **Je distinguais mal les jumelles *l'une de l'autre*.**
> I had difficulty telling one twin from the other.

> **Ils parlaient doucement *les uns aux autres*.**
> They were speaking quietly to each other.

> **Ils se tenaient serrés *les uns contre les autres*.**
> They were standing close together.

> ***Les uns* buvaient, *les autres* fumaient.**
> Some were drinking, others were smoking.

> **Les uns parlent français mieux que *les autres*.**
> Some (of them) speak French better than (the) others.

l'un(e) l'autre*; *l'un(e) et/ou l'autre*; *ni l'un(e) ni l'autre 'each other; both/one or the other; neither'

L'un l'autre expresses reciprocity – frequently emphasizing a reflexive pronoun.

> **Ils s'aiment *l'un l'autre*.**
> They love each other.

> **Elle a invité Patrick et Laurent. *L'un et l'autre* viendront.**
> She has invited Patrick and Lawrence. They'll both come.

> **Je les ai invitées toutes les deux. *L'une ou l'autre* va venir.**
> I have invited both of them. One or the other will come.

> **On a posé la question aux deux frères. *Ni l'un ni l'autre* n'a répondu.**
> We asked both brothers. Neither replied.

Each set of pronouns has plural forms:

> **Ni les un(e)s ni les autres n'ont voulu commencer.**
> Neither group wanted to begin.

> **Je l'ai communiqué *aux uns et aux autres*.**
> I've informed both groups.

On

On is a subject pronoun, usually accepted as masculine singular in contexts where agreement is required. **On** can be translated by most of the English personal pronouns 'I, you (s/pl), he, she, we, they, one', or by general nouns such as 'people'. **On** is *always* used with a third person singular verb; its corresponding possessive adjectives are **son**, **sa**, **ses**; its emphatic pronoun is **soi**; its reflexive pronoun is **se**; and its direct *and* indirect object pronoun is **vous**.

> ***On* le ferait volontiers.**
> We'd do it willingly.

> ***On* verra.**
> We'll see.

> ***On* y va, *nous*?**
> Shall we go?

> ***On* a des amis autour de *soi*.**
> They have friends round them (for support).

If **on** clearly refers to a feminine and/or plural noun, adjectives or past participles referring to the noun must agree with the noun. The verb remains singular.

> **Alors, *on* est *contentes*, les petites?**
> Well, are we happy now, girls?

> ***On* est *devenus* bon copains.**
> We became good friends.

On is also used to form the passive (see **41.3, 41.4.1**).

> ***On* a refait le toit.**
> The roof has been repaired.

The form **l'on** may occur instead of **on**, especially following **et, ou, où, si** 'and, or, where, if'. This is probably simply to improve the sound:

> ***Ou l'on* écoute, *ou l'on* se tait.**
> Either you listen or be quiet.

11.9 *Même(s)* (m/fpl)

(a) adjective 'same, very'

When **même** means 'same' it *precedes* the noun and is itself preceded by a definite article:

> **Elle a mis *la même* robe que moi.**
> She's wearing the same dress as me.

> **J'ai toujours *les mêmes* cours.**
> I still have the same classes.

When **même** means 'very' it *follows* the noun:

> **Ce sont *les paroles mêmes* du professeur.**
> They are the teacher's very words.

When **même** is joined by a hyphen to an emphatic pronoun it means 'self' (see **14.2i**):

> **Il le fera *lui-même*.**
> He will do it himself.

> **Nous avons trouvé la maison *nous-mêmes*.**
> We found the house ourselves.

(b) pronoun

le, la, les + **même(s)** 'the same'

> **J'aime ton chapeau; moi, j'ai *le même*.**
> I like your hat; I've got one the same.

> **Pour lui un café; pour elle *le même*.**
> A coffee for him; the same for her.

> **Ce sont toujours *les mêmes* qui sont les derniers.**
> It's always the same (ones) who are last.

(c) adverb

Même (invariable) 'even' usually *follows* the verb, but *precedes* the past participle. **Même** may be followed by an emphatic pronoun.

> **On pourrait refuser *même* d'y aller.**
> We could even refuse to go.

> **Il ne l'a *même* pas vue.**
> He did not even see her.

> ***Même lui* ne s'en souvient plus.**
> Even he does not remember it any more.

(d) some expressions using **même**:

quand même/tout de même	all the same/nevertheless
de même	similarly
même pas	not even (that)

11.10   *Tel(le)(s)*

(a) adjective

Tel 'such' is usually preceded by **un(e)**, **de**: **un tel, une telle** . . . 'such a'. Note the different word order in French and English.

> ***Une telle* réponse est parfaite.**
> Such a reply is perfect.

> **On n'a jamais vu *de tels* films.**
> We've never seen such films.

If one wants to use an expression such as 'such a lovely day!' or 'such expensive presents!', one has to say:

> ***Une si* belle journée!**
> **Des cadeaux *tellement coûteux*!**

This is because **tel** cannot be used to qualify another adjective. It is replaced by **si** or **tellement**.

Tel may also be followed by **que** 'such as, like':

> **Les problèmes sont *tels que* vous nous les avez racontés.**
> The problems are as you told us.

> **Une solution *telle que* celle que vous proposez est impossible.**
> A solution such as you suggest is impossible.

(b) pronoun

Tel occurs as a pronoun in a few expressions:

M. un *tel*	Mr So and So	**Mme une *telle***	Mrs So and So

> **N'importe si *tel* et *tel* ne l'aiment pas.**
> It doesn't matter if some people don't like it.

(c) some expression using **tel**:

de telle façon/manière/sorte que (see 39.2.2)	so that, in such a way that
à tel jour	on such and such a day
en tant que tel	as such
en telle ou telle circonstance	in such and such a situation

11.11 *Quelque*

(a) adjective: **quelque(s)** (mf/pl) 'some, a few'

> **Nous avons *quelques* difficultés à parler allemand.**
> We have some difficulties speaking German.

> **Attends *quelques* instants!**
> Wait a few minutes!

(b) adverb: **quelque** (invariable) 'some, approximately'

> **Il y a *quelque* trente ans qu'elle a quitté la France.**
> She left France some thirty years ago.

> ***Quelque* stupides qu'ils soient ils s'en tireront.**
> However stupid they are, they'll manage.

11.11.1 **Quelqu'un** (ms) pronoun 'someone, somebody'. If **quelqu'un** is qualified by an adjective, the adjective is preceded by **de, d'**:

> ***Quelqu'un* est à la porte.**
> Someone is at the door.

> **Il faut *quelqu'un de* sérieux.**
> We need a responsible person.

11.11.2 **Quelque chose** (ms) pronoun 'something' – always *two* words in French, *one* in English. If **quelque chose** is qualified by an adjective, the adjective is preceded by **de, d'**:

> **Tu veux boire *quelque chose*?**
> You want something to drink?

> **C'est *quelque chose d'*incroyable.**
> That's something unbelievable.

11.11.3 **Quelques-un(e)s** (pl) pronoun 'some, a few' formed of **quelques** (adjective) + **un(e)s**. **Quelques-un(e)s** agrees in gender with the noun it refers to:

> ***Quelques-uns* lisaient leurs journaux.**
> Some (of them) were reading their papers.

> ***Quelques-unes* de ces femmes sont très belles.**
> Some of these women are very beautiful.

11.12 *Qui que, quoi qui/que* 'whoever, whatever' – always used with the subjunctive (see 39.2.2)

> ***Qui que ce soit qui appelle*, je ne suis pas là.**
> Whoever calls, I'm not in.

> ***Quoi qu'elle t'offre*, prends-le.**
> Whatever she offers you, take it.

Be very careful not to confuse **quoi que** 'whatever' with **quoique** 'although'.

11.13 *N'importe + quel; lequel, qui, quoi; combien, comment, où, quand*

(a) adjective

n'importe quel(le)(s) 'any'

> **Elle écoute *n'importe quelle* histoire.**
> She listens to any (old) story.

> **Il arrivera à *n'importe quel* moment.**
> He'll arrive at any time.

(b) pronoun

n'importe + lequel, laquelle, lesquel(le)s 'any one'

> **Il m'a donné trois boîtes de chocolats. Tu peux avoir *n'importe laquelle*.**
> He has given me three boxes of chocolates. You can have any one you want.

> **Il y a trop de livres: prenez donc *n'importe lesquels*.**
> There are too many books, so take any (of them).

n'importe + qui 'anyone, anybody' (**n'importe qui** can be replaced by **quiconque**)

> ***N'importe qui* peut venir.**
> Anyone can come.

> **Parle à *n'importe qui*/*quiconque*.**
> Speak to anyone.

n'importe + quoi 'anything'

> **Il dit *n'importe quoi*.**
> He (just) says anything.

(c) adverb

n'importe + combien, comment, où, quand 'however much, somehow, wherever, whenever'

> **Tu fais ça *n'importe comment*.**
> You're making a real mess of this.

> ***N'importe comment*, j'y arriverai.**
> I'll manage somehow.

11.14 *Maint(e)(s)* adjective 'many, many a, several'

Maint(e)(s) is usually reserved for written French. In spoken French it is normally replaced by **plus d'un(e)**, **plusieurs**, **de nombreux/nombreuses**:

> **Elle y est allée *maintes* fois./Elle y est allée *plus d'une* fois.**
> She went there many times.

> **Pour *maints* étudiants la vie est dure./Pour *beaucoup* d'étudiants la vie est dure.**
> Life is hard for many students.

12 ## Personal pronouns

12.1 ### Subject, direct object, indirect object pronouns

	Subject		Direct Object		Indirect Object	
1st person singular	**je**	I	**me (m')**	me	**me (m')**	to/for me
2nd person singular	**tu**	you	**te (t')**	you	**te (t')**	to/for you
3rd person singular	**il**	he, it	**le (l')**	him, it	**lui**	to/for him, it
	elle	she, it	**la (l')**	her, it	**lui**	to/for her, it
1st person plural	**nous**	we	**nous**	us	**nous**	to/for us
2nd person plural	**vous**	you	**vous**	you	**vous**	to/for you
3rd person plural	**ils**	they	**les**	them	**leur**	to/for them
	elles	they	**les**	them	**leur**	to/for them

12.2 ### Use of the subject pronouns

(a) **Tu** is the informal, singular pronoun used when the person addressed is well known to the speaker or writer, or is a child.

> *Tu* **veux venir ou non?**
> You want to come or not?

Vous is used both as the formal, singular pronoun – usually when the person addressed is not so well known to the speaker or writer – and as the plural pronoun.

> *Vous* **voulez venir, Madame?**
> Do you want to come, (Mrs Smith)?

> **Jean et Isabelle, où étiez-***vous* **ce matin?**
> Jean and Isabelle, where were you this morning?

(b) When there are two or more subjects care must be taken to ensure that the correct plural forms of the pronoun and verb are used (see **22**). If a first person subject is involved, then the plural pronoun is **nous** and the verb agrees with **nous**. If second and third person subjects are combined, then the plural pronoun is **vous** and the verb agrees with **vous**.

> **Moi et mon frère,** *nous irons* **au cinéma.**
> My brother and I will go to the cinema.

> **Vous et Madame Guiat,** *vous allez* **nous représenter à la réunion.**
> You and Mme Guiat will represent us at the meeting.

> **Véronique et toi,** *vous viendrez* **demain?**
> Will you and Véronique come tomorrow?

(c) **Il(s)** and **elle(s)** refer to masculine and feminine nouns, singular and plural – whether the nouns are people or things.

> **C'est une ville magnifique!** *Elle* **attire de nombreux visiteurs chaque année.**
> It's a wonderful city! It attracts many visitors every year.

Il(s), **elle(s)** are frequently replaced by the demonstrative pronoun **ce/c'** if the verb is **être**.

> **L'homme qui m'attendait tous les soirs au coin de la rue?** *C'était* **mon père.**
> The man who waited for me every evening at the street corner? It was my father.

> **Qui faisait ce bruit affreux?** *C'était* **la police.**
> Who was making that awful noise? It was the police.

(d) **Il** is used as the impersonal, or neuter, subject in impersonal verb phrases, and with **être** and **avoir** (see **46**):

il **importe de** + infinitive	it is important to
il **reste à** + infinitive	it remains to
il **est nécessaire de** + infinitive	it is necessary to
il **y a**	there is/are

> *Il* **y a des gens qui n'ont jamais fumé.**
> There are people who have never smoked.

Il est, il était . . . il y a, il y avait . . . are invariably singular, whereas **c'est, c'était** can become plural if the subject referred to is third person plural (see **6.3a**).

12.3 **Position and use of the direct object pronouns**

(a) The direct object pronouns normally precede the verb, or the auxiliary verb **avoir**.

> **Il** *me* **voit.**
> He/It can see me.

> **Elle** *t'***a vu(e) hier au cinéma.**
> She saw you at the cinema yesterday.

> **Cette élève, je** *la* **connais.**
> I know that pupil.

> **On** *les* **a entendu(e)s chanter.**
> We heard them singing.

(b) The pronouns **le** and **les** are *never* combined with **à** or **de** – unlike the articles **le, les** (**au, aux, du, des**) (see **2**).

> **Il s'est décidé à le faire.**
> He has decided to do it.

(c) The impersonal direct object pronoun **le/l'** may replace, or refer back to, an entire idea or sentence, or **cela**. It is frequently used to finish off a sentence, and it is frequently used in comparative constructions.

> **Il aura bientôt terminé. Il** *l'***a dit.**
> He'll have finished soon. He said so.

> **Elle n'est pas heureuse. Je** *le* **vois.**
> She isn't happy. I can tell.

> **A-t-il entendu cela? Il *l*'a entendu.**
> Did he hear that? He heard it.

> **Elle est beaucoup plus intelligente qu'on ne *le* croyait.**
> She is much more intelligent than we thought.

English does not always require the addition of 'it' in equivalent contexts. But, in some cases where English *does* include 'it', French does not. This occurs with verbs such as **considérer, trouver**:

> **Elle considère inutile de répéter la phrase.**
> She considers *it* pointless to repeat the sentence.

In certain verb phrases **le/l'** is actually part of the phrase and *must* be included: e.g. *l'*emporter sur 'to get the better of', *l'*échapper belle 'to have a narrow escape'.

> **Ils *l*'emportaient sur leurs ennemis.**
> · They were getting the better of their enemies.

<table><tr><td>**12.4**</td><td>**Use of the indirect object pronouns**</td></tr></table>

These pronouns include 'to' and/or 'for' in their meaning. So when verbs have **à** in their construction, the pronoun form used is the indirect object.

> **Mais elle *lui* a écrit. (écrire à qn)**
> But she has written to him.

> **Vous allez *nous* permettre de partir? (permettre à qn)**
> You will allow us to leave?

Some French verbs carry the meaning 'to/for someone': e.g. **payer, chercher**. Such verbs use the indirect object pronoun form.

> **Je vais *te* chercher un mouchoir.**
> I'm going to get a handkerchief for you.

> **On va *lui* payer un café.**
> We're going to buy him a coffee.

<table><tr><td>**12.5**</td><td></td></tr></table>

Y is an adverbial pronoun which refers to a place or location, but *never* to a person in formal use.

(a) adverb: **y** 'there' may replace several prepositions or prepositional phrases, but *not* **de**.

> **Je vais à Paris. (J'*y* vais.)**
> I'm going to Paris.

> **Il va au lycée. (Il *y* va.)**
> He is going to the lycée.

> **La reine est arrivée à la mairie à midi. (Elle *y* est arrivée à midi.)**
> The queen arrived at the town hall at noon.

> **Son manteau est dans l'armoire. (Son manteau *y* est.)**
> His/Her coat is in the wardrobe.

> **Elle s'est tenue près de la porte. (Elle s'*y* est tenue.)**
> She stood by the door.

(b) pronoun: **y** 'it' replaces **à** + noun.

> **On répondra à ta lettre. (On *y* répondra.)**
> They'll reply to your letter.

> **Nous pensons à ton anniversaire. (Nous *y* pensons.)**
> We are thinking about your birthday.

> **Il faut réfléchir à cette proposition. (Il faut *y* réfléchir.)**
> We'll have to give some thought to that proposal.

Note that **y** can occasionally refer to a person in informal use:

> **A-t-elle pensé à son frère? Oui, elle a pensé à lui/elle *y* a pensé.**
> Has she thought about her/his brother? Yes, she has (thought about him).

> **Parles- *y*.**
> Talk to him/her.

12.6 **En** is an adverbial pronoun meaning 'from there, some, of them'.

(a) adverb: **en** refers to a place or location and always replaces a phrase introduced by **de**.

> **Nous n'allons pas à Paris. Nous *en* revenons. (revenir de)**
> We're not going to Paris. We're just back from there.

> **Elles sortent de l'école. Elles *en* sortent. (sortir de)**
> They are (just) coming out of school. They are coming out (of it).

(b) pronoun: **en** replaces the preposition **de** (usually part of a verb construction) + noun.

> **Quel est son nom? Hélas, je ne m'*en* souviens plus. (se souvenir de)**
> What is his name? I'm sorry, I can't remember (it).

> **Tu prends un pot? Merci, je n'*en* ai pas envie. (avoir envie de)**
> Would you like a drink? No thanks, I don't want one.

> **Connaît-elle ce roman? Oui, elle *en* a lu plusieurs chapitres. (lire plusieurs chapitres de)**
> Does she know the novel? Yes, she has read several chapters (of it).

En may refer to a quantity or number of things *or* people. The actual quantity or number may be specified.

> **A-t-elle un frère? Oui, elle *en* a *un*.**
> Does she have a brother? Yes, she does/she has one (brother).

> **Prends encore du vin. Non, merci, j'*en* ai eu *assez*.**
> Have some more wine. No thanks, I've had enough (of it).

> **De quelle amie parles-tu? J'*en* connais *trois*.**
> Which friend were you talking about? I know three (of them).

> **Je ne veux pas d'argent. J'*en* ai *trop*.**
> I don't want any money. I have too much (of it).

(c) **En** may replace, or be substituted for, or refer to, an entire statement or idea.

> **Avez-vous besoin de sommeil? Non, je n'*en* ai plus besoin.**
> Do you need some sleep? No, I don't any more.

> **Tu ne m'aimes plus? J'*en* suis bouleversé!**
> You don't love me any more? I'm terribly upset!

(d) **En** also occurs in certain expressions: e.g. *en* **vouloir à qn** 'to bear a grudge against someone', s'*en* **prendre à qn** 'to take it out on someone'.

> **Je lui *en* veux.**
> I have a grudge against him/her.

13 Reflexive pronouns

13.1 Reflexive pronouns occur with verbs – making them reflexive verbs – and always agree in person and number with the subject:

	Singular	Plural
1st person	je *me*	nous *nous*
2nd person	tu *te*	vous *vous* (also polite singular)
3rd person	il/elle *se*	ils/elles *se*

> **Elle *se* lave.** (*se* **laver**)
> She is getting washed.

> **Nous allons *nous* lever bientôt.** (*se* **lever**)
> We're going to get up soon.

> **Après *t'*être reposé(e) un peu, viens manger avec nous.** (*se* reposer)
> After you've had a rest come and eat with us.

NOTE | These verbs are not normally reflexive in English.

14 Emphatic pronouns; position and order of pronouns

14.1 The emphatic (stressed) pronouns have separate forms in the third person for masculine and feminine genders, in both singular and plural. There is also a third person singular form **soi** which corresponds to the indefinite pronouns **chacun, on, personne, tout le monde** (see **11.4b, 11.8, 47.8, 11.1b**).

	Singular	Plural
1st person	moi	nous
2nd person	toi, vous	vous
3rd person	lui/elle and soi	eux/elles

14.2 **Uses of the emphatic pronouns**

The emphatic pronouns are used in a variety of contexts.

(a) after a preposition or prepositional phrase, such as **de, au lieu de, pour, chez**:

> **Elle est arrivée *chez moi*.**
> She arrived at my house.

> **On veut partir *avant lui*.**
> We want to leave before him.

> **Vous pourrez le faire *sans eux*.**
> You can do it without them.

(b) after the preposition **à**:

Indirect object pronouns **me, te, lui, nous, vous, leur** are used with verbs such as **donner, obéir, promettre** and mean 'to me, to you, to him/her . . .'

> **Elle *lui* a *permis* de sortir.**
> She allowed him/her to go out.

> **On *nous* a *donné* le livre.**
> They gave the book to us.

If **me, te, nous, vous** acting as *direct* objects are present these pronouns cannot co-occur with the *indirect* object pronouns. To express 'to me, to you, to him/her . . .' in such cases **à moi, à toi, à lui, à elle** . . . are used.

> **Tu *me* présenteras *à elle*?**
> You will introduce me to her?

> **Il *nous* a recommandé(e)s *à eux*.**
> He recommended us to them.

Certain verbs such as **venir, courir**, involving actual movement towards someone, are followed by **à** + emphatic pronoun.

> **Elle *est venue à nous*.**
> She came to us.

> **Les enfants *sont allés à lui*.**
> The children went to him.

A few fairly common verbs are also followed by **à** + emphatic pronoun. These verbs do not involve any movement towards a person: **penser à, avoir recours à, être à, s'intéresser à**:

> **Il *pense à elle*.**
> He is thinking about her.

> **Ils *ont* souvent *recours à nous*.**
> They often consult us.

> **C'*est à toi*.**
> It's yours.

> **Ils *s'intéressent à nous*.**
> They are interested in us.

(c) after **c'est** and **ce sont**:

C'est *moi*.	It's me.
C'est *toi, vous*.	It's you (informal, formal).
Ce ne sera pas *lui/elle*.	It won't be him/her.
Ce sera *nous*.	It'll be us.
C'est *vous*.	It's you (pl).

but for the third person plural:

Ce sont *eux/elles*.	It's them.

(d) to emphasize the subject:

Lui, il n'en sait rien.
He knows nothing about it.

Moi, j'irai sans toi.
I'll go without you.

Aussi, seul(e)(s) 'too, alone', or a cardinal number, may be included for additional emphasis, and **autres** may be added to **nous**, **vous** for additional emphasis.

Lui aussi pourra le faire.
He will be able to do it as well.

C'est pour la vie, *nous deux*.
We'll be together, the two of us, for always.

Nous en sommes ravi(e)s, *nous autres*.
As for us, *we* are delighted with/about it.

(e) in expressions without verbs:

Qui l'a fait? *Nous. Pas elle.*
Who did it? Us./We did. Not her.

Tu ne veux pas y aller? *Moi non plus.*
You don't want to go (there)? Neither do I.

(f) in comparative phrases:

Elle est *plus* intéressante *que lui*.
She is more interesting than he is/him.

Il a la *même* voiture *que moi*.
He has the same car as me/I have.

(g) in the negative phrase **ni . . . ni . . . ne . . .**:

Ni toi ni nous n'avons *accepté* de répondre à la question.
Neither you nor we agreed to answer the question.

(h) in double subjects:

Son père et *lui* sont allés en ville.
His father and he went into town. (see **22.2, 22.3.2**)

(i) with **-même(s)** 'self/selves':

moi-même	nous-mêmes
toi-même/vous-même	vous-mêmes
lui-même	eux-mêmes
elle-même	elles-mêmes

Je le ferai *moi-même*.
I'll do it myself.

(j) **Soi** is used with indefinite pronouns (see **1.8**), and with the impersonal **il** (see **12.2d**).

> ***Tout le monde* doit rentrer chez *soi*.**
> Everyone must go home.

> ***On* a souvent des amis plus intelligents que *soi*.**
> We often have friends who are more intelligent than we are.

> ***Chacun* pour *soi*.**
> Every man for himself.

14.3   Position of pronouns

(a) Pronouns are normally placed immediately before the verb, the auxiliary verb, or an infinitive to which they are linked in meaning – in statements, questions and negative forms:

Il *l'adore*.	He adores her/him/it.
J'*y vais*.	I'm going.
J'*en ai* vu(e)s.	I've seen some (of them).
Elle ne *l'a* pas lu.	She hasn't read it.
Je vais *lui envoyer* un mot.	I'll write him a note.
Va *leur dire* au revoir.	Go and say goodbye to them.
On peut *en trouver* plusieurs.	You may find several.

(b) Pronouns *precede* a negative imperative, but *follow* a positive imperative and are linked to it by a hyphen.

Ne me parlez *pas* comme ça!	Don't speak to me like that!
N'en parlons *pas!*	Let's forget about it!
Dites-*lui* de revenir bientôt!	Tell him/her to come back soon!
Bois-*en* un peu!	Drink a little (of it)!
Prends-*le* mais ne *le* donne pas à ton frère!	Take it but don't give it to your brother!

With the positive imperative **me** and **te** are replaced by **moi** and **toi**.

Donnez-moi votre billet!	Give me your ticket!

An **s** is added to the singular positive imperative of **-er** verbs before **y** and **en**.

Vas-y!	Come on!/Get on with it!
N'*y* va pas!	Don't go (there)!
Manges-en!	Eat some!
N'*en* mange plus!	Don't eat any more!

(c) There are two small groups of verbs, each followed by an infinitive, and with them the pronoun is placed before the *principal* verb: **faire, laisser, envoyer** and **regarder, voir, écouter, entendre, sentir.**

On *y fera* installer un placard.	We'll have a cupboard installed.
Il va *la laisser* partir.	He's going to let her leave.
Ne *les laissez* pas tomber!	Don't drop them!
Le professeur *l'a envoyé(e)* chercher ses clés.	The teacher sent him/her to fetch his keys.
Elle *nous regarde* travailler.	She is watching us work.
Je *le sens* brûler.	I smell it burning.

When the principal verb is in the positive imperative form, the pronoun is placed after the imperative and linked to it by a hyphen.

Faites-les entrer!	Show them in!
Laisse-nous dormir!	Let us sleep!
Regarde-la pleurer!	Look at her crying!

14.4 Order of pronouns

When more than one of the pronouns occur in a verb phrase, there is a special order in which they are placed. The following table is a useful guide:

me te se nous vous	le/l' before la/l' les	lui before leur	before **y**	before **en**

(a) examples with **me, te, se, nous, vous, le/l', la/l', les**:

Il *me l'a* donné(e).	He has given it to me.
Ne *nous les* montre pas!	Don't show them to us!
Elle *se le* gardera.	She'll keep it for herself.
Nous *vous l'*enverrons chercher.	We'll send you to get it.

(b) examples including **lui, leur**:

| Ne *les lui* donnez pas! | Don't give them to him/her! |
| Il *la leur* a montrée. | He showed it to them. |

(c) examples including **y** and **en**:

Elle *m'y* a vu(e).	She saw me there.
Nous *vous y* attendrons.	We'll wait for you there.
Il *les y* a laissé(e)s tomber.	He dropped them there.
Elle ne *s'en* souvient jamais.	She never remembers it.
Je vais *leur en* parler.	I'm going to speak to them about it.
On *lui en* donne tous les jours.	We give him/her some every day.
Il n'*y en* a plus.	There's none left.

(d) The exception to the above guidelines has to do with the positive imperative. The pronouns *follow* the positive imperative and are linked to it by hyphens (see **14.3b**).

Donne-*le-lui*!	Give it to him!
Montrez-*le-nous*!	Show it to us!
Cherchez-*les-y*!	Look for them there!

Offrez-*leur-en!*	Offer them some!
Demande-*lui-en!*	Ask him for some!

With the positive imperative **mol** and **toi** are used instead of **me** and **te**, and are moved right to the end of the group:

Rends-*la-moi!*	Give it back to me!

These two changes are not required if **y** and **en** are involved:

Donne-*m'en!*	Give me some!
Va-*t'en!*	Go away!

15 Relative pronouns

The relative pronouns link the information contained in a relative clause to a preceding noun, pronoun, or noun phrase (antecedents). The gender and number of verbs and adjectives in the relative clause agree with the antecedent.

15.1 **Qui** (invariable) 'who, which, that' is the subject in the relative clause. It is used for people, animals or things:

> **L'homme *qui* attendait au coin de la rue était son père.**
> The man who was waiting at the corner of the street was his/her father.

> **Toi, *qui* as l'air content, dis-moi pourquoi.**
> You look happy. Tell me why.

> **Ce sont un étudiant et une lectrice *qui* vont nous représenter.**
> It's a student and an assistant who are going to represent us.

> **Le chat *qui* est toujours dans mon jardin n'est pas à moi.**
> The cat that's always in my garden is not mine.

and in some set expressions and proverbs:

Qui plus est . . .	And what's more . . .
Voilà *qui* est agréable!	That's super!
Qui se ressemble s'assemble.	Birds of a feather flock together.

15.2 **Que/qu'** (invariable) 'who(m), which, that' is the direct object in the relative clause. It is used for people, animals or things:

> **Voilà le livre *que* tu as cherché partout.**
> There/Here is the book you looked/have been looking for everywhere.

> **Les étudiants *qu'*elle a invités sont ses amis.**
> The students she invited are her friends.

English does not need the pronouns 'who, who(m), which, that' in the relative clause. But in French, in contrast, the relative pronouns *must* be used.

15.3 Preposition + **qui** refers only to people:

> **La femme *chez qui* j'habitais était française.**
> The woman whose house I was living in was French.

> **Le jeune homme à *qui* elle a donné les clés de la voiture était un voleur.**
> The young man she gave the car keys to was a thief.

> **C'est un professeur *en qui* tu peux avoir confiance.**
> He's/She's a teacher you can have confidence in.

15.4 **Lequel, lesquels, laquelle, lesquelles** 'who, which' are used as the subject in a relative clause, instead of **qui**, only in administrative or literary language:

> **Cette femme, *laquelle* était fort élégante, était en réalité des services de police.**
> That woman, who was extremely elegant, was in fact a police officer.

15.5 Preposition + **lequel** . . . refers to people, animals or things:

> **C'est la jeune femme *avec laquelle* (*or avec qui*) il est allé à l'école.**
> It's the young woman he went to school with.

> **Où est le sac *dans lequel* j'ai mis l'argent?**
> Where is the bag I put the money in?

15.6 **De, à** are combined with **lequel** to form the pronouns:

> **duquel, desquels, de laquelle, desquelles**
> **auquel, auxquels, à laquelle, auxquelles**

These changes are similar to changes made with the articles (see **2**). The contracted forms are used whenever **de** or **à** form part of a prepositional phrase or the construction following a verb:

> **Sa mère, *grâce à laquelle* (*or* à qui) il s'en est tiré, est très malade.**
> His mother, thanks to whom he was able to cope, is very ill.

> **Un garçon d'accord, mais *duquel* (*or de qui*) s'agit-il?**
> A boy, yes, but which one?

15.7 When referring to people, and following a preposition, either **lequel** or **qui** can be used. The exception to this rule occurs with the prepositions **parmi**, **au nombre de** and **entre**. Following these prepositions the appropriate form of **lequel** is always used:

> **Les otages, *parmi lesquels* se trouvaient les trois religieuses, étaient morts.**
> The hostages, amongst whom were the three nuns, were dead.

15.8 **Dont** 'of/about whom, which; whose' is used for people, animals or things, and can be used instead of **de qui, duquel, desquels, de laquelle, desquelles**:

> **Voici l'argent *dont* (*or duquel*) il a besoin.**
> Here's the money he needs.

> **C'est la fille *dont* (*or de qui, de laquelle*) il parle.**
> It's the girl he's talking about.

> **C'est la maison *dont* (*or de laquelle*) je me souviens.**
> It was the house I remember.

15.8.1 The order of words following **dont** is important – subject, verb (+ object):

> Voilà la maison *dont* les volets sont verts.
> This/That is the house whose shutters are green.

> Les étudiants *dont* le nom figure ci-dessous sont priés de passer à mon bureau dès que possible. Merci.
> Would the students whose names are below call at my office as soon as possible. Thank you.

15.8.2 **Dont** always follows its antecedent directly. From the examples at 15.8 above: **l'argent** *dont* . . ., **la fille** *dont* . . ., **la maison** *dont* . . .

15.8.3 **Dont** cannot be used instead of **de qui, duquel** . . . if the relative 'whose' is dependent on a noun governed by a preposition: *sous* **la présidence de** '*during* whose . . .', *avec* **l'aide de** '*with* whose . . .', *à la fenêtre de* '*at* whose . . .':

> On a vu la maison *à* la porte *de laquelle* (*not dont*) la jeune fille a frappé.
> We saw the house where the girl knocked at the door.

> C'est l'homme *sous* la présidence *duquel/de qui* (*not dont*) la Communauté a fait le plus de progrès.
> He's the man during whose presidency the Community has made most progress.

> Voici l'étudiante *avec* l'aide *de laquelle/de qui* (*not dont*) vous allez compléter vos recherches.
> This is the student with whose help you will complete your research.

The English translations indicate that these are formal structures. Informally, in spoken French, these complex structures would probably be divided into two sentences:

> Ton ami . . . je ne me souviens jamais de son adresse . . .

15.9 **Où** 'where, in which, when' is a relative adverb which can express place or time. It refers only to things. **Où** can be used with several prepositions: **d'où** 'from where/which', **par où** 'by which', **jusqu'où** 'how far, to what extent'. **Où** can replace relatives such as **dans lequel** . . ., **duquel** . . ., **par lequel** . . .

> Restez *où* vous êtes!
> Stay where you are!

> Voilà la maison *où* (*or dans laquelle*) je suis né(e).
> That's the house where I was born.

> C'est le pays *d'où* il vient.
> It's the country he comes from.

> Je connais les sentiers *par où* (*or par lesquels*) on arrive à l'église.
> I know the paths to the church.

> On verra *jusqu'où* il peut aller.
> We'll see how far he'll go.

Some examples where **où** expresses time:

> le mois *où*   the month when
> l'année *où*   the year when

> le moment *où*   the moment when
> C'était le jour *où* elle est arrivée.   It was the day she arrived.

If the antecedent is not specified, **là** often precedes **où**:

> *Là où* elle va, elle trouve des amis.
> Wherever she goes she makes friends.

15.10   Preposition + **quoi** refers only to things. It is also used to refer to neuter pronouns such as **ce, cela, quelque chose, rien**:

> On sait *de quoi* il s'agissait.
> We know what it was about.

> Il a écouté le discours *après quoi* il est allé prendre un verre.
> He listened to the speech and afterwards went for a drink.

> Il n'y a vraiment pas *de quoi* s'inquiéter.
> There's nothing to worry about.

> Ce à *quoi* nous pensons ce sont nos examens.
> What we are thinking about is our exams.

15.11   Ce qui, ce que/qu', ce dont 'which, what' are compound relative pronouns. Ce (invariable) refers back to information which may be contained in an entire sentence, or paragraph. The pronouns **qui, que/qu', dont** function exactly as if they were being used on their own (see above):

> Elle a toujours refusé de se soumettre, *ce qui* ne lui plaît pas. (*qui* is the subject of the relative clause)
> She's always refused to obey, which doesn't please him/her.

> Elle fera *ce qu'elle* veut. (*que* is the object of the relative clause)
> She will do what she wants.

> Ils ne se souviennent jamais de *ce dont* nous leur parlons. (*dont* < parler *de*)
> They never remember what we talk to them about.

15.11.1   **Tout** can precede **ce qui** . . . 'everything (that, which)'.

> Elle adore *tout ce qui* est écossais.
> She loves everything Scottish.

> Je ferai *tout ce qu'elle* me demande.
> I'll do everything she asks me to do.

> Nous avions appris *tout ce dont* nous avions besoin.
> We'd learned everything we needed to.

15.12   C'est (ce sont) . . . qui, que (qu'), dont 'it's . . . who, that, which' is used to emphasize someone or something. **C'est** is used for all persons, singular and plural. **Ce sont** is used for the third persons plural in formal spoken and written contexts.

> *C'est* Isabelle *qui* va comme d'habitude assurer le cours.
> It's Isabelle who will take the class as usual.

> *C'est/Ce sont* nos amis *qui* posent des questions.
> It's our friends asking questions.

> *C'est* votre passeport dont j'ai besoin.
> It's your passport I need.

The relative pronouns function exactly as if they were being used on their own, without the **ce**. The verb in the relative clause agrees with the subject, that is, with whoever or whatever is introduced by **c'est** or **ce sont**. Normally the present tense of **être** is used, but other tenses are also possible:

> *Ce sera* avec sa mère *qu'*il ira en Italie.
> It's/It will be his/her mother he'll go to Italy with.

If the subject emphasized is in the pronominal form, the emphatic pronoun is used (see **14.2c**).

> *Ce n'est pas moi qui* sera responsable.
> It's not me who'll be responsible.

> *C'est* grâce à *elle qu'*il s'en est tiré.
> It's thanks to her he succeeded.

Note the structure **c'est . . . que**, frequently used to emphasise something. In this case **que** is a conjunction. **C'est . . . que** is also used to draw attention to someone or something:

> *C'est* demain *qu'*on va partir. (emphasising 'demain')
> It's tomorrow we're leaving.

> *C'était* avec toute la famille *qu'*on allait partir en vacances.
> (emphasising 'toute la famille')
> It was with the whole family that we were going on holiday.

16 Interrogative pronouns, adjectives and adverbs

There are different sets of interrogative pronouns for people and for things, and some of the pronouns have two forms: a short form, and a longer compound form which includes the interrogative inversion **est-ce?** The longer forms are more likely to be used in contexts which are less formal such as spoken French, or informal letters. Some of the forms are also different depending on whether the pronoun is the subject or object of the interrogative clause, or whether it follows a preposition. The interrogative pronouns are usually accepted as masculine singular – for adjective and verb agreement – unless the pronouns clearly refer to feminine and/or plural nouns.

16.1 Forms for people

Subject	**qui?** or **qui est-ce qui?**	who?
Object	**qui?** or **qui est-ce que/qu'?**	who(m)?
Following a preposition	**de, à, avec . . . qui?** or **qui est-ce que/qu'?**	of, to, with . . . who(m)?

In the following examples, note the use – or not – of inversion.

Qui est à la porte?/*Qui est-ce qui* est à la porte?
Who is at the door?

Qui vous a vu(e/s)?/*Qui est-ce qui* vous a vu(e/s)?
Who saw you?

Qui as-tu trouvé?/*Qui est-ce que* tu as trouvé?
Who did you find?

Qui a-t-on entendu pleurer?/*Qui est-ce qu'*on a entendu pleurer?
Who did we hear crying?

A qui parle-t-elle?/*A qui est-ce qu'*elle parle?
Who is she talking to?

Près de qui est-il assis?/*Près de qui est-ce qu'*il est assis?
Who is he sitting beside?

16.2 Forms for animals and things

Subject	**qu'est-ce qui?**	what?
Object	**que/qu'?** or **qu'est-ce que/qu'?**	what?
Following a preposition	**de, à . . . quoi?** or **quoi est-ce que/qu'?**	of, to . . . what?

Once again, in the examples, note the use – or not – of inversion.

Qu'est-ce qui t'intéresse?
What are you interested in?

*Qu'est-ce qu'*il dit?
What is he saying?

Que veux-tu?/*Qu'est-ce que* tu veux?
What do you want?

Que pense-t-il de la maison?/*Qu'est-ce qu'*il pense de la maison?
What does he think of the house?

En quoi consiste-t-il?/*En quoi est-ce qu'*il consiste?
What does it consist of?

Avec quoi va-t-elle payer les billets?/*Avec quoi est-ce qu'*elle va payer les billets?
What is she going to pay for the tickets with?

16.3 Guidelines on the use of inversion

(a) **qui?** (subject pronoun, used for people) – no inversion.
(b) compound forms already include **est-ce?**, so additional inversion is *not* needed.
(c) **que/qu'?** (object pronoun, used for things) – inversion needed.
(d) **quoi?** (pronoun following prepositions, used for things) – inversion needed.

16.4 *Qui?* and *quoi?* can occur in phrases without verbs – usually in spoken French.

> **M. Martin est à la porte.** *Qui?*
> Mr Martin is at the door. Who?

> **Je n'ai pas entendu.** *Quoi?*
> I didn't hear. What?

> *Quoi* **de neuf?**
> What's new?

> *Quoi* **de plus joli que l'Ecosse?**
> What is lovelier than Scotland?

16.4.1 The interrogative pronoun **lequel?** 'who, which, what?'

Lequel implies that a choice is being made from a limited number of known people or things.

	Singular	Plural
Masculine	**lequel?**	**lesquels?**
Feminine	**laquelle?**	**lesquelles?**

There are also contracted forms following **de** and **à**:

	Singular	Plural
Masculine	**duquel?**	**desquels?**
Feminine	**de laquelle?**	**desquelles?**
Masculine	**auquel?**	**auxquels?**
Feminine	**à laquelle?**	**auxquelles?**

> *Laquelle* **des étudiantes cherchez-vous?**
> Which of the students are you looking for?

> **De tous les cours à la fac,** *lequel* **préfères-tu?**
> Which of all the classes at university do you prefer?

> **Il m'a dit qu'il a besoin d'un de ces livres. Mais** *duquel?*
> He told me he needs one of these books. But which (one)?

> *Auxquelles* **de vos amies avez-vous écrit?**
> Which of your friends did you write to?

16.4.2 The interrogative adjective **quel?** 'which, what?'

Quel has four forms:

	Singular	Plural
Masculine	**quel?**	**quels?**
Feminine	**quelle?**	**quelles?**

> *Quelle* **réponse?**
> What/which answer?

> *Quelle réponse* a-t-elle donnée?
> Which answer did she give?

Note the inversion when **quel?** modifies the subject of the sentence, as in the first two of the following examples:

> *Quels professeurs* seront là?
> Which teachers will be there?

> *Quelle* était la *femme* qui t'a donné le pourboire?
> Which woman gave you the tip?

> *Quelle heure* est-il?
> What time is it?

> *Quel jour* sommes-nous?
> What is the date?

> Dans *quelle poche* a-t-elle mis la clé?
> Which pocket did she put the key in?

16.4.3 The interrogative adverbs **combien de/d'?** 'how many?', **comment?** 'how?', **où?** 'where?', **quand?** 'when?'

In spoken French, simply by using interrogative intonation, a statement can become a question:

> **Il est là?**   He's here?

When any interrogative words are included in this kind of question, they are placed at the end of the sentence:

Elle attend *depuis combien de mois?*	She has been waiting how many months?
Vous l'avez fait *comment?*	How did you do it?
Ils vont *où?*	Where are they going?
Elle fait *quoi?*	She's doing what?
Ils aiment *quel* programme?	They like what (which) programme?

When an interrogative word *starts* the question there are various ways of dealing with the interrogative inversion:

(a) if the subject is a noun, simple inversion:

Où habite la vieille dame?	Where does the old lady live?
Quand partira le train?	When does the train leave?
Comment va le malade?	How is the patient?
Combien coûte cette bouteille de vin?	How much is this bottle of wine?

(b) if the subject is a pronoun, it is linked to the verb by a hyphen:

Où habite-t-elle?	Where does she live?
Quand *partira-t-il?*	When will it leave?
Comment *va-t-il?*	How is he?
Combien *coûte-t-elle?*	How much is it?

Another way of asking the same questions is to change the order of words, with the noun subject placed before or after the interrogative word – usually in informal, spoken French.

La vieille dame, elle habite où?	Où la vieille dame habite-t-elle?
Le train, il partira quand?	Quand le train partira-t-il?
Le malade, il va comment?	Comment le malade va-t-il?
Cette bouteille de vin, combien elle coûte?	Combien cette bouteille de vin coûte-t-elle?

The questions may also be asked by inserting **est-ce que?** after the question word. There is no additional inversion. This way of asking questions is much more common in informal, spoken French.

> Où *est-ce que* la vieille dame habite?
> Quand *est-ce que* le train partira/va partir?

NOTE Inversion of the verb and a noun subject is often avoided with interrogative words of more than one syllable: **comment?, combien?**

16.4.4 There is no inversion of the verb and a noun subject if the verb has a direct object or is closely linked to an adverbial phrase. In this case, you make inversion by adding a pronoun which agrees with the subject, and, in fact, you have a double subject.

> Quand *les enfants* mangent-*ils* leur petit déjeuner?
> When do the children have their breakfast?

> Comment *le premier ministre* va-t-*il* expliquer cela?
> How is the prime minister going to explain that?

> Comment *le professeur* l'a-t-*il* traduit en anglais?
> How did the teacher translate it into English?

16.4.5 Some of the interrogative adverbs may be preceded by a preposition:

D'où viennent-ils?	Where have they come from?
Jusqu'où compte-t-elle aller?	How far does she intend going?
Depuis quand les enfants attendent-ils?	How long have the children been waiting?
Pendant combien de temps êtes-vous resté(e/s)?	How long did you stay?

16.4.6 The interrogative adverb **pourquoi?** 'why?'

There are three possibilities with **pourquoi**:

(a) if the subject is a noun:

> *Pourquoi* l'étudiant va-t-il à la fac? *or* L'étudiant, *pourquoi* va-t-il à la fac?
> Why is the student going to the university?

(b) the informal version:

> Pourquoi *est-ce que* l'étudiant va à fac?

(c) if the subject is a pronoun:

> *Pourquoi* êtes-vous là?
> Why are you here?

17 Cardinal and ordinal numbers (see **49.4, 49.7**)

Cardinal numbers are adjectives and precede their noun. They can be grouped according to their form: simple or compound.

17.1 Simple forms

0	zéro	6	six	12	douze	30	trente
1	un, une	7	sept	13	treize	40	quarante
2	deux	8	huit	14	quatorze	50	cinquante
3	trois	9	neuf	15	quinze	60	soixante
4	quatre	10	dix	16	seize	100	cent
5	cinq	11	onze	20	vingt	1000	mille

17.2 Compound forms

Units are linked to tens by a hyphen – with the exception of the six numbers linked by **et** (**17.2.1**).

17   **dix-sept**   18   **dix-huit**   19   **dix-neuf**

22–29	**vingt-deux** *to* **vingt-neuf**
32–39	**trente-deux** *to* **trente-neuf**
42–49	**quarante-deux** *to* **quarante-neuf**
52–59	**cinquante-deux** *to* **cinquante-neuf**
62–99	**soixante-deux** *to* **quatre-vingt-dix-neuf**

In Belgium, Canada and Switzerland the old forms of 70, 80 and 90 are sometimes used:

70   **septante**   80   **octante** *or* **huitante**   90   **nonante**

17.2.1 Compound forms linked by **et**, *no* hyphens

21 **vingt et un**	31 **trente et un**
41 **quarante et un**	51 **cinquante et un**
61 **soixante et un**	71 **soixante et onze**

17.2.2 Compound forms without **et** and without hyphens

101 **cent un**	1,001 **mille un**

17.3 Numbers are invariable, but there are four exceptions to this rule – **un, zéro, vingt, cent.**

(a) **un, une: un** is used in counting, and with masculine nouns; **une** is used with feminine nouns.

un,deux, trois . . .	one, two, three . . .
un verre de vin	a/one glass of wine
Vingt et une étudiantes sont venues.	Twenty-one students came.

(b) **zéro, vingt, cent:** these numbers add **s** in the plural.

sept zéros	seven zeros/nothings
quatre-vingts	80
cinq cents	500

but the **s** is dropped whenever they are followed by another number:

quatre-vingt-douze	92
trois cent soixante-sept	367

17.4 Mille is invariable.

7,000 **sept mille** 9,021 **neuf mille vingt et un**

In dates **mille** may be shortened to **mil** – but this is a bit old-fashioned:

1941 *mille (or mil)* **neuf cent quarante et un**

When dates are spoken, as opposed to written, **dix-neuf cent** may be used instead of **mille neuf cent:**

dix-neuf cent quarante et un

NOTE **Cent** *must* be included in the date, whereas in English 'hundred' is usually omitted.

Mille and **cent** are *never* preceded by **un**, whereas in English 'thousand' and 'hundred' may be preceded by 'one' or 'a':

mille one/a thousand **cent** one/a hundred

17.4.1 Care should be taken with the following series (see **49.7d**):

mille (invariable, and *never* followed by **de**) 'thousand'

dix *mille* personnes ten thousand people

un millier (de/d'), des milliers (de/d') 'about a thousand, thousands'

Il y a *des milliers d'*étudiants dans les rues.
There are thousands of students in the streets.

un million (de/d'), cinq millions (de/d') 'a million, five million'

*un million d'*habitants a million inhabitants

un milliard (de/d'), douze milliards (de/') 'a billion, twelve billions'

La banque lui a prêté *cinquante milliards* d'euros.
The bank has lent him/her fifty billion euros.

17.5   Cardinal numbers

Cardinal numbers are used in the following:

(a) dates:

le 15 (*quinze*) mars	the 15th (of) March
le 3 (*trois*) janvier	the 3rd (of) January
Quel jour sommes-nous?	What's the date?
Nous sommes le 7 (*sept*).	It's the 7th.

but, exceptionally, the ordinal number is used for the first of the month:

le 1er (*premier*) avril	the 1st (of) April

NOTE   Months and days of the week begin with *small letters* in French.

(b) names of kings and queens:

Henri IV (*quatre*), Louis XIV (*quatorze*) *but* François 1er (*premier*)

(c) chapter and page numbers:

chapitre *deux, trois, quatre* . . . *but* chapitre *premier* or chapitre *un* à la page 18 (*dix-huit*)

(d) time:

à *cinq* heures	at five o'clock

The 24 hour clock is used in timetables:

à *quatorze* heures	at two o'clock

17.6   Punctuation in numbers

French	English
1000 or 1.000	1,000 or 1000
15294 or 15.294	15,294
8,5	8.5 (decimal point)

17.7   Ordinal numbers

Ordinal numbers are adjectives, but may be used as nouns.

17.7.1   **Le premier, la première 'first'; le second, la seconde or le/la deuxième 'second':**

Elle est *la première* de la classe.	She is top of the class.
Ils étaient *les premiers* à partir.	They were the first to leave.
Voilà un billet de *seconde* classe.	Here is a second class ticket.

C'est un politicien de *second* rang.	He's a minor politician.
C'est *la deuxième* fois qu'il est en retard.	It's the second time he's been late.

For most ordinal numbers **ième** is added to the cardinal.

trois > *troisième*	third
dix-sept > *dix-septième*	seventeenth
vingt et un > *vingt et unième*	twenty-first
cent > *centième*	hundredth

but there are some exceptions:

un > *premier* (see 17.7.1)	first
deux > *second, deuxième* (see 17.7.1)	second
cinq > *cinquième* (add **u**)	fifth
neuf > *neuvième* (**f** > **v**)	ninth

and there is a small group where the final **e** of the cardinal number is dropped:

quatre > *quatrième*	fourth
trente > *trentième*	thirtieth
mille > *millième*	thousandth

and in two cases the final **s** of the cardinal number is dropped:

quatre-vingts > *quatre-vingtième*	eightieth
six cents > *six centième*	six hundredth
neuf cents > *neuf centième*	nine hundredth

The abbreviated forms are the number + **-ème** (note that **-ème** is sometimes further shortened to a superscript **e**):

la 33*ème* étage	the 33rd floor
le 57*ème* livre	the 57th book

but

Jean-Paul *1er*	John-Paul 1

(You say: **Jean-Paul premier**.)

Some examples with numbers used as nouns and adjectives:

Je suis en *première* (année).	I'm in the sixth form.
Qui est le *onzième*? (*no* elision)	Who is eleventh?
C'est le *quinzième* siècle.	It's the fifteenth century.
Pour la *énième* fois!	For the umpteenth time!

18 Fractions (see **49.7**)

½	**un demi** *but* when 'half' is not a fraction use **la moitié (de)**		
⅓	**un tiers**	⅔	**deux tiers**
¼	**un quart**	¾	**trois quarts**

and for all the rest, the ordinal forms are used:

$\frac{1}{10}$	**un dixième**	$\frac{1}{11}$	**un onzième**	$\frac{2}{5}$	**deux cinquièmes**
$1\frac{1}{2}$	**un et demi**	$1\frac{1}{3}$	**un et un tiers**	$6\frac{3}{4}$	**six (et) trois quarts**
$\frac{1}{100}$	**un centième**	$\frac{1}{1000}$	**un millième**		

Some examples:

une *demi*-bouteille	a half bottle
trois kilos et *demi*	3½ kilos
une *demi*-heure	a half hour
une heure et *demie*	1.30 (a.m.)

NOTE | **Demi** is invariable, but **et demi(e)** agrees in gender (*not* number) with its noun (see **10.6c**).

Je serai là dans *un quart* d'heure.	I'll be there in quarter of an hour.
On a bu *les trois quarts* de la bouteille.	We've drunk three-quarters of the bottle.

19 Approximate quantities (see **49.7**)

Approximate quantities are all followed by **de/d'** if a noun is specified.

une *dizaine*	about ten
une (*demi*-)/*douzaine*	(half) a dozen
une *vingtaine*	about twenty
une *centaine*	about a hundred
un *millier*	about a thousand

and

plus de/d'	more than	*moins de/d'*	less than

Some examples:

Je voudrais *une demi-douzaine* d'œufs.	I'd like half a dozen eggs.
Il y avait *des centaines de* cafards.	There were hundreds of cockroaches.
Elles étaient *plus de/moins* de trente.	There were more/less than thirty (of them).

20 Dimensions (see **49.6**)

There are various ways of expressing length, breadth, height, depth, etc., some of which are given below. Perhaps the best way to deal with them is to select the form that you find easiest to remember.

20.1 Length

for things and animals:

Quelle est la longueur de la corde?	How long is the rope?
Quelle est la largeur de la rue?	How wide is the street?
Quelle est la hauteur de l'immeuble?	How high is the building?
Quelle est la profondeur de l'étang?	How deep is the pond?

and for people:

Combien mesure-t-il?	How tall is he?

20.2 *Long de, large de, haut de, profond de*

une corde *longue de* **5 mètres**	a rope 5 metres long
une rue *large de* **3 mètres**	a street 3 metres wide
un immeuble *haut de* **quatre étages**	a building four storeys high
un étang *profond d'***un mètre**	a pond one metre deep

and if a verb is required: **avoir/faire** + size + **de long** *or* **être** + **long de** + size:

Cette corde *a* **5 mètres** *de long.*	This rope is 5 metres long.
Cette rue *fait* **3 mètres** *de large.*	This street is 3 metres wide.
Cette corde *est longue de* **5 mètres.**	This rope is 5 metres long.
Ce fossé *est profond d'***un mètre.**	This ditch is one metre deep.

Different verbs are required for expressing the height of *people*:

C'*est* **un homme** *d'un mètre quatre-vingts.*
He's 6 feet tall.

Elle *mesure* **à peu près** *un mètre quatre-vingts.*
She's almost 6 feet tall.

Il *est plus grand qu'***elle.**
He's bigger than she is.

Elle *est plus petite que* **lui.**
She's smaller than him.

Ils n' *ont* **pas** *la même taille.*
They're not the same height.

C'est vrai, elle n'*a* **pas** *la même taille* **que lui.**
That's right, she isn't the same height as him.

20.3 Weight

for things and animals:

***Combien pèse* l'éléphant?**	What does the elephant weigh?

or

*Quel poids fait-*il?	What does it weight?
Il *pèse* environ . . . je ne sais pas.	It weighs about . . . I don't know.
Il *pèse* plus lourd que toi.	It's heavier than you.
Il *est moins lourd* (*or plus léger*) *qu'*elle.	It's lighter than her.

and for people:

*Combien pèse-*t-il?	What is his weight?
Il *pèse plus de* 127 *kilos.*	He's over 127 kilos/20 stone.
C'est une femme *de* 60 *kilogrammes* 500.	She's 60½ kilos/10 stone.

and when shopping:

Je voudrais 500 *grammes de fromage.*
I'd like 500g of cheese.

Environ 250 *grammes de cerises*, s'il vous plaît.
About 250g of cherries, please.

Et *un kilo de tomates.*
And a kilo of tomatoes.

Et enfin *une demi-livre de* sucre. Merci!
And finally 250g of sugar. Thank you!

Note the different order in English and French in the following:

a two-kilo packet	**un paquet** *de deux kilos*

21   Adverbs of quantity (see 4.3, 49.7)

These adverbs can introduce a noun, or modify a verb. If they introduce a noun they are followed by **de/d'** (see **4.3**). Some may also be followed by **que** in comparisons.

assez (de)	enough	**autant (de/que)**	so/as much/many
un peu (de)	a little, some	**beaucoup (de)**	a lot of, many
peu (de)	little, few	**plus (de/que)**	more
tant (de)	so much/many	**combien (de)?**	how much?
trop (de)	too much/many	**moins (de/que)**	fewer, less

Il a *assez d'*argent.	He has enough money.
Elle a *assez* entendu.	She has heard enough.
Nous avons *beaucoup de* travail.	We have a lot of work.
Moi aussi, j'al *beaucoup* travaillé.	I've worked hard too.
*Combien d'*influence a-t-il?	How much influence does he have?
Ce livre vaut *combien*?	How much is this book?
Il y a *moins de* gens ce soir.	There are fewer people tonight.
Il gagne *moins que* son frère.	He earns less than his brother.

Note that **un peu de** has a more positive meaning than **peu de**:

J'ai *un peu d'*argent.	I have a little money.
J'ai *peu d'*argent.	I haven't much money.

trop (de) can be modified by **beaucoup** or **un peu**:

Il a *beaucoup trop d'*argent.	He has far too much money.
Elle a bu *un peu trop.*	She has drunk a bit too much.

beaucoup is *never* preceded by **très**:

Merci *beaucoup*!	Thank you very much.

▌▌ The verb group

22   Agreement of verb and subject

The verb is formed of the stem, and an ending. For example in the infinitive
donner, the stem is **donn-** and the ending is **-er**. Most verbs are listed in a
dictionary in their infinitive form, which is the part of the verb which does not
indicate a subject (first, second or third person) or number (singular or plural).
The English equivalent of the infinitive is 'to' + verb. There are three main groups,
or conjugations, of verbs, identified according to their infinitive ending: **-er, -ir,
-re**.

donner	**donn- + -er**	to give
finir	**fin- + -ir**	to finish
vendre	**vend- + -re**	to sell

There are also verbs which have an infinitive ending **-oir: recevoir** 'to receive', **s'asseoir**
'to sit down'. Verb endings – in contrast to the infinitive – indicate the person, the
number, time (tenses) and mood (indicative, subjunctive). With these endings the verb
is called a finite verb.

22.1

The verb ending *always* agrees with the subject: singular subject + singular verb ending,
plural subject + plural verb ending.

> *Elle* chant*e* bien.   She sings well.
> *Nous* parl*ons* français.   We speak French.

22.2   Guidelines for verb/subject agreement

Normally, it is clear whether the subject is singular or plural, but there are some subjects
which cause difficulty. When the subject of the verb is **qui**, the verb agrees with the
antecedent (see **15.1**).

> *Toi et ton frère, qui avez été* tous les deux très paresseux, *vous allez*
> redoubler cette année.
> You and your brother, who have both been very lazy, are going to repeat
> this year.
>
> C'est *nous qui serons* responsables.
> We'll be responsible.

C'est is used with all the singular emphatic pronouns, and also, in informal contexts, for all the plural emphatic pronouns. In more formal written and spoken French the third person plural form is **ce sont** (see **6.3a, 14.2c**).

> *C'est elles* **qui font toujours la vaisselle.**
> *They* always do the washing-up.

> *Ce sont eux* **qui vont donner la réponse au ministre.**
> *They* are going to reply to the Minister.

and note the expression **si ce n'est** 'unless, except for, if not' (invariable):

> *Si ce n'est* (*pas*) *eux*, **qui est-ce?**
> If it's not *them*, who is it?

22.3 ### Compound subject + singular and/or plural verb

> *Un* des *films* **qui lui** *a/ont* **beaucoup plu, c'est 'La liste de Schindler'.**
> One of the films he liked very much was 'Schindler's List'.

> *Plus d'un* **de mes amis** *va/vont* **en France cet été.**
> Several of my friends are going to France this summer.

A singular noun referring to a group, or a quantity, has a singular verb: **la famille** 'family', **le comité** 'committee', **le parti socialiste** 'the socialist party', **la foule** 'crowd' . . . :

> *Le parti socialiste a* **trop de candidats.**
> The socialist party has too many candidates.

In the case of singular nouns expressing quantity followed by a plural noun, the verb can be singular *or* plural: **le manque de** 'lack of', **le reste de** 'remainder of, other, rest of', **la foule de** 'crowd of' . . . :

> *Le manque d'argent est* **un problème peu supportable.**
> The lack of money is a major problem.

> *Le manque d'auditeurs est* **vraiment décevant.**
> The lack of an audience is really disappointing.

But the speaker or writer may want to focus firmly on the plural part of the compound subject, and in this case, the verb agrees with that plural subject.

> *Une foule de gens manifestaient* **dans les rues.**
> A crowd of people were demonstrating in the streets.

22.3.1 **Beaucoup de, combien de?, peu de, la plupart de** are followed by plural verbs when they are used as subjects.

> *Beaucoup d'étudiants* **n'**ont **pas de bourse.**
> Many students don't have a grant.

> *Combien d'Anglais sont allés* **au match?**
> How many English people went to the match?

> *Peu de gens ont aimé* **la pièce.**
> Few people liked the play.

> *La plupart des étudiants travaillent* durant l'été.
> Most students work during the summer.

If **combien de?** and **la plupart de** are followed by a singular noun, the verb is also in the singular.

> *Combien de la tarte reste-t-il?*
> How much of the tart is left?

> *La plupart est déjà mangée.*
> Most of it has already been eaten.

22.3.2   Compound subjects linked by **et:** the verb is always plural.

> *Pierre et Marie iront* ensemble.
> Peter and Mary will go together.

> *L'un et l'autre sont fatigués.*
> They are both tired.

> *Isabelle et moi allons* prendre un café.
> Isabelle and I are going for a coffee.

22.3.3   Compound subjects linked by **ou** or **ni:** the verb is usually plural – unless the subject is, in fact, really singular.

> *Michel ou Marc viendront* te chercher.
> Michel or Marc will come and pick you up.

> *Vous ou elles devez* rester à la maison.
> You or they must stay at home.

> *Ni* mon frère *ni* ma sœur *n'aident* ma mère.
> Neither my brother nor my sister help(s) my mother.

> *Ni lui ni moi n'avons reçu* un cadeau.
> Neither he nor I received a present.

Ni l'un ni l'autre may be followed by a singular verb, but the plural is also possible (see **11.7.1**):

> *Ni l'un ni l'autre n'est allé/ne sont allés* lui parler.
> Neither of them went to talk to him/her.

Note that **l'un ou l'autre** *always* has a singular verb:

> *L'un ou l'autre pourra* venir.
> One or the other will be able to come.

The following rule of thumb for compound subjects and their verbs may prove useful:

- if the subjects are linked by **et** use a plural verb
- if the subjects are linked by **ou** or **ni** a plural verb is preferred *unless*

  1 the subject is logically singular
  2 the speaker or writer is thinking of a singular subject
  3 the subject is **l'un ou l'autre**

In these three cases the verb is singular.

22.3.4 Impersonal verbs, such as **il y a** 'there is/are', **il reste** 'there remain(s)', **il est arrivé** 'something happened/occurred' (see **46**), usually remain singular, *whatever* the subject is.

> *Il y aura des manifestations* si vous n'acceptez pas la décision du comité d'entreprise.
> There will be demonstrations if you don't accept the decision of the works council.

> *Il est venu des gens d'affaires* à l'aéroport comme prévu mais le vol avait été annulé.
> Some business people arrived at the airport as arranged, but the flight had been cancelled.

23   Formation of tenses

Guidelines on the formation of tenses are given below, but unless and until you are absolutely sure of the forms and the irregularities – often very small irregularities – it is good practice to check in verb tables which include the most useful irregular verbs (see Verb tables). The guidelines refer to verbs *and* their compounds, e.g. **venir, devenir, revenir, convenir**.

In each of the conjugations there are irregular verbs, that is, verbs which have the infinitive endings **-er, -ir, -re, -oir** but whose stems change under certain conditions. Two of the irregular verbs – **avoir** and **être** – are the most important of all the irregular verbs because they are used to form the compound tenses.

23.1 All of the tenses have a basic meaning – they are used to refer to present, future or past time. Each of them is also used with additional meanings. These additional meanings are usually made clear in an adverbial phrase in the sentence which indicates exactly what the speaker or writer means. However, it is not always necessary to confirm the exact meaning – the tense, or context, may be enough. For example, the present tense alone may be enough to express a habit.

> **Elle** *se lève* **tôt.**   She gets up early.

But the speaker or writer may feel it necessary to indicate quite clearly that the action *is* a habit.

> **Elle** *se lève* **tôt** *tous les jours.*   She gets up early every day.

24   The indicative tenses; the present tense

24.1 There are two main groups of indicative tenses, and they can be divided according to their form: the *simple* tenses and the *compound* tenses. Each of the simple tenses has a corresponding compound tense, formed with **avoir** or **être**.

Simple tenses	Compound tenses
present (**présent**) (see **24.2, 24.4**)	*perfect* (**passé composé**) (see **28, 29**)
future (**futur**) (see **25**)	*future perfect* (**futur antérieur**) (see **28, 30**)

| *imperfect* (**imparfait**) (see **26**) | *pluperfect* (**plus-que-parfait**) (see **28, 31**) |
| *past historic* (**passé historique**) (see **27**) | *past anterior* (**passé antérieur**) (see **28, 32**) |

The past historic is also called the *simple past* (**passé simple**) or the *preterite* (**prétérit**).

The *conditional* tense (**conditionnel**) and its corresponding compound form, the *conditional perfect* (**conditionnel passé**) (see **33**), are treated separately because they form a bridge, in terms of meaning, between the indicative and the subjunctive (see **34**).

24.2 | **The present tense**

(a) **-er** verbs: **donner** 'to give', composed of the stem **donn-** + the endings **-e, -es, -e, -ons, -ez, -ent**:

je	*donne*	I give, am giving	nous	*donnons*
tu	*donnes*		vous	*donnez*
il/elle	*donne*		ils/elles	*donnent*

All **-er** verbs have the same present tense forms as **donner** with the exception of **aller** 'to go': je *vais*, tu *vas*, il/elle *va*, nous *allons*, vous *allez*, ils/elles *vont*

(b) **-ir** verbs: **finir** 'to finish', composed of the stem **fin-** + the endings **-is, -is, -it, -issons, -issez, -issent**:

je	*finis*	nous	*finissons*
tu	*finis*	vous	*finissez*
il/elle	*finit*	ils/elles	*finissent*

Regular verbs in the **-ir** group have **-iss-** inserted in the plural forms of the present tense, throughout the imperfect tense: **je finissais** (see **26**), in the present participle: **finissant** (see **43**), and in the plural imperative forms: **finissons, finissez** (see **44**).

Some verbs with an **-ir** infinitive have the endings of the **-er** group in the present tense:

> **ouvrir** 'to open': j'*ouvre*, tu *ouvres*, il/elle *ouvre*, nous *ouvrons*, vous *ouvrez*, ils/elles *ouvrent*

Some verbs with an **-ir** infinitive have the endings of the **-re** group (see below) in the present tense. They may also have changes in the stem, for example **cueillir** 'to pick', **dormir** 'to sleep', **mentir** 'to tell a lie', **offrir** 'to offer', **partir** 'to leave', **se repentir** 'to repent', **sentir** 'to feel', **servir** 'to serve' . . . and their compounds.

> **dormir** 'to sleep': je *dors*, tu *dors*, il/elle *dort*, nous *dormons*, vous *dormez*, ils/elles *dorment*

(c) **-re** verbs: **vendre** 'to sell', composed of the stem **vend-** + the endings **-s, -s, -t** or **-d, -ons, -ez, -ent**:

je	*vends*	nous	*vendons*
tu	*vends*	vous	*vendez*
il/elle	*vend*	ils/elles	*vendent*

Verbs whose stem ends in **d** do not add **-t** or **-d** in the third person singular: **il/elle** *vend*; **il/elle** *répond* 'he/she answers'; **il/elle** se *rend* 'he/she goes'; **il/elle** *prend* 'he/she takes' – the **d** of the infinitive stem is enough. Otherwise, the verbs have **-t**:

boire 'to drink'	**il/elle** *boit*
rompre 'to break'	**il/elle** *rompt*
faire 'to do, make'	**il/elle** *fait*

The one exception to this rule is **vaincre** 'to conquer' (and its compound **convaincre** 'to convince'). The third person singular ending is **-c**: **il/elle** *vainc* (*convainc*).

With verbs ending in **-aindre**, **-eindre**, **-oindre**, **-nd-** changes to **-gn-** before a vowel:

> **joindre** 'to join': **je** *joins*, **tu** *joins*, **il/elle** *joint*, **nous** *joignons*, **vous** *joignez*, **ils/elles** *joignent*

There is also a group of verbs ending in **-aître**, **-oître**, some of which are very common: **accroître** 'to grow', **apparaître** 'to appear', **connaître** 'to know', **disparaître** 'to disappear', **paraître** 'to appear' . . . These verbs have **î** before **t**, but **i** (no circumflex) everywhere else:

> **connaître** 'to know': **je** *connais*, **tu** *connais*, **il/elle** *connaît*, **nous** *connaissons*, **vous** *connaissez*, **ils/elles** *connaissent*

(d) **-oir** verbs: **recevoir** 'to receive':

These verbs all have the same endings as **-re** verbs: **-s**, **-s**, **-t**, **-ons**, **-ez**, **-ent**, but the stem may have changes.

je	*reçois*	nous	*recevons*
tu	*reçois*	vous	*recevez*
il/elle	*reçoit*	ils/elles	*reçoivent*

In most cases the first and second persons plural keep the infinitive stem, with changes occurring in the singular and in the third person plural.

> **devoir** 'to owe; must, should': **je** *dois*, **tu** *dois*, **il/elle** *doit*, **nous** *devons*, **vous** *devez*, **ils/elles** *doivent*
> **pouvoir** 'to be able to; can, may': **je** *peux* , **tu** *peux*, **il/elle** *peut* , **nous** *pouvons*, **vous** *pouvez* , **ils/elles** *peuvent*. (Note the interrogative form of **je peux**: **puis-je?**)
> **savoir** 'to know; know how to': **je** *sais*, **tu** *sais*, **il/elle** *sait*, **nous** *savons*, **vous** *savez*, **ils/elles** *savent*
> **vouloir** 'to want (to); wish': **je** *veux*, **tu** *veux*, **il/elle** *veut*, **nous** *voulons*, **vous** *voulez*, **ils/elles** *veulent*
> **falloir** – always in the infinitive or the 3rd person singular: **il faut** 'it is necessary; must'

24.2.1 | **avoir** 'to have' and **être** 'to be'

avoir:

j'*ai*	nous *avons*
tu *as*	vous *avez*
il/elle *a*	ils/elles *ont*

être:

je *suis*	nous *sommes*
tu *es*	vous *êtes*
il/elle *est*	ils/elles *sont*

24.2.2 | Points to remember about some present tense forms:

● three verbs have the ending **-tes** (*not* **-ez**) with **vous**:

être 'to be'	vous êtes
dire 'to say'	vous dites
faire 'to do; make'	vous faites

● four verbs have the ending **-ont**, or form **ont** (not **-ent** or **ent**) with **ils/elles**:

aller	ils/elles vont	avoir	ils/elles ont
faire	ils/elles font	être	ils/elles sont

24.2.3 | Some further guidelines on changes in the spelling and form of **-er** verbs – the changes may also occur in other parts of the verbs (see **verb tables**).

● verbs ending in **-e-** + consonant + **-er**

The following verbs are examples of verbs which strengthen the sound of the middle e when the following syllable is not pronounced:

renouveler 'to renew' doubles the **l**: je *renouvelle*, tu *renouvelles*, il/elle *renouvelle*, ils/elles *renouvellent but* nous *renouvelons*, vous *renouvelez*
jeter 'to throw' doubles the **t**: je *jette*, tu *jettes*, il/elle *jette*, ils/elles *jettent but* nous *jetons*, vous *jetez*
acheter 'to buy' changes the middle e to **è**: j'*achète*, tu *achètes*, il/elle *achète*, ils/elles *achètent but* nous *achetons*, vous *achetez*

● verbs ending in **-cer**

These verbs change the **c** to **ç** before **a** and **o**: **commencer** 'to begin' – nous *commençons*

● verbs ending in **-ger**

These verbs add **e** before **a** and **o**: **partager** 'to share' – nous *partageons*

● verbs ending in **-oyer** and **-uyer**

These verbs change the **y** to **i** before an **e** that is silent:

employer 'to employ': j'*emploie*, tu *emploies*, il/elle *emploie*, ils/elles *emploient but* nous *employons*, vous *employez*

● verbs ending in **-ayer**

These verbs may change the **y** to **i** before an **e** that is silent, but they *can* keep the **y**:

> **payer** 'to pay (for)': **je** *paye* (or *paie*), **tu** *payes* (or *paies*), **il/elle** *paye* (or *paie*), **nous** *payons*, **vous** *payez*, **ils/elles** *payent* (or *paient*)

● verbs ending in **-é-** + consonant + **-er**

These verbs usually change the **é** to **è** before a *final* **e** that is not pronounced:

> **espérer** 'to hope (for)': **j'**espère, **tu** *espères*, **il/elle** *espère*, **ils/elles** *espèrent* but **nous** *espérons*, **vous** *espérez*

24.2.4 Spelling changes in verbs ending in **-dre**

● verbs ending in **-aindre, -eindre, -oindre** change the **-nd-** of the stem to **-gn-** in the plural forms:

> **craindre** 'to be frightened of': **je** *crains*, **tu** *crains*, **il/elle** *craint* but **nous** *craignons*, **vous** *craignez*, **ils/elles** *craignent*

● verbs ending in **-oudre** change the **-ud-** of the stem to **-lv-** in the plural forms:

> **résoudre** 'to resolve; solve': **je** *résous*, **tu** *résous*, **il/elle** *résout* but **nous** *résolvons*, **vous** *résolvez*, **ils/elles** *résolvent*

These are *some* of the changes which occur in the stem or the endings of verbs. It is always advisable to check the forms in verb tables.

24.3 **How the present tense is used**

● to express any action that takes places, or is taking place, in the present:

> **Il** *répare* son auto. He is repairing his car.

● to express facts, proverbs and general or universal truths:

> **Nous** *sommes* le 15 mars. It's the 15th of March.
> **Je ne** *fume* pas. I don't smoke.
> **3 et 4** *font* 7. 3 and 4 make 7.
> **Pierre qui** *roule* n'*amasse* pas mousse. A rolling stone gathers no moss.

● to narrate a story – the tense is then called the historic present and occurs in the informal narrating of a story, or in literature. In both contexts it is intended to make a story more vivid. The following extract is taken from *Un Jeune Homme Seul* by Roger Vailland, published in 1951. The main narrative tense of the novel is the past historic:

> **Il passe sans répondre, court à sa chambre et se jette sur le lit. Il garde les yeux fixés, au delà de la fenêtre, sur la Tour Eiffel, mais il ne la voit pas. Il répète à voix haute: 'Je suis l'homme le plus seul au monde, je suis . . .'**
> He went past without answering, ran to his room and threw himself on the bed. He stared out of the window at the Eiffel Tower, but he didn't see it. He said over and over again, 'I am the loneliest man in the world, I am . . .'

● to express the near, or very near, future or past, especially in a spoken, informal context:

J'y *vais*.	I'm off/leaving right now. (*or* I'll see to it.)
Elle *sort* dans un instant.	She's coming out in a minute.
Il *part* dimanche prochain.	He's leaving next Sunday.
Nous *allons* au cinéma ce soir.	We're going to the cinema tonight.
Je *reviens* tout de suite.	I'll be right back.
Le train *arrive* de Paris.	The Paris train is (just) in.
Il *sort* à l'instant.	He has just left.

and note the verb phrase **venir de** + infinitive 'to have just' + past participle (see **26.1**).

Nous *venons de* commencer.	We have just begun.

● to express habit or repetition:

Il se *couche* tard.	He goes to bed late.
Il *taille* la haie toutes les trois semaines.	He cuts the hedge every three weeks.

● to express a condition, in the si clause (see **33.1.1**):

S'il *arrive* bientôt, nous pourrons/pouvons partir.
If he arrives soon, we can leave.

24.4   Differences in French and English present tenses

It is important to remember that French has *one* present tense form but English has three forms: a simple present – 'I take, I listen, I write', a continuous (or progressive) present – 'I am taking, I am listening, I am writing', and the emphatic or negative form with 'do' – 'I do/don't take, listen, write'.

Il *chante*.	He sings. (*or* He is singing.)

The verb phrase **être en train de** + infinitive can be used to indicate that an action is in progress:

Il *est en train d'*écrire une lettre.
He is writing a letter. (at this very moment)

The verb phrase **aller** + (**en**) + present participle can also be used to express an action, or event, in progress at the present time:

Certains secteurs de l'économie britannique *vont en s'améliorant*.
Some sectors of the British economy are improving.

24.4.1

When a continuous and *continuing* action is expressed along with the time it began ('since . . .') or along with the period of time it has been going on ('for . . .'). French uses the present tense:

Il *pleut* depuis dimanche.
It has been raining since Sunday.

Ça/Cela *fait* un quart d'heure que je l'attends.
That's a quarter of an hour I've been waiting for him/her.

> **Depuis quand *êtes*-vous en Ecosse?**
> How long have you been in Scotland?
>
> **Depuis combien de temps *est*-elle étudiante?**
> How long has she been a student?
>
> **Il y a trois mois que nous *sommes* là.**
> We've been here for three months.

and

> **Voilà une heure que nous vous *attendons*!**
> We've been waiting for you for an hour!

In the previous example the phrase **voilà . . . que . . .** is used only with the present tense: **voilà** refers to the present moment.

In each of the examples, the continuous and *continuing* action is expressed by the present tense in French: the English equivalent is 'have/has been' (+ present participle).

25 The future tense

The future tense of most French verbs is composed of the infinitive + the endings -ai, -as-, -a, -ons, -ez, -ont.

donner:

je	*donnerai*	I shall give	nous	*donnerons*
tu	*donneras*		vous	*donnerez*
il/elle	*donnera*		ils/elles	*donneront*

finir:

je	*finirai*	I shall finish	nous	*finirons*
tu	*finiras*		vous	*finirez*
il/elle	*finira*		ils/elles	*finiront*

The -**re** infinitives drop the final -**e**: **j'*écrirai*** 'I shall write', **je *prendrai*** 'I shall take'

vendre:

je	*vendrai*	I shall sell	nous	*vendrons*
tu	*vendras*		vous	*vendrez*
il/elle	*vendra*		ils/elles	*vendront*

25.1 Many of the -**oir** verbs, and the irregular verbs of the -**er**, -**ir** and -**re** conjugations, have changes in the stem, but they *all* have the same endings. Some examples of the stem changes are given here, but it is good practice, as always, to check in the verb tables for possible changes.

| 25.1.1 | Examples of **-oir** verbs: |

	recevoir:	je *recevrai*	I shall receive
	voir:	je *verrai*	I shall see

| 25.1.2 | **devoir, pouvoir, savoir, vouloir, falloir:** |

	devoir:	je *devrai*	I shall have to; I must
	pouvoir:	je *pourrai*	I shall be able to; I can
	savoir:	je *saurai*	I shall know (how to)
	vouloir:	je *voudrai*	I shall want/wish to
	falloir:	il *faudra*	pronoun + will have to; must

| 25.1.3 | Some of the irregular verbs of the other conjugations: |

	aller:	j'*irai*	I shall go
	courir:	je *courrai*	I shall run
	avoir:	j'*aurai*	I shall have
	cuellir:	je *cueillerai*	I shall pick
	être:	je *serai*	I shall be
	venir:	je *viendrai*	I shall come
	faire:	je *ferai*	I shall do; make
	tenir:	je *tiendrai*	I shall hold

| **25.2** | **How the future tense is used** |

● to express an action or event in future time:

Il *viendra*.	He'll come.
Elle le *fera* demain.	She will do it tomorrow.

● to express habit, or repeated action (with an adverbial phrase):

Nous *lirons* un journal *tous les jours*.
We'll read a paper every day.

● to express conjecture, supposition or probability (see **30**):

Quelqu'un vient d'arriver. Ce *sera* tes invités.
Someone has just arrived. It will be your guests.

● to express absolute refusal:

N'insiste pas, je n'*irai* pas.
Don't go on about it. I won't go.

● to indicate some distance from someone:

Voudrez-vous encore du thé?
Would you like some more tea?

J'*avouerai* que je préfère un verre d'eau.
I would prefer a glass of water.

● as a stylistic device, in a narrative in literature or in journalism:

C'était un jeune homme très timide, et il le *restera* toute sa vie.
He was a very shy young man, and remained so all his life.

- as the tense of the main verb, accompanying **si** + present tense expressing condition (see **33.1.1**):

> On *fera* la vaisselle, si on a le temps.
> We'll do the washing-up, if we've time.

25.3 Differences in French and English usage

French and English usage are different in certain contexts:

- with **quand/lorsque** 'when': French uses the future tense; English uses the present tense.

> *Quand* tu les *rejoindras*, tes parents seront vraiment ravis.
> When you join your parents, they'll be really delighted.

- with reference to a future action French is much more precise than English.

> Il fera ce qu'il *voudra*.   He'll do what he wants.

25.3.1 - to express a continuous action in the future:

> Je *serai* en train de préparer un repas quand tu arriveras.
> I'll be preparing a meal when you arrive.

> L'économie *ira* (en) *s'aggravant*.
> The economy will continue to get worse.

25.3.2 To express the near future (**le futur proche**): **aller** + infinitive, with **aller** normally in the present, or imperfect, tense. This verb phrase is used in spoken and written, formal and informal French, and often replaces the future tense. Despite its name it can refer to an action in a remote future. It carries with it an idea of certainty about the action, which is not necessarily there in the future tense. It may express intention.

> Elle *va réussir*/réussira.
> She will succeed.

> Les cours *vont commencer*/commenceront la semaine prochaine.
> Classes begin next week.

> Le congrès *va avoir lieu* l'année prochaine.
> The conference will take place next year.

If an action is *really* immediate, the present tense is used (see **24.3**):

> Elle *vient* dans un instant.   She will be here in a moment.

The near future is used to express certainty:

> Si tu continues, tu *vas m'ennuyer*.
> If you continue, you'll bore me (stiff).

and to express an intention:

> Tu *vas voir*!
> You'll see!

> Il *va* nous *montrer* comment le faire.
> He'll show us how to do it.

The imperfect tense

The imperfect tense of most verbs is formed by using the stem of the first person plural of the present tense and adding the endings **-ais, -ais, -ait, -ions, -iez, -aient**. It is recommended that you use the first person plural of the present tense because the imperfect tense of every French verb, with the exception of **être**, can be composed with this form.

donner:

je	*donnais*	I was giving/gave	nous	*donnions*
tu	*donnais*		vous	*donniez*
il/elle	*donnait*		ils/elles	*donnaient*

and some more examples:

nous *finissons*: je *finissais*   nous *faisons*: je *faisais*
nous *vendons*: je *vendais*   nous *pouvons*: je *pouvais*
nous *recevons*: je *recevais*   nous *avons*: j'*avais*
nous *mettons*: je *mettais*   nous *mangeons*: je *mangeais*

but être:

nous *sommes*: j'*étais*

How the imperfect tense is used

● in description of people, animals, things, states, events (of any length) in the past:

> **Nous nous sommes retrouvés dans un camp dans le centre de la France. Nous *logions* dans des tentes. C'*était* en juillet, nous *avions* froid.**
>
> *(The Guardian* 14.2.95)
>
> We found ourselves in a camp in the centre of France. We lived in tents. It was July, and we were cold.

● in description, as opposed to action:

> **J'*étais* l'aînée, je *parlais* parfaitement le français, je *travaillais* bien à l'école. Mes parents ont eu besoin de moi. Je leur ai servi d'interprète.**
>
> *(The Guardian* 14.2.95)
>
> I was the eldest, I spoke perfect French, I worked well at school. My parents needed me. I was their interpreter.

● to express habit, or repeated action (frequently an adverbial phrase confirms the habit, or repeated action):

> **Nous *attendions* là *tous les jours*.**
> We waited there every day.
>
> ***Chaque vendredi elle allait* au marché.**
> Every Friday she went to market.

- to express suggestion:

  Si je le *faisais* pour toi?
  What if I were to do it for you?

- to express discretion (usually in the first person):

  ***Je venais* vous parler de son mari.**
  I came to talk to you about her husband.

- to express simultaneity of actions (usually combined with the perfect tense or the past historic):

  Il *traversait* la rue quand il a entendu/entendit son cri.
  He was crossing the street when he heard his/her shout.

The two actions occur at the same time; the imperfect expresses a continuous or prolonged action, the perfect or past historic express a sudden, completed action.

- as a stylistic device, replacing the perfect or past historic, when narrating a story (in literature or in journalism):

  Son représentant dans l'ex-Yougoslavie se disait persuadé que le cessez-le-feu n'était pas encore définitivement enterré.
  (*Le Monde* 23.3.95)
  His/Her/Its representative in the former Yugoslavia said he was convinced that the cease-fire had not completely broken down.

- to express conjecture, supposition or probability, referring to a possible event in the past (see **33.1.5**):

  Un pas de plus et il *tombait*.
  One more step, and he'd have fallen.

- to express the immediate past (see **24.3**):

  Le train *arrivait* de Paris.
  The train had just arrived from Paris.

  Elle *sortait* de la salle de classe.
  She had just left the classroom.

These examples could also mean 'The train was arriving from Paris', 'She was leaving the classroom'. The imperfect tense of **venir** in the verb phrase **venir de** + infinitive may be used to express the immediate past (see **24.3**).

  Nous *venions de* commencer.　　We had just begun.

- to express a condition, in the **si** clause (see **33.1.1**):

  S'il *travaillait*, il réussirait.
  If he worked, he would be successful.

26.1.1　When a continuous but *completed* action in the past is expressed along with the time it began ('since . . .') or along with the period of time it lasted ('for . . .'), French uses the imperfect tense (see **24.4.1**):

  Il *neigeait* depuis trois semaines.
  It had been snowing for three weeks.

> Ça/Cela faisait un mois que nous le *savions*.
> We had known for a month.
>
> Depuis combien de temps *habitait*-il en France?
> How long had he been living in France?
>
> Il y avait dix jours qu'il *attendait* la lettre.
> He had been waiting for the letter for ten days.

In each of the examples, the continuous and *completed* action is expressed by the imperfect tense in French: the English equivalent is 'had been' + present or 'had' + past participle.

27 | The past historic

The past historic (or simple past or preterite) of most verbs is formed by using the stem of the infinitive and adding the endings of the past historic (see **27.1**). However, irregular verbs may not follow this rule, and it is advisable to check the stem in verb tables.

27.1 | Past historic endings

The following endings are added to **-er** verbs: **-ai, -as, -a, -âmes, -âtes, -èrent.**

donner:

je	*donnai*	I gave	nous	*donnâmes*
tu	*donnas*		vous	*donnâtes*
il/elle	*donna*		ils/elles	*donnèrent*

and the following endings to regular **-ir** verbs: **-is, -is, -it, -îmes, -îtes, -irent.**

finir:

je	*finis*	I finished	nous	*finîmes*
tu	*finis*		vous	*finîtes*
il/elle	*finit*		ils/elles	*finirent*

Some **-oir** verbs, and almost all **-re** verbs, also have the **-ir** group endings. Some examples with changes in the stem:

> **voir:** je *vis*, tu *vis*, il/elle *vit*, nous *vîmes*, vous *vîtes*, ils/elles *virent*
> **faire:** je *fis*, tu *fis*, il/elle *fit*, nous *fîmes*, vous *fîtes*, ils/elles *firent*
> **mettre:** je *mis*, tu *mis*, il/elle *mit*, nous *mîmes*, vous *mîtes*, ils/elles *mirent*

Note the exceptions **venir** and **tenir:**

> **venir:** je *vins*, tu *vins*, il/elle *vint*, nous *vînmes*, vous *vîntes*, ils/elles *vinrent*
> **tenir:** je *tins*, tu *tins*, il/elle *tint*, nous *tînmes*, vous *tîntes*, ils/elles *tinrent*

There is a third group of endings – identical to the **-ir** group except for the vowel. Instead of **i**, they have **u**: **-us, -ut, -ûmes, -ûtes, -urent**. These endings are used with most **-oir** verbs, including **devoir, pouvoir, savoir, vouloir** and **falloir**.

> **recevoir: je** *reçus*, **tu** *reçus*, **il/elle** *reçut*, **nous** *reçûmes*, **vous** *reçûtes*, **ils/elles** *reçurent*
> **devoir: je** *dus*, **tu** *dus*, **il/elle** *dut*, **nous** *dûmes*, **vous** *dûtes*, **ils/elles** *durent*
> **pouvoir: je** *pus*, **vouloir: je** *voulus*, **savoir: je** *sus*, **falloir: il** *fallut*

and

> **avoir: j'***eus*, **tu** *eus*, **il/elle** *eut*, **nous** *eûmes*, **vous** *eûtes*, **ils/elles** *eurent*

The **-us** . . . endings are also used with a small group of **-re** verbs, including **être**:

> **être: je** *fus*, **tu** *fus*, **il/elle** *fut*, **nous** *fûmes*, **vous** *fûtes*, **ils/elles** *furent*

and some other examples:

> **connaître** 'to know':   je *connus*
> **lire** 'to read':   je *lus*
> **vivre** 'to live':   je *vécus*

There are two irregular **-ir** verbs which have the **-us** . . . endings:

> **courir** 'to run':   je *courus*
> **mourir** 'to die':   il/elle *mourut*

27.2   **How the past historic is used**

The past historic is not used very frequently, and is usually replaced in modern French by the perfect tense. However, it may occur in formal written or spoken contexts: in some newspapers and magazines, in literary works, in lectures and in public speeches. It is most commonly found in the third person singular and plural. The past historic is used to express:

● an event or action, of long or short duration, that is complete, and over, but not necessarily remote in time:

> **Le Général de Gaulle** *vécut* **80 ans.**
> General de Gaulle lived for eighty years.

> **Le sport** *s'épanouit* **dans les démocraties: mais il** *fut* **à l'honneur sous le totalitarisme stalinien.**
> Sport was encouraged in democratic countries: but it was worshipped under Stalin's totalitarian régime.

> **En 1991, l'équipe de France de tennis** *gagna* **la coupe Davis.**
> In 1991, the French team won the Davis Cup.

Note that the English equivalent in each of the examples is the past tense: 'lived, was encouraged (passive), was worshipped (passive), won'.

● a series of completed events, perceived as points in time:

The following examples are taken from an article in *Le Monde* (23.3.95), the day after a campaign meeting held by the Socialist candidate in the Presidential elections:

> . . . l'image *fut* bonne . . . cela *parut* pour son entourage l'essentiel . . .
> on *sentit* tout de même . . . son épouse lui *fit* signe de . . .
> . . . the impression was good . . . that seemed to be the essential thing
> for his entourage . . . they felt nevertheless . . . his wife signalled to
> him to . . .

● and in combination with and in contrast to the imperfect tense, which describes
the background of the event or series of events (see **26.1**):

> Puis, il *tourna* le robinet de l'évier, se *lava* les mains, s'*essuya* au
> linge accroché sous le grêle tuyau . . . Et elle *guettait* ses moindres
> gestes . . .
>
> (Henri Troyat (1936) *Grandeur Nature*)
>
> Then he turned on the tap, washed his hands, dried them on the towel
> hanging under the thin pipe. . . . And she watched his slightest
> movement . . .

In the following example the past historic is accompanied by a supporting adverbial
phrase:

> Il regardait passer toutes les voitures et *tout à coup comprit* pourquoi
> elle était partie.
>
> He was watching all the cars going past and suddenly understood why
> she had left.

The description of what the man was doing (**regardait**) is interrupted suddenly by an
event (**comprit**).

28 The compound tenses

The compound tenses of the indicative are formed by adding the past participle of a
verb to one of the simple tenses of the auxiliary verbs **avoir** and **être**. The compound
tenses of the majority of verbs are formed with **avoir**. Reflexive (pronominal) verbs
(see **40**), some intransitive verbs (see **42.2**), and the passive (see **41**) are formed with
être.

28.1 *Avoir* + past participle

the perfect tense	*j'ai donné*	I gave, I have given, I have been giving
the future perfect tense	*j'aurai donné*	I shall have given
the pluperfect tense	*j'avais donné*	I had given, gave
the past anterior tense	*j'eus donné*	I had given, gave

28.1.1 The past participle in the compound tenses formed with **avoir** agrees with a *preceding
direct object* in gender and number. The preceding direct object may be a personal
pronoun (see **12**), a relative pronoun: **que/qu'**, **lequel** (see **15**); the interrogative
adjective: **quel?** (see **16.4.3**); or **combien de?** (see **16.4.4**).

> *Je les* ai vu(*e*)*s.*
> I have seen them.

> **J'ai vu l'étudiante *que* vous avez mentionn*ée*.**
> I have seen the student you mentioned.

> **Je ne sais pas *laquelle* des voitures il a achet*ée*.**
> I don't know which of the cars he bought.

> ***Quels* conseils lui avez-vous donn*és*?**
> What advice did you give him/her?

> ***Combien de* lettres as-tu écrit*es*?**
> How many letters did you write?

The past participle *never* agrees with **en**:

> **On disait que trente jeunes filles attendaient à la porte mais je n'*en* ai vu que dix.**
> They said that thirty girls were waiting at the door, but I only saw ten.

28.2 *Être* + **past participle**

the perfect tense	je *suis allé(e)*	I went, have gone
the future perfect tense	je *serai allé(e)*	I shall have gone
the pluperfect tense	j'*étais allé(e)*	I had gone, went
the past anterior tense	je *fus allé(e)*	I had gone, went

28.2.1 The past participle in the compound tenses formed with **être** agrees with the *subject* in gender and number.

je suis *allé, allée*	nous sommes *allés, allées*
tu es *allé, allée*	vous êtes *allé, allés, allée, allées*
il est *allé*	ils sont *allés*
elle est *allée*	elles sont *allées*

---

29 # How the perfect is used

The perfect tense is the most widely used of all the past tenses, in spoken, written, formal and informal contexts. It is used to express:

● completed actions or events, without any implication of duration:

> **J'*ai vu* le film.**   I saw the film.

Frequently a precise time is given:

> **Elle *est arrivée* à six heures.**   She arrived at six o'clock.

● a series of completed actions or events:

> **Il *a voulu* aller en vacances. Il *a consulté* une carte. Il *a loué* une voiture. Il *est parti* hier.**
> He wanted to go on holiday. He looked at a map. He hired a car. He left yesterday.

Adverbs such as **d'abord, puis, ensuite, enfin** may be added to make it clear that one action or event follows another.

> **D'abord elle s'est levée, puis elle s'est lavée, ensuite elle s'est peignée, et enfin elle est sortie.**
> First she got up, then she got washed, then she combed her hair, and finally she went out.

Examples of the perfect in a formal context:

> **Dans le récent entretien qu'il a accordé au 'Monde' (18.3.95) Boris Eltsine a réaffirmé son opposition à une extension immédiate de l'OTAN.**
>
> (*Le Monde* 23.3.95)
> In the recent interview with 'Le Monde', Boris Yeltsin reaffirmed his opposition to an immediate enlargement of NATO.

> **L'ampleur du 'non' au référendum suédois du 14 septembre a surpris tout le monde.**
>
> (*Le Monde* 17.9.03)
> The size of the 'no' vote in the Swedish referendum of 14 September took everyone by surprise.

and in an informal context:

> **Tu vas faire tes devoirs maintenant! – Mais je les ai faits!**
> You're going to do your homework now! – But I've done it!

The action or event may be related to the present, but this is not always the case. Note how remote some of the following events are:

> **J'ai mangé, on peut sortir si tu veux.**
> I've had something to eat. We can go out, if you like.

> **J'ai vu le film cet après-midi.**
> I saw the film this afternoon.

> **Ils ont vu le film il y a un mois.**
> They saw the film a month ago.

> **Elle est morte il y a cinquante ans.**
> She died fifty years ago.

> **Le Général de Gaulle est né en 1890.**
> General de Gaulle was born in 1890.

In the following examples note how the context creates additional meanings for the perfect:

● the action is completed and in the past, but one could take it that the windows are still shut:

> **On a fermé les fenêtres.**
> We've shut (We shut) the windows.

● the action – probably of some duration – was completed in the past, but the speaker feels the effects of the action as he/she is speaking. The context suggests a relation of cause and effect between the two actions. Note the English tense form:

> **Je le sens! C'est affreux! Tu *as fumé*.**
> I can smell it! It's awful! You've been smoking!

● the actions were completed in the past but were clearly repeated several times:

> **Cette phrase? Je l'*ai répétée* cinquante fois!**
> That phrase? I've repeated it fifty times!

> **Nous *avons écouté* le bulletin météorologique tous les matins.**
> We listened to the weather forecast every morning.

The perfect is often found in close proximity to the imperfect. When this occurs, the perfect is expressing an action or event, the imperfect is describing the background, and/or giving an explanation (see **26.1**).

> **Nous nous *sommes levé(e)s* tôt ce matin. Il *faisait* beau et nous *sommes parti(e)s* passer la journée à la campagne.**
> We got up early this morning. The weather was lovely and we left for a day in the country.

In the following example the imperfect describes the background and the perfect expresses an event which cuts across the background. The adverbial indicates the suddenness of the event.

> **Il *regardait* passer toutes les voitures et *tout à coup* il *a compris* pourquoi ses amis préfèrent la bicyclette.**
> He was watching all the cars going past and suddenly he understood why his friends prefer to go by bike.

The immediate past is often expressed in French by **venir de** + infinitive (see **24.3, 26.1**) where English has the perfect or pluperfect:

> **Je *viens de* le lui dire.**   I've just told him/her.
> **Elle *venait de* partir.**   She'd just left.

The perfect may be used to express a completed action or event in the near future. An adverbial would be required to confirm the future meaning.

> **J'*ai fini* dans une demi-heure.**
> I'll have finished in half an hour.

30 How the future perfect is used

The future perfect always refers to an action or event which takes place in the future. The tense may occur in a main clause or in a dependent clause. It is used:

● in *main* clauses to express a completed action or event:

> **Elle *aura* bientôt *fini*.**
> She'll have finished soon.

> **Nous *serons parti(e)s* à cette heure-là.**
> We'll have left at/by that time.

> **Dans deux semaines ils *auront terminé* leurs études.**
> In two weeks they'll have finished their studies.

● in *dependent* clauses, which are always introduced by conjunctions such as **dès que**, **aussitôt que; quand, lorsque; après que**, or by a relative pronoun, to express completion of an action or event *before* another action or event in the future. The verb in the main clause is usually in a future tense (see **25.3**):

> *Dès que* nous *aurons mangé* nous *irons* les chercher.
> As soon as we've eaten we'll go and look for them.

> Elle *pourra* le faire *quand* tu *auras* tout *expliqué*.
> She will be able to do it when you have explained everything.

> Je te *prêterai* le livre *que j'aurai lu* avant la fin de la semaine.
> I'll lend you the book which I'll have read before the end of the week.

Note the English equivalent of the future perfect:

> **dès que nous *aurons mangé***   as soon as we *have eaten*
> **quand tu *auras expliqué***   when you *have explained*
> **que j'*aurai lu***   which I'*ll have read*

● to express conjecture, supposition or possibility – just like the future tense (see **25.2**):

> **Sa mère lui *aura dit* que nous sommes là.**
> His mother will (probably) have told him that we are here.

> **Ils ne sont pas arrivés! Ils *auront manqué* le train.**
> They haven't arrived! They (must) have missed the train.

● to express a mild imperative or warning:

> **Tu *auras rangé* ta chambre cet après-midi!**
> You'll tidy your room this afternoon!

31   How the pluperfect is used

The pluperfect always refers to an action or event which takes place in the past. It may occur in a main clause or in a dependent clause. In both types of clause it expresses, or suggests, completion of an action or event *before* another event.

● in *main* clauses:

> **Elle *avait terminé* ses études.**
> She had finished her studies.

> **Nous *avions parlé* au président avant sa démission.**
> We had spoken/spoke to the president before he resigned.

> **Tu *étais entré(e)* au moment où elle commençait à chanter.**
> You had (just) entered/entered at the moment she began to sing.

Note the English equivalent of the pluperfect:

> **avait terminé**   had finished
> **avions parlé**   had spoken/spoke
> **étais entré(e)**   had entered/entered

- in *dependent* clauses, where it is frequently accompanied by a perfect or imperfect in the main clause. The dependent clause, containing the pluperfect, is always introduced by a conjunction such as **puisque; après que; depuis que; quand, lorsque; parce que** or by a relative pronoun.

> *C'était* sans espoir *puisqu'*il n'*avait* pas *eu* le courage de poser la question.
> It was hopeless because he hadn't had the courage to ask the question.

> *Après qu'*elle *avait écrit* sa lettre de démission, elle *était tombée* malade.
> After she wrote her letter of resignation, she fell ill.

> *J'ai dépensé* tout l'argent *que* j'*avais reçu* de mon père avant son départ.
> I have spent all the money I received from my father before he left.

In the following example the pluperfect conveys a sense of diffidence or politeness or discretion. It may even imply mild criticism – just as it can in English, with the appropriate stress on the auxiliary verb:

> Il *était venu* t'inviter dîner ce soir.
> He *had* come to invite you to dinner tonight.

The pluperfect is also used to express a condition (see **33.1.1**), but in this case the condition is unfulfilled – the action or event never took place:

> On lui aurait donné l'argent dont il avait besoin, s'il l'*avait demandé*.
> We would have given him the money if he had asked for it.

The pluperfect is used in indirect (or reported) speech if the verb in the main clause refers to an action or event in past time.

> Ma mère ne *savait* pas/n'*a* pas *su*/n'*avait* jamais *su* quand nous *étions rentré(e)s*.
> My mother didn't know/never knew when we got home.

32 How the past anterior is used

The past anterior belongs essentially to written, formal French. It can occur in a main clause or a dependent clause.

- when it is used in a *main* clause it is accompanied by an adverb of time and it usually indicates that the action or event is sudden or rapid. Verbs in other main tenses in the text will be in the past historic. The English equivalent is 'had' + past participle, or simply the past tense.

> Il *eut bientôt* trop *bu*. On lui *donna* à manger.
> He'd soon had too much to drink. We gave him something to eat.

> A peine *fut*-elle *arrivée* qu'il *commença* à chanter la Marseillaise.
> She had scarcely arrived when he began to sing the Marseillaise.

- in a *dependent* clause, the past anterior is *always* introduced by one of the following conjunctions: **après que; quand, lorsque; aussitôt que, dès que; à peine**, and the main verb is *always* in the past historic.

Il *rougit dès qu'il eut dit* le mot.
As soon as he had said/said the word, he blushed.

If the main verb is *not* in the past historic, the past anterior is *not* used.

Il *a rougi dès qu'il a dit* le mot.

33 The conditional and the conditional perfect

The conditional tense is composed of the stem of the future (see **25**) + the endings of the imperfect: **-ais, -ais, -ait, -ions, -iez, -aient**.

donner:

je	*donnerais*	I would give	nous	*donnerions*	
tu	*donnerais*		vous	*donneriez*	
il/elle	*donnerait*		ils/elles	*donneraient*	

finir:

je	*finirais*	I would finish	nous	*finirions*	
tu	*finirais*		vous	*finiriez*	
il/elle	*finirait*		ils/elles	*finiraient*	

vendre:

je	*vendrais*	I would sell	nous	*vendrions*	
tu	*vendrais*		vous	*vendriez*	
il/elle	*vendrait*		ils/elles	*vendraient*	

The conditional perfect is composed of the conditional of **avoir** or **être** + past participle:

avoir: j'*aurais,* tu *aurais,* il/elle *aurait,* nous *aurions,* vous *auriez,* ils/elles *auraient*
être: je *serais,* tu *serais,* il/elle *serait,* nous *serions,* vous *seriez,* ils/elles *seraient*

j'*aurais donné*   I would have given
je *serais allé(e)*   I would have gone

33.1 How the conditional and the conditional perfect are used

The conditional has three main functions. It is used to express time, mood and conditions. In an indirect (or reported) context, when the verb in the main clause is in one of the past tenses, the conditional is used in the dependent clause to refer to a future action or event in the context of past time (see **50.5d, 51.b**).

Elle m'*a dit* qu'elle me *verrait* tout à l'heure. ('Je te verrai . . .')
She said she would see me soon. ('I'll see you . . .')

Il m'*écrivait* qu'il n'*arriverait* pas avant la fin du mois.
He wrote (to say) that he would not be here before the end of the month.

Je *savais* qu'il *pleuvrait.*
I knew it would rain.

The conditional perfect normally implies that the action or event is complete before another action or event:

Pierre *a promis* qu'il l'*aurait terminé* quand nous *serions rentré(e)s.*
Peter promised (that) he would have finished before we got back.

Le professeur *a dit* qu'il *aurait rendu* les copies avant les vacances.
The teacher said he would return the papers before the holidays.

Je *savais* qu'il n'*aurait* toujours pas *reçu* ta lettre.
I knew he would still not have received your letter.

The conditional and the conditional perfect often occur in dependent clauses introduced by **dès que, aussitôt que; quand, lorsque** (see **30**). The main verb is in one of the past tenses. Note the tense in the English translation:

Il *répondait* que *dès qu'*il *aurait* assez d'argent il *irait* voir le film.
He replied that as soon as he had enough money he would go to see the film.

Je lui *ai demandé* d'allumer la télévision *quand* elle *aurait fini* ses devoirs.
I asked her to put on the television when she had finished her homework.

33.1.1 The conditional and the conditional perfect with **si** meaning 'if'.

There is a sequence of tenses which has to be used when conditions are expressed in French. The sequence is the same as the sequence of tenses in English conditional tenses. The dependent **si** clause can precede or follow the main clause.

Dependent verb	Main verb
si + present	future or imperative
*S'*il *fait* beau demain	– **j'***irai* à la plage.
If it's fine tomorrow	– I'll go to the beach.
Si tu *sors*	– **branche** le répondeur téléphonique.
If you go out	– switch on the answering machine.
si + imperfect	conditional
Si vous *aviez* de l'argent	– **vous** *pourriez* partir en vacances.
If you had some money	– you could go on holiday.

In the following sequence, the action or event expressed in the conditional clause never actually took place – the condition was unfulfilled:

si + pluperfect	conditional perfect
Si mon réveil *avait* sonné	– je *serais arrivé(e)* à temps.
If my alarm had rung	– I would have arrived in time.

The following examples show how the order of the clauses in conditional sentences can be changed round:

> *Si* tu n'*avais* pas *donné* la tarte aux cerises à ton frère ta sœur l'*aurait mangée*.
> If you hadn't given the cherry tart to your brother your sister would have eaten it.

> Ta sœur *aurait mangé* la tarte aux cerises *si* tu ne l'*avais* pas *donnée* à ton frère.
> Your sister would have eaten the cherry tart if you hadn't given it to your brother.

33.1.2 When there is more than one condition in a sentence, **si** is used with the appropriate sequence of tenses for the first condition. For subsequent conditions **si** is replaced by **que** + subjunctive.

> *Si* vous *avez* assez d'argent et *que* vous *fassiez* des économies, vous *pourrez* partir en vacances.
> If you have enough money and you save a bit, you can go on holiday.

33.1.3 The conditional is used – especially with **aimer, préférer, devoir, pouvoir** and **vouloir**:

- to express politeness:

> Elle a très chaud, *pourrais*-tu ouvrir la fenêtre?
> She is very hot, could you open the window?

> Vous *devriez* lui dire merci.
> You should say thank you to him/her.

> Il *voudrait* un billet aller et retour Paris-Londres.
> He'd like a return ticket Paris-London.

- to express a wish or desire to do something:

> J'*aimerais* visiter les musées de Paris.
> I'd like to visit the museums in Paris.

33.1.4 The conditional perfect is used with **aimer, préférer, devoir, pouvoir** and **vouloir**:

- to express regret:

> Il *aurait* bien *aimé* voir la peinture de Picasso mais l'exposition s'est terminée la semaine dernière.
> He would have liked to see the Picasso but the exhibition ended last week.

> Le snack-bar est fermé. J'*aurais* bien *voulu* t'offrir un café.
> The snack-bar's shut. I'd have liked to buy you a coffee.

33.1.5 The conditional and the conditional perfect are used:

- to give information that is doubtful, unconfirmed or alleged – especially in the media:

Est-ce vrai qu'il n'y *aurait* pas de réunion demain matin?
Is it true there won't be a meeting tomorrow morning?

L'accident ferroviaire d'hier *aurait fait* trente-trois victimes.
Thirty-three people are feared dead in yesterday's rail crash.

● to imply conjecture, supposition or probability (see **25.2, 30**):

On *dirait* qu'il va pleuvoir.
You'd think it was going to rain.

Selon elle une foule énorme *devrait* attendre l'arrivée du Président.
According to her a huge crowd was waiting for the President to arrive.

Il n'est toujours pas là. Il *aurait manqué* l'autobus?
He's still not here. Could he have missed the bus?

Tu vas être en retard; tu *aurais dû* prendre un taxi.
You are going to be late. You should have taken a taxi.

34 The subjunctive

The essential difference between the indicative and the subjunctive has to do with meaning: whereas the indicative refers to actions and events in past, present or future time (see **24**), the subjunctive is used to express feelings, possibilities, doubts, wishes, orders, etc. In other words, the subjunctive is used when an action or event is not a fact – or not *yet* a fact, or when there is some sort of doubt or reservation about a possible action or event.

The subjunctive is sometimes used as a main verb, but it usually occurs in dependent clauses following verbs such as **avoir peur que** 'to fear', **croire que** 'to think', **vouloir que** 'to want, wish' or conjunctions such as **avant que** 'before', **pourvu que** 'provided that', **supposé que** 'supposing/assuming that'.

The subjunctive is not frequently used in English today, and translations of the French subjunctive tenses may be indistinguishable from the indicative tenses. However, sometimes it is appropriate to include 'may, might, should . . .' in English translations.

34.1 The subjunctive tenses

There are four subjunctive tenses:

Simple tenses	Compound tenses
present (**subjonctif présent**) (see **35**)	*perfect* (**subjonctif passé**) (see **37**)
imperfect (**subjonctif imparfait**) (see **36**)	*pluperfect* (**subjonctif plus-que-parfait**) (see **38**)

35 The present subjunctive

The present subjunctive of most verbs is composed of the stem of the third person plural of the present indicative + the endings -e, -es, -e, -ions, -iez, -ent.

> donner: que je *donne*, que tu *donnes*, qu'il/elle *donne*, que nous *donnions*, que vous *donniez*, qu'ils/elles *donnent*
> finir: que je *finisse*, que tu *finisses*, qu'il/elle *finisse*, que nous *finissions*, que vous *finissiez*, qu'ils/elles *finissent*
> vendre: que je *vende*, que tu *vendes*, qu'il/elle *vende*, que nous *vendions*, que vous *vendiez*, qu'ils/elles *vendent*

35.1 Some of the endings of the present subjunctive are the same as certain endings in indicative tenses:

● some verbs have the same forms for *all the singular* and the *third person plural* of the present indicative and the present subjunctive:

donner:

present	je	*donne*	present	que je	*donne*
indicative	tu	*donnes*	subjunctive	que tu	*donnes*
	il/elle	*donne*		qu'il/elle	*donne*
	ils/elles	*donnent*		qu'ils/elles	*donnent*

● some verbs have the same forms for the *third person plural* of the present indicative and the present subjunctive, for example:

finir:	ils/elles *finissent*	qu'ils/elles *finissent*
mettre:	ils/elles *mettent*	qu'ils/elles *mettent*
recevoir:	ils/elles *reçoivent*	qu'ils/elles *reçoivent*
venir:	ils/elles *viennent*	qu'ils/elles *viennent*

● most verbs have the same forms for the *first* and *second persons plural* of the imperfect indicative and the present subjunctive:

donner:	nous *donnions*	que nous *donnions*	vous *donniez*	que vous *donniez*
finir:	nous *finissions*	que nous *finissions*	vous *finissiez*	que vous *finissiez*
vendre:	nous *vendions*	que nous *vendions*	vous *vendiez*	que vous *vendiez*

The exceptions to this are **avoir, être, faire, pouvoir** and **savoir:**

avoir:	nous *avions*	que nous *ayons*	vous *aviez*	que vous *ayez*
être:	nous *étions*	que nous *soyons*	vous *étiez*	que vous *soyez*
faire:	nous *faisions*	que nous *fassions*	vous *faisiez*	que vous *fassiez*
pouvoir:	nous *pouvions*	que nous *puissions*	vous *pouviez*	que vous *puissiez*
savoir:	nous *savions*	que nous *sachions*	vous *saviez*	que vous *sachiez*

35.1.2 Verbs which have stem changes in the present indicative (see **24.2**), have similar changes in the present subjunctive:

> boire: que je *boive*, que tu *boives*, qu'il/elle *boive*, qu'ils/elles *boivent* – que nous *buvions*, que vous *buviez*

devoir: que je *doive*, que tu *doives*, qu'il/elle *doive*, qu'ils/elles *doivent* – que nous *devions*, que vous *deviez*
prendre: que je *prenne*, que tu *prennes*, qu'il/elle *prenne*, qu'ils/elles *prennent* – que nous *prenions*, que vous *preniez*
venir: que je *vienne*, que tu *viennes*, qu'il/elle *vienne*, qu'ils/elles *viennent* – que nous *venions*, que vous *veniez*

| 35.1.3 | There is a small, but important, group of irregular verbs in which the present subjunctive has a completely different form from the present indicative: |

faire: que je *fasse*, que tu *fasses*, qu'il/elle *fasse*, que nous *fassions*, que vous *fassiez*, qu'ils/elles *fassent*
pouvoir: que je *puisse*, que tu *puisses*, qu'il/elle *puisse*, que nous *puissions*, que vous *puissiez*, qu'ils/elles *puissent*
savoir: que je *sache*, que tu *saches*, qu'il/elle *sache*, que nous *sachions*, que vous *sachiez*, qu'ils/elles *sachent*
falloir: qu'il *faille*

| 35.1.4 | A few verbs not only have a different form from the present indicative – they also have changes in the first and second persons plural: |

aller: que j'*aille*, que tu *ailles*, qu'il/elle *aille*, qu'ils/elles *aillent* – que nous *allions*, que vous *alliez*
avoir: que j'*aie*, que tu *aies*, qu'il/elle *ait*, qu'ils/elles *aient* – que nous *ayons*, que vous *ayez*
être: que je *sois*, que tu *sois*, qu'il/elle *soit*, qu'ils/elles *soient* – que nous *soyons*, que vous *soyez*
vouloir: que je *veuille*, que tu *veuilles*, qu'il/elle *veuille*, qu'ils/elles *veuillent* – que nous *voulions*, que vous *vouliez*

36 The imperfect subjunctive

The imperfect subjunctive is composed of the stem of the second person singular of the past historic minus the **s** + the endings -sse, -sses, -ât/-ît/-ût, -ssions, -ssiez, -ssent. The imperfect subjunctive keeps the vowel (**a, i, u**) of the past historic. The third persons singular and plural are the ones you are most likely to meet, so they are the forms given below.

donner: qu'il/elle *donnât*, qu'ils/elles *donnassent*
finir: qu'il/elle *finît*, qu'ils/elles *finissent*
vendre: qu'il/elle *vendît*, qu'ils/elles *vendissent*

There is a small group of verbs which keep the **u** of the past historic – most of the -oir verbs, including the **devoir** group, and a few -re verbs such as **boire**, **connaître**, **lire**.

recevoir: qu'il/elle *reçût*, qu'ils/elles *reçussent*
devoir: qu'il/elle *dût*, qu'ils/elles *dussent*

Avoir and **être** also keep the **u** of their past historic form:

avoir: qu'il/elle *eût*, qu'ils/elles *eussent*
être: qu'il/elle *fût*, qu'ils/elles *fussent*

37 The perfect subjunctive

The perfect subjunctive is composed of the present subjunctive of **avoir** or **être** + past participle.

donner: que j' *aie donné*	**venir:** que je *sois venu(e)*
finir: que j'*aie fini*	**arriver:** que je *sois arrivé(e)*
vendre: que j'*aie vendu*	**se reposer:** que je me *sois reposé(e)*

38 The pluperfect subjunctive

The pluperfect subjunctive is composed of the imperfect subjunctive of **avoir** or **être** + past participle.

donner: que j'*eusse donné*	**venir:** que je *fusse venu(e)*
finir: que j'*eusse fini*	**arriver:** que je *fusse arrivé(e)*
vendre: que j'*eusse vendu*	**se reposer:** que je me *fusse reposé(e)*

39 Sequence of tenses; uses of the subjunctive

There are rules governing the sequence of tenses used in the main clause and a dependent clause, when the main verb is in the indicative and the dependent verb is in the subjunctive.

Main clause (indicative)		Dependent clause (subjunctive)	
present	J'attends		
future	J'attendrai		
future perfect	J'aurai attendu	either the present	qu'il finisse
perfect	J'ai attendu	or the perfect	qu'il ait fini
imperative	Attends		
imperfect	J'attendais		
past historic	J'attendis		
pluperfect	J'avais attendu	either the imperfect	qu'il finît
conditional	J'attendrais	or the pluperfect	qu'il eût fini
conditional perfect	J'aurais attendu		

There is a tendency in contemporary French to avoid using the imperfect and pluperfect tenses of the subjunctive. The present and the perfect tenses take their place in written, spoken, and informal French. In formal written French and in *very* formal spoken French the imperfect and the pluperfect subjunctive may still occur.

A guideline for the sequence of tenses in contemporary French: whether the tense of the main verb is present, future or past, use the present or perfect subjunctive in the dependent clause. Reference to present, future or past actions or events will help in deciding whether to use the present subjunctive (actions and events in the present or future), or the perfect subjunctive (actions and events in the past).

Elle *veut que* tu *partes.*
She wants you to go.

Elle *voulait que* tu *sois couché(e)* à 9 heures.
She wanted you to be in bed by 9 o'clock.

39.1   **The subjunctive in main clauses**

The subjunctive may occur in main clauses – frequently in exclamations, and usually in the third person singular or plural.

● to express a wish or desire that an action or event should happen:

(*Que*) *Viennent* les vacances! (note the inversion)
I wish it were (was) the holidays!

*Pourvu qu'*il *fasse* beau demain!
I hope it's fine tomorrow!

● as a form of imperative, or of encouragement, usually following **que**:

*Qu'*elles *viennent* à mon bureau!	Tell them to come to my office!
Que ces idées te *soutiennent*!	I hope these ideas help you!

● to express indignation, following **que**:

Que je t'*offre* un cadeau? Jamais de la vie!
Me give you a present? Not likely!

● to express possibility, or assumption. The subjunctive may follow **que**, and inversion may occur:

*Qu'*elle *réponde* et nous verrons bien si elle a appris sa leçon!
Let her answer and we'll see if she has learned the lesson!

Soit un triangle ABC . . .
Let ABC be a triangle . . .

Soit les deux hypothèses suivantes . . .
Given the two hypotheses which follow . . .

● in certain idiomatic expressions:

Que Dieu te *bénisse*!	May God bless you!
Sauve qui peut!	Run for your life!/Every man for himself!
Vive la République!	Long live France!

39.2   **The subjunctive in dependent clauses**

The subjunctive *has to be used* following certain verbs or conjunctions (see **39.2.2**). The lists which follow give the most common of the verbs and conjunctions which introduce the subjunctive: the lists are *not* exhaustive. One or two of the verbs may also be followed by an indicative, depending on the meaning, for example:

> **dire que** 'to say' + indicative *but* **dire que** 'to tell someone to do something' + subjunctive

The subjunctive may also be used without any introductory verb or conjunction when a speaker or writer wants to suggest that he/she has some doubt or uncertainty about something.

39.2.1   The subjunctive must be used following verbs or verb phrases expressing

● doubt, uncertainty, possibility:

douter que	to doubt (that)

il est *douteux que*	it's doubtful (that)
il est *improbable que*	it's unlikely (that)
il est *peu probable que*	it's unlikely (that)
il est *impossible que*	it's impossible (that)
il est *peu sûr que*	it's not certain (that)
il est *incertain que*	it's not certain (that)

Il est *peu probable qu*'elle le *sache*.
It's unlikely that she knows.

Note that **ne pas douter que** means 'to have *no* doubt that' and is followed by the indicative:

Je *doute que* vous *ayez* raison.
I don't think you are right.

Je *ne doute pas que* vous *avez* raison.
I have no doubt that you're right.

Expressions such as **il est possible que/il se peut que** 'It is possible', **il semble que** 'it seems' are followed by the indicative *or* the subjunctive depending upon whether the speaker or writer feels certainty (indicative) or doubt (subjunctive) about what is said or written. When the expressions are interrogative or negative they are followed by the subjunctive. **Croire** and **penser** are also followed by the subjunctive if they are interrogative or negative. Today, however, this rule is not always observed, as in the fifth example below.

Il est *possible qu*'elle *viendra*.
It's possible (very likely) that she'll come.

Il est *possible qu*'elle *vienne*.
It's possible (not really likely) that she'll come.

Est-il *possible qu*'elle *vienne*?
Is it possible that she'll come?

Il *n*'est pas possible qu*'elle *vienne*.
It is not possible that she'll come.

Je *ne crois pas qu*'elle *sera* là demain.
I don't think she'll be here tomorrow.

● necessity, obligation, restriction, advantage:

il *faut que*	necessary
il est *utile que*	worth it
il est *essentiel que*	essential
il *convient que*	should be
il *importe que*	important
il *vaut mieux que*	be better

Il *faudra que* tu *sois* là à midi.   You must be there at noon.

Il *vaut mieux que* tu y *ailles*.   You'd better go.

● wanting, wishing, agreeing, accepting:

vouloir que want	**préférer que** prefer	**permettre que** allow
exiger que demand	**éviter que** + ne avoid	**s'attendre à ce que** expect
tenir à ce que insist	**ordonner que** order	**dire que** order

Que veux-**tu** *que* je *fasse*?
What do you want me to do?

(and note the very informal way of saying the same thing: **Qu'est-c' tu veux que j'y fasse?**)

Je *ne supporte pas* **que tu me** *répondes* **comme ça!**
I will not stand for you answering me like that!

● feelings, emotions, attitudes (whenever they carry an element of doubt). Note the expletive **ne** in certain cases (see **47.12**):

craindre que + ne fear	**être** *content que* pleased
avoir peur que + ne fear	**être** *ravi que* delighted
redouter que (+ ne) fear	**être** *étonné que* astonished
regretter que (+ ne) regret	**être** *désolé que* upset
se réjouir que be delighted	**être** *satisfait que* satisfied
s'étonner que be astonished	**c'est** *dommage que* it's a pity

J'*ai peur qu'*il *ne soit* en retard.
I'm afraid he may be late.

C'est *dommage qu'*elles ne *puissent* pas t'accompagner.
It's a pity they can't go with you.

39.2.2 The subjunctive must be used after the following conjunctions expressing

● time:

avant que (+ ne)	before
en attendant que	while
jusqu'à ce que	until

Il faut partir *avant qu'*il (*ne*) *fasse* **nuit.**
We must leave before it gets dark.

Elle est restée *jusqu'à ce que* **l'enfant** *soit endormi*(*e*).
She stayed until the child was asleep.

Note that in informal French, the subjunctive sometimes occurs following **après que** when the conjunction refers to an action or event in the past (see **31**). This probably happens because the speaker or writer is associating **après que** with the rule for **avant que**.

> *Après qu*'elle *ait/a annoncé* les résultats nous sommes allé(e)s prendre un petit verre.
> After she announced the results we went for a quick drink.

● concession:

bien que/quoique/malgré que/encore que	although, even though
qui que	whoever
quoi que	whatever
quel que (usually with **être**)	whatever
où que	wherever

and the adverbs **si/quelque/pour** + adjective + **que** 'however' + adjective:

> *Bien que* je le *sache*, je n'arrive pas à y croire.
> Although I know it, I can't believe it.

> *Quoi que* tu *fasses*, tu ne vas pas changer sa décision.
> Whatever you do, you won't change his/her mind.

> *Quelles que soient* leurs raisons, ils n'auraient pas dû dire cela.
> Whatever their reasons, they shouldn't have said that.

> *Si* dur *qu*'elle *travaille*, elle ne réussit jamais.
> However hard she works, she doesn't succeed.

Note the following use of the third person singular of the imperfect subjective of **être** in the set phrase **fût-ce**:

> *Fût-ce* pour les encourager un peu!
> If only to give them a little encouragement!

> On a constaté les signes d'un changement, *fût-ce* d'un changement progressif!
> There have been signs of change, even if it's only gradual!

● hypothesis, introduced by **que** and frequently followed by an alternative such as **ou non** 'or not':

> *Qu*'il *aille* (*ou non*) avec moi, je vais au match.
> Whether he goes with me or not, I'm going to the match.

● condition:

pourvu que/à condition que	provided that
supposé que	assuming that
à moins que + ne	unless

> Ils t'aideront *à condition que* tu ne *dises* rien à tes amis.
> They'll help you provided (that) you say nothing to your friends.

- aim/*intended* result; result/consequence:

pour que / afin que	in order to
trop / assez + adjective + **pour que**	too + adjective + to
de peur que + **ne/de crainte que** + **ne**	for fear that, so that . . . not
éviter que + **ne**	to avoid (something happening)
sans que	without

Les enfants sont assez *grand(e)s* pour qu'*on* puisse *les laisser seul(e)s.*
The children are old enough to be left on their own.

De crainte que vous *ne manquiez* l'avion, je vous ai réservé un taxi.
So that you don't miss the plane, I've called you a taxi.

Elles sont parties sans que *leurs parents les* aient entendues.
They left without their parents hearing them.

and some expressions such as **l'intention est que** 'the intention is to', **le fait que** 'the fact that' . . .:

L'intention est qu'il puisse *travailler chez lui.*
The intention is that he should be able to work at home.

Sometimes (especially in spoken and informal French, and usually following an imperative) **que** alone is enough to express an intended result:

Approchez que je vous *voie*!
Come closer so that I can see you!

Note the conjunction **au point que** 'to the extent that' which is followed by the subjunctive when it is used to express (unfulfilled) result, provided the main verb is negative or interrogative:

Ces paquets ne *sont* pas *lourds* au point que *nous* devions *les porter à trois.*
These parcels are not so heavy that it will need three of us to carry them.

And there are three conjunctions which are followed by the subjunctive *or* the indicative depending upon whether the aim was only intended, or hoped for, or merely a possibility (+ subjunctive), or whether in fact the result or consequence actually occurred (+ indicative).

de sorte que/de manière que/de façon que	so that

Lève-toi de façon que *tu puisses voir le défilé.*
Stand up so that (hopefully) you can see the procession.

Lève-toi de façon à *voir le défilé.* (same subject in both clauses, so use *à* + the infinitive)
Stand up and you'll (definitely) be able to see the procession.

Finally, there is the expression **non (pas) que** 'not that' which is used to deny, or dismiss, a cause or reason. The following clause frequently provides the real cause. In the example, note how the consequence precedes the cause:

Elle ne va pas venir. *Non qu'*elle n'en *ait* pas envie, mais elle sera à
l'étranger.

She isn't coming. Not that she doesn't want to, but she'll be abroad.

● place:

où que	wherever
d'où que	from where
jusqu'où	how far

*Où qu'*elle *aille*, j'irai aussi.
Wherever she goes. I'll go too.

The subjunctive or indicative in a relative clause

The choice of subjunctive or indicative in a relative clause depends upon whether
the information in the clause is merely a possibility (subjunctive), or whether it is a
reality (indicative).

Je veux vivre dans up pays arabe *qui aille* avec mon prénom, ma
couleur de peau, ma culture.

(*The Guardian* 16.2.95)

I want to live in an Arab country which suits my name, the colour of my
skin, and my culture. (But *is there* such a country?)

Je veux vivre dans un pays arabe *qui va* avec mon prénom, ma
couleur de peau, ma culture.

I want to live in an Arab country which suits my name . . . (And there
is one!)

Elle cherche une maison *qui soit* plus petite.
She is looking for a smaller house. (There *might* be one.)

Elle cherche une maison *qui est* plus petite.
She is looking for a smaller house. (And there *are* some on the market.)

And only the subjunctive is used following some negative clauses such as:

il n'y a rien qui	there is nothing that
il n'y a personne qui	there is nobody who
il n'y a aucun homme/livre qui	there isn't a man/book that

Il n'y a rien qui puisse m'aider.
There is nothing that can help me.

The subjunctive following superlative adjectives and expressions such as

premier/dernier	first/last
le meilleur/le pire	the best/worst
le plus grand/le moins grand	bigger or the biggest/smaller or the smallest
seul	only
ne . . . personne/ne . . . jamais/ ne . . . aucun	nobody/never/not one

These expressions are usually followed by a relative pronoun: **qui, que, dont.**

C'est/Ce sont *les derniers* qui *aient répondu*.
They were the last people who replied.

C'est *la meilleure* histoire *que* j'*aie* jamais *entendue*.
It's the best story I've ever heard.

Il est le *seul* élève *qui ait compris* la question.
He is the only pupil who understood the question.

Elle *ne* connaît *personne qui soit* aussi jolie qu'elle.
She doesn't know anyone as pretty as she is.

NOTE | The expressions **la première/dernière fois** 'the first/last time' are adverbial phrases and do not influence the use of the indicative or the subjunctive.

39.5 | **Ways of avoiding the subjunctive**

It is sometimes possible to avoid the subjunctive. This usually depends upon the availability of alternative constructions following verbs and conjunctions, and on the main and dependent clauses having the *same* subject. Some examples:

- verbs and impersonal verbs:

avoir peur de + infinitive	instead of	**avoir peur que** + **ne** + subjunctive
éviter de + infinitive	instead of	**éviter que** + **ne** + subjunctive
vouloir + infinitive	instead of	**vouloir que** + subjunctive
il faut + infinitive	instead of	**il faut que** + subjunctive
il est possible de + infinitive	instead of	**il est possible que** + subjunctive
il convient de + infinitive	instead of	**il convient que** + subjunctive

- conjunctions:

sans + infinitive	instead of	**sans que** + subjunctive
pour + infinitive	instead of	**pour que** + subjunctive
avant de + infinitive	instead of	**avant que** (+ **ne**) subjunctive
afin de + indicative	instead of	**afin que** + subjunctive
à moins de + infinitive	instead of	**à moins que** + **ne** + subjunctive
de peur de + infinitive	instead of	**de peur que** + **ne** + subjunctive
de manière à + infinitive	instead of	**de manière que** + subjunctive
de façon à + infinitive	instead of	**de façon que** + subjunctive

Some conjunctions may also be used as prepositions and introduce nouns:

avant son arrivée, il/elle . . . *malgré* leur départ, ils/elles . . . *jusqu'à* ton retour, tu . . .

40 | # Reflexive verbs

Reflexive verbs (also called pronominal verbs) are verbs which are preceded by reflexive object pronouns: **me, te, se, nous, vous, se** (see **13**). With the infinitive and with participles the reflexive pronoun used is always the one which corresponds to the subject of the clause or sentence. The position of the reflexive pronouns follows the same rules as those for other object pronouns (see **14.3**). For past participle agreement see **42.3**.

Je vais *me reposer* un peu.　　　I'm going to rest for a bit.

40.1　Tenses of reflexive verbs

(In the following examples only the masculine singular of the past participle is given.)

Infinitive			
Present	**se reposer** 'to rest'	Perfect	**s'être reposé** 'to have rested'
Indicative			
Present	**je *me repose***	Perfect	**je *me suis reposé***
Future	**je *me reposerai***	Future perfect	**je *me serai reposé***
Imperfect	**je *me reposais***	Pluperfect	**je *m'étais reposé***
Past historic	**je *me reposai***	Past anterior	**je *me fus reposé***
Conditional	**je *me reposerais***	Conditional perfect	**je *me serais reposé***
Subjunctive			
Present	**que je *me repose***	Perfect	**que je *me sois reposé***
Imperfect	**que je *me reposasse***	Pluperfect	**que je *me fusse reposé***

40.2　How reflexive verbs are used

Some verbs are genuinely reflexive – their action *reflects back* to the subject. In the following example, in French *and* in English, the transitive verb **couper** 'to cut' is used reflexively:

Elle s'est coupée.　　　She cut herself.

Remember that there is *no* agreement of the past participle when a reflexive verb is used with a part of the body (see **2.4b, 42.3**).

Elle s'est lavé *les cheveux*.　　　She washed her hair.

40.2.1　Some transitive verbs are used reflexively when the action they refer to is in fact reflexive. The corresponding English verb is *not* necessarily reflexive.

laver　　to wash　　　**se laver**　　to get washed/wash

Il *lave* la vaisselle.
He is washing the dishes.

Il *se lave* avant de se coucher.
He gets washed before he goes to bed.

Examples of verbs which can be transitive or reflexive in French, but only transitive or intransitive in English.

coucher	to put (someone) to bed	**se coucher**	to go to bed
habiller	to dress (someone)	**s'habiller**	to get dressed/dress
promener	to take (someone/something) for a walk	**se promener**	to go for a walk

40.2.2 Some verbs are reflexive in French – the English equivalent is *not*. Some examples:

s'asseoir	to sit down	**s'approcher**	to approach
se diriger vers	to go to/towards	**se servir de**	to use

40.2.3 Some reflexive verbs have a reciprocal meaning: 'each other' (see **11.7**). Some examples:

se téléphoner:

> *Nous nous téléphonons le weekend.*
> We telephone each other at the weekend.

s'écrire:

> *Elles* ne *se sont* jamais *écrit.*
> They have never written to each other.

se rencontrer:

> *Ils se rencontrent sans dire un mot.*
> They meet but don't speak to each other.

se détester:

> *Ils se détestent.*
> They hate each other.

40.2.4 Some verbs have a different meaning when they are used as reflexives:

agir	to act	**s'agir de**	to be a matter/question of
aller	to go	**s'en aller**	to go away

40.2.5 Reflexive verbs may have a passive meaning (see **41.3**) – although **on** + an active verb is frequently used for the passive instead of a reflexive (see **41.3**):

> *Cela* ne *se dit* jamais en anglais!/*On* ne *dit* jamais cela en anglais!
> That is never said in English!

40.2.6 The subject of impersonal reflexive verbs is always **il** (see **12.2d**):

> *Il se trouve que nous sommes né(e)s dans la même ville.*
> We happen to have been born in the same city.

41 The passive

The passive in French is very similar to the passive in English: it is composed of the verb **être** (in the appropriate tense) + past participle, in English the verb 'to be' (in the appropriate tense) + past participle. The participle *always* agrees with the subject.

Active form:

> **Le directeur *a reçu* les nouveaux élèves.**
> The headmaster welcomed the new pupils.

Passive form:

> **Les nouveaux élèves *ont été reçus* par le directeur.**
> The new pupils were welcomed by the headmaster.

The object (**les nouveaux élèves**) of a directly transitive verb (**recevoir**) in an active clause > the subject in a passive clause. The subject (**le directeur**) in the active clause > the agent in the passive clause. The agent is introduced by **par** or by **de**. **Par** tends to be used more frequently than **de**, but, if in doubt, the following guidelines may help: use **par** for an action and for reference to specific people or things, and use **de** for a state of affairs, feelings or thoughts, habit, and for general reference to people or things.

> **Elle *a été invitée* au cinéma *par* un ami.**
> She has been invited to the cinema by a friend.

> **Il *sera accompagné de* plusieurs amis.**
> He'll be accompanied by several friends.

41.1 The agent is *not* always present:

> **Si elles continuent à traverser la rue sans faire attention, elles vont être blessées.**
> If they go on crossing the street without looking, they're going to get hurt.

41.1.1 The passive is typically found with directly transitive verbs, that is, verbs which can have a direct object: e.g. **respecter, aimer, raconter**. Some verbs which are directly transitive in French may not be directly transitive in English – and vice versa:

écouter **la radio**	to listen *to* the radio
chercher **la femme**	to look *for* the woman
to *enter* the house	**entrer *dans* la maison**
to *remember* her name	**se souvenir *de* son nom**

41.2 **Formation of the passive**

(In the following examples only the masculine singular of the past participle is given.)

	Active	Passive	
Infinitive			
Present	**inviter** to invite	**être invité**	to be invited
Perfect	**avoir invité** to have invited	**avoir été invité**	to have been invited

Indicative			
Present	j'*invite*	je *suis invité*	was invited
Future	j'*inviterai*	je *serai invité*	shall be invited
Imperfect	j'*invitais*	j'*étais invité*	was invited
Past historic	j'*invitai*	je *fus invité*	was invited
Perfect	j'*ai invité*	j'*ai été invité*	have been invited
Future perfect	j'*aurai invité*	j'*aurai été invité*	shall have been invited
Pluperfect	j'*avais invité*	j'*avais été invité*	had been invited
Past anterior	j'*eus invité*	j'*eus été invité*	had been invited
Conditional	j'*inviterais*	je *serais invité*	should be invited
Conditional perfect	j'*aurais invité*	j'*aurais été invité*	should have been invited

Subjunctive			
Present	que j'*invite*	que je *sois invité*	am/may be invited
Imperfect	que j'*invitasse*	que je *fusse invité*	was/might be invited
Perfect	que j'*aie invité*	que j'*aie été invité*	(may) have been invited
Pluperfect	que j'*eusse invité*	que j'*eusse été invité*	had (might have) been invited

41.3 **Other ways of expressing the passive**

- **on** + third person singular of an active tense:

> Le terroriste *a été interrogé.*/*On a interrogé* le terroriste.
> The terrorist was interrogated.

> Ils *seront avertis* du danger./*On* les *avertira* du danger.
> They'll be warned of the danger.

- reflexive verbs (remember not all verbs can be used reflexively, see **40**):

> Le champagne *se boit* très frais.
> Champagne is drunk chilled.

> Ces légumes *se vendent* partout.
> These vegetables are sold everywhere.

In less formal French, **se faire, se voir, s'entendre** . . . + infinitive can also be used to express the passive:

> Le garçon *s'est fait renverser* par un autobus.
> The boy was knocked over by a bus.

> Elle *s'est vue exclure* du parti.
> She was excluded from party membership.

- impersonal verbs (which are always in the third person singular (see **46**)), especially with **être** + past participle, or in the reflexive form:

Il a été dit des choses terribles.
Awful things were said.

Il se présente quelques problèmes.
There are some problems.

41.4 A few directly transitive verbs cannot be used in the passive, for example **avoir** when it means 'to possess'. The following example could not be passive in English either:

Elle *a* un très bel appartement.
She has a very beautiful flat.

41.4.1 It is important to remember that whereas in English a passive form is possible with an indirect object, it is *not* in French.

He gave me the book.
Il m'a donné le livre.

I was given the book./The book was given to me.
On m'a donné le livre.

41.4.2 There are three verbs with an indirect object which *can* be used in the passive – the indirect object > the subject of the passive clause. The verbs are **obéir à qn** 'to obey someone', **désobéir à qn** 'to disobey someone', **pardonner à qn** 'to forgive someone'.

Les élèves *obéiront à* l'institutrice.
The pupils will obey the teacher.

L'institutrice *sera obéie* de ses élèves.
The teacher will be obeyed by her pupils.

42 ## The past participle

Some guidelines on the formation of past participles:

Verbs whose infinitive ends in **-er**: the stem of the infinitive + **é**;
e.g. **donner: donné** 'given'
Verbs whose infinitive ends in **-ir**: the stem of the infinitive + **i**; e.g. **finir: fini** 'finished'
Verbs whose infinitive ends in **-re**: the stem of the infinitive + **u**;
e.g. **vendre: vendu** 'sold'

But *many* verbs, including the **-oir** group, do not follow these guidelines, and the past participles simply have to be learned (see verb tables). Some examples:

être:	**été**	been	**boire:**	**bu**	drunk
avoir:	**eu**	had	**convaincre:**	**convaincu**	convinced
connaître:	**connu**	known	**venir:**	**venu**	come
prendre:	**pris**	taken	**craindre:**	**craint**	feared
devoir:	**dû** (accent on ms only)				

42.1 Past participles may be used as nouns, adjectives, verbs, prepositions and conjunctions.

● nouns:

la *prise* de notes	notetaking
la *mise* en œuvre	implementation
le *mort*	the dead man
la *vue*	sight, view
l'*arrivée*	arrival
le *reçu*	receipt

- adjectives (agreeing with their nouns):

la *porte fermée*	the closed door
des *films connus*	well-known films

Frequently, the English equivalent of a past participle in French is a present participle:

agenouillé	kneeling	**penché**	leaning
assis	sitting	**pendu**	hanging

On l'a vu *agenouillé(e)* devant l'autel.
We saw him/her kneeling before the altar.

- verbs (agreeing with nouns or pronouns):

Les devoirs *terminés*, les élèves sont sorti(e)s.
When their homework was finished the pupils left.

Bien qu'*équipée* d'un nouveau système d'alarme, la voiture a été volée.
Although it had a new alarm system, the car had been stolen.

Tu y vas demain? – *Entendu*!
You're going tomorrow? – OK!

- prepositions (some of these are very useful in business correspondence). They normally precede the noun and there is no agreement:

approuvé	agreed	**vu**	given
excepté	apart from	**supposé**	assuming
entendu	decided/agreed	**ci-joint/ci-inclus**	enclosed
y compris	including		

Vous trouverez *ci-joint* les pièces demandées.
The documents requested are enclosed.

But some of them, such as **excepté, y compris, ci-joint**, may follow the noun and when they do, they agree with it in gender and number:

La Grande Bretagne *exceptée*, tous les pays membres ont accepté le contrat social.
Apart from Great Britain, all the member countries have accepted the Social Contract.

Note **étant donné** 'given' – agreement is variable with this prepositional phrase:

étant données/donné les circonstances given the circumstances

- conjunctions (*no* agreement):

vu que	since
attendu que	given
supposé que	assuming

Vu qu'il était si tard, elle est partie de la réunion.
Since it was so late, she left the meeting.

42.2   **The past participle with *être*** (see 28.2)

Some intransitive verbs (verbs which cannot have a direct object) and all reflexive verbs are conjugated with **être** in their compound tenses. Their past participle agrees in gender and number with the subject. Intransitive verbs which have **être** are:

aller	to go	**partir**	to leave
arriver	to arrive	**rentrer**	to return
demeurer	to stay, live	**rester**	to stay
descendre	to go down	**retourner**	to return
entrer	to enter	**sortir**	to go out
monter	to go up	**tomber**	to fall
mourir	to die	**venir**	to come
naître	to be born		

and all their compounds, for example: **venir, convenir, devenir, parvenir, redevenir.** Some of these verbs can be used transitively, and then their compound tenses are formed with **avoir: descendre, monter, rentrer, retourner, sortir**. The meaning of the verbs changes when they are used transitively.

Elle *est sortie* avant leur arrivée.
She went out before they arrived.

Elle *a sorti* son argent.
She got her money out.

42.3   **Agreement of the past participle with reflexive verbs**

The past participle agrees with the subject of reflexive verbs:

Elles *se sont rencontrées* devant le cinéma.
They met at the cinema.

If the reflexive pronoun is equivalent to an *indirect* object – as it is with such verbs as **se dire** 'to say to each other', **s'écrire** 'to write to each other', **se téléphoner** 'to telephone each other' – there is *no* agreement.

Vous *vous étiez dit* bonjour au moins!
You said hello to each other at least!

Elles *se sont téléphoné* hier.
They phoned each other yesterday.

But, if there is a direct object in the sentence and it *precedes* the verb, the past participle agrees with that preceding direct object.

Voilà les gants *qu'elle s'est achetés.*
Here are the gloves she bought herself.

> *Combien d'actions s'est-il achetées?*
> How many shares did he buy himself?

If there is a direct object and it *follows* the verb, there is *no* agreement.

> Elle *s'est cassé le nez.*
> She broke her nose.

> **Pour préparer l'examen, ils** *s'étaient posé des questions* **très difficiles.**
> In preparation for the exam, they asked each other some very difficult questions.

Agreement of the past participle with *avoir*

The past participle *never* agrees with subject of verbs conjugated with **avoir.**

> *Elle avait travaillé* **toute la nuit.**
> She had worked all night.

> *Ils ont assisté* **à cette réunion.**
> They were present at that meeting.

If there is a direct object in the sentence which precedes the verb, the past participle agrees with that preceding direct object. The direct object may be a personal pronoun (**me, te, le** . . .); the relative pronouns **que, lequel, laquelle, lesquels, lesquelles**; or a noun introduced by the interrogative or exclamatory adjective **quel(le)(s)** or the interrogative adverb **combien de.**

> **Ces lettres, je** *les ai* **déjà** *lues.*
> I've already read these letters.

> **Voilà la jeune femme** *qu'on a rencontrée* **hier.**
> There's the young woman we met yesterday.

> **Je ne savais pas** *lesquels* **des discours vous** *aviez enregistrés.*
> I didn't know which of the speeches you had recorded.

> *Quelles propositions aurait-il faites?*
> Which proposals will he have made, do you think?

> *Combien de cadeaux as-tu reçus* **pour ton anniversaire?**
> How many presents did you get for your birthday?

The past participle *never* agrees with **en.**

> **Des chocolats, elle** *en a mangé* **beaucoup trop!**
> She's eaten far too many chocolates!

The past participle with impersonal verbs

There is *no* agreement of the past participle with impersonal verbs.

> **Il** *avait manqué* **des détails importants.**
> Important details were missing.

> **Il** *a été trouvé* **toutes sortes d'objets sur les pistes de ski.**
> All kinds of things have been found on the ski slopes.

42.6 Verbs of the senses and past participle agreement

Past participles of verbs of the senses: **écouter, entendre, regarder, voir, sentir** +
infinitive – there is agreement if the preceding direct object is the object of the verb of
the senses, but not if it is the object of the infinitive.

> **Ce sont les jeunes filles** *qu'on a entendues chanter* **à la radio.**
> It's the girls we heard singing on the radio.

> **C'est la chanson que j'ai entendu chanter à la radio.**
> It's the song I heard sung on the radio.

and with *laisser* + infinitive, the past participle usually agrees with the preceding direct
object.

> **Voilà la voiture** *qu'il a laissée passer* **hier.**
> There's the car he let through yesterday.

Note that there is an increasing tendency today not to make the agreement.

42.7 The past participle of *faire* + infinitive

There is *no* agreement of the past participle in this construction.

> **As-tu vu la maison** *que j'ai fait restaurer*?
> Have you seen the house I've had restored?

> **Elle** *les a fait sortir.*
> She made them leave.

43 The present participle

The present participle is usually formed of the stem of the first person plural present
indicative + **-ant**:

> **donnant** giving   **finissant** finishing   **vendant** selling

Some exceptions to the above guideline:

avoir: ayant having   **être: étant** being   **savoir: sachant** knowing

43.1 Present participles may be used as nouns, adjectives, verbs, gerunds, prepositions and
conjunctions.

● nouns

> le/la *participant(e)*   participant, delegate
> le/la *représentant(e)*   representative

● adjectives

These participles, agreeing with the noun or pronoun in gender and number, are really
verbal adjectives describing a quality or state.

> **C'était une question** *étonnante.*
> It was an astonishing question.

Ils ont des voisins *charmants.*
They have delightful neighbours.

● verbal adjectives may have a different spelling from the corresponding present participle. Some examples:

Verbal adjective		Participle	
différent	different	**différant**	differing
excellent	excellent	**excellant**	excelling
fatigant	tiring	**fatiguant**	tiring
précédent	preceding	**précédant**	preceding
négligent	negligent	**négligeant**	neglecting

● verbs

In contrast to verbal adjectives, the present participle used as a verb is invariable.

C'était une décision *intéressant* tous les spectateurs.
It was a decision of interest to all the spectators.

Because the participles are functioning as verbs they may have objects, they may be used in the negative, they may be reflexive and they may be qualified by adverbs.

***Relisant* le texte, elle a trouvé beaucoup de fautes de frappe.**
When she read the text again, she found many typing errors.

***S'étant* cassé le bras, il n'arrivait pas à écrire.**
Because he'd broken his arm, he couldn't write.

● gerunds

The gerund is a verbal noun and follows **en** or **tout en**. The English equivalent is 'while, in, on by, if . . .' + present participle. (**Tout**) **en** + present participle may have a variety of different meanings, some of which are given here.

***En enlevant* votre manteau, vous serez plus à l'aise.** (condition)
If you take your coat off, you'll be more comfortable.

Elle a donné l'impression d'être plus calme, (*tout*) *en cachant* ses pleurs. (cause)
She appeared calmer because she was hiding her tears.

Ils perdront tout leur argent *en* le *gaspillant* comme ça. (explanation)
They'll lose all their money wasting it like that.

Prenez un siège *en attendant.* (simultaneity)
Take a seat while you're waiting.

Nous avons rougi *en entendant* ces mots. (anteriority)
We blushed when we heard those words.

● prepositions

Examples include: **durant, pendant** . . .

Il écoutait les CD *pendant* des heures.
He listened to CDs for hours on end.

- conjunctions

Examples include: **en attendant que** (see **39.2.2**), **pendant que** . . .

> **Je peux travailler *pendant qu'il* regarde la télé.**
> I can work while he is watching telly.

44 The imperative

There are three imperative forms in French. For the majority of verbs the present
indicative tense provides the verb forms used – *without* the personal pronoun: the
second person singular, and the first and second persons plural. In the case of **-er** verbs
the second person singular drops the **s**. For the position of personal pronouns see **14.3**.

> **donner: donne** 'give', **donnons** 'let's give', **donnez** 'give'
> **finir: finis, finissons, finissez**
> **vendre: vends, vendons, vendez**

If the **-er** verb is *followed* by the pronouns **y, en** the second person singular imperative
keeps the **s**:

> *Vas-y!*   Go on!
> N'*y va* pas!   Don't go there!
> *Donnes-en* à la petite fille!   Give some to the little girl.

44.1 The imperative forms of some verbs, e.g. **être**, **avoir**, **savoir**, **vouloir**, are irregular. The
forms should always be checked in verb tables.

> **être: sois, soyons, soyez**
> **avoir: aie, ayons, ayez**
> **savoir: sache, sachons, sachez**
> **vouloir: veuille, veuillons, veuillez**

> *Veuillez* agréer, Madame, l'expression de mes sentiments
> respectueux.
> Yours faithfully, . . .

44.1.1 Reflexive verbs use the emphatic pronoun in the second person singular imperative.
The negative form and the plural forms keep the personal pronouns.

> *Repose-toi* un peu!
> Have a little rest!

> Ne *te hâte* pas!
> Don't hurry!

> *Habillez-vous* vite!
> Hurry up and get dressed!

> Ne *nous couchons* pas avant minuit!
> Let's not go to bed before midnight!

44.2 **How the imperatives are used**

The second persons singular and plural can be used to give an order, an instruction,
advice, an invitation, make an appeal, or express a warning, a wish, etc.:

Viens!   Come here! (order)
Ne *recommencez* pas!   Don't start again! (order)

Faites tout d'abord cuire les pommes de terre.
First cook the potatoes. (instruction)

Téléphonez-lui avant d'aller la voir.
Ring her before you go and see her. (advice)

Venez dîner ce soir!
Come to dinner tonight! (invitation)

Ne m'*oubliez* pas.
Don't forget me. (appeal)

Continue comme ça et tu vas à la catastrophe.
Go on like that and you're asking for trouble. (warning)

Dors bien, ma petite!
Sleep well, dear! (wish)

The first person plural imperative is often used to give encouragement, advice:

Allons-y!   OK! Let's go!/Let's get started!
                     (encouragement)
Restons tranquilles!   Let's take it easy! (advice)

44.2.1 The imperative may also be used as an exclamation:

Tiens! Prends-le!
Here! Take it/him!

Voyons! On peut partir immédiatement!
OK! We can leave right away!

44.2.2 There are various ways of giving an order instead of using the imperative (see **70.3**).

- **que** + subjunctive (main verb):

  Que tout le monde *mette* un casque de protection!
  Everyone must wear a safety helmet!

- future tense:

  Les hommes *sortiront* par la gauche!
  Men leave by the left!

- infinitive:

  Ne pas *se pencher* au-dehors!
  Don't lean out!

- and for a polite imperative, use an interrogative form and/or the conditional tense:

  Pouvez-vous/Pourriez-vous ouvrir la fenêtre (s'il vous plaît)?
  Please open the window.

45   The infinitive

There are two infinitive forms – the present infinitive, e.g. **donner, finir, vendre** and the perfect infinitive, composed of **avoir** or **être** + past participle:

> **avoir donné** 'to have given', **avoir fini** 'to have finished', **avoir vendu** 'to have sold', **avoir reçu** 'to have received', **s'être reposé** 'to have rested', **être allé** 'to have gone', **avoir eu** 'to have had', **avoir été** 'to have been'

45.1   Infinitives used as other parts of speech

Infinitives can be used as nouns:

> *Nager* est très agréable.
> Swimming is very enjoyable.

> *Avoir fini* ses devoirs est aussi très agréable.
> Having finished one's homework is also very nice.

45.1.1

The infinitive can be used as an imperative, an exclamation, and as an interrogative:

Prendre un billet à la porte.	Take a ticket at the door.
Ne laissez pas *parler* ce représentant.	Don't let that representative speak.
Croire à tes salades!	Believe your rubbish!
Que *faire*?	What can we do?
Où *aller*?	Where can we go?
Qui *croire*?	Who can we believe?

45.1.2

The infinitive may be used – following **de** or **et de**, mainly in written French and replacing a tense – to add a little variety to a text:

> 'Le vin doit se déguster à table', a dit le jeune étudiant. *Et d'ajouter*: 'Lentement!'
> 'Wine must be tasted at table,' the young student said. And he added, 'Slowly!'

45.1.3

The infinitive may follow the prepositions:

> **pour, sans, avant de** + present (and sometimes perfect) infinitive,
> **après** + perfect infinitive

These constructions can be used providing the subject of both parts of the sentence is the same, otherwise a different construction would have to be used – note the English equivalents:

> **Ces bottes sont faites *pour marcher*.**
> These boots are made for walking.

> **Elle est entrée *sans avoir fait/ faire* de bruit.**
> She came in without making any noise.

> ***Après avoir mangé*, nous nous sommes reposé(e)s.**
> After eating we had a rest.

> *Avant de manger*, nous nous sommes lavé les mains.
> Before eating we washed our hands.

45.2 Same subject in both parts of the sentence

When the subject of both parts of the sentence is the same, some verbs are followed directly by the infinitive. Some examples: **aimer, aller, compter, devoir, entrer, espérer, falloir, manquer, penser, pouvoir, préférer, savoir, venir, vouloir.**

> **Nous** *comptons* **y** *aller* **demain.**
> We hope to go there tomorrow.

45.3 *Faire* + infinitive – note the English equivalent:

> **Elle** *a fait venir* **le médecin.**
> She called the doctor.
>
> **C'est bien! Ça** *fait dormir.*
> That's good. It makes you sleep.
>
> *Fais réparer* **la voiture, si tu veux.**
> Have the car repaired, if you like.
>
> **Il** *a fait travailler* **les étudiants.**
> He made the students work.

If there are two objects in this type of sentence and one of the objects is a person, that object is preceded by **à**:

> **Elle** *fait parler* **français à ses enfants.**
> She makes her children speak French.

If the infinitive is reflexive the reflexive pronoun is dropped:

> *Faites taire* **ces enfants!**
> Make the children shut up!

45.4 Verbs of the senses + infinitive

Verbs of the senses: **écouter, entendre, regarder, voir, sentir** + infinitive, and **laisser, envoyer** + infinitive – note the alternative relative clause, and the English equivalent:

> **Je l'***entends pleurer.* **(Je l'entends qui pleure.)**
> I can hear him/her crying.
>
> **On** *a vu* **des étudiants** *faire* **du stop. (. . . qui faisaient . . .)**
> We saw students hitch-hiking.

45.5 Verbs + preposition (à, de, pour . . .) + infinitive

This type of construction is possible when the subject of both clauses is the same. It is very important to know the correct preposition to use, and to know if the meaning of the verb changes if a different preposition is used. The preposition and the meaning should be checked in a dictionary.

finir de + infinitive	**Il** *a fini de manger.*	He has finished eating.
finir par + infinitive	**Il** *a fini par* **le/la** *casser.*	He finished up breaking it.

Some verbs may have different prepositions with *no* change in meaning:

> **commencer à** *or* **de** + infinitive   to begin to do/doing
> **continuer à** *or* **de** + infinitive   to continue to do/doing
> **s'efforcer à** *or* **de** + infinitive   to try hard to do

45.5.1 Some examples of verbs + **à** + infinitive:

> **apprendre à, s'attacher à, avoir à, consentir à, s'habituer à, inviter à**

and some examples of verbs + **de** + infinitive:

> **accepter de, cesser de, convenir de, détester de, s'empresser de, essayer de**

> Nous *nous sommes mis à faire* le ménage.
> We began to do the housework.

> Il *a cessé de parler* pendant le film.
> He stopped talking during the film.

45.6 **Nouns and adjectives may also be followed by a preposition** + infinitive

> **l'aptitude à** 'aptitude for', **la détermination à** 'determination to', **l'intérêt à** 'interest in'
> **la raison de** 'reason for', **le besoin de** 'need to', **les moyens de** 'means to'

(And note **une maison à vendre** 'a house for sale', **une femme à craindre** 'a woman to be feared', **une machine à coudre** 'a sewing machine' . . .)

> **dispose à** 'willing to', **lent à** 'slow to', **préparé à** 'prepared to', **capable de** 'capable of', **responsable de** 'responsible for', **certain de** 'certain to'

Note:

> *Il* est difficile *de* comprendre le finnois.
> It is difficult to understand Finnish.

> *Ce* livre est difficile à lire.
> This book is difficult to read. (see **6.3b**)

And note **assez** and **trop** + adjective + **pour** + infinitive:

> Ils sont *trop petits pour sortir* seuls.
> They are too little to go out alone.

46 **Impersonal verbs**

Impersonal verbs are fairly common in French. The subject is either **il** or **ce, cela, ceci**, and the verb is always in the third person singular of the tense required, indicative or subjunctive. Past participles are invariable.

> *Il est venu* plusieurs personnes.
> Several people came.

> *Il n'est pas tombé* beaucoup de pluie.
> There wasn't a lot of rain.

Impersonal verbs are used for expressing dates, time and weather

> *C'est* aujourd'hui le 16 avril. It's the 16th of April today.
> *Il était* six heures. It was six o'clock.
> *Il pleuvra* demain. It will rain tomorrow.

The weather may also be expressed by **il fait** . . . :

> *Il fait* beau, mais *il ne fait* pas chaud.
> It's fine, but it's not warm.

Examples of impersonal verbs

il faut que + subjunctive 'must, need to, have to' or **il (me) faut** + infinitive (using indirect object pronouns: **me, te, lui** . . .):

> *Il faudra que* tu *obéisses à* ton père.
> You must do what your father tells you.

> *Il leur fallait montrer* leur carte d'identité.
> They had to show their identity cards.

il y a 'there is/are' (note that the verb in this expression is **avoir** *not* être):

> *Y a-t-il* quelqu'un à la porte? Non. *Il n'y a* personne à la porte.
> Is there someone at the door? No. There's nobody.

il s'agit de + noun or infinitive 'it is a matter/question of':

> *Il s'agit d'*une grosse *somme d'argent.*
> It's a matter of a large amount of money.

> *De plus il s'agira de* la *payer* immédiatement.
> And it's a matter of paying it immediately.

Some more examples:

> *Il n'est venu* personne.
> Nobody came.

> *Il me manquera* du temps pour faire cela.
> I won't have enough time to do that.

> *Il a été convenu* d'une date.
> A date was agreed.

Note the passive form of the last example:

> **Une date a été convenue.** (not an impersonal verb in this case)

il (me) semble 'it seems (to me) that'

il semble que + subjunctive:

> *Il semble qu'*elle *aille* en France cet été.
> It seems she's going to France this summer.

il semble que + indicative occurs in spoken French, and when the verb in the dependent clause is in the imperfect:

> *Il semble qu'*elle ne *pouvait* pas y aller.
> It seems she couldn't go.

and when **il semble que** adds a pronoun (indirect object pronoun):

> *Il me semble que* je l'*ai entendu* chanter.
> I think I've heard him sing.

il ne + indirect object pronoun + **semble pas que** + subjunctive:

> *Il ne leur semble pas qu'*elle *puisse* le faire avant jeudi.
> They don't think she can do it before Thursday.

il (me . . .) semble + infinitive (same subject in both clauses) *or* + adjective:

> *Il me semble l'avoir vue* quelque part.
> I think I may have seen her somewhere.

> *Cela* ne *nous semblait* pas très *intéressant.*
> That didn't seem very interesting to us.

47 Adverbs

Adverbs are generally formed from adjectives, but unlike adjectives, adverbs are *invariable*. They are used with verbs – **travailler dur** 'to work hard', with adjectives – **très facile** 'very easy', and with other adverbs – **assez bien** 'quite good/well'. There are three main types of adverb: of manner – **vite** 'quick/quickly', place – **ici** 'here', and time – **demain** 'tomorrow'. To these should be added adverbs of quality – **bien** 'well' and negation – **jamais** 'never'. Adverbs may consist of one word – **difficilement** 'with difficulty', a compound word – **après-demain** 'the day after tomorrow', or of a phrase – **tout à fait** 'completely'.

47.1 Formation of adverbs of manner

In general adverbs of manner are composed of the feminine form of an adjective + **-ment**.

> **doux, douce, doucement** 'quietly, gently'
> **premier, première, premièrement** 'first of all, firstly'
> **complet, complète, complètement** 'completely, totally'
> **sérieux, sérieuse, sérieusement** 'seriously'

47.1.1 Adjectives ending in **-ent** or **-ant** drop the **-nt** of the masculine form and add **-mment**.

> **évident, évidemment** 'evidently'
> **suffisant, suffisamment** 'sufficiently, enough'

There are some exceptions to this rule:

> **lent, lente, lentement** 'slowly'
> **présent, présente, présentement** 'at present'

47.1.2 Adjectives which end in a vowel other than **e** normally simply add **-ment** to the masculine form:

poli, **poliment** 'politely'
absolu, **absolument** 'absolutely'
aisé, **aisément** 'easily'

| 47.1.3 |

Some adjectives are used as adverbs, without any change of form: **dur** 'hard', **bon** 'good', **net** 'short' (as in 'to stop short'):

refuser tout net to refuse point blank

In some cases different adverbial forms are available, but they are *not* interchangeable. They are used in different contexts and may have slightly different meanings.

dur; durement 'hard; deeply, badly'
fort; fortement 'extremely; strongly, highly'

C'est *fort* dommage.
It's a great pity.

Il est *fortement* recommandé de se munir d'un vêtement de pluie.
It's strongly recommended that you/we take some waterproof clothing.

Some adverbial phrases of manner:

avec soin 'carefully', **d'un coup** 'suddenly', **côte à côte** 'side by side', **en danger** 'in danger', **hors d'haleine** 'out of breath', **sous peu** 'soon', **sur un ton triste** 'sadly'

| **47.2** | **Comparative and superlative adverbs**

These adverbs are formed by placing **plus, aussi, moins** before the adverb and, if appropriate, adding **que** in the comparative and **de** in the superlative: **plus vite (que)** 'quicker (than)', **aussi vite (que)** 'as quick as', **moins vite (que)** 'less quick (than)'; **le plus vite (de)** 'the quickest (of)', **le moins vite (de)** 'the slowest (of)'.

Elle parle *plus vite* (*que lui*).
She speaks more quickly (than he does).

Nous avons mangé *aussi rapidement* (*que toi*).
We ate as quickly (as you).

Ils voyagent *moins* (*que leurs enfants*).
They travel less (than their children).

Je suis venu(e) *le plus vite possible*.
I came as quickly as possible.

C'est le cheval blanc qui court *le moins vite*.
It's the white horse that's going slowest.

| 47.2.1 |

Comparative and superlative forms of the irregular adverbs **bien, mal, beaucoup, peu**:

bien 'well'; **mieux (que)** 'better (than)'; **le mieux (de)** 'the best (of)'
mal 'badly'; **pis/plus mal (que)** 'worse (than)'; **le pis/le plus mal (de)** 'worst (of)'
beaucoup 'much'; **plus/autant (que)** 'more/as much (than/as)'; **le plus (de)** 'most (of)'
peu 'little'; **moins/aussi peu (que)** 'less/as little (than/as)'; **le moins (de)** 'least'

Tu aimes ce livre? – Non, je ne l'aime pas *beaucoup*.
You like this book? – No, not much.

J'aime *mieux* celui-ci (*que* celui-là).
I like this one better (than that one).

Moi, c'est ce livre-là que j'aime *le mieux* (*de* tous).
I like *that* book best (of all).

Eh *bien*! Tant *pis*!
Oh well! Too bad!

Some expressions using **plus** and **moins**:

de plus en plus	increasingly
de mal en pis	from bad to worse
de moins en moins intéressant	less and less interesting

Plus elle travaille, *plus* elle gagne de l'argent.
The more she works, the more she earns.

Moins je mange, *plus* j'ai envie de manger.
The less I eat, the more I want to.

Note the **ne** before the verb in a dependent clause, following a positive comparison:

Johan travaille *plus que* je *ne* (le) croyais.
Johan works more than I thought.

47.2.2 **Bien** used with **vouloir**: the position of **bien** may indicate a level of formality or informality:

Elle *veut bien* répondre à la question. (formal/informal)
She will be pleased to answer the question.

Il *voudrait bien* que tu l'écoutes. (informal)
Il vous prie de *vouloir bien* l'écouter. (formal)
He would like you to listen to him/her.

47.3 **Adverbs of quantity** (see **4.3, 21**)

Some examples:

assez 'enough', **peu** 'little, not much', **autant** 'as much', **plus** 'more', **beaucoup** 'much', **moins** 'less', **combien?** 'how much?', **trop** 'too much', **davantage** 'more', **très** 'very', **tellement** 'so much', **tant** 'so much'

Some adverbial phrases of quantity:

à peine 'hardly', **tout à fait** 'completely', **à peu près** 'almost'

47.4 **Adverbs of time**

Some examples:

alors 'then', **après** 'after', **aujourd'hui** 'today', **auparavant** 'before', **aussitôt** 'immediately', **bientôt** 'soon', **déjà** 'already', **demain**

'tomorrow', **désormais** '(from) now (on)', **enfin** 'at last, finally', **hier** 'yesterday', **longtemps** 'for a long time', **maintenant** 'now', **puis** 'then'

Some adverbial phrases of time:

à présent 'at present', **de temps en temps** 'from time to time', **tout à l'heure** 'soon, later'

47.5 Adverbs of place

Some examples:

autour 'round', **contre** 'against', **dedans** 'inside', **dehors** 'outside', **derrière** 'behind', **dessous** 'underneath', **devant** 'before', **ici** 'here', **là** 'here, there', **où** 'where'

Some adverbial phrases of place:

en arrière 'backwards', **en avant** 'forwards', **nulle part** 'nowhere'

47.6 Position of adverbs

With simple tenses, adverbs usually follow the verb, and with compound tenses they are usually placed between the auxiliary verb and the past participle. Normally they precede an infinitive.

Elles *travaillent beaucoup.*	They work a lot.
Elles *ont beaucoup travaillé.*	They have worked a lot.
Il faut *bientôt* **partir.**	We'll have to leave soon.

For emphasis, they are placed at the beginning – or at the end – of the sentence.

Vraiment, **tu m'ennuies!**
Really, you are annoying me!

They are placed before an adjective, a past participle or another adverb which they modify.

Elles sont *toujours bien* **habillées.**
They are always well dressed.

Cet Allemand parle *assez mal* **le français.**
That German speaks French rather badly.

But, these are only guidelines on the position of adverbs, and they may, for various reasons, be moved from their usual position. For example, if the adverb is quite long it is frequently placed at the end of the sentence.

Elle viendra nous voir *tout à l'heure.*
She'll come and see us later on.

If more than one adverb is being used in the sentence, the order they come in is manner, then place, then time – just as in English.

Il est arrivé *hors d'haleine chez nous à minuit.*
He arrived out of breath at our house at midnight.

47.7   **Adverbs of negation** (see **53**)

The forms are:

non	no	**ne . . . guère/(à peine)**	hardly
pas	no	**ne . . . ni . . . ni . . .**	neither . . . nor . . .
ne . . . pas	not	**ne . . . que**	only
ne . . . plus	no more, longer	**ne . . . aucun(e)/nul(le)**	not a, not one
ne . . . personne	nobody, no-one	**ne . . . nullement**	not at all, by no means
ne . . . rien	nothing	**ne . . . aucunement**	not at all, not in any way
ne . . . jamais	never	**ne . . . nulle part**	nowhere

47.7.1   **Non** and **pas**

Non is the main adverb of negation.

> **Tu veux du sucre?** *Non* (or **Merci**).
> Like some sugar? No.

Pas is used like **non** in some ways, but is less formal.

> **Il veut chanter mais** *pas* **moi!**
> He will sing but not me!

> **J'aime le français mais** *non/pas* **l'italien.**
> I like French but not Italian.

> **Pourquoi** *pas*?
> Why not?

> *Pas* **possible!**
> That's not possible.

Some expressions with **non** and **pas**:

Mais non!/Absolument pas!/Pas du tout!	No!
Pas un seul!	Not one!
Jamais de la vie!	Never!
Moi je *n'ai pas* **bu** *du tout*!	I haven't been drinking!
Il *n'y a même pas* **un verre d'eau!**	There's not even a glass of water!

And more gently:

Je crois *que non*.	I don't think so.
Sans doute que non./Probablement pas.	Probably not.

47.7.2   A positive answer, which contradicts a negative question or statement, is usually introduced by **si** (not **oui**).

> **Vous** *ne* **voulez** *pas* **m'accompagner?** *Mais si*!
> You don't want to come with me? Yes, I do!

47.7.3 For the partitive article in a negative context see **4.1**.

47.8 **Position of negative adverbs**

In simple tenses **ne** *precedes* the verb and **pas, plus, jamais** *follow* the verb. In compound tenses **ne** *precedes* the auxiliary verb and **pas, plus, jamais** *follow* the auxiliary verb.

Je *ne* **vois** *rien.*	I can't see anything.
Elles *n'***y sont** *jamais* **allées.**	They have never been there.

But **personne, rien, aucun**(e) can follow the verb, the past participle, or a preposition.

Nous *n'***avons entendu** *personne.*
We didn't hear anyone.

Elle *ne* **poserait cette question** *pour rien au monde.*
She wouldn't ask that question for anything (in the world).

Personne and **rien** may be used as subjects of the verb, but they *must* have their **ne**!

*Personne n'***est venu hier soir.**
Nobody came last night.

Aucun(e) may be replaced by **nul**(le) in formal French, and by **pas un**(e) in informal French.

Nous *n'***avons** *aucun* **souci concernant cette étudiante.**
We have no worries about this student.

Nulle **réponse** *n'***a été donnée au ministre.**
No reply was given to the minister.

Il *ne* **sait** *pas un* **mot de français.**
He doesn't know a word of French.

Both parts of the negative precede an infinitive if they refer to that infinitive.

Je *ne* **veux** *pas* **y aller.**	I don't want to go.
Il préfère *ne jamais* **y aller.**	He prefers never to go there.

NOTE Personal pronouns are placed between the **ne** and the verb or the auxiliary (see **14.3**).

47.8.1 ne . . . ni . . . ni . . .

Il *n'***a vu** *ni* **sa mère** *ni* **sa sœur.**
He hasn't seen his mother or his sister.

Ni **sa mere** *ni* **sa sœur** *ne* **viendra/viendront.** (see 22.3.3)
Neither his mother nor his sister will come.

47.8.2 **Nulle part** always follows the verb or the auxiliary.

Je *ne* **l'ai vu** *nulle part.*
I haven't seen him/it anywhere.

47.9   **Omission of *ne* and *pas***

Ne may be omitted in informal spoken French, and often in short phrases without a verb.

> J'sais pas.   Don't know.
> C'est pas vrai!   Not true!
>
> **Tu veux un chocolat? – Merci, pas de chocolat. Je suis au régime.**
> You want a chocolate? – No thanks, no chocolate. I'm on a diet.

Pas may be omitted after **cesser, oser, pouvoir, savoir**.

> **Elle ne *cesse* de parler.**   She never stops talking.

47.9.1   **Sans** + negative adverbs (*not* **pas**): examples include **sans plus, sans rien, sans aucun(e)**.

> **Nous sommes parti(e)s *sans rien* dire.**
> We left without saying a word.

47.10   ***Ne . . . que***

Que is always placed before the word it refers to. Note **ne . . . que si** 'not unless'.

> **Il *n'*est sorti avec la jeune fille *que* le samedi.**
> He only went out with the girl on Saturdays.
>
> **Cette femme, elle *ne* fait *que* faire des histoires!**
> That woman! All she does is make a fuss!
>
> **Je *ne* te donnerai une réponse *que si* j'ai des nouvelles.**
> I won't give you an answer unless I have any news.

47.11   ***Ne . . . pas toujours*** 'not always'; ***ne . . . toujours pas*** 'still not'

> **Elles *ne* sont *pas toujours* à la maison.**
> They're not always at home.
>
> **Elles *ne* sont *toujours pas* à la maison.**
> They're still not at home.

47.12   **The expletive *ne***

This **ne** occurs in formal, or very correct French, but only in certain contexts. It is frequently omitted from informal French. It is used:

● after verbs expressing feeling, and verbs expressing avoidance:

> **Il a peur qu'elle *ne* soit malade.**
> He's afraid (that) she may be ill.

● after verbs expressing doubt, when these verbs are negative:

> **On ne doute jamais qu'ils *ne* seront là.**
> We never doubt that they'll be there.

● following **à moins que** and **avant que**:

Je prendrai un imper *à moins qu'il ne* fasse très chaud.
I'll take a mac unless it's very warm.

● in comparisons:

C'est *plus* difficile *que je ne* (le) croyais.
It's more difficult than I thought.

47.13 **Formation of negative adjectives**

The negative prefixes **im-, in-, il-, ir-, mé-, mal-** are used to form these adjectives:

| patient *impatient* | légal *illégal* | content *mécontent* |
| correcte *incorrecte* | régulier *irrégulier* | honnête *malhonnête* |

Peu may be used instead of the prefixes:

Le livre est *peu intéressant.*
The book is not very interesting.

48 Prepositions

Prepositions may be single words, e.g. **à, devant**, or phrases, e.g. **au-dessous de, du côté de**. Some uses are very similar to English uses, but they do not always correspond to each other. Some examples are given here, but it always good practice to check in a dictionary – unless you are absolutely sure about their use, *and* about which verb, noun, adjective, or adverb the preposition is used with. The examples given here are grouped according to their function(s).

48.1 **Manner or means**

*Au moyen d'*une échelle nous sommes entré(e)s dans la maison.
We got into the house by a ladder.

*A force d'*étudier, il a réussi ses examens.
By studying hard, he passed his exams.

en voiture by car   *par* le train by train   *par* avion by plane

48.2 **Place**

à la campagne	in the country
à la télé	on telly
au bas de la page	at the foot of the page
auprès de la fenêtre	near the window
autour du feu	around the fire
chez moi	at my place
dans le train	on the train
en face de la gare	opposite the station
entre guillemets	in inverted commas
jusqu'à l'église	as far as the church

loin de l'école	far from the school
par terre	on the ground
parmi les étudiants	among the students
vers la banque	towards the bank

48.3 Time

à trois heures	at three o'clock
après ton anniversaire	after your birthday
avant le repas	before the meal
au printemps	in spring
depuis vendredi	since Friday
dès ce jour	from today
en 1996	in 1996
il y a huit jours	a week ago
jusqu'à minuit	until midnight
par jour	by day
pendant la nuit	during the night
vers cinq heures	about five o'clock

48.4 Cause

When the cause is *negative*:	When the cause is *positive*:
à cause du travail	*grâce à* cette aimable jeune fille
because of the work	thanks to that friendly girl
*en raison d'*un désaccord	*à la faveur de* sa compétence
because of a disagreement	on account of his/her efficiency

48.5 Restriction of some kind

excepté le boulanger	except for the baker
sauf l'ordre du jour	except for the agenda
quant à nous	as far as we are concerned
faute de temps	through lack of time
hors de prix	too expensive
en dehors de vous trois	apart from you three

48.6 Aim or purpose

afin de réussir	in order to succeed
de façon à comprendre	so as to understand
de manière à clarifier	so as to clarify
de peur de t'ennuyer	so as not to bore you
en vue de finir	with a view to finishing
pour terminer	in conclusion

Section B

Functions

Functions

III
Exposition

49 **Referring to people, things and places**

49.1 **Physical characteristics**

The simplest way to describe someone or something is to use **être** + adjective:

> **Il *est grand* et *beau* comme au cinéma.**
> He's tall and handsome like a film star.

or **être** + noun phrase introduced by **de**:

> **Mais non! Il *est de taille moyenne* et *d'une laideur indescriptible*.**
> No! He's average height and indescribably ugly.

Many adjectives may be used to describe hair, eyes, etc. Note that compound adjectives of colour such as **châtain foncé** or **gris vert** and some nouns like **marron** are invariable in French:

> **Elle est grande, mince, aux yeux *marron*, aux cheveux bouclés *châtain clair*.** (see **2.4b**)
> She's tall, thin, with brown eyes and light brown curly hair.

The definite article or **avoir** + definite article are used to refer to parts of the body:

> **Comme il est mignon . . . tu crois qu'il va garder *les yeux bleus*?** (see **2.4b**)
> He's a little darling! Do you think he'll keep his blue eyes?

> **A la suite de sa chute, elle *avait l'épaule* démise et *les deux jambes* dans le plâtre.**
> After she fell she had a dislocated shoulder and both legs in plaster.

But note that the indefinite article is also used, in particular when the adjective precedes the noun:

> **T'as *d'beaux yeux*, tu sais!** (see **4.2**)
> You've lovely eyes, you know!

> **Mère-grand, comme vous avez *de grandes dents*!**
> What big teeth you've got, Grandmother!

Prepositions such as **à** or **avec** may also be used:

> Comme je voudrais avoir une petite fille *à la peau* blanche comme la neige, *aux lèvres* rouges comme le sang et *aux cheveux* noirs comme l'ébène! (see **2.4b**)
> How I would love a little girl with skin as white as snow, lips as red as blood, and hair as black as ebony!

> **La serveuse** *au teint blême* **et** *à la chevelure blonde* **lui rendit sa monnaie.**
> The waitress with the pale face and the blonde hair gave him his change.

In the following lines – featuring **avec** – from a well-known French song, note how physical characteristics are emphasized by the possessive adjectives **ma, mes** which are used to paint a complete portrait – body and soul!

> *Avec* **ma gueule de métèque, de juif errant, de pâtre grec et mes cheveux aux quatre vents,**
> *Avec* **mes yeux bleus délavés qui me donnent l'air de rêver moi qui ne rêve plus souvent,**
> *Avec* **mes mains de maraudeur, de musicien et de rôdeur qui ont pillé tant de jardins,**
> *Avec* **ma bouche qui a bu, qui a embrassé et mordu sans jamais assouvir sa faim . . .**
>
> (Moustaki)

> With my foreign face – a wandering Jew and peasant Greek – unruly hair
> And pale blue eyes and dreamer's gaze – but I don't dream much any more
> My thieving hands – musician's hands – my plundering hands
> My greedy mouth has tasted wine – and flesh – a thirst that's never satisfied . . .

When describing an object, use **c'est, il s'agit de** 'it's, it's for' with verbs such as **se servir de** 'to use' in relative clauses such as **qui sert à, qui est utilisé pour** 'which is used for', **dont on a besoin lorsque** 'which you need when', **que l'on utilise pour** 'which you use for':

> **C'est** un petit outil, avec un manche, *dont on se sert pour* visser et dévisser.
> It's a small tool with a handle (which you use) for tightening or loosening screws.

> **Il s'agit d'un** ustensile de cuisine percé de petits trous *qui permet* par exemple *d'*écumer un bouillon.
> It's a kitchen utensil with small holes which you can use for skimming stock, for example.

49.2 **Personality**

Once again, many adjectives or past participles are used following **avoir** + noun or **être** in order to describe someone's qualities:

> Mademoiselle Frain *a* toujours *été ponctuelle* et *consciencieuse* dans son travail. Elle *a* une personnalité *enjouée* qui facilite le contact avec la clientèle.

Miss Frain has always been punctual and conscientious in her work.
She has a cheerful personality which makes for good customer
relations.

or defects:

**Si vous voulez mon avis, il *est prétentieux* et *a* un comportement
paternaliste avec les secrétaires qui ne me plaît pas du tout!**
If you want my opinion, he's a pretentious man and behaves in a
paternalistic manner towards the secretaries which I don't like one
little bit.

Note how the article is sometimes omitted, for example before expressions involving
bon or **mauvais**:

Il *est bon vivant* mais *a* aussi très *mauvais caractère*.
He's a nice guy but he can also be very bad-tempered.

Avoir + **air** may be used in two ways:

(a) **avoir un air** + adjective 'to look' + adjective:

Elle *a* toujours *un air condescendant*, ça m'énerve!
She always looks condescending, it really annoys me!

(b) **avoir l'air** + adjective (**sembler** + adjective) 'to seem' + adjective:

Ils *ont l'air* plutôt *sympathique(s)* tes copains!
Your friends seem quite nice guys.

NOTE | Agreement of the adjective in the previous example – with **air** or with **Ils**.

49.3 | **Relationships**

When introducing yourself or someone else, you may want to refer to personal and
social relationships, or professional relationships.

(a) For personal and social relationships use **être** + adjective or past participle, or a
noun phrase:

**Mon frère *est marié*, ma sœur *est divorcée* et moi, je *suis* encore
célibataire.**
My brother's married, my sister's divorced, and I'm still single.

Elle *est mère de famille* depuis peu. (see 3.1b)
She recently became a mother.

Note that most of these adjectives and past participles may be used as nouns:

Lui, c'est un *célibataire* endurci, et elle une *divorcée*.
He's a confirmed bachelor and she's a divorcee.

Avoir may also be used with expressions such as **à charge** or **à** + infinitive:

J'*ai* deux enfants *à charge*.
I have two dependent children.

Il *avait* six enfants *à nourrir*.
He had six children to feed.

(b) In order to state your identity, you may simply give your name, or give it following an appropriate verb:

Jean-Paul Murat

Je *m'appelle Alice Mirabeau* et vous êtes . . .?
My name is Alice Mirabeau and you are . . .?

In order to introduce someone else, again simply state the name. In a fairly informal situation, you can add **c'est** or **voilà**:

Laurence, viens voir . . . tiens, *c'est Jacques* et Cyrille. (see 6.3a)
Laurence, come and see . . . look, it's Jacques and Cyrille.

Bernard, un vieux copain d'école . . . et *voilà Camille* et Béatrice.
Bernard, an old school friend . . . and this is Camille and Béatrice.

You can make clear exactly what the relationship is using a possessive adjective (see 7):

Ma fille, Bernadette.
My daughter, Bernadette.

Mon collègue, Frédéric Rolland.
My colleague, Frédéric Rolland.

In a more formal situation, introductions might be slightly more complex and include the verb **présenter** 'to introduce':

Madame Moreau, je vous présente Monsieur Detrait.
Madame Moreau, let me introduce Monsieur Detrait.

You may also use polite verbal expressions, combined with expressions in apposition or relative clauses in order to be more specific about occupation or circumstances . . . :

J'ai le plaisir de vous présenter Mlle Lamie, journaliste au 'Monde'.
It is my pleasure to introduce Mlle Lamie, a reporter with 'Le Monde'.

Note the lack of article before **journaliste** in apposition.

Permettez-moi de vous présenter Luc Bessonier, du service relations publiques.
Allow me to introduce Luc Bessonier of Customer Relations.

Puis-je vous présenter mes parents, qui viennent d'arriver à Londres et ne parlent pas un mot d'anglais.
May I introduce my parents who have just arrived in London and don't speak any English.

(c) Occupations may be given by simply using **être** + noun without an article (see 3.1b):

Vous êtes avocat, n'est-ce pas?
You're a lawyer, aren't you?

> *Je suis directeur* du marketing et *ma femme est directrice* des ressources humaines dans la même société.
> I'm the marketing manager and my wife is director of personnel in the same company.

In the previous example, note how the definite article (**de** + **le** < **du**, **de** + **les** < **des**) has to be used after **directeur/directrice**. Keep in mind that a number of nouns used for professions have no feminine form (see **9.5**)

> J'ai deux *sœurs*, il y en a *une qui est prof(esseur)* et *l'autre ingénieur*.
> I have two sisters. One's a teacher and the other's an engineer.

Many other verbs and verb phrases are available such as **travailler** 'to work', **être chargé de** + infinitive, **être responsable de** + noun 'to be responsible for', and many different prepositions (see **48**) can be used – depending on what follows:

chez is used with proper names – of organizations or people:

> Maintenant, il *travaille chez Peugeot* mais avant, il *était chez Chaumont & Frères* à Loches.
> He works for Peugeot now but he used to be with Chaumont & Frères in Loches.

dans is used with sectors or organizations – when the name is not specified:

> Elle aurait voulu entrer *dans l'enseignement* et voilà qu'elle se retrouvait employée *dans une banque* du centre-ville.
> She would have liked to go into teaching, but there she was working in a bank in the centre of town.

à is used with names involving a definite article, with institutions and also in order to be specific about departments within a company, for example:

> Ma belle-sœur est responsable des achats *à* Marks & Spencer et mon frère travaille *à la* Mairie, *au* Département de l'Etat Civil.
> My sister-in-law is head buyer for Marks & Spencer and my brother works for the local authority in the Registry Office.

Naturally, these prepositions are often combined in one statement:

> Je suis chargée d'organiser les expéditions *dans* une grande société d'informatique, *au* service exportation.
> I'm in charge of dispatching goods in a big computer company, in the export department.

49.4 Age

Avoir is used to give precise details of age. Do not forget **ans** after the number:

> Catherine *a deux ans et trois mois*.
> Catherine is 2 years and 3 months (old).

> Il *aura trente-cinq ans* en l'an deux mille vingt.
> He'll be 35 in the year two thousand and twenty.

With other verb phrases you can be less precise:

> Ma fille *vient d'avoir quinze ans* et mon fils *va sur ses douze ans.*
> My daughter has just turned 15 (had her fifteenth birthday) and my son is almost 12.

Nouns may also be used to give an indication of age without being precise:

> C'est *un octogénaire* très dynamique!
> He's a very lively 80-year-old!

> A mon avis, elle *a une quarantaine d'années.* – Tu plaisantes!? Je dirais plutôt *la cinquantaine* bien tassée.
> In my opinion, she's about 40. – You must be joking! She's well past 50.

Verbs such as **être**, **paraître** may be combined with adjectives and past participles such as **jeune, âgé**:

> Il *paraît* très *jeune* pour être PDG (Président-Directeur Général) de l'entreprise!
> He seems very young to be Chairman and Managing Director of the company!

Note that the adjective or past participle is sometimes omitted, in particular in comparative expressions:

> Entrée gratuite pour les enfants (*âgés*) *de moins de cinq ans.*
> Admission free for children under 5.

It is useful to be able to talk or write about age groups, for example when analysing an age pyramid. There are various ways of doing it:

You can use **âgé de . . . à**:

> les générations 1915–1919, *âgées de* 68 *à* 72 ans au ler janvier 1988
> the generations born between 1915–1919, aged from 68 to 72 on 1st January 1988

or **avoir entre . . . et**:

> les générations *ayant* actuellement *entre* 15 *et* 35 ans
> the generations in the present age-band 15 to 35

or **à** or **de** and a hyphen between the two age limits:

> *A* 70–74 ans, il ne reste que 70 hommes pour 100 femmes et, *à* 80–84 ans, seulement 50.
> In the age group 70–74, there are now 70 males for 100 females and in the age group 80–84, only 50.

> 19% pour les femmes *de* 21–24 ans et 17% pour les hommes *de* 24–29 ans
> 19% for females in the age group 21–24 and 17% for males in the age group 24–29

and use the definite and partitive articles with comparative forms or age bands:

> Au recensement de 1954, *les plus de dix ans* forment une pyramide d'un genre nouveau, en forme de 'meule de paille' (*l'effectif des*

10–19 ans étant moins nombreux que celui des 20–29 ans), mais *les moins de 10 ans*, nés du baby boom, *sont* nettement *plus nombreux*. Au dernier recensement (1982), enfin, la pyramide tout entière a cette forme de meule de paille, *la part des 20–29 ans* à peu près *à égalité avec celle des 10–19 ans*, est nettement *supérieure à celle des 0–9 ans*, marquée par la baisse récente de la fécondité.

(Vallin, J. (1989) *La Population française*, Paris: La Découverte)

In the 1954 census, the number of children over 10 influenced the profile of the age pyramid (the proportion of those between 10 and 19 was lower than the proportion of those between 20 and 29), but there was a significant increase in the number of those under 10, born during the baby boom. Finally, in the last census (1982), the age structure (pyramid) of the population had changed completely, with the proportion of those aged between 20 and 29 at almost the same level as those aged between 10 and 19, but significantly higher than the numbers of children under 9, caused by the recent downward trend in fertility rates.

49.5 **Ownership**

(a) A simple way to refer to what someone owns is to use a verb such as **avoir** or **posséder**:

> **Il *a* un appartement à Paris et une résidence secondaire en province.**
> He has a flat in Paris and a second home in the country (provinces).

> **La famille de Lisieux a perdu peu à peu tous les terrains qu'elle *possédait* autrefois.**
> The Lisieux family gradually lost all the land it used to own.

Note that sometimes you have to use **de** after the verb when the quantity is indefinite:

> **Son fiancé *a de l'argent* et *pas mal de terrain* dans la région.** (see **4**)
> Her fiancé has (some) money and quite a bit of land in the area.

In the following example, **de** is used before an adjective preceding a noun:

> **Mère-grand, comme vous *avez de grandes oreilles*!** (see **4.2**)
> What big ears you've got, Grandmother!

Nouns denoting ownership may also be used, and are most often preceded by **être**:

> **Elle *est* depuis peu *possesseur d'*une immense fortune.**
> She's recently inherited a large fortune.

In the previous example, note that **possesseur** has no feminine form. (see **9.5**):

> **L'antiquaire *était détenteur de* nombreux objets volés.**
> The antique dealer had a lot of stolen goods in his possession.

> **Monsieur le Procureur, ces documents *sont* désormais *en notre possession*.**
> Your Honour, the documents are now in our possession.

C'est is used to introduce a reference to ownership, followed by various phrases such as **à moi, à toi . . .**, or **de mes, de tes . . .**, or **mon propre, ton propre . . .** (see **7**):

C'est à vous ces beaux yeux-là!? (see 6.3a, 8.2)
Are they yours, those beautiful eyes!?

Aussi incroyable que cela puisse paraître, *c'est* un *de mes* cadeaux de mariage!
Unbelievable though it may seem, it's one of my wedding presents!

Mais non! *C'est ma propre* brosse à dents!
No! It's my own toothbrush!

(b) In some of the above examples, the possessive adjectives **mon, ton** . . . are included (see **7**). These and possessive pronouns **le mien, le tien** . . . 'mine, yours . . .' are frequently used to express ownership (see **8.1**):

Il a vendu tous *ses* **vieux disques.**
He has sold all his old records.

Sur cette photo, vous voyez *mon* **mari et moi-même,** *notre* **maison en arrière-plan, et ici** *nos* **chiens.**
In this photo, you can see my husband and me, our house in the background, and here are our dogs.

C'est ma **chambre** *à moi* **et je veux que tu enlèves tous** *tes* **jouets de là!** (see **6.3a**)
It's *my* room and I want you to take all your toys out of it!

Après la réunion, les directeurs sont partis dîner avec *leurs* **femmes** (or *leur* **femme**).
After the meeting, the managers went for dinner with their wives.

Tu crois que *son* **horloge est à l'heure?**
Do you think his/her clock is right?

N'oublie pas *ton* **bonnet et** *ton* **écharpe!**
Don't forget your cap and your scarf!

NOTE **Son/ton**, and *not* **sa/ta**, are used with **horloge** and **écharpe** (feminine nouns) because they begin with a mute **h**/vowel. (see **78.1, 7.1a**).

The possessive adjective is not always repeated with a list of nouns (see **7.1c**):

Veuillez indiquer *vos* **nom, prénoms, titres et qualités sur ce formulaire.**
Please enter your name, first names, titles and occupation on this form.

To avoid repeating the noun a possessive pronoun may also be used:

Ton **nouveau sac ne me plaît pas,** *le mien* **est beaucoup plus pratique.**
I don't like your new bag. Mine is much more practical.

Le matin, je prends *ma* **voiture et mon mari prend** *la sienne*.
In the mornings, I take my car and my husband takes his (one).

Leur **maison est plus grande que** *la sienne*.
Their house is bigger than his/hers.

Nos enfants sont turbulents mais *les leurs* sont encore pires! (see 8.1b)
Our children are rowdy, but theirs are worse!

Note the difference between **les leurs** (possessive pronoun) in the previous example and **les leur** (personal pronouns) in the following one:

J'ai reçu les photos, tu *les leur* montreras? (see 12, 14.4)
I've got the photos. Will you show them to them?

In some expressions, the article may be dropped before the possessive pronoun:

C'était une petite maison sans cachet, elle la fit *sienne* en y disposant tous ses bibelots.
It was an ordinary little house, but she made it hers once she had arranged her own things in it.

(c) Within a noun phrase, ownership may be expressed using **de** (and **du, de la, des, d', de l'**) (see 2):

Le manteau *de* Patrick est resté dans la classe.
Patrick's coat is still in the classroom.

L'instituteur a relevé les cahiers *des* élèves.
The teacher took in the pupils' notebooks.

Le passeport *de l'*écrivain était en règle.
The writer's passport was in order.

On n'a pas retrouvé le permis de conduire *de l'étudiante.*
They/We haven't found the student's driving licence.

Note that in these four examples, the **de** structure could be replaced with a possessive adjective:

L'instituteur a relevé *leurs* cahiers.
Son passeport était en règle.

However, if the possessor is an inanimate object or thing as in the following example:

Il est allé consulter le cadastre *de la Mairie.*
He went to check in the land register in the Town Hall.

then a change of structure will involve a change of personal pronoun:

Il est allé à la Mairie pour *en* consulter le cadastre.
He went to the Town Hall to check in the (its) land register.

The combination **de mon, de ton** . . . is also used, in particular after an indication of quantity:

Trois *de mes* fichiers ont disparu!
Three of my files have disappeared!

and the combination **de** + possessive pronouns **du mien, du tien** . . . 'of mine, of yours . . .':

Mon tracteur est en panne; les propriétaires de la ferme voisine m'ont prêté un *des leurs.*
My tractor has broken down; the owners of the neighbouring farm have lent me one of theirs.

(d) The preposition **à** has to be used with certain verbs such as **appartenir** 'to belong':

> **Cette voiture *appartient à* mon frère.**
> This car belongs to my brother.

or replaced, when appropriate, with a personal pronoun:

> **Cette voiture *lui appartient*.**
> This car belongs to him/her.

The preposition **à** + emphatic pronoun may also be used with **être** (see **6.3a, 8.2**):

> **A qui *est* ce livre? – Pas *à nous*, Monsieur. II *est à* Paul.**
> Whose is this book? – Not ours, Sir. It's Paul's.

> **Tout ce qui *est à moi est à toi*.**
> Everything that's mine is yours.

> **A qui *sont* ces vêtements? – Le manteau *est à lui* et les gants *sont à elle*.**
> Who do these clothes belong to? – The coat is his and the gloves are hers.

In the spoken, rather than written, language and to emphasize ownership or avoid any ambiguity, the following forms may be found:

> **Touche pas, *c'est* ma poupée *à moi*!**
> Don't touch, it's my doll!

> **Tu veux dire qu'il a pris *sa* Jaguar? – Non, il a pris *sa* voiture *à elle*, la Clio.**
> You mean he's taken his Jaguar? – No, he's taken her Clio.

(e) Before parts of the body or items of clothing – where English uses the possessive adjective – French uses the definite article (see **2.4**):

> **Je voudrais que tu te laves *le* visage et *les* mains, et que tu te brosses *les* dents et *les* cheveux avant de partir.**
> I'd like you to wash your face and hands, and brush your teeth and hair before you leave.

> **Levez *la* main droite et dites 'Je le jure . . .'**
> Raise your right hand and repeat after me, 'I swear . . .'

> **Il se tenait là, *les* mains dans *les* poches.**
> He was standing there with his hands in his pockets.

However, this is not a hard and fast rule and there are many exceptions to it, in particular when you want to emphasize possession or ownership:

> **J'ai posé *ma* main sur *mon* cœur.**
> I put my hand on my heart.

or when the part of the body is qualified by an adjective:

> **Le bébé a ouvert *ses grands* yeux *bleus*.**
> The baby opened his/its big blue eyes.

or to avoid ambiguity. For example, compare:

> **Donne-moi *la main* pour traverser la route.**
> Give me your hand to cross the street.

and

> **Donnez-moi *votre main*, je vais examiner la blessure.**
> Give me your hand (the one that's hurt), I'm going to examine the injury.

It is worth noting the difference in the use of the reflexive pronoun in **se laver le visage et les mains, se brosser les dents** . . . and also in the following example:

> **Rassurez-vous, vous ne *vous* êtes pas cassé *le* poignet.** (see 13, 40)
> Don't worry, you haven't broken your wrist.

and the use of the indirect object pronoun in the following example to indicate that an action affects someone other than the subject of the sentence:

> **Elle *nous* a serré *la* main en arrivant.**
> She shook our hands when she arrived.

> **Sa mère *lui* a brossé *les* cheveux avant qu'il parte.**
> His mother brushed his hair before he left.

(f) Finally, note that the meaning of some verbs and nouns allows you to refer more specifically to the action leading to ownership, for example:

> **La famille *s'est approprié* cette terre qui me revenait de droit.**
> The family took over this land which was rightfully mine.

> **Que penses-tu de *ma dernière acquisition*?**
> What do you think of my latest acquisition?

49.6   Dimensions (see 20)

Specific verbs may be used in order to refer to length, width, depth, height, thickness, size, surface area, capacity, etc., e.g. **mesurer, chausser, faire.**

> **Cette planche *mesure* 2 mètres.**
> This plank is 2 metres long.

> **Il *mesure* un mètre quatre-vingts et *pèse* quatre-vingt-quinze kilos.**
> He's 6 foot tall and weighs 13 stone.

> **Je *chausse* du 38.**
> I take a (size) 38 shoe.

The verb **faire** is often used to refer to dimensions and size:

> **La corde *fait* 3 mètres.**
> The rope is 3 metres long.

> **Ma cousine *fait* un mètre soixante-quinze.**
> My cousin is 5 foot 10.

> **En chaussures de ski, je *fais* du 40.**
> I take a 40 in ski boots.

> **La piscine *fait* 4 mètres.**
> The swimming-pool is 4 metres deep.

In the absence of context for the previous example, you might need to specify that you are referring to depth (as opposed to length, for example) and the structure used requires **de**:

> **La piscine *fait 25 mètres de long(ueur)* et *2 mètres de profondeur*.**
> The swimming-pool is 25 metres long and 2 metres deep.

In the case of length, width and height (*not* depth), an adjective can be used instead of the noun, after **de**:

> **Cette pièce *fait 3 mètres de haut(eur)*.**
> This room is 3 metres high.

After the object being described, when the noun is not the subject, it is followed by **de** + the expression of size:

> **C'est un petit chemin *d'environ 2 kilomètres*.**
> It's a small road about 1¼ miles long.

> **Il a une cicatrice *de 10 centimètres* sur la jambe.**
> He has a 4-inch scar on his leg.

Similarly, when the noun expressing dimension is subject of the verb **être**, you need to use **de**:

> **Mesdames et messieurs, notre *altitude est* actuellement *de* 5000 mètres.**
> Ladies and gentlemen, we are flying at (an altitude of) 5,000 metres.

> **La *profondeur* de ce puits *est d'*environ 10 mètres.**
> This well is about 10 metres deep.

The same applies after using an adjective of dimension:

> **Le réseau routier danois *est long d'*environ 70900 km.**
> The road network in Denmark totals some 70,900 km.

Different prepositions such as **à, de, par** + definite article can be used to refer to different measurement tools (see **49.12**):

Examples with **à**:

> **Les experts *ont mesuré* la profondeur du lac *à la sonde*.**
> The experts have measured the depth of the lake with a sounding line.

> **Le maçon *vérifie* son travail *au niveau à bulle*.**
> The mason checks his work with a level.

Note that if you use an alternative expression such as **à l'aide de**, the definite article becomes indefinite:

> **La profondeur *a été mesurée à l'aide d'une sonde*.**
> **Il *vérifie* son travail *à l'aide d'un niveau à bulle*.**

Examples with **de** and **par**:

> *L'ayant mesurée des yeux*, il sut tout de suite qu'elle serait trop grande pour le rôle.
> He looked her up and down and knew right away that she would be too tall for the part.

> Les résultats *ont été estimés par l'observation* et *vérifiés par le calcul.*
> The results were assessed by (further) observation and verified by calculation.

Finally, note the use of reflexive verbs combined with prepositions (**à** + singular, **en** + plural) to indicate the unit of measurement:

> Chez nous, les pommes *se vendent au kilo* et le cidre *au litre.*
> In our country, apples are sold by the kilo and cider by the litre.

> Suivant leur importance, les terrains *se mesurent en mètres carrés* ou *en hectares.*
> Depending on their size, areas of land are measured in square metres or hectares.

49.7 Quantity and number (see 21, 17)

When you want to be precise about quantity and number, you use cardinal numbers. In the following examples, note certain small changes, in particular in the spelling of **cent** and **vingt** (see **17.3b**):

> Il y a *trois cent soixante-cinq* jours dans l'année.
> There are 365 days in the year.

> Sur *quatre cent cinquante* étudiants inscrits en première année d'anglais, *quatre-vingts* passeront en deuxième année.
> Of 450 students registered in first year English, 80 will go into second year.

> Le chiffre d'affaires du Groupe est d'environ *trois cents millions* de euros, dont *quatre-vingt-dix millions* représentent les ventes à l'étranger. (see **17.3**)
> The Group's turnover is approximately 300 million euros, of which 90 million represent exports.

When you do not need to be so precise, nouns such as **dizaine, centaine, millier** may be used (see **19**):

> J'ai *une vingtaine de* livres de cuisine.
> I've got about twenty cookery books.

> Des amis? Il s'*en* fera *des centaines.*
> Friends? He'll make hundreds of them.

> *Plusieurs milliers de* personnes ont assisté au match.
> Several thousand people were at the match.

If you want to rank things, or express fractions, use ordinal numbers – **premier, deuxième, dixième, centième** . . . (see **17.7**).

(a) as adjectives:

> **Attention, les *deux premiers* barreaux de l'échelle sont cassés.**
> Careful, the first two rungs of the ladder are broken.

Note the order of numbers in the previous example.

> **C'est *le cinquième pays le plus riche du monde*.**
> It's the fifth richest country in the world.

Note the place of the superlative adjective in the previous example (see **10.11**).

The following example illustrates the use of **premier** (*not* **un**) in dates:

> **Le congrès a lieu *le premier* ou le deux *juin*?** (see **17.5a**)
> Will the conference take place on the first or second of June?

(b) as nouns, with an article (or a possessive adjective for riddles!):

> **C'est *le quatrième* à se plaindre au chef de rayon, nous devons intervenir!** (see **17.7.2**)
> He's the fourth to complain to the departmental manager. We'll have to do something.

> ***Mon premier* est l'opposé de rien, *mon second* est un oiseau réputé voleur, mon tout est un jouet!** (see **17.7.2**)
> My first is the opposite of nothing. My second is a bird that's a well-known thief. I'm a toy.

> **Je n'ai fait qu'*un quart de* mon travail.** (see **18**)
> I've only done a quarter of my work.

> **Les îles représentent *un cinquième de* la superficie totale de la Grèce.** (see **18**)
> The islands account for about one fifth of the total land area of Greece.

(c) Difficulties can arise with collective expressions of quantity (for example, **la moitié** 'half') and with fractions (for example, **les deux tiers** 'two thirds') when they are part of the subject of a verb, because you have to decide whether the verb should be singular or plural (see **22.3.1**):

> ***Plus de la moitié des personnes interrogées* se sont déclarées favorables au projet.**
> More than half of the people questioned said they were in favour of the project.

> **La moitié des élèves a opté pour le voyage en Angleterre, *l'autre moitié* pour le voyage en Allemagne.**
> Half of the pupils have chosen the trip to England, and the other half the trip to Germany.

In the previous example, the emphasis is on the quantity (**la moitié**) and therefore the verb agrees with the singular noun.

> ***Les quatre cinquièmes* du budget *ont* été absorbés.**
> Four-fifths of the budget have been spent.

> *Une bonne partie* du budget *a* été absorbée (or absorbé).
> A considerable part of the budget has been spent.

You often have the choice of focusing on the complement (here – **budget**) or on the quantity (**une bonne partie**) and have to make the verb agree with the subject. In this example the feminine past participle indicates focus on the quantity. This applies to many expressions such as **le plus grand nombre, un certain nombre, une partie, la majorité, la plupart.** The noun following them can often be considered as the subject in terms of gender and number (see **22.3**):

> *La plupart des Grecs appartiennent* à l'Eglise chrétienne orthodoxe.
> The majority of Greeks belong to the Greek Orthodox Church.

(d) Other ways of expressing fractions of a whole include the use of **sur** or **dont**:

> *Un* Allemand *sur quatre* travaille pour l'exportation.
> One in every four Germans is employed in the export sector.

> **Le Danemark comprend 483 îles, *dont 100* environ sont habitées.**
> Denmark has approximately 483 islands of which about 100 are inhabited.

You may need to express quantity and numbers when referring to an illustrative document such as a table. The following table contains information from the 1982 census in France:

Taille des unités urbaines	Nombre de communes	Nombre d'unités urbaines	Population (en milliers)	Part de la population totale (%)
Unités urbaines				
Agglomération parisienne	335	1	8 707	16,0
Plus de 100 000 hab.	1 078	56	15 142	27,9
10 000 à 100 000 hab.	1 413	365	9 947	18,3
Moins de 10 000 hab.	2 062	1 360	6 079	11,2
Total unités urbaines	4 888	1 782	39 875	73,4
Communes rurales	31 545	–	14 460	26,6
TOTAL	36 433	(1 782)	54 335	100,0

You may simply want to draw attention to some of the numbers presented in the table:

> **Le nombre total de communes s'élève à *4888*.** (When reading this aloud, you *say* **quatre mille huit cent quatre-vingt-huit**.)
> The total number of (urban) communities is 4,888.

> **Il y a *1 413* communes de *10 000* à *100 000* habitants.** (and you *say* **quatorze cent treize** or **mille quatre cent treize/dix mille à cent mille**)
> There are 1,413 districts with a population of 10,000 to 100,000.

Note that you do not use a comma, but leave a space – except for dates, 1995 – in big numbers. However, you do use a comma before decimal points:

26,6% de la population totale vit dans des communes rurales.
(and you *say* **vingt-six virgule six pour cent**)
26.6% of the total population lives in rural communities.

In the above example, **population** is taken as the subject of the verb **vivre**, so the verb is singular. If you place the emphasis on the percentage, you have a plural verb:

26,6% de la population vivent dans des communes rurales.

When describing a table, one of the difficulties lies in transferring numbers from written to spoken form. Here, for example, when using the fourth column **Population en milliers**, you would write **8,707 millions** and you would *say*:

Huit *millions* sept cent sept mille personnes vivent dans l'agglomération parisienne.
Eight million seven hundred and seven thousand people live in Paris and its suburbs.

Another way of dealing with the numbers, and less precisely than the version above, would be the following (note the addition of **de** in this case after the noun **millions**):

Près de neuf millions de **personnes vivent dans l'agglomération parisienne.**
Almost nine million people live in Paris and its suburbs.

An alternative adverb for **près de** is **environ**:

Environ huit millions et demi de **personnes vivent dans l'agglomération parisienne.**
Around eight and a half million people live in Paris and its suburbs.

Finally, if the unit indicated in brackets at the top of a column of four figure numbers were **en millions**, you would *say* the number in **milliards** 'billions':

Accroissement prévu de la population mondiale en l'an deux mille et en l'an deux mille vingt-cinq

	Population (en millions)
2000	6 000
2025	8 000

Expected increase in world population:
6 billion in 2000 and *8 billion* in 2025.

Another useful way of expressing numbers consists of using brackets when writing:

Outre l'agglomération parisienne très peuplée (*8 700 000* habitants), *56* agglomérations hébergent près de *20 millions* de Français.
In addition to the densely populated area of Paris and its suburbs (8,700,000 inhabitants), 56 other suburban areas have a population of 20 million.

Quality

(a) To describe something according to distinguishing features you can use the verb **être** + adjective or **être** + **de** + noun phrase:

> **En Allemagne, 43% des habitants *sont protestants* et 43,3% *de confession catholique romaine.***
> In Germany, 43% of the population are Protestants and 43.3% are Roman Catholic.

or simply **être** + noun:

> **La France *est une république.***
> France is a republic.

The verb **être** also features in a number of expressions where it is combined with past participles, e.g. **être marqué par**, or nouns, e.g. **être un exemple de**:

> **Le relief de l'Espagne *est marqué par* une alternance entre les chaînes de montagne et les vallées fluviales.** (see **41**)
> The Spanish landscape is characterized by alternating mountain chains and river valleys.

> **Madrid *est un exemple* unique *des* différentes cultures qui ont laissé leurs traces en Espagne.**
> Madrid is a unique example of the different cultures which have left their mark on Spain.

> ***Particulièrement riche*, la peinture espagnole de l'époque baroque *est* exceptionnellement bien *représentée* au musée du Prado.**
> The glory of Spanish baroque painting is exceptionally well represented in the Prado.

Note how the pair adverb + adjective (**particulièrement riche**) in apposition to **la peinture espagnole** also contributes a distinguishing characteristic of Spanish baroque paintings. See also **49.2** to refer to a person's qualities.

(b) A number of reflexive verbs are used with the preposition *par* such as *se caractériser par, se distinguer par*:

> **La Grèce *se caractérise par* le contraste entre de hautes montagnes et les eaux bleues de la Méditerranée.** (see **41**)
> Greece is characterized by the contrast between high mountains and the blue waters of the Mediterranean.

(c) Many transitive verbs, that is, verbs with a direct object, may be used, such as *présenter, posséder*. Note the place of the adjectives in the following example:

> **La France *présente une grande diversité de paysages* et *possède un riche patrimoine* historique et culturel.**
> France has a wide diversity of landscapes and a rich historical and cultural heritage.

(d) The passive form is often used when describing a system or a procedure and referring to quantity and quality (see **41**):

En Grèce, le pouvoir législatif est exercé par le Parlement et par le président de la République. Les 300 membres du Parlement, sauf 12 d'entre eux, sont élus au suffrage universel direct [. . .]. Les 12 députés d'Etat sont désignés par les partis politiques.

In Greece, legislative power is exercised by the parliament and by the President of the Republic. The 300 members of parliament are elected by direct universal suffrage, except for 12 who are appointed by the political parties.

49.9 **Comparison** (see **10.10–12**)

(a) You can compare two different objects in terms of one quality:

> *La chaise* est plus haute que *le banc.*
> The chair is higher than the bench.

or two different qualities in one object:

> Le jardin est *plus long que large.*
> The garden is longer than it is wide.

The comparative forms **plus** or **moins**, which express inequality, are often used with adjectives, as in the two previous and the two following examples:

> Je suis *plus grande que* lui.
> I am taller than he is.

> Il est *plus petit que* moi.
> He is smaller than I am.

and with adverbs:

> Paris est *moins loin que* Lyon.
> Paris is not as far as Lyons. (*or* Paris is less distant than Lyons.)

> Lyon est *moins près que* Paris.
> Lyons is less near than Paris. (*or* Lyons is not as near as Paris.)

or with nouns:

> Il a montré *plus de culot que de talent.*
> He's demonstrated more cheek than talent.

> Il a montré *moins de talent que de culot.*
> He's demonstrated less talent than cheek.

In order to express total superiority or inferiority, you use superlative forms (see **10.11**):

> Ne va pas traîner par là, c'est *un des quartiers les plus pourris de la ville.*
> Don't hang around there, it's one of the worst parts of the city.

> Ne me provoquez pas, vous savez bien que *de nous trois*, je suis *le plus fort* et *le moins bête*!
> Don't provoke me! You know very well I'm the strongest and the least stupid of the three of us.

> **C'est *l'élève le moins assidu de tous.***
> He's the laziest pupil of the lot.

> **La France est *le deuxième grand producteur de vin après l'Italie.***
> France is the second biggest producer of wine after Italy.

> **Je suis *le meilleur en maths* mais *le dernier en anglais.***
> I'm top in maths but bottom in English.

In the previous example, note the use of the irregular form **meilleur** (see **10.12**) and also how you can compare or rank things using **le dernier**.

(b) Sometimes, you make a comparison to show equality, or similarity, using phrases such as **aussi . . . que** with adjectives (see **10.10**):

> **La chaise *est aussi haute que* le banc.**
> The seat is as high as the bench.

> **Le jardin est *aussi large que* long.**
> The garden is as broad as it's long.

or with adverbs:

> **Je cours *aussi vite que* lui.**
> I can run as fast as him.

or with nouns. Here, you can use a verb **être, avoir, faire** . . . + article + **même** + noun (see **20.2**):

> **Le banc et la chaise *sont de la même hauteur.***
> The bench and the chair are the same height.

> **Ma mère et moi *faisons la même taille.***
> My mother and I are the same size.

> **Ces deux supermarchés *sont à la même distance de chez moi.***
> These two supermarkets are the same distance away from where I live.

> **Ils *ont le même costume.***
> They've got the same suits.

When referring specifically to equal *quantity*, use **autant de . . . que**:

> **Elle a *autant de* livres *que* son frère.**
> She has as many books as her brother.

(c) Other ways of comparing include:

● using prepositions in phrases such as **à la manière de, à la façon de** to emphasize similarity:

> **Elle traversa la pièce en ondulant, *à la manière d'*une lionne.**
> She went slinking across the room like a lioness.

or **contrairement à, à la différence de** to emphasize difference:

> ***Contrairement à* son frère, Jacques ne s'intéressait pas aux femmes.**
> Unlike his brother, Jacques was not interested in women.

● using conjunctions such as **comme, ainsi que, de même que** for straightforward comparison (see **10.10d**):

> **Il est stupide,** *comme* **sa sœur d'ailleurs!**
> He's stupid, just like his sister!

> **Il travaille la terre** *ainsi que l'ont fait* **son père et son grand-père avant lui.**
> He works on the land, like his father and grandfather before him.

● using **d'autant plus/moins . . . que** or **plus/moins . . . plus/moins** in order to indicate proportional comparison (see **10.10**):

> **Il semblait que** *plus son frère réussissait, moins elle consacrait* **de temps à ses propres études.**
> It seemed as if the more her brother succeeded, the less time she spent on her own studies.

> **Cet homme est** *d'autant plus détesté qu'il est riche.*
> They hate the man even more because he is rich.

> **Sa trahison le** *rendait d'autant moins fier qu'il savait* **combien elle avait foi en lui.**
> His betrayal (of her) made him all the more ashamed because he knew how much she trusted him.

● using comparative or superlative forms with two clauses (see **10.10**):

> **La société n'a pas** *autant de* **dettes** *qu'on* **voudrait nous le faire croire.**
> The company does not have as many debts as we've been led to believe.

> **Le dernier film de Besson est** *le meilleur que* **j'aie jamais vu.** (see **39.4**)
> Besson's last (latest) film is the best I've ever seen.

In the following example, note the use of the expletive **ne**, in particular when writing (see **47.12**), and note the difference between:

> **Depuis huit jours, elle** *ne boit pas plus qu'elle ne mange.* **(= elle ne boit, ni ne mange)**
> She hasn't eaten or drunk anything for a week. (She doesn't eat anything.)

and

> **Alcoolique? Non! elle** *ne boit pas plus qu'elle mange.*
> An alcoholic? No! She drinks as moderately as she eats. (She does eat something.)

Note that after superlative forms, it is possible to use the subjunctive or the indicative – the subjunctive to indicate uniqueness, the indicative to emphasize a fact:

> **C'est** *la plus belle femme que j'aie* **jamais** *vue!* (see **39.4**)
> She's the loveliest woman I've ever seen!

> **C'est** *le plus jeune des enfants dont j'ai* **la garde.**
> He's the youngest child I have in my care.

- using adjectives such as **tel** (or the conjunction **tel que**), **identique**, **pareil**:

> **Elle se jeta sur lui** *tel (or telle)* **un tigre.** (see **11.10**)
> She threw herself at him like a tigress.

In the previous example, **tel** agrees with **tigre**, **telle** with **Elle**.

> **Les deux frères étaient restés** *tels qu'elle les avait connus* **dix ans plus tôt.**
> The two brothers had stayed just as she had known them ten years earlier.

> **Ils ont des costumes** *identiques.*
> They have identical suits.

> **Le propre d'une cité pavillonnaire, c'est qu'une habitation est** *pareille* **à toutes les autres.**
> What is peculiar to a housing estate is that one house is the same as all the others.

- using verbs or nouns which express comparison through explicit meaning:

> **Dans sa construction, ce roman** *s'apparente à* **un film.**
> In the way it's constructed, this novel is like a film.

> **Tu crois qu'il** *ressemble à* **son père? Moi, je vois plutôt** *la ressemblance avec* **sa mère et je trouve qu'***on reconnaît* **aussi le grand-père.**
> You think he's like his father? As far as I'm concerned, I see more of a resemblance to his mother and I think you can see a bit of his grandfather too.

49.10 Directions

(a) Typically, you have to give directions orally when someone asks you the way. Imperatives are often used for this (see **44**):

> **Après la sortie d'autoroute,** *continuez* **tout droit jusqu'à la place Duval.** *Traversez* **cette place puis** *prenez* **la deuxième rue à gauche après le feu . . .**
> After leaving the motorway, go straight ahead to the Place Duval. Go across the Place, then take the second street on the left after the lights . . .

You can also use the future tense with **vous** or **tu** in order to divide the explanation into several stages:

> **Après la sortie d'autoroute, continuez toujours tout droit.** *Vous déboucherez* **dans le boulevard Heurteloup. Prenez à gauche jusqu'au bout.** *Vous laisserez* **l'hôtel de ville et le tribunal sur votre gauche. En arrivant sur la place centrale au bout du boulevard,** *vous apercevrez* **une sorte de tour, juste derrière les fontaines . . .**
> After leaving the motorway, keep straight on. You'll come out in the Boulevard Heurteloup. Turn left and go right to the end. You'll pass the Town Hall and the Law Courts on your left. When you get to the main square at the end of the Boulevard Heurteloup, you'll see a sort of tower, just behind the fountains . . .

Alternatively, it is not unusual in *spoken* French to switch between tenses, for example the present and the future, and to use **tu** or **vous** forms instead of the imperative:

> **Alors, pour le théâtre, *tu continues* toujours tout droit. *Tu vas arriver* dans le boulevard Heurteloup. Là, *tu prendras* à gauche et *tu vas tomber* sur l'avenue Pompidou . . .**
> So, for the theatre go straight on. You'll get to the Boulevard Heurteloup. Turn left and you'll be in the Avenue Pompidou . . .

Markers are often given using **il y a**:

> **Là, vous verrez, *il y a* un Monoprix qui fait l'angle . . .**
> There, you'll see, there's a Monoprix on the corner . . .

> **Tu vas prendre la direction Armentières, *il y a* environ deux kilomètres de voie rapide . . .**
> Follow the directions for Armentières, there's about two kilometres of expressway . . .

Expressions in apposition can be used to give detailed descriptions:

> **Vous déboucherez dans le boulevard Heurteloup, *une grande avenue avec des marronniers* . . .**
> You'll come out in the Boulevard Heurteloup, a wide avenue with chestnut trees . . .

> **Au feu, à gauche, jusqu'à la Mairie, *une bâtisse blanche avec des massifs de fleurs devant et la piscine à côté* . . .**
> At the lights, on the left, as far as the Town Hall, a white building with flowerbeds in front of it and the swimming-pool beside it . . .

Finally, people often sum up what they have said, particularly when the explanations have been quite long and detailed. In the following example, note the language shortcuts – there is no verb and **rue** is dropped after **première**:

> **Donc, en sortant ici à gauche, *première à droite*, tout droit, tout droit, et encore à droite au feu.**
> So, you'll come out here on the left, first right, straight on, and another right at the lights.

And, if you're really stuck and you can't find your way, you can resort to:

> **S'il vous plaît, où est la réception?**
> Where is the reception desk, please?

> **Pardon, pour aller au Musée d'Orsay?**
> Excuse me, where is the Musée d'Orsay?

(b) In writing, for example in a tourist guide, directions are often given using verbs in the infinitive. The following examples are taken from an Edinburgh tourist guide:

> **Comment vous *rendre* au musée? En voiture: *suivre* la direction de l'aéroport d'Edimbourg puis les panneaux indiquant le musée. En autobus et à pied: *prendre* le nº 16 de la Compagnie Eastern Scottish.**

Descendre à l'arrêt Airport Interchange. *Descendre* les escaliers et
emprunter le passage souterrain . . .

How to get to the museum? By car: go in the direction of Edinburgh
Airport, then follow the signs for the museum. By bus and on foot: take
the No. 16 Eastern Scottish bus. Get off at the Airport Interchange stop.
Go down the steps and through the subway . . .

Alternatively, the present or future tenses, and/or impersonal verbs (see **46**) can be
used:

Vous *pouvez* également prendre l'autobus assurant la navette entre
Waverley Bridge et l'aéroport.
You can also take the shuttle bus between Waverley Bridge and the
airport.

Il est également *possible* de descendre à l'arrêt Norton Cottages mais
il vous faudra alors traverser la route directement, ce qui est
dangereux.
It's also possible to get off at the Norton Cottages stop but then you have
to cross the road, which is dangerous.

49.11   **Location**

(a) A noun phrase or emphatic pronoun introduced by a preposition (see **48**) is often
used to indicate location, origin or destination:

Les enfants jouent *dans le jardin.*
The children are playing in the garden.

La Grèce forme une péninsule *au sud de l'Europe.*
Greece is a peninsula in southern Europe.

Ce matin-là, elle s'était assise *à côté de lui dans le compartiment.*
That morning, she'd sat beside him in the compartment.

Votre père *revient d'Espagne* demain mais il *ira* d'abord *en ville* avant
de *rentrer chez nous.*
Your father's coming back from Spain tomorrow but he'll go into town
first before he comes home.

Comme la route nationale est barrée *entre Tours et Le Mans*, il nous
faudra *passer par les petites routes.*
Since the main road between Tours and Le Mans is closed, we'll have to
use the minor roads.

Sometimes, the preposition is dropped, for example in an address:

J'habite rue des Lilas depuis dix ans.
I've been living in the Rue des Lilas for ten years.

Ils ont été obligés de se garer place Grécourt.
They have had to park in the Place Grécourt.

In the following examples, note the use of the pronouns **y** and **en** instead of the
complements (**en Ecosse** and **de chez eux**) (see **12.5, 12.6**):

Si je connais l'Ecosse?! J'*y* ai vécu pendant douze ans et je m'*y* plaisais beaucoup.
Do I know Scotland? I lived there for twelve years and I liked it very much.

Inutile d'essayer de les appeler, j'*en* reviens, il n'*y* a personne.
No point trying to call them. I've just tried and there's nobody there.

Informal or colloquial use may lead to *misuse* of prepositions:

Elle est où ta sœur? *Au coiffeur!* (instead of *chez le coiffeur*)
Your sister's where? The hairdresser's!

(b) Many adverbs and adverbial phrases indicate location:

Elle s'était amusée à cacher tous les livres de son frère, *ici et là, au-dessus de* l'armoire, *sous* les lits, *derrière* les tableaux, *auprès des* bouteilles *dans le cellier* et même *dehors, en dessous des* haies qui bordaient le jardin.
She had a great time hiding all her brother's books, all over the place – on top of the wardrobe, under the beds, behind the pictures, beside bottles in the wine-cellar, and even outside under the hedges round the garden.

Va donc voir *ailleurs* si j'y suis!
Get lost!

Colloquial use may lead to redundancies, especially with verbs of movement:

Maman, je *sors dehors* faire un foot!
Mum, I'm going out to play football.

Je vais *descendre en bas* chercher une autre bouteille.
I'm going down to get another bottle.

(c) Relative clauses with no antecedent are sometimes used to refer to location:

Va *où* le vent te mène, va! (from a song by Branduardi)
Go where the wind takes you, go!

Tu le vois, là-haut? *D'où* il est, la vue doit être extraordinaire.
D'you see him up there? From where he is, the view must be extraordinary.

and the structure **c'est + ici, là** . . . **que** for particular emphasis:

C'est ici que nous nous sommes rencontrés il y a vingt ans.
It was here we met twenty years ago.

C'est en Belgique que l'on trouve les meilleurs chocolats. (see **10.12a**)
It's in Belgium that you get the best chocolates.

(d) Place names are obvious indicators of location, whether they are used on their own, e.g. countries, cities, or in noun phrases such as **la mer Egée** 'the Aegean Sea', **l'éléphant d'Afrique** 'the African elephant'. Note that the preposition **à** is usually used with countries of masculine gender and **en** with countries of feminine gender. When there is no gender, for example, **Chypre** 'Cyprus', **à** is normally used (see **2.4e**):

> J'ai vécu deux ans *au Brésil*, un an *à Madagascar*, trois ans *en Bolivie* et je suis *aux Etats-Unis* depuis six mois.
> I lived in Brazil for two years, Madagascar for one, Bolivia for three, and I've been in the United States for six months.

The preposition à is also used with towns and cities. Do not forget to make the necessary changes when an article is part of the name:

> **Il pleut plus souvent *à Glasgow* qu'*à Edimbourg*.**
> It rains more often in Glasgow than in Edinburgh.

> **J'ai décidé de partir (pour) une semaine *au Caire*.**
> I've decided to go to Cairo for a week.

However, remember that there are numerous exceptions concerning the use of prepositions and countries (**en Iran** 'in Iran'), islands (**en Sardaigne** 'in Sardinia', but **à La Réunion**), departments and regions, and that in some cases more than one preposition may be used – even with cities – but in such cases the meaning is usually affected.

> **Des fourgons de police ont patrouillé *dans Paris* durant tout le week-end.**
> Police vans patrolled Paris the whole weekend.

Note how the definite article is dropped in some noun phrases involving place names:

> **Les *vins de France* se vendent partout dans le monde.**
> French wines are sold all over the world.

> **L'*éléphant d'Afrique* est différent de l'*éléphant d'Asie*.**
> The African elephant is different from the Indian elephant.

Note the difference in meaning, and different preposition, between:

> **Allô Paris! Je me trouve actuellement *dans* le nord de la France.**
> (Alternatively, with a capital letter: **Je me trouve dans le Nord** – the name of the region)
> Hello, Paris! I'm in the north of France at the moment. (present location)

and

> **La Manche se trouve *au* nord de la France.**
> The Channel is on the northern coast of France. (permanent state)

(e) In the previous example, there is a good illustration of a verb (*se trouver*) used to introduce location. There are others such as *se situer*:

> **Copenhague *se situe* sur l'île d'Amager.**
> Copenhagen is on the island of Amager.

Passive forms of these verbs, e.g. **être situé, localisé, orienté**, are also frequently used (see **41**):

> **L'île de Sardaigne *est située* à l'ouest de l'Italie.**
> Sardinia is situated to the west of Italy.

> **La pente que tu aperçois *est orientée* au sud.**
> The hillside you can see is south-facing.

Naturally, points of the compass are frequently used to refer to geographical location

> **Les Pays-Bas s'étendent *du nord au sud* sur environ 300 km et *d'est en ouest* sur environ 200 km.**
> The Netherlands are approximately 300 km from north to south and about 200 km from east to west.

and sometimes they are combined:

> **Il n'y a de collines que dans les régions *du sud-est.*** (see **47.10**)
> The only hills are in the south-east.

> **La ville de Cherbourg se trouve *au nord-ouest* de la France.**
> Cherbourg is in the north-west of France.

(f) Finally, there is a series of nouns, and corresponding adjectives, which may also be used to indicate geographical location:

> **Cette année, nous ne passerons pas nos vacances dans *le Midi.***
> This year we will not be spending our holidays in the Midi.

> **Le versant *méridional* des Alpes descend de façon abrupte jusqu'à la plaine du Pô.**
> On their southern side the Alps drop steeply to the Po plain.

49.12   **Manner** (see **47.1–47.2.2**)

When referring to manner, that is, broadly answering the question 'How?' in relation to an action or event, it is useful to distinguish between (a) the means used to do something, (b) the manner in which something is done and (c) the presence or absence of other people or things during the action or event.

(a) You may use a noun phrase or pronoun introduced by a preposition such as **à**, **avec**, **sans**, **de**, **au moyen de**, **à l'aide de** (see **48**):

> **Tu tricotes *à la main* ou *à la machine?***
> Do you knit by hand or do you use a machine?

> **Il s'est hissé jusqu'au sommet *au moyen d'une corde.***
> He pulled himself to the summit by a rope.

Sometimes these prepositions occur within more complex structures, for example, in relative clauses:

> **Voici la lime *avec laquelle il a scié* les barreaux de sa cellule.** (see **15.5**)
> Here's the file he used to saw through the bars of his cell.

A number of verbs may be used to refer to the means or methods used such as **user de**, **employer, utiliser, se servir de**:

> **Elle *a usé de son charme* pour s'introduire dans l'organisation.**
> She used her charm to get into the organization.

> ***En employant la langue du pays*, vous gagnerez la faveur de la population locale.**
> If you use their language, local people will love you for it. (see **43.1**)

(b) Again, the manner in which something is done may be stated using a noun phrase or a pronoun introduced by a preposition such as **sans, de, en, à**:

> **C'est *sans enthousiasme* que les ouvriers ont accueilli l'ordre de grève.** (see **56.2**)
> The workers greeted the strike call without enthusiasm.

> **L'écrire, c'est bien mais je veux te l'entendre dire *de vive voix*.** (see **47.1.3**)
> Writing it, that's fine, but I want to hear you say it.

Sometimes, there is no preposition – the parts of the sentences are simply in apposition:

> **Les passants observaient la scène, *l'air médusé*.**
> The passers-by watched what was going on dumbfounded.

In the previous example, note the use of the definite article **l'**. In some expressions it is omitted, and to be certain whether it is used or not, it is best to check in a dictionary.

> **Il est interdit d'entrer *jambes nues* dans les églises italiennes.** (see **45.6**)
> It is forbidden to go into an Italian church with bare legs.

Note that the preposition **sans** is sometimes followed by an infinitive:

> **Il prit son manteau et sortit *sans dire un mot*.** (see **45.1.3**)
> He took his coat and left without a word.

The gerund and the present participle will also allow you to state the manner in which something is done, with or without **en** (see **43.1**):

> **Les candidats posent souvent cette question *en rougissant*.**
> Candidates often blush when they ask that question.

> **Elle continuait à monter, ses pieds *cherchant* appui sur les aspérités de la roche.**
> She continued to climb, her feet searching for footholds in the uneven surface of the rock.

> ***Haussant* les épaules, il rétorqua qu'il n'en savait rien.**
> Shrugging his shoulders, he replied that he knew nothing about it.

In the previous example, note that the complement of manner is in apposition. Adjectives or relative clauses may also be used in this way:

> ***Courtois mais direct*, le commissaire l'interrogea sur sa vie privée et ses activités nocturnes.**
> Polite but firm, the superintendent questioned him about his private life and what he did at night.

> **Regarde bien cette image: un des jeunes manifestants, *qui brandit un bâton*, se précipite vers les CRS (Compagnie Républicaine de Sécurité).** (see **15.1**)
> Look carefully at this picture: one of the young demonstrators, who is wielding a stick, is running towards the CRS (riot police).

Many adverbs are available for referring to the manner of doing something:

> **Il parlait vite en la regardant fixement.** (see **43.1**)
> He spoke quickly and he stared at her as he did so.

and a number of adjectives may be used as adverbs – and therefore become invariable (see **47**). This is the case in set verb phrases such as **parler fort** 'to speak loudly', **chanter juste** 'to sing in tune', **voir clair** 'to see clearly'.

> **Il me semble qu'elles *ont visé un peu haut*.**
> I think they've aimed a bit high.

But remember that new phrases of this type are constantly being created for particular stylistic effect. Thus, advertising has given us:

> **Les lessives qui lavent *plus blanc*!** (= mieux?)
> Washing powders that wash whiter (= better?)!

(c) Naturally, **avec** and **sans** are the main prepositions used to introduce a noun phrase or pronoun to indicate the presence, or absence, of another person or thing:

> **Je prends l'avion demain *avec mes deux collègues*.**
> I'm taking the plane tomorrow with my two colleagues.

> **Puisque c'est comme ça, j'irai *sans toi*!**
> OK! If that's how it is, I'll go without you!

Note that the article is sometimes omitted before the noun:

> **Cela fait du bien de partir en week-end *sans enfants*!** (see **4.4**)
> It does you good to go away for the weekend without the children!

> **Vous voulez faire la visite *avec ou sans guide*?**
> Do you want to do the visit with or without a guide?

Alternatively, an expression such as **en compagnie de** may be used:

> **Le comédien a célébré son succès *en compagnie de toute la troupe*.**
> The actor celebrated his success with the entire company.

Finally, verbs such as **se joindre à** or **accompagner** may be used:

> **Je descends prendre un verre, voulez-vous vous *joindre à moi*?**
> I'm going down for a drink. Do you want to come with me?

> **Lorsque les époux Duval se sont présentés au Commissariat, ils *étaient accompagnés par/de* leurs deux enfants.** (see **41**)
> When M. and Mme Duval went to the police station, they were accompanied by their two children.

> ***Accompagne* ton frère au magasin, s'il te plaît!**
> Go to the shop with your brother, please!

50 Narrating

This section is about how we use tenses. It focuses on the organization of a narrative in past, present and future time. There are many instances of uses of specific tenses in 'another time', for example, the use of the present tense to express past actions. By way of introduction, it is interesting to look at the various points of view which the speaker or writer – the narrator – may adopt.

You may envisage an action in its duration:

> **Les spectateurs *lisaient* (*lisent, liront*) le programme en attendant que le rideau s'ouvre.**
> The audience were (are, will be) reading the programme while they were (are) waiting for the curtain to go up.

or as being completed and having occurred at a particular point in time:

> **Mes parents *ont passé* (*passèrent*) deux mois de vacances au bord de la mer.**
> My parents have had (had) two months' holiday at the seaside.

or as a repeated action or habit:

> **Elle *prenait* (*prend, prendra*) tous les matins le train de 8h30.**
> She caught (catches, will catch) the 8.30 train every morning.

or you may want to describe an action as being completed or not completed:

> **Il *a* (*avait, aura*) *ouvert* la fenêtre.**
> He has (had, will have) opened the window.

> **J'*ai obtenu* une bourse.**
> I've obtained a grant.

> **Ils *recherchent* les coupables.**
> They are looking for the culprits.

> **Les premières fleurs *apparaissaient*.**
> The first flowers were appearing.

50.1 Present time (see 24.3, 24.7)

(a) In order to indicate that an action or event is taking place at the present moment, you can use the present tense – however long or short the actions or events may be:

> **La lune *luit*, un cri *retentit* dans la nuit.**
> The moon is shining and a cry rings out in the night.

Some verbs and verb phrases, such as **se mettre à** + noun or infinitive, **être en train de** + infinitive, **ne pas arrêter de** + infinitive, allow you to emphasize the start or development of an action in the present time:

> **Ah quand même, tu *te mets au travail*.**
> About time too! You're starting your work!

> **Rappelle tout à l'heure, il *est en train de regarder* son feuilleton à la télé.**
> Call back later, he's watching his serial (*or* soap opera) on telly.

The present tense can also convey the notion of repetition, which may be made more explicit through the use of expressions such as **tous les jours, chaque dimanche . . .** , or verbs with the prefix **re-** such as **redire**:

> **Il passe et *repasse toutes les cinq minutes* devant le magasin.**
> He walks up and down in front of the shop every five minutes.

(b) Naturally, the present tense is used for direct speech:

> **'Il ne *pleut* plus, vous *pouvez aller* jouer dehors maintenant.'**
> 'It isn't raining any more. You can go and play outside now.'

And when another tense, for example, the imperfect, is used with indirect speech, as in:

> **Il a dit qu'il *faisait* beau.**
> He said the weather was fine.

it refers to the present time of the corresponding direct speech:

> **Il a dit: 'Il *fait* beau'.**
> He said, 'It's fine weather.'

(c) The present tense is also used to indicate that something, such as a proverb or a definition, has timeless universal value:

> **L'union *fait* la force.**   **Cinq fois trois *égale* quinze.**
> Unity is strength.   Five times three equals fifteen.

So the present tense may well occur in a past narrative. In the following example, the assumption is that there is one universal way one talks about one's children:

> **Les militants de ce mouvement ont parlé des animaux comme on *parle* de ses enfants.**
> The activists/militants in the movement spoke about animals as you speak about your children.

See **50.2d** for other examples of the present tense in a past narrative.

(d) Other tenses are sometimes used with actions or events or behaviour occurring in the present time. In speech, for example, the imperfect, future, conditional, or pluperfect tenses may be used as a way to be more polite:

> **'*Vous désiriez? – Je voulais* un kilo de tomates et une livre de haricots verts, s'il vous plaît.'** (see **33.1.3**)
> 'What would you like?' 'I'd like a kilo of tomatoes and a pound of French beans, please.'

> **'*Voudriez-vous* que je vous conduise à la gare? – *J'accepterai* volontiers.'**
> 'Would you like me to drive you to the station?' 'I'd like it very much.'

> **J'étais *venu* vous demander un petit service.** (see **31**)
> I've come to ask a little favour of you.

Note also the use of the imperfect for expressing endearment, in particular with pets and babies:

> **Il *avait* bobo à sa patte ce petit chien-là.**
> That little dog has hurt his paw.

(e) Remember that each 'time' – past, present, or future – is defined in relation to the others and that therefore there are connections between them. For example, the perfect is often used for a past action when there is a connection with the present time (see **29**):

> Comme on *n'a pas* encore *découvert* l'assassin, l'enquête *se poursuit*.
> Since they haven't found the murderer yet, the inquiry is continuing.

> Il *ne fait pas* chaud ici! J'*ai ouvert* les fenêtres avant de partir pour aérer, tu *peux les fermer* maintenant.
> It's not very warm in here! I opened the windows before I left to air the place – you can shut them now.

<h2>50.2   Past time</h2>

(a) In order to focus on the duration of the action or event in the past, you should use the imperfect for description or to indicate a state of affairs (see **26.1**):

> La nuit *tombait* sur la ville et il *faisait* froid.
> Night was falling over the city and it was cold.

The imperfect is also used for repeated actions or habits in the past (see **26.1**):

> Quand j'*étais* étudiante, je me *levais* tôt, je *pouvais* travailler toute la journée, sortir le soir, puis je *recommençais* le lendemain . . . , et je n'*étais* jamais fatiguée!
> When I was a student, I used to get up early, I used to work all day, go out in the evening, then I started again the next day . . . , and I was never tired!

The imperfect also occurs in historical narratives for stylistic effect. In this case, it refers to an action which is completed, and presents it as a 'photograph' for the reader:

> En mai 1981, François Mitterrand *entrait* dans l'histoire. (see **26.1**)
> In May 1981, François Mitterrand made history.

(b) When referring to one, or a series, of completed actions occurring at a particular point in the past, you use the past historic. Note, however, that the past historic is usually restricted to the written narrative (see **27.2**):

> Son véhicule, lancé à 120 km/h, *manqua* le virage, *heurta* la barrière, *fut déporté* et *alla* s'écraser contre un arbre de l'autre côté de la route.
> His car, travelling at 75 mph, missed the bend, hit the barrier, swerved and crashed into a tree on the other side of the road.

When speaking, and increasingly when writing, the perfect is used instead of the past historic. The functions of the two tenses are, for the purpose of referring to one or a series of actions complete in the past, to all intents and purposes, identical (see **29**).

> Il *a manqué* le virage et *heurté* la barrière, puis la voiture *a été déportée* et il *s'est écrasé* contre l'arbre de l'autre côté de la route.
> He missed the bend and hit the barrier, then the car swerved and he crashed into the tree on the other side of the road.

When combined with the imperfect in a complex sentence, the past historic allows you to emphasize the suddenness of an action (see **27.2**):

Elle *cheminait* en chantonnant quand un loup *surgit* de derrière un fourré.
She was walking along humming to herself when a wolf came out from behind a thicket.

(c) Other tenses, namely the pluperfect (see **31**) and the past anterior (see **32**), will allow you to consider a completed action from the point of view of its duration:

Le professeur *avait* longuement *exposé* les raisons de sa démission.
The teacher had explained the reasons for his resignation at length.

from the point of view of its result:

Tous remarquèrent combien elle *avait changé*.
Everyone noticed how much she had changed.

or of its occurrence at a particular point in (past) time. Note that the past anterior is only used in specific written contexts:

Quand il eut terminé sa sieste au soleil, le lièvre *décida* de reprendre la course. (see **32**)
When the hare had finished its siesta in the sun, it decided to continue the race.

(d) Note that other tenses 'intrude' into past time; for example, the present tense – especially in historical narratives:

Napoléon *entreprend* alors une nouvelle campagne qui *coûte* la vie à un grand nombre de soldats.
Then Napoleon undertook another campaign which cost the lives of many soldiers.

In the following extract, the present and future tenses are used, for stylistic effect, in a narrative otherwise written in the past tense:

Dès 1957, . . . les six membres *décidèrent* de construire une communauté économique. . . . Les droits de douane *seront* totalement *éliminés* le premier juillet 1968 et les politiques communes *seront mises en place* durant cette décennie. . . . En 1981 et en 1986, les adhésions de la Grèce, de l'Espagne et du Portugal *renforcèrent* le flanc sud de la Communauté. . . . Parallèlement, la Communauté *s'affirme* sur le plan international en renforçant les liens contractuels noués avec les pays du sud de la Méditerranée.
(Fontaine, P. (1992), 'Les Grandes Phases historiques', in *Dix leçons sur l'Europe*, Documentation européenne)

In 1957, . . . the six member countries decided to create an economic community. . . . Customs duties would be completely eliminated on 1st July 1968 and common policies would be put in place during that ten-year period . . . In 1981 and 1986 the entry of Greece, Spain and Portugal would strengthen the southern flank of the Community. . . . At the same time, the Community established itself internationally by strengthening contractual links with countries to the south of the Mediterranean.

Note some further 'intrusions' of the present tense in past time in the following narrative. The first one relates to the character's thoughts 'in real time', and the second is an intervention by the narrator:

> Il avait pris le métro comme tous les matins à 7h30. Soudain, la rame s'immobilisa. *Que se passe-t-il? Je vais être en retard* . . . furent ses premières pensées. Puis voyant que personne ne réagissait et qu'un silence passif s'installait, il décida qu'après tout il n'y pouvait rien et que mieux valait attendre patiemment comme tous les autres. *Y a-t-il* un besoin plus irrésistible que celui de se conformer au groupe auquel *on se trouve* mêlé?
>
> He had taken the metro as he did every morning at 7.30. Suddenly, the train stopped. What's happening? I'm going to be late . . . were his first thoughts. Then seeing that nobody was reacting and that a passive silence ensued, he decided that he could do nothing about it anyway and it would be better to wait patiently like the rest of them. Is there any more irresistible need than to conform to the group in which one finds oneself?

The present tense is also used, when speaking, to refer to an action in the near past (see **24.3**):

> *Je sors* de chez le coiffeur et tu n'as rien remarqué!
> I've just left the hairdresser's and you didn't even notice!

> Allô oui? . . . tu as de la chance, *j'arrive* à l'instant!
> Hello, yes? . . . you're lucky! I'm just in!

Alternatively, you may use a verb phrase such as **venir de** + infinitive (see **24.3**):

> Vous avez de la chance de me trouver, *je viens d'arriver*!
> You're lucky to catch me, I've just arrived.

50.3 Future time (see 25.3)

(a) With the future tenses, you can refer to actions which will occur at a later date or time. Note the equivalent English tenses.

> *Je prendrai* rendez-vous chez le dentiste demain matin.
> I'll make an appointment at the dentist's tomorrow morning.

You can also focus on the future result of an action:

> Asseyez-vous, Monsieur Maillou *sera là* dans un instant.
> Take a seat. M. Maillou will be here in a moment.

> Nous attendons avec impatience les résultats des premières circonscriptions qui *seront communiqués* à partir de 20h30. (see **41**)
> We are waiting impatiently for the results from the first constituencies which will be announced from 8.30 onwards.

> Tu verras, d'ici un mois *tu auras reçu* ton premier salaire et *tu n'auras plus* de problèmes d'argent. (see **30**)
> You'll see, in a month from now you'll have had your first salary and you'll have no more money problems.

When the realization of a future action depends on another action, you use future tenses in both clauses – the future perfect for the first action and the future for the second:

On *ira* où tu *voudras*, quand tu *voudras*, et l'on *s'aimera* encore lorsque l'amour *sera mort*. (from a song by Joe Dassin)
We'll go where you want, when you want, and still make love when our love has died.

Quand elle *sera partie*, nous *serons* plus tranquilles. (see 25.3, 30)
When she has gone, we'll be happier.

(b) In the following example in indirect speech, the conditional tense is used in the transfer from direct speech in the future tense (see **51b**):

Il a dit qu'il *viendrait* ce soir. = Il a dit: 'Je viendrai ce soir.'
He said he would come tonight. = He said, 'I'll come tonight.'

(c) The present tense (see **24.3**), and the perfect (see **29**), are often used for an action which will take place in the near future, especially when speaking:

Ne bougez pas, *j'arrive* tout de suite.
Don't move, I'll be right there.

Ils partent en Guadeloupe demain soir.
They are leaving for Guadeloupe tomorrow evening.

Un peu de patience les enfants, ce n'est plus très loin maintenant, encore quelques minutes et *nous sommes arrivés*.
Have patience, children, it's not very far now. Just a few more minutes and we'll be there.

Alternatively, verb phrases such as **aller** + infinitive, or **être sur le point de** + infinitive, or **devoir** + infinitive, may be used:

Attention, le train en provenance de Paris et à destination de Bordeaux *va entrer* en gare.
Attention. The train from Paris for Bordeaux is about to arrive at the station.

Je vous laisse les clés, *nous sommes sur le point de partir*.
Here are the keys, we're about to leave.

As-tu des nouvelles de Jacques? Non, mais j'en aurai demain, *il doit m'appeler*.
Any news of Jacques? No, but I'll have some tomorrow, he's supposed to call me.

50.4 **Dates and time** (see **2.4c**)

(a) In order to situate an event in time, you have to be able to give the date when it occurs, using **en** with years and **en** or **au mois de** with months:

La Communauté européenne du charbon et de l'acier a été créée *en* 1950. (see **41**)
The European Coal and Steel Community was established in 1950.

Normalement, j'aurai terminé mes études *en* juin 2005 (*or au mois de juin* 2005).
If everything goes well, I'll have finished my studies in June 2005.

or **le** with specific dates:

> **Les droits de douane industriels ont été totalement éliminés *le* 1er juillet 1968.**
> Customs tariffs for industry were abolished completely on 1st July 1968.

> **Le Conseil Européen de Brême a eu lieu *les* 6 et 7 juillet 1978.**
> The European Council in Bremen was on the 6th and 7th of July 1978.

The definite article is also used with days of the week when referring to regular events:

> **Les enfants n'ont pas d'école *le mercredi* après-midi.**
> Children don't have school on Wednesday afternoon.

> **Les journaux du dimanche sont très lus en Grande-Bretagne.** (see **41**)
> Sunday papers are widely read in Britain.

> **Les éboueurs passent *tous les vendredis*.**
> There is a refuse collection every Friday.

> **Mon salaire est viré sur mon compte *le premier lundi* de chaque mois.** (see **41**)
> My salary is paid into my account on the first Monday in the month.

With specific days, there is no article:

> ***Mercredi*, je pars en vacances!**
> On Wednesday I'm going on holiday!

> **Il a sa photo dans *le journal de mardi*.**
> His photo is in Tuesday's paper.

> ***Lundi soir?* Non, je ne peux pas, plutôt un jeudi soir, je n'ai pas cours le lendemain.**
> Monday evening? No, I can't. Better on a Thursday evening, I haven't any lectures next day.

In correspondence, there are various ways of indicating a precise date. In letter headings, you may find:

> **Edimbourg, *le 13 avril 2002* (*or 13.4.2002*)**

Similarly, in the text of the letter, you may find:

> **Suite à *votre lettre du 22 février*, je . . .**
> Further to your letter of 22nd February, I . . .

or

> **Ayant reçu votre bon de commande *daté du 22.2.04*, je . . .**
> I have received your order of 22.2.04 . . .

(b) If the precise date is not known, you use prepositions such as **vers** + article, **autour de** + article:

> **Sa famille a dû émigrer *vers la fin des années 40*.**
> His/Her family must have emigrated at the end of the 1940s.

>Je compte rentrer de vacances *autour du 10 août*.
>I intend to return from holiday about the 10th of August.

Note that **début, fin, mi-, vers le milieu de, au milieu de** can be used with or without an article:

>Tu comptes te mettre en congé *fin juillet?* Non, plutôt *vers la mi-août*.
>You intend to take some time off at the end of July? No, more towards the middle of August.

(c) Approximate time of occurrence is usually introduced by **vers**:

>Je vous attends *vers midi*.
>I'll expect you about noon.

Note that the 24-hour clock is widely used in 'official' French. The English a.m./p.m. device is not available. Equivalent phrases would be **du matin** 'a.m.', **de l'après-midi**, **du soir** 'p.m.'. In less formal situations you would say:

>Tu passes me prendre *à quatre heures et demie*?
>Will you come for me at 4.30?

If you wanted to be a bit more formal, you could use **trente**:

>Votre taxi est réservé pour *cinq heures trente*.
>Your taxi is reserved for 5.30.

Similarly, **et quart** and **moins le quart** are less official than **quinze** and **quarante-cinq**:

>Lève-toi, il est neuf heures *moins le quart*!
>Get up, it's a quarter to nine!

>Le train en provenance de Bordeaux entrera en gare à huit heures *quarante-cinq*.
>The train from Bordeaux will arrive at the station at 8.45.

Although **heures** cannot usually be omitted, **minutes** often is except in very rare instances:

>L'accident est arrivé devant chez moi *à huit heures vingt*.
>The accident happened outside my house at 8.20.

>RTL, il est quatorze heures (et) trois minutes.
>This is Radio Television Luxembourg, it's three minutes past two.

(d) You might also want to indicate the duration of an event, for example between two dates with **de . . . à**:

>Le magasin sera fermé *du 1er au 31 août*.
>The shop will be shut from the 1st to the 31st of August.

>Le parc de loisirs est ouvert *de juin à octobre*.
>The fairground is open from June to October.

>*De 1954 à 1988*, l'aide communautaire a permis la création de 180 000 nouveaux emplois dans ce secteur.
>From 1954 to 1988, Community funding enabled 180,000 new jobs to be created in this sector.

The same structure can be used with times:

> **Les banques sont généralement ouvertes** *de 9h00 à 17h00.*
> Banks are generally open from 9 to 5.

Alternatively, **entre . . . et** may be used, for example if an event is likely to occur at a particular time between two times:

> **Il a dit qu'il passerait me prendre** *entre 8h00 et 8h30.*
> He said he'd pick me up between 8 and 8.30.

Indications of date(s) and time(s) can of course be combined:

> **La piscine est ouverte** *de 8h00 à 18h00 du lundi au vendredi, de 9h00 à 17h00 le samedi et de 10h00 à 17h00 le dimanche.*
> The swimming pool is open from 8 to 6 Monday to Friday, 9 to 5 on Saturday and 10 to 5 on Sunday.

(e) You may of course want to focus on the initial date or time with **depuis, dès** or **à partir de:**

> **Je travaille dans cette société** *depuis 1992.*
> I've been working in this company since 1992.

> *Dès 1957,* **les six membres décidérent de construire une communauté économique.**
> In 1957, the six member countries decided to establish an economic community.

> **Le musée est ouvert tous les jours** *à partir de 9h30.*
> The museum is open every day from 9.30.

or on the final date or time with **jusqu'à:**

> **Le magasin reste ouvert** *jusqu'à 20h00* **du lundi au vendredi.**
> The shop stays open till 8 p.m. Monday to Friday.

> **J'ai un contrat de travail** *jusqu'à juin 97.*
> I have a contract of employment until June '97.

In the following example, note the use of **d'ici** for a deadline:

> *D'ici l'an 2009,* **il aura terminé sa thèse.**
> He'll have finished his thesis by the year 2009.

and that a deadline may also be expressed as a period of time:

> **La troisième étape de l'UEM (Union économique et monétaire) débutera** *au plus tôt le 1er janvier 1997* **et** *au plus tard le 1er janvier 1999.*
> The third stage of the EMU (Economic and Monetary Union) will begin at the earliest on 1st January 1997 and at the (very) latest on 1st January 1999.

50.5   **Sequence**

As already mentioned (see **50.1e**), past, present and future actions or events are not considered in isolation but in relation to one another. The correct sequence of tenses has to be used in order to relate actions in time. This means that in a given sentence with at least two clauses, the main action takes place at a time we can call the 'reference' time and the other action occurs before, at the same time as, or after the main one.

(a) Actions or events taking place before the main action, situated in its reference time:

> Je *pense* qu'elle n'*a* pas suffisamment *révisé.*
> I don't think she has done enough revision.

> Je *pense* qu'elle n'*était* pas prête pour cet examen.
> I don't think she was ready for this exam.

> Ils *croiront* que nous nous *sommes moqués* d'eux.
> They'll think that we've been making fun of them.

> Il *saura* que tu ne lui en *voulais* pas.
> He'll know you don't bear him a grudge.

> Je ne *savais* pas que tu *avais été opéré.*
> I didn't know you had had an operation.

> **Nous** *avons entendu* **dire que vous** *aviez* **déjà** *eu* **des difficultés avec ce fournisseur.**
> We heard that you'd already had problems with this supplier.

> **Ses parents** *sont déçus* **qu'elle** *ait échoué.*
> Her parents are disappointed that she has failed.

> **Notre délégation** *a* **fort** *apprécié* **qu'un accueil aussi chaleureux lui** *soit* (*or fût*) *réservé* **à son arrivée.**
> Our delegation was delighted that they were given such a warm welcome.

In the previous two examples, note that past subjunctives have to be used after certain verbs and verb phrases. This is also the case in (b) and (c) below.

Nowadays, the imperfect and pluperfect subjunctives are rarely used, even in written French (see **39**).

(b) Action(s) taking place at the same time as the main action:

> Je *crois* qu'elle *est* prête.
> I think she's ready.

> Je lui *dirai* que tu ne *veux* plus *venir.*
> I'll tell him/her you don't want to come any more.

> **En la voyant, il** *sut* **immédiatement qu'elle** *était* **en pleine dépression.**
> When he saw her he knew immediately that she was terribly depressed.

> **Nous** *sommes enchantés* **que vous** *soyez* **parmi nous aujourd'hui.**
> We are delighted you are with us today.

Elle *aimait* qu'il la *fasse* (*or fît*) rire.
She loved it when he made her laugh.

(c) Action(s) taking place after the main action:

Une bonne partie des électeurs ne *savent* pas pour qui ils *voteront*.
Many of the electors don't know who to vote for.

Je lui *dirai* que tu nous *rejoindras* après le cours.
I'll tell him/her that you'll join us after the lecture.

Elle *comprit* qu'il ne *reviendrait* plus.
She realized that he would never come back.

Nous *savions* que la facture *serait envoyée* le lendemain.
We knew that the invoice would be sent the next day.

Je ne *veux* pas que tu *partes* si tôt.
I don't want you to leave so early.

Elle *demanda* qu'on *prenne* (*or prît*) la peine de lui envoyer le document.
She told them/us to make an effort to send her the document.

(d) There may be more than two clauses in a sentence and the use of different tenses allows you to establish a sequence of actions and events. In the following examples, the sequence of actions is represented by numbers:

Comme elle *a* consciencieusement *révisé* (1), elle *pense* (2) qu'elle *décrochera* (3) son diplôme.
Since she has revised thoroughly, she thinks she will get her diploma.

Les grévistes qui jusque-là *avaient manifesté* (1) calmement, *décidèrent* (2) vers midi qu'ils *attaqueraient* (3) les fourgons de police.
The strikers demonstrated peacefully up until midday, when they decided to attack the police vans.

Etant donné que vous n'*avez* pas *répondu* (1) à ma réclamation, je me *vois* dans l'obligation (2) d'en aviser la direction qui *prendra* (3) les mesures nécessaires.
Since you have not answered my complaint, I am compelled to inform the management who will take the necessary action.

Quand vous *aurez terminé* ce travail (2) , je *souhaite* (1) que vous *veniez* (3) dans mon bureau pour que toute l'équipe *puisse préparer* (4) le programme de la semaine prochaine.
When you have finished this work, I would like you to come to my office so that the whole team can prepare the programme for next week.

(e) A strict sequence of tenses is not always observed, for example, when the 'universal' present tense is used (see **24.3, 50.1c**):

Beaucoup de Français ne *savaient* pas que le Président *est* (*instead of était*) élu pour sept ans.
Many French people did not know that the President is elected for seven years.

or when there is a succession of short actions or events and in order to maintain the dramatic effect of the actions or events:

> **Dès qu'il *toucha*** (*instead of eut touché*) **la pierre, le ciel *s'assombrit* et le tonnerre *retentit*.**
> As soon as he touched the stone, the sky darkened and the thunder rolled.

or when you focus on the result of the actions or events:

> **Nous *attendons* qu'il *ait obtenu*** (*instead of obtienne*) **son permis de conduire avant de partir en vacances.**
> We are waiting for him to get his driving licence before going on holiday.

> **Quand le raisin de la rangée *était coupé*** (*instead of avait été coupé*), **il *s'asseyait* au bout pour fumer une cigarette.**
> When the grapes had been picked, he sat down at the end of the row to have a cigarette.

51 Reporting

(a) Speech may be reported directly in the words actually used. Note the differences in punctuation in French and English:

> **Il m'a dit: '*On se voit ce soir?*' – '*Ça m'étonnerait!*', ai-je répondu.**
> He said to me, 'Are we meeting this evening?' 'I'd be surprised,' I answered.

Note how punctuation is used in French: a colon before reported speech, inverted commas to include all reported speech and a dash to introduce a new speaker. Instead of a colon, a verb such as **dire, affirmer, déclarer** + **que** + indicative may be used to introduce direct speech:

> **Et si, pour une fois, Jacques Chirac avait raison quand il *affirme que* 'l'opposition a un problème avec la jeunesse'?**
> And what if Jacques Chirac were right for once when he says that 'the opposition has a problem with the young'?

Alternatively, the verb may follow the quotation:

> **'C'est agréable, le train', *a dit* Edouard Balladur dans le train qui l'emmenait à Montélimar.** (see 15.1)
> 'It's nice travelling by train,' said Edouard Balladur in the train taking him to Montélimar.

(Note the English translation of the relative clause in the previous example.)

> **'Le gouvernement dévalorise nos diplômes': telle *est* l'antienne entendue dans les manifs.**
> 'The government's devaluing our degrees' was the cry heard during the demos.

(Note the elliptical past participle **entendue**, instead of a relative clause **qu'on entendait**, in the previous example.)

or the verb may even be in the middle of the quotation:

> **'On ne rêve pas, on ne prétend pas obtenir l'abrogation des
> lois Pasqua, *commente* Charlie, mais on veut sensibiliser . . .'**
> (see **45.4**)
> 'It's not a pipedream, we're not saying we'll get the Pasqua
> legislation overturned,' said Charlie, 'but we want to make the
> public aware . . .'

When speaking *and* using a quotation, the convention is to use (**et**) **je cite** at the beginning and sometimes **fin de citation** at the end of the quotation:

> **Jacques Chirac a sans doute raison quand il affirme, *et je cite*,
> que 'l'opposition a un problème avec la jeunesse'.**
> Jacques Chirac is probably right when he says, and I quote, 'the
> opposition has a problem with the young'.

(b) Sometimes, only part of the original speech is directly reported – in inverted commas below – while the rest is presented as indirect speech:

> **'Bien sûr', rétorque d'emblée le Premier Ministre à ceux qui osent lui
> demander s'il existe encore une place sur le marché de la presse
> économique.**
> 'Of course', is the Prime Minister's immediate retort to those who
> venture to ask him if there is room for another economic journal in
> the market.

In the previous example, a direct question: **'Existe-t-il encore une place sur le marché de la presse économique?'** is indirectly reported. Note that some features of the direct question have gone (inversion and the question mark) and that **si** has to be used after the verb (**demander**). For other types of indirect question, interrogative adverbs and adjectives are used and **que?** 'what?' (object) becomes **ce que** while **qui?** 'what?' (subject) becomes **ce qui**. Take the following example:

> **La secrétaire m'a dit: 'Vous voulez vous inscrire en deuxième
> année? Où avez-vous fait votre première année? Comment vous
> appelez-vous? Quelle est votre adresse? Que font vos parents?'** (direct)
> The secretary said to me, 'You want to go into the second year? Where
> did you do your first year? What is your name? What is your address?
> What do your parents do?'

> **La secrétaire m'a demandé *si* je voulais m'inscrire en deuxième
> année, *où* j'avais fait ma première année, *comment* je m'appelais,
> *quelle* était mon adresse, *ce que* faisaient mes parents.** (indirect)
> The secretary asked me about my request to go into the second year,
> where I'd done my first year, what my name was, what my address was,
> and what my parents did.

In addition, some changes have to be made with tenses when the introductory verb is in the past (**m'a demandé**). However, when the introductory verb is in the present or future, the tenses used are the same as for direct speech:

> **Mon père *dit qu'il votera* si les candidats sont sérieux.** ('Je *voterai*
> **si . . .'**)
> My father says he'll vote if the candidates are serious. ('I'll vote if . . .')

> **Mon père *dit qu'il voterait* si les candidats étaient sérieux. ('Je *voterais* si . . .')**
> My father says he would vote if the candidates were serious. ('I'd vote if . . .')

Both of these with an introductory verb in the past become:

> **Mon père *a dit qu'il voterait* si les candidats étaient sérieux.**
> (see **33.1**)
> My father said he would vote if the candidates were serious.

In the previous example the sequence of tenses is invariable, and in the absence of context, there is a little ambiguity about what was actually said ('I will vote' or 'I would vote').

Sometimes, the introductory verb is followed by **que** + subjunctive, in particular when the corresponding direct speech is an order, a request, etc.:

> **Dis-lui qu'il le *fasse* tout de suite! ('Fais-le tout de suite!')** (see **39.2.1**)
> Tell him to do it at once! ('Do it at once!')

> **L'agent *a exigé que* je lui *remette* mon permis de conduire.**
> **('Donnez-moi votre permis de conduire, s'il vous plaît.')**
> The policeman told me to hand over my driving licence. ('Give me your driving licence, please!')

Alternatively, an infinitive may be used, sometimes introduced by **de**:

> **Dis-lui *de* le *faire* tout de suite.**
> Tell him to do it at once.

> **Elle *m'a prié* plusieurs fois *de l'accompagner* à la gare.**
> She asked me several times to accompany her to the station.

In the following example, there is no **de** because of the verb **estimer** + infinitive.

> **D'après l'interview que j'ai lue, il *estime avoir fait* tout ce qui était humainement possible pour réparer ses erreurs.** (see **4.4, 15.11.1**)
> According to the interview I read, he thinks he has done everything humanly possible to make up for his mistakes.

Reflexive verbs such as **se déclarer, s'avouer** + adjective provide another way of reporting indirectly:

> **En conclusion, le Président du Conseil *s'est déclaré satisfait* des progrès réalisés durant la réunion.**
> In conclusion, the chairman of the board declared he was satisfied with the progress made at the meeting.

> **La déposition indique que le suspect *s'est avoué coupable* après une heure d'interrogatoire.**
> The evidence indicates that the suspect confessed after an hour of questioning.

Some changes need to be made with personal pronouns and possessive adjectives when using indirect speech:

Paul a promis qu'*il* viendrait avec son camion pour *m*'aider à déménager. ('*Je* viendrai *t*'aider avec mon camion.')
Paul promised to come with his lorry to help me move house. ('I'll come and help you with my lorry.')

Il a rappelé à Paul qu'*il* devait venir avec son camion.
He reminded Paul that he was to come with his lorry.

The previous example is ambiguous in the sense that, in the absence of context, you do not know whether **il** (**devait venir**) was the original speaker or not, that is, whether he or Paul said: '**Je viendrai avec mon camion.**' ('**I'll come with my lorry.**')

When transferring from direct to indirect speech, other changes have to be made when you are referring to time and place:

Le directeur a annoncé: 'Le rapport sera prêt *demain/dans une semaine.*'
The manager announced, 'The report will be ready tomorrow/in a week.'

If this is part of a narrative, and the speech is reported, then it becomes:

Le directeur a annoncé que le rapport serait prêt *le lendemain/ une semaine plus tard.* (see 33.1)
The manager announced that the report would be ready the next day/a week later.

Adverbs of time vary, naturally, according to the timing of the original statement and the information given:

Il a annoncé *hier* que le rapport serait prêt *aujourd'hui/dans une semaine.*
He announced yesterday that the report would be ready today/in a week.

Il a annoncé *l'autre jour* que le rapport serait prêt *le lendemain/une semaine plus tard.*
He announced the other day that the report would be ready the next day/a week later.

Le 19 juin, lendemain du crime, vous avez déclaré dans votre déposition, et je cite: 'Je suis chez ma sœur *depuis avant-hier soir.*' Pouvez-vous confirmer aujourd'hui que le jour du crime, vous vous trouviez bien 8, rue du Lac chez votre sœur, et ce, *depuis la veille au soir*?
On the 19th of June, the day after the crime, you stated in your evidence, and I quote: 'I have been at my sister's since the evening before last.' Can you confirm today that on the day of the crime you were in fact at 8, rue du Lac at your sister's, and had been since the night before?

Similarly, changes are required with place:

Elle m'avait promis: 'Je te retrouve *ici* dans deux heures', je ne l'ai jamais revue.
She'd promised me, 'I'll meet you back here in two hours', I never saw her again.

Two and a half hours after the direct speech actually occurred:

> **J'étais avec cette fille . . ., je ne sais pas ce qu'elle fait. Elle m'avait promis de me retrouver *là* à quatre heures/il y a une demi-heure.**
> I was with the girl . . ., I don't know what she's doing. She'd promised me that she would meet me back there at four o'clock/half an hour ago.

A week later:

> **Ce jour-là, j'ai rencontré cette fille, mais je ne l'ai jamais revue alors qu'elle m'avait promis de me retrouver deux heures après *là-bas*/*devant la Mairie*.**
> That day, I met the girl, but I never saw her again although she'd promised to meet me two hours later there/in front of the Town Hall.

(c) Various ways of reporting – especially reporting what was *said* – are often found in minutes of meetings. Many transitive verbs are used to write minutes – compare the tenses in French and English:

> **En ouvrant la séance, Mme Dupuis *souhaite la bienvenue* aux délégués présents et énonce l'ordre du jour.**
> Opening the meeting, Mme Dupuis welcomed the delegates and set out the agenda.

> **M. Courreau *relève des anomalies* dans le bilan présenté.**
> M. Courreau noted anomalies in the balance sheet.

Many verbs are followed by **que**, which has to be repeated with three or more clauses:

> **M. C. *rappelle qu'*au 1er janvier 2004, nous avons une réserve de 23 500 000 euros.**
> M. C. recalled that on 1st January 2004, we had reserves of 23,500,000 euros.

> **M. F. *souligne que* nous avons voté un budget en déséquilibre et *que* nous n'avons pas d'autre solution que de rappeler nos difficultés.**
> M. F. stressed that we had approved a deficit budget and all we could do was note our difficulties.

Sometimes, **c'est** or **cela** have to be used with indirect speech:

> **Il *ajoute que ce sont* les ressources propres qui sont touchées.**
> He added that it was the shareholders' equity that was affected.

> **Mme G. lui *répond que cela* n'est pas prévu.**
> Mme. G. replied that that had not been expected.

Passive forms are also frequently used in minutes (see **41, 41.1**):

> **Après discussion, la rédaction du mémorandum *est reportée* à la fin de la séance.**
> Following discussion, the drafting of the memorandum was postponed till the end of the meeting.

> **La proposition *est soutenue* par M. C. . . . , *rejetée par* Mme B. . . . , elle *est* finalement *votée* à l'unanimité.**
> The proposal was supported by M. C. . . . , rejected by Mme B. . . . , and eventually passed unanimously.

Questions are reported using verbs and verb phrases:

> **M. E. *demande* à Mme G. *si* elle ira au Rectorat défendre les problèmes de la section d'anglais.**
> M. E. asked Mme G. whether she would go to the university administration to put the case for the English department.

> **M. N. *veut savoir s'*il y a une ventilation précise des dépenses pour chaque section.**
> M. N. wanted to know whether there was a detailed breakdown of spending for each department.

Expressions in apposition, with the second, or subsequent ones, containing a response are also used in minutes. These very compact structures are useful for combining question(s) and answer(s), and they also provide stylistic variation:

> ***Invité à commenter* les 20 000 euros de frais divers enregistrés en 2001, M. T. *présente* une facture de la Société Duchemin.**
> Asked to comment on the 20,000 euros miscellaneous expenditure in 2001, M. T. presented an invoice from the Société Duchemin.

> ***En réponse à une question* de Mme V. sur la meilleure façon de réaliser des économies, M. P. *précise* que ses charges sont déjà compressées au maximum.** (see **41**)
> In answer to a question from Mme V. on the best way of making savings, M. P. stated that his costs/expenses had already been reduced as far as possible.

Answers or explanations can also be provided using **comme** after the introductory verb:

> **M. V. *cite comme raison* profonde des mauvais résultats la chute des ventes de véhicules neufs . . .**
> M. V. cited the fall in new car sales as the principal reason for the poor results . . .

> **. . . il *avance comme deuxième raison* la conjoncture mondiale conséquente à la Guerre du Golfe.**
> . . . he added that a further reason was the world economic situation following the Gulf War.

52 Asking questions

(a) A simple and informal way of asking questions consists of making a statement and using appropriate intonation when speaking, and adding a question mark when writing:

> **Vous venez, on y va?**
> Are you coming, shall we go?

> **Tu me prêtes ton vélo?**
> You'll lend me your bike?

> **T'en veux pas?**
> You don't want any?

(b) Alternatively, you may introduce a question with **est-ce que?**. This expression is also fairly informal:

> *Est-ce que* **tu pourrais me garder les enfants vendredi soir?** (see **50.4**)
> Can you look after the children for me on Friday evening?

> *Est-ce que* **le magasin est ouvert le dimanche?** (see **2.4c, 50.4**)
> Is the shop open on Sunday(s)?

(c) Note that all of the questions in (a) and (b) require 'yes/no' answers. There is a more formal way of asking this type of question, using inversion of the verb and the subject – a pronoun subject is linked to the verb or the auxiliary verb by a hyphen, a noun or proper noun subject is *not*:

> *Etes-vous* **prête à répondre à la première question, Danielle?**
> Are you ready to answer the first question, Danielle?

> **Les gouvernements** *sauront-ils* **répondre à cet appel de détresse lancé par la Somalie?**
> Will the governments be able to respond to the appeal for help from Somalia?

Inversion usually occurs in writing but may also occur when speaking, in particular in polite conversation, and in discussion (see **16.3**):

> *Puis-je* **fumer?**
> May I smoke?

> *Voulez-vous* **que je vous accompagne?**
> Would you like me to go with you?

(d) When a question does not call for a 'yes/no' answer, it is focusing on one particular aspect of exposition, for example, location or ownership, and therefore on one particular part of the sentence such as the complement. Interrogative adjectives or pronouns (see **16.1**) may be used in this case, as well as the forms presented above: intonation, **est-ce que?**, and inversion.

When you want to find out who or what is the subject of the verb, you usually use **qui?** 'who?' or **qu'est-ce qui?** 'what?':

> *Qui* **a fait ça?**
> Who did that?

> *Qu'est-ce qui* **lui permet d'être aussi arrogant?**
> What is it that allows him to be so arrogant?

Qui est-ce qui? 'who?' and particularly **c'est qui qui?** 'who?' are more colloquial forms:

> **Ah non!** *C'est qui qui* **a touché mon ordinateur?**
> Oh no! Who's been at my computer?

Note that you can be more precise and direct if you use **parmi, d'entre** 'of, among' + noun or pronoun after **qui?**:

> *Qui parmi vous* **se porte volontaire pour cette mission?**
> Which of you will volunteer for this task?

and remember that in an indirect question **qu'est-ce qui?** becomes **ce qui**:

> Je *me demande ce qui* lui permet d'être aussi arrogant.
> I wonder what it is that allows him to be so arrogant.

In order to ask who or what is the direct object of the verb, use **qui?**, **que?**, **quoi?**:

> *Que vois-tu* par la fenêtre? *Qu'est-ce que tu vois*?
> What can you see out the window? What can you see?

> *Qui vois-tu* en ce moment? *Qui est-ce que tu vois*?
> Who can you see at the moment? Who can you see?

And there is the very informal:

> Tu vois *quoi?/qui?*
> You can see what?/who?

Note that **quoi** or **que** are often used with an infinitive:

> Je ne sais plus *quoi* (*or que*) *dire* ni *quoi* (*or que*) *faire* à son
> sujet.
> I don't know what to say any more or what to do about
> him/her/it.

Interrogative pronouns can be used to refer back or forward to a noun (see **16.4.2**):

> J'ai plusieurs variétés de pommes de terre: *lesquelles* voulez-vous?
> (back)
> I've several varieties of potato: which do you want?

> *Lequel* choisirais-tu parmi tous ces manteaux? (forward)
> Which of all these coats would you choose?

And less formally:

> J'en ai plusieurs sortes, vous voulez *lesquelles*?
> I've several kinds, which do you want?

> Tu choisirais *lequel*, toi, de tous ces manteaux?
> Which of all these coats would *you* choose?

To find out who or what is the *indirect* object, you need to use a preposition such as **à** or **de**. The preposition always precedes the interrogative term (see **16.2**):

> *A qui/A quoi* faites-vous allusion quand vous dites cela?
> Who/What are you referring to when you say that?

> *De qui* se moque-t-on?
> Who are you making fun of?

and less formally:

> *A qui/A quoi est-ce que* vous faites allusion quand vous dites cela?
> Who/What are you referring to when you say that?

and definitely informal:

> Tu fais allusion *à quoi* exactement?
> You're talking about what exactly?

When you want to know about location, time, cause, manner, quantity, etc., use interrogative pronouns and adjectives on their own:

Où et *quand* **aura lieu la prochaine réunion?** (see **16.4.4**)
Where and when is the next meeting?

Cela arrive *tous les combien*?
That happens how often?

Pourquoi **cette société a-t-elle licencié tant de personnel?** (see **16.4.7**)
Why has this company made so many staff redundant?

Tu comptes y aller *comment* **si ta voiture est en panne?**
How do you intend to get there if your car has broken down?

and following prepositions:

Avec qui **est-ce qu'ils partent?**
Who are they leaving/going with?

Tu vas monter *sur quoi* **pour peindre le plafond?**
What are you going to stand on to paint the ceiling?

Finally, interrogative adjectives (see **16.4.3**) and pronouns may be used as determiners – with or without a preposition:

Quel formulaire **est-ce que je dois remplir pour effectuer un versement?**
What form must I fill in in order to make a payment?

Quelles villes **voulez-vous visiter pendant votre séjour?**
What cities do you want to visit during your stay?

C'est le manteau de qui, **là par terre?**
Whose coat is it on the ground?

Dans laquelle **de ces pièces voulez-vous faire installer le double vitrage?**
Which of these rooms do you want to have the double glazing in?

(e) Sometimes, the question does not call for an answer but is simply a way of creating a particular effect or conveying a particular feeling:

Il a fait quoi? Il t'a dit ça? . . . **Je n'en reviens pas!** (surprise)
He did what? He said that to you? . . . I'm amazed!

Comment voulez-vous que je m'en sorte **avec tout ça?** (complaint, call for sympathy)
How on earth can I manage with all that (to do)?

Note that some questions, especially with **pouvoir**, which in terms of form are of the 'yes/no' type, are in fact aimed at eliciting a fuller answer:

Pouvez-vous me donner l'heure, **s'il vous plaît?**
Can you give me the time, please?

Est-ce que vous pourriez nous exposer la position **de votre parti sur cette question?**
Can you give us your party's position on this issue?

Finally, there is the question tag which you can add to any statement when you are seeking someone's agreement with your question – **n'est-ce pas?** This little expression is unique. It can be used formally or informally. It never varies in its form and it is equivalent to every single question tag in English 'isn't he/she/it?, can't you?, didn't we?, won't I?, shouldn't they?'. Sometimes, it is used simply to end a sentence and has no real interrogative function. Sometimes it is used to reinforce a statement. Sometimes, it is merely the equivalent of a nervous tic!

> **Vous aimez la grammaire française, *n'est-ce pas*?**
> You like French grammar, don't you?

> **La question, *n'est-ce pas*, reste ouverte.**
> The question, of course, remains open.

53 | **Negating** (see **47.7–47.13**)

As in asking questions (see **52d**), you have to distinguish between negation applied to the *whole* sentence or clause – full negation, and negation applied to only one *part* of the sentence or clause – partial negation.

(a) The most obvious way to apply full negation is to use **ne . . . pas** (see **47.8**):

> **Si les Dupont *ne sont pas* là maintenant, c'est qu'ils *ne viendront pas*.**
> If the Duponts are not here now, it's because they won't be coming.

Ne is often omitted in informal speech (see **47.9**):

> **Elle est pas venue, Jacqueline, je sais pas pourquoi.**
> Jacqueline hasn't come. I don't know why.

When speaking, other shortcuts may be taken and only **pas** is used, for example, with an adverb, in answer to a question:

> **Non, merci, *pas* tout de suite. (= Je ne veux pas prendre un verre (de vin) tout de suite.)**
> No, thanks, not right away.

Pas is replaced by **ni . . . ni . . .** (see **47.8.1**) when there are two elements in the negation, for example, two nouns or two verbs:

> **Pauvre petite, elle *n'a ni père ni mère*.** (Note the omission of the article.)
> Poor little thing, she has neither a father nor a mother.

> **Je crois que nous *n'avons ni le droit* d'ignorer ce conflit, *ni celui* de ne pas condamner les responsables des massacres.**
> I believe we do not have the right to ignore this conflict, nor the right not to condemn those responsible for the massacres.

(Note the double negation: **nous *n'avons pas* le droit de *ne pas* condamner – nous devons condamner**. This usage is for emphasis.)

> **Il *ne parle ni ne rit* (*plus*) depuis longtemps.**
> He has not said a word or laughed in a long time.

Note that the previous structure is rarely used when speaking informally. On the other hand, when speaking informally, it is possible to avoid **ne . . . ni . . . ne . . .** 'neither . . . nor . . . nor . . .':

> **Voilà Docteur, il *ne* mange *plus*, (et/ni) *ne* dort *plus*.**
> Well, Doctor, he won't eat or sleep.

Pas is sometimes omitted, in a more formal context, after the verbs **cesser, oser, pouvoir, savoir** (see **47.9**):

> **Il *ne* sait où aller.**
> He doesn't know where to go.

Instead of **ne . . . pas**, you can use the negative form of a noun or adjective (see **47.13**):

> **Ce n'est pas possible! = C'est *impossible*!**
> It's impossible!

or a preposition:

> **Elle est *sans domicile fixe*. (see 4.4) = Elle *n'a pas* de domicile. (see 4.1)**
> She is homeless.

(b) The negation may apply to one part of the sentence only, such as the subject (see **47.8**):

> ***Personne n'*est venu.**
> Nobody came.

> ***Rien* au monde *ne* me fera changer d'avis.**
> Nothing in the world will make me change my mind.

> ***Aucun* de vous *n'*est qualifié pour faire ce travail.**
> Not one of you is qualified to do this work.

> **Il *n'*y a *aucune* raison de s'énerver.**
> There's no need to get excited.

or the negation may focus on the verb:

> **Tu *ne viens jamais* me voir.**
> You never come to see me.

> **Elle *n'*en *a rien voulu savoir*.**
> She didn't want to know anything about it.

> **Nous *ne voulons plus* vous voir.**
> We don't want to see you again.

Adverbs expressing full negation replace **pas** in the negative structures **ne . . . jamais, ne . . . rien, ne . . . plus**. This is not the case when less powerful adverbs are involved:

> **Tu *ne* viens *pas souvent* me voir.**
> You don't come to see me very often.

> **Elle *n'*a *pas* voulu en savoir *davantage*.**
> She didn't want to know any more about it.

> **Nous *ne* voulons *pas* vous voir *constamment*.**
> We don't want to see you all the time.

(c) Finally, note that a question or a command may also be negative:

> ***Pourquoi n'est-il pas* encore *arrivé?***
> Why hasn't he/it arrived yet?

> ***N'oublie pas* de faire tes devoirs!**
> Don't forget to do your homework!

and don't forget that when it is a question of the 'yes/no' type, the answer is **si/non**:

> ***N'êtes-vous pas convaincu* de son innocence? Moi, *si.***
> Are you not convinced of his innocence? *I* am.

Be careful when there is a double negation:

> **Tu *ne* crois *pas* qu'il *ne* faut *pas* réveiller les enfants maintenant? Si, tu as raison, laissons-les dormir./Non, on a assez attendu maintenant!**
> Don't you think we shouldn't wake the children now? Yes, you're right, let's leave them asleep./No, we've waited long enough!

IV
Attitude

54   Greeting and leave-taking

54.1   Greeting

The verb **aller** is often used after introductory terms such as **salut** (informal) 'hi' or **bonjour** 'good morning/afternoon':

> *Salut*, **les mecs,** *ça va?*
> Hi there, you guys! OK?

> **Monsieur Duverger,** *bonjour*, **comment** *allez*-**vous?**
> M. Duverger, good morning. How are you?

The reply may be modulated with intonation or using verbs or adverbs, and it is quite common to thank someone at the same time:

> **Ouais, ça** *peut aller*, **et toi?**
> Yeah, OK, you?

> *Très bien*, *merci*, **et vous-même?**
> Very well, thank you. And yourself?

The term of greeting is often combined with a title, which precedes or follows it:

Bonsoir, Messieurs Dames!	Good evening, ladies and gentlemen!
Chers amis, bonjour!	Friends/Colleagues, good morning!
Bonjour Docteur!	Good morning, Doctor!

When introduced to a person for the first time, you can use the above terms (**bonjour, bonsoir, salut . . .**) and/or adjectives or past participles, such as **heureux, enchanté + de** + infinitive, or simply on their own:

> **Bonjour Mademoiselle,** *très heureux de faire* **votre connaissance.**
> Good morning, Miss Smith, very pleased to meet you.

> *Enchantée*!
> Delighted!

> *Salut* **Danielle, je suis** *content de* **te** *rencontrer*, **on m'a beaucoup parlé de toi.**
> Hello Danielle, I'm pleased to meet you. I've heard a lot about you.

The standard opening formula in correspondence, when you do not know the person you are writing to, is:

> **Madame/Monsieur,**
> Dear Madam/Sir,

You add the definite article and title in a very formal letter:

> **Monsieur le Directeur,** (under the title/name and address)
> Dear Sir,

> **Madame le Maire,** (under the title/name and address)
> Dear Madam,

The use of **cher** indicates that you know the person quite well – very well if you add a possessive adjective – or wish to be informal:

Chers **amis,**	Dear Mr and Mrs Smith,/My dear friends,
Chère **Madame,**	Dear Mrs Smith,
Mon cher **Jean,**	My dear John,

54.2 Leave-taking

Note that some of the terms of greeting: **salut, bonsoir** . . . may also be used for leave-taking. **Bonjour** is used as a term of greeting *only*:

> **Allez** *salut*, **à demain!**
> OK! Bye! See you tomorrow.

> *Bonsoir*, **Messieurs Dames et** *bonne fin de soirée*!
> Goodnight, ladies and gentlemen. Enjoy the rest of the evening!

It is fairly common to use phrases introduced by the preposition **à** in order to refer to a future meeting, such as **à demain** above:

> *Au revoir* **Docteur,** *à la semaine prochaine*!
> Goodbye, Doctor. Till next week!

> **Salut Martin,** *à plus tard*!
> Bye, Martin. See you later!

> *Au plaisir* (de vous revoir)!
> Till the next time!

It is not uncommon to express some form of best wishes when taking leave, and this often involves using **bon**, as in **bonne fin de soirée** above:

> **Au revoir les enfants,** *bon voyage*!
> Bye kids! Have a good journey!

> **Salut Anne,** *bonne chance* **pour tes examens!**
> Bye, Anne! Good luck for your exams!

In correspondence, informal leave-taking may be expressed using short phrases with adverbs or adjectives:

Bien amicalement.	With best regards,
(*Grosses*) *bises* **et à bientôt.**	Lots of love, see you soon,
Bien des choses **à toute la famille.**	Best wishes to all the family,

or verbs:

> **Je t'** *embrasse bien fort.*   Lots of love,

In a more formal register, you would use the imperative (see **44.2**):

> *Croyez*, **Monsieur, à l'expression de mes sentiments les meilleurs.**
> Yours faithfully,

> *Veuillez* **agréer, Madame le Maire, mes salutations distinguées.**
> Yours faithfully, (*or* Yours sincerely, if you use the name of the person you are writing to.)

> *Recevez*, **je vous prie, nos meilleures amitiés.**
> With best regards,

or a verb with the pronoun **vous**:

> **Je** *vous prie de croire* **à l'assurance de mes sentiments distingués.**
> Yours faithfully,

> **Je** *vous adresse* **mon très amical souvenir.**
> Regards,

55 Expressing congratulations and appreciation

55.1 Congratulations

Single terms may be used with appropriate intonation or punctuation:

> **Bravo!**   Well done!
> **Chapeau!**   Well done!

Nouns may be used on their own or reinforced by **tout** and a possessive adjective:

> **Compliments!**   Well done!
> **Toutes mes félicitations!** Congratulations!
> (see **11.1a**)

In order to compliment someone with various degrees of emphasis, you can use **c'est** + adverb or adjective (see **6.3b**):

> **Mais dis donc,** *c'est pas mal du tout* **ce que tu as fait!**
> Hey! It's not bad at all what you've done!

> **Votre exposition,** *c'est formidable*, **bravo!**
> Your exhibition, it's wonderful, well done!

More formally, when writing and for social contexts, e.g. birth, marriage, new job, you can use a phrase with a preposition such as **à**, **pour**, **avec** and no verb:

> **A Paul et Virginie,** *avec* **toutes nos félicitations pour votre mariage.**
> (on a card)
> For Paul and Virginie, with our warmest congratulations on your wedding.

or a transitive verb such as **présenter, adresser, souhaiter**:

> **Je vous *présente les félicitations* du jury pour votre performance à cet examen.**
> Congratulations from the board of examiners on your performance in this exam.

> **Nous vous *adressons tous nos vœux* de bonheur et de prospérité.**
> We wish you every happiness and prosperity.

or a verb followed by the preposition **de** + noun or infinitive:

> **Je me *réjouis* avec vous *de la naissance* de Catherine.**
> I congratulate you on the birth of your daughter Catherine.

> **Nous te *félicitons d'avoir obtenu* ton permis de conduire du premier coup.**
> Congratulations on passing your (driving) test at the first attempt.

or **être** + adjective + **de** + infinitive:

> **J'ai été très *heureuse d'apprendre* la naissance de Patrick.**
> I was very pleased to learn of the birth of your son Patrick.

> **Jean-Claude et moi *sommes ravis d'apprendre* que tu as été admis à Sciences Po.**
> Jean-Claude and I are delighted to hear that you've been accepted by Sciences Po (Institute of Political Science).

or **c'est avec . . . que**:

> **C'est avec une grande joie *que* nous avons appris le mariage de votre fils avec Carole Maillou.**
> It is with great pleasure that we have learned of the marriage of your son to Carole Maillou.

55.2 Appreciation

The simplest form of appreciation is of course **merci**. This can be emphasized with an adverb:

Merci beaucoup.	Thank you very much.
Merci encore.	Thanks again.

or a short phrase:

Merci pour tout.	Thanks for everything.
Merci mille fois.	Thanks a million.

Merci takes the preposition **de** when it is followed by a verb:

> *Merci d'avoir pensé* à moi.
> Thank you for thinking about me.

Note that **merci** is sometimes used to refuse politely:

> **Encore un verre?** *Merci.*
> Another glass? Thanks, but no thanks. (*or* No, thank you.)

When accepting an invitation or a suggestion, you can use short expressions such as

Avec plaisir! *or* **Volontiers!**	With pleasure!
OK! *or* **D'accord!**	Right!
Excellente idée!	An excellent idea!

or verb phrases:

Je veux bien!	Yes, love to!
C'est une bonne idée!	That's a good idea!

In a more formal context, you may first of all acknowledge the invitation with verbs or verb phrases such as **remercier de** + noun or infinitive 'to thank for', **c'est très gentil . . . de** + infinitive 'it's very kind (of you) to . . .', **faire plaisir à** 'to give pleasure to':

Nous vous *remercions de votre aimable invitation*.
Thank you for your kind invitation.

C'est très gentil à vous *de m'inviter*.
It's very kind of you to invite me.

C'est très aimable de votre part *de nous avoir invités* tous les deux.
(see **42.4**)
It's very kind of you to have invited both of us.

Votre invitation *nous a fait grand plaisir*.
We were delighted to receive your invitation.

and then accept the invitation with verbs or verb phrases such as **accepter avec plaisir de** + infinitive 'to accept with pleasure', **se réjouir de** + infinitive 'to be delighted to', **c'est avec plaisir que . . .** 'I am pleased to . . .':

Nous *acceptons avec plaisir de* nous *rendre* au vin d'honneur.
We will be delighted to come to the reception.

Je me *réjouis d'*être des vôtres. (see **8.1c**)
I am delighted to join you.

C'est avec le plus grand plaisir que je vous accompagnerai.
I shall be delighted to come with you.

Naturally, both are often combined, using a relative clause:

Claude Lambert *remercie* M. et Mme Duforestel *de* leur aimable invitation *à laquelle* il se rendra *avec grand plaisir* le 18 décembre à 21 heures.
Claude Lambert is delighted to accept the kind invitation of M. and Mme Duforestel on 18th December at 9 o'clock.

Je vous *remercie de* votre cordiale invitation *que* j'accepte *avec grand plaisir*.
Thank you for your kind invitation which I am delighted to accept.

56 Expressing apologies and sympathy

56.1 Apologies

The simplest form is **pardon** 'sorry/pardon', – if you bump into someone, for example – used on its own or in various verb phrases such as **demander pardon**:

> Je vous *demande pardon.* I beg your pardon.

Imperative forms are also used:

> **Pardonne-moi!** Pardon me!
> **Excusez-nous!** Excuse us!

and verb forms and verb phrases such as **regretter** 'to regret', **être désolé mais . . .** 'to be sorry but . . .':

> **Je m'excuse.**
> I'm sorry.

> **Nous ne pouvons pas venir et *nous le regrettons.***
> We are sorry but we cannot come.

> **D'après le message que nous avons reçu, *elle est désolée mais* son fils est malade et elle n'a pas pu se libérer.**
> According to the message we've received, she is sorry but her son is ill and she is not able to get away.

You may apologize more profusely using polite forms or adverbs:

> **Je vous *prie de* m'excuser.**
> I ask you to forgive me.

> ***Veuillez* me pardonner.**
> Please accept my apologies./Please forgive me.

> **Nous sommes *terriblement désolés*.**
> We are dreadfully sorry.

> ***Avec toutes nos excuses*, veuillez agréer, Monsieur (Madame/ Mademoiselle), nos salutations distinguées.**
> Please accept our sincere apologies. Yours faithfully.

When explaining what you are apologizing for, you can use **pour** + noun, **de** + infinitive or noun, verb + **que** + subjunctive (see **39.2.1**), or the relatives **ce qui/que/dont**:

> **Je m'excuse *pour le retard* mais j'ai crevé sur l'autoroute!**
> I'm sorry for the delay, but I had a puncture on the motorway.

> **Je regrette *d'arriver* si tard mais il y avait des bouchons sur le périph!**
> I'm sorry for arriving so late, but there were tailbacks on the ring road.

> **Nous *sommes désolés que* vous *n'ayez pas été prévenu* à temps.**
> We are sorry you weren't informed in time.

The following examples are taken from official or business contexts:

> **La Direction vous *prie d'accepter toutes ses excuses pour cette erreur de facturation*.**
> The management hopes you will accept its apologies for the error in the invoice.

> **Nous *regrettons de ne pouvoir donner suite à* votre appel.** (see **47.9**)
> The number you have dialled has not been recognized. Please check and try again.

Nous *sommes navrés de ce malentendu* et *regrettons* vivement les complications qu'il a entraînées.
We are very sorry about this misunderstanding and we sincerely regret the difficulties it has caused.

Cette facture vous a en effet été adressée par erreur, *ce dont* nous vous prions de bien vouloir nous excuser. (excuser de > ce dont)
The invoice was in fact sent to you by mistake, and we hope you will accept our apologies.

When suggesting an explanation, the expression of apology may be followed by a verb in the imperfect or pluperfect tenses:

Excusez-moi, je ne *voulais* pas vous déranger.
I'm sorry, I didn't want to disturb you.

Excusez-moi, j'*avais cru* bien faire.
I'm sorry, I thought I was doing the right thing.

Excusez-moi, j'*essayais* simplement de vous aider.
Excuse me, I was only trying to help.

by the verb **pouvoir** or an impersonal phrase such as **il est impossible de** + infinitive:

Je *regrette* infiniment, mais je ne *pouvais* pas faire autrement.
I'm terribly sorry, but there was nothing else I could do.

Malheureusement, *il* m'*est impossible de* vous *recevoir* aujourd'hui.
Unfortunately, I cannot see you today.

The verb **devoir** is also used to give an explanation or express regret, and when it does express regret, the perfect or conditional perfect tenses are used:

Excusez-moi, mais j'*ai dû* prendre des dispositions en votre absence.
I'm sorry, I had to make arrangements in your absence.

Pardonne-moi, je *n'aurais pas dû* te parler comme ça!
Forgive me, I shouldn't have spoken to you like that!

If you have to apologize, you may also want to give assurances about the future, using the future tense:

Je le jure, je ne le *ferai* plus!
I swear, I'll never do it again.

Soyez assuré que cela ne *se reproduira* pas.
Rest assured it will never happen again.

Nous *ferons* tout notre possible pour éviter ces erreurs à l'avenir.
We'll do everything possible to avoid these errors in future.

56.2 **Sympathy**

In order to express sympathy when speaking, you can use an exclamation, involving the adjective **pauvre**, sometimes with the definite article or a possessive adjective:

> *Pauvre vieux*! Je le voyais tous les jours en sortant du bureau.
> Poor old chap! I used to see him every day when I left the office.

> *La pauvre . . .*, elle n'en a plus pour très longtemps!
> Poor thing! She hasn't long to go.

> *Mon pauvre chéri*! Tu n'as vraiment pas de chance!
> My poor darling, you certainly don't have much luck!

Alternatively, you may use an adjective such as **quel** with a noun, or an adverb such as **comme** with a verb:

> *Quelle tristesse* dans les yeux de ces enfants!
> What sadness in these children's eyes!

> *Comme* je les plains!
> How I pity them!

In writing, elliptical forms are used and often include **tout** + noun or the preposition **avec** + noun:

> Toutes mes condoléances.
> All my sympathy,

> Avec notre profonde sympathie.
> With our deepest sympathy,

Also in writing, a number of verbs may be used with nouns such as **condoléances** or **sympathie** and the cause of grief may be introduced with terms such as **à l'occasion de** or **en**:

> Nous vous adressons nos plus sincères condoléances *à l'occasion de* la disparition tragique de votre fils.
> We send you our deepest sympathy on the tragic death of your son.

> Je vous fais toutes mes condoléances *en* ces moments difficiles.
> I extend to you my deepest sympathy at this difficult time.

Imperative forms, which are much more formal, can also be used (see **54.2**):

> *Crois* bien, chère Anne, à l'expression de ma profonde sympathie.
> Please accept, (my) dear Anne, my deepest sympathy.

> *Croyez* que nous sommes de tout cœur avec vous et soyez assurés de notre sincère sympathie.
> Our hearts go out to you and we send you our deepest sympathy.

Alternatively, you may use the emphatic form **c'est . . . que**:

> *C'est* avec une immense tristesse *que* nous avons appris le décès de Victor.
> It is with immense sadness that we have learned of Victor's death.

57   Expressing surprise and disgust

57.1   Surprise

When speaking, surprise is often conveyed by intonation alone, and marked in writing by punctuation:

> **Elle a pris l'verre de bière et . . . elle lui a versé sur la tête!**
> She took the glass of beer and . . . poured it over his head!

The correct written equivalent would be:

> **Elle a pris le verre de bière et elle le lui a versé sur la tête!**

Interjections such as **oh!** and **ah!** may be used, to express surprise and admiration:

> *Oh!* **quel beau bleu!**
> Oh, what a beautiful blue!

> *Ah!* **voilà Claire! Je me demande ce qui l'amène.**
> Oh, there's Claire! I wonder what brings her here.

> *Ouah!* **C'est vraiment cool chez toi!**
> Wow! It's really cool/brilliant at your place!

And there are many short expressions, which are used to express surprise or disbelief: **ça alors!, ah bon?!, pas possible!, sans blague!, non!** . . .

> *Ça alors*, **Jean-Pascal, ça fait une paille!**
> Well, Jean-Pascal, long time no see!

> *Tiens*, **il a neigé!**
> Well now! It's been snowing!

C'est/ce n'est pas + adjective are also frequently used (see **6.3a, 6.3b**):

> **Ah bon,** *c'est vrai*?!
> Really? Is that true?!

> **Non,** *c'est incroyable*!
> No! That's unbelievable!

> **Sans blague,** *ce n'est pas possible*!
> No kidding! That's not possible!

And verbs such as **plaisanter** 'to joke', some including **en,** are also used to express surprise:

> **Tu** *plaisantes*?!
> Are you joking?

> **Je n'***en reviens* **pas.**
> I can't get over it.

> **Quand elle lui a dit ça, il** *en est resté* **baba!**
> When she told him that, he was flabbergasted!

An adjective such as **quel** may be used to introduce a noun phrase:

> **Vous ici, *quelle surprise*!**
> You here! What a surprise!

or an adverb such as **comme** introducing a clause:

> **C'est ton fils? *Comme* il a grandi!**
> That's your son? Hasn't he grown!

In a more formal register, you can use expressions in apposition:

> ***A mon étonnement*, il n'a rien répondu.**
> To my surprise, he didn't answer.

> ***A notre grande surprise*, les sanctions ont été levées.**
> To our great surprise, the sanctions were lifted.

or **être** + past participle expressing surprise:

> **Nous *avons été* très *surpris par* ce changement d'attitude.**
> We were very surprised by this change of attitude.

> **Je *suis sidérée par* sa réaction.**
> I'm astonished at his reaction.

> **Elle *a été très étonnée de* constater qu'on avait augmenté son salaire.**
> She was amazed to find that her/his salary had been increased.

or **avoir** + noun expressing surprise:

> **Nous *avons eu la surprise* de le voir arriver en pleine nuit.**
> We were surprised to see him/it arriving in the middle of the night.

or verbs expressing surprise such as **s'attendre à** 'to expect', **surprendre** 'to surprise':

> **J'avoue que je ne *m'y attendais* pas.**
> I admit I didn't expect that.

> **Je dois dire que cette décision m'*a surprise*.**
> I must say that decision surprised me.

57.2   Disgust

Again, interjections are available:

> ***Pouah*, ça pue ici!**   Ugh! It stinks here!
> ***Berk!***   Yuk!

or **c'est** + adjective expressing disgust (see **6.3b**):

> **C'est horrible!**   It's horrible!
> **C'est dégueulasse!**   That's disgusting!
> **C'est révoltant!**   It's revolting!

or **c'est** + noun expressing disgust:

> **C'est une honte!**   It's a disgrace!
> **C'est vraiment un scandale!**   That's a real scandal!

And there is the adjective **quel** + noun expressing disgust – used as an interjection:

| Quelle horreur! | That's horrible! |
| Quelle puanteur ici! | What a stink here! |

or **ce** + noun + **être** + adjective, sometimes reinforced by an adverb (see **5.2.1**):

Ce steak est absolument immangeable!
This steak is inedible!

Cet appartement est indescriptible!
This flat is indescribable!

or **c'est** + adjective + **de** + verb:

C'est tout de même *écœurant d'avoir* à payer les honoraires de la famille royale avec nos impôts!
It's disgusting to have to pay the expenses of the royal family with all our taxes!

or verb + adjective + **que** + subjunctive (see **39.2.1**):

Je *trouve scandaleux que* l'on *puisse* ainsi mettre les gens à la porte!
I find it scandalous that one can throw people out in this way!

When explaining what you are disgusted about, you can use a passive form + preposition + explanation (see **41**):

Je *suis révoltée par le traitement* qui est réservé aux SDF (sans domicile fixe).
I'm disgusted by the treatment given to homeless people.

Indignés de l'accueil qu'on leur avait fait, ils sont partis sans dire au revoir.
Annoyed by the reception they got, they left without saying goodbye.

or you can offer the explanation followed by a verb or noun expressing disgust:

L'attitude des hommes politiques me *révolte*.
The attitude of the politicians disgusts me.

Le prix des légumes est *un scandale*!
The price of vegetables is a disgrace.

58 Expressing contrasting attitudes, emotions, feelings

58.1 Likes and dislikes

To express likes and dislikes, you can use a variety of verbs and verb phrases such as **aimer** 'to like, love', **agacer** 'to annoy', a verb such as **aimer** + noun:

Tu *aimes* la littérature anglaise?
You like English literature?

sometimes used with **bien**:

J'*aime* bien les œufs à la coque.
I really like soft-boiled eggs.

> **Tu l'*aimes bien* Jean-Pierre? – Non, ce type m'*agace*!**
> Do you like that Jean-Pierre? – No, that guy annoys me.

noun + a verb such as **plaire** 'to please' or **déplaire** 'to displease':

> **Ce *film* m'*a plu*, et (à) toi?**
> I liked the film, did you?

> **Non, moi je *n'ai pas* tellement *aimé*.**
> No, I didn't like it very much.

a verb expressing liking/disliking + infinitive, or frequently, + **que** + subjunctive (see **39.2.1**):

> **Je n'*aime* pas *faire* la cuisine.**
> I don't like cooking.

> **Elle *aime qu'*on lui *fasse* des cadeaux.**
> She loves getting presents.

> **L'institutrice n'*aime* pas *qu'*on lui *dise* des gros mots.**
> The teacher doesn't like people using bad language.

and phrases introduced by **c'est** or **ça** (see **6.3b, 6.3d**):

> **Ça t'*a plu* 'Les Visiteurs'? – Oui, *c'est très bien*!**
> Did you like 'The Visitors'? – Yes, it's very good!

Impersonal verbs can also be used (see **46**):

> **Il lui *était pénible* d'avoir à effectuer toujours les mêmes tâches.**
> It was boring for him/her always doing the same jobs.

and the structures used for emphasis, **ce qui/ce que . . . c'est** or **c'est que/qu'** 'what . . . is that' (see **15.11**):

> ***Ce qui* me déplaît chez cet auteur, *c'est qu'il* donne toujours l'impression de prendre ses lecteurs pour des imbéciles.**
> What I don't like about this writer is that he always gives the impression of taking his readers for fools.

> ***Ce que* j'aime quand je suis en vacances, *c'est* le soleil, *c'est qu'*il n'y a pas d'heure, *c'est* rester au lit jusqu'à midi et les longues soirées passées dehors sur la terrasse.**
> What I love when I'm on holiday is the sun, the fact that you don't have to watch the clock, you can stay in bed till lunchtime and spend long evenings out on the terrace.

Other introductory verbs may be used, such as **éprouver, trouver** + noun + **à** + infinitive, and **être** + adjective or noun + **de**, with no definite article:

> **J'*éprouve du plaisir à me promener* seule en forêt.**
> I enjoy walking alone in the forest.

> **Il *trouve de la satisfaction à écouter* de la musique.**
> He enjoys listening to music.

> **Les enfants *sont friands de* bonbons.**
> The children love sweets.

Il *est amateur de* jazz.
He's a jazz enthusiast.

58.2   **Preference**

To express preference there are a number of verbs and verb phrases available, including
préférer x **à** y 'to prefer x to y':

Je *préfère* le vin rouge *au* vin blanc.
I prefer red wine to white wine.

and the construction **préférer** + infinitive + **plutôt que** + infinitive:

Nous *préférons sortir* tous les deux *plutôt que* rencontrer des tas de
gens.
We prefer to go out just the two of us rather than meeting crowds of
people.

Preference can of course be expressed in an elliptical way, for example in a dialogue:

Tu aimes l'écharpe jaune? Non, *plutôt* la verte.
You like the yellow scarf? No, (I prefer) the green one.

Avoir + noun expressing preference + **pour** is an alternative:

J'aime certains morceaux modernes mais j'*ai une prédilection pour* la
musique classique.
I like some modern pieces but I prefer classical music.

Si ça ne vous ennuie pas, nous *avons une préférence pour* le samedi
plutôt que le vendredi.
If it doesn't bother you, we prefer Saturday rather than Friday.

Impersonal forms are also used: **il vaut mieux que** + subjunctive 'it would be better to
. . .' (see **39.2.1**), **il paraît/est préférable de** + infinitive 'it seems/is preferable to . . .':

Il me *paraît préférable de garder* l'ancien système, le nouveau est trop
compliqué.
It seems to me to be preferable to keep the old system, the new one is too
complicated.

Il *vaudrait mieux que* ce *soit* vendredi soir puisque nous ne
travaillons pas le lendemain.
It would be better for it to be Friday evening because we don't work the
day after.

Note the use of the conditional tense in the previous example. This is quite frequent for
expressing preference politely: verb (in the conditional) + **que** + subjunctive (see **39.2.1**):

J' *aimerais mieux que tu viennes* me chercher à la gare, ça m'évitera
de prendre un taxi.
I'd prefer it if you came to get me at the station, then I won't have to take
a taxi.

Sa mère *préférerait qu'il aille* la voir plus de deux fois par an.
His mother would prefer it if he went to see her more than twice a year.

or **cela/ce** + verb (in the conditional) + **mieux**:

> **A neuf heures?** *Cela* m'*arrangerait mieux* à huit heures.
> Nine o'clock? It would suit me better at eight.

or a noun phrase + verb (in the conditional):

> **Dix-huit heures me** *conviendrait* **mieux/davantage.**
> Six o'clock would suit me better.

59 Love and hate

In order to reinforce expressions of liking and disliking, you can use adverbs:

> **J'aime** *énormément* **la cuisine chinoise, et vous?**
> I love Chinese food, do you?

> *Ah non, moi pas du tout!*
> Oh no, I don't like it at all!

> **Il éprouve** *beaucoup de plaisir* **à se moquer des autres.**
> He loves making fun of other people.

> **La robe qu'elle a choisie** *ne* **me plaît** *pas du tout*.
> I don't like the dress she has chosen at all.

> **Ce que j'aime** *plus que tout*, **c'est avoir le temps de lire un bon roman policier.**
> What I like more than anything is having the time to read a good thriller.

or adjectives:

> **On dirait qu'il trouve un** *plaisir intense* **à créer des conflits.**
> You would think he gets immense pleasure from creating trouble.

> **Je** *n'*éprouve *aucune satisfaction* **à effectuer des tâches répétitives.**
> I get no pleasure from doing repetitive tasks.

Naturally, there are specific verbs expressing love and hate such as **adorer, détester**:

> **J'***adore* **le chocolat blanc mais je** *déteste* **le noir.**
> I love white chocolate but I hate dark chocolate.

> **Elle le** *haïssait* **autant qu'il l'***adorait*.
> She hated him as much as he adored her. (**le, il** and **l'** are ambiguous)

These verbs may also be followed directly by infinitives (see **45.2**):

> **Il** *adore se promener* **sous la pluie.**
> He loves walking in the rain.

> **Je** *déteste voir* **souffrir des enfants.**
> I hate seeing children suffer.

These and other verbs may also be followed by **que** + subjunctive (see **39.2.1**):

> **Brigitte Bardot ne** *supporte* **pas** *que* **l'on** *fasse* **du mal aux animaux.**
> Brigitte Bardot cannot tolerate people hurting animals.

Rien as the subject is an alternative for expressing love and hate (see **47.8**):

> **Pour moi, *rien ne vaut* une soirée entre amis au coin du feu.**
> For me there's nothing better than an evening by the fire among friends.

> **Tu sais bien que pour lui, *rien n'est pire que* le mensonge.**
> You know very well that for him nothing is worse than telling lies.

60   Enthusiasm and indifference

Some of the expressions used for like/love may, of course, be used to express enthusiasm. In addition to these, spontaneous enthusiasm can be expressed, in particular when speaking, with short phrases such as:

> **Super!**   Super!
> **Excellente idée!**   An excellent idea!

or **c'est** + adjective or noun:

> ***C'est génial* comme idée!**
> It's a brilliant idea!

> ***C'est une excellente suggestion*!**
> It's an excellent suggestion!

In more formal contexts, you can use reflexive verbs such as **s'enthousiasmer pour** 'to be enthusiastic about':

> **Il *s'est* immédiatement *enthousiasmé pour* ce projet.**
> He was immediately enthusiastic about the project.

> **Au cours des prochains mois, je vais *me donner à fond* dans la rédaction de ce manuscrit.**
> Over the next few months I'm going to devote myself to writing/drafting this manuscript.

or passive forms such as **être enthousiasmé par** + noun, **être ravi de** + infinitive:

> ***Nous sommes enthousiasmés par la perspective* de travailler avec vous.**
> We are delighted at the prospect of working with you.

> ***Je serais ravie de prendre* mes fonctions dès que possible.**
> I would be delighted to take up my post as soon as possible.

A number of short phrases are also available for expressing indifference:

> **Bof!**   Not so hot!
> **Comme tu veux!**   If you like!
> **Ça m'est égal!**   I don't care!
> **Peu importe.**   Doesn't matter!

and phrases introduced by ça, cela, c'est (see **6.3a**, **6.3c–d**):

> ***Ça* n'a pas vraiment d'importance.**
> It really isn't very important.

> *Cela* ne change rien.
> That doesn't make any difference.

> *C'est* comme tu veux.
> As you wish.

and when you want to place emphasis on your own indifference, stating that you really don't mind:

> *Je* n'ai aucune préférence. *Toi*, tu décides. (see **14.2d**)
> I don't mind. *You* can decide.

61 Hopes, fears and regrets

There are many ways of expressing hopes, fears and regrets. You can express hope using verbs such as **souhaiter** + infinitive 'to wish', **compter bien** + infinitive 'to count on doing something', **espérer** + infinitive 'to hope' or + **que** 'to hope that':

> Il *souhaite* nous *rejoindre* en Italie.
> He wants to meet/join us in Italy.

> Je *compte bien* ne pas *avoir* à attendre la retraite pour profiter de la vie.
> I'm counting on not having to wait for retirement in order to enjoy life.

> Le secrétaire général du parti *espère que* les adhérents sauront se mobiliser pour les prochaines élections.
> The Secretary General of the party hopes that members will be able to mobilize themselves for the next election.

or verb + noun:

> Nous te *souhaitons beaucoup de bonheur et de succès.*
> We wish you every happiness and success.

Emphatic forms such as **ce que/ce qui . . . c'est que** are also available:

> *Ce que* j'espère plus que tout, *c'est que* nous pourrons nous revoir bientôt.
> What I hope more than anything is that we can see each other again soon.

Verbs such as **vouloir** – with its various constructions – may be used. Note the nuances in the present tense, which is used to express a strong hope, and note the use of **que** + subjunctive when the subjects of the two clauses are different (see **39.5**):

> Avant tout, *je veux que tu sois* heureux dans la vie.
> More than anything I want you to be happy (in your life).

> Toi, tu *voudrais* la lune!
> You'd ask for the moon.

Alternatively, you can use an expression such as **si seulement je** + imperfect:

> *Si seulement je pouvais* un jour faire ce grand voyage . . .
> If only I could make this great journey one day . . .

The same phrase may also be used to express regrets:

> *Si seulement* j'avais suivi tes conseils, je n'en serais pas là aujourd'hui.
> I wish I had followed your advice. I would not be in such trouble today.

The conditional perfect tense, of course, reinforced by adverbs, may also be used to express regret:

> *J'aurais* tellement *voulu* me joindre à vous. Malheureusement, je ne peux pas.
> I wish I was (were) in a position to join you. Unfortunately, I can't.

Fears in various contexts can be expressed with short phrases or interjections, such as **Ah!** 'Ah!', **Oh non!** 'Oh no!', **Au secours!** 'Help!', **Mon Dieu!** 'My God!'. There are also verb phrases such as **avoir peur** + **de** + noun *or* infinitive, or + **que** + subjunctive, **craindre que** + **ne** + subjunctive 'to fear' (see **39.2.1**):

> Maman, j'*ai peur du* loup dans ma chambre.
> Mum, I'm frightened of the wolf in my room.

> Avec ce qui s'est passé ici, nous *avons très peur de laisser* sortir nos enfants.
> After what's happened here, we are very frightened to allow our children out.

> Elle *craint que* les intrus qui ont forcé sa porte *ne reviennent*.
> She is afraid the intruders who broke open her/his door may come back.

Expressions such as **pourvu que** + subjunctive or **espérons que** + subjunctive may express both hopes and fears:

> *Pourvu qu'il* n'*aille* pas le répéter à tout le monde!
> Let's hope he doesn't repeat it to everybody!

> *Espérons que* le temps *se mette* au beau d'ici samedi!
> Let's hope the weather has turned better by Saturday.

62 Approval and disapproval

You can express approval or disapproval of something or someone with verbs: **approuver** 'to approve of', **désapprouver** 'to disapprove of'. Note that the French verbs are directly transitive, whereas the English verbs have an indirect object:

> J'ai décidé de me mettre en disponibilité pendant un an et mes collègues m'*approuvent*.
> I've decided to take leave of absence for a year and my colleagues are in agreement.

> Vos professeurs *désapprouvent* votre comportement.
> Your teachers disapprove of your behaviour.

or the passive form can be used (see **41**):

> La décision *a été approuvée* par tous.
> The decision has been approved by everyone.

Alternatively, **être** + adjective *or* past participle + **à** may be used:

> Le directeur *est favorable au* redéploiement des ressources que vous avez suggéré.
> The manager is in agreement with the redeployment of resources that you have suggested.

> Ton père et moi *sommes* entièrement *opposés à* ce mariage.
> Your father and I are entirely opposed to this marriage.

Avoir features in a number of verb phrases which may be used, such as **avoir bien fait de** + infinitive 'to have done well to, done the right thing to', **avoir raison de** + infinitive 'to be right', **avoir tort de** + infinitive 'to be wrong':

> Vous *avez bien fait de* m'*envoyer* les documents avant de venir me voir.
> You were right to send me the documents before coming to see me.

> Il *a raison de* ne pas *se laisser faire*!
> He's right not to let himself be pushed around.

> A mon avis, tu *aurais tort de* le *quitter* pour ça.
> In my opinion, you would be wrong to leave him/it for that.

NOTE | Expressing approval or disapproval is often an opportunity to give an opinion (**à mon avis** in the previous example) and is related to agreeing and disagreeing (see **63.1c**).

You can also use adverbial expressions introduced by prepositions such as **à**, **avec**:

> Vous vous êtes plaint *à juste titre* auprès de vos supérieurs.
> You were right to complain to your superiors.

> Il a évité *avec raison* de parler de ses précédents accidents de voiture.
> He was right not to speak about his previous car accidents.

and there is a variety of other ways of expressing approval and disapproval:

> Tu pars en vacances? *Très bien*, il *était grand temps que* tu penses un peu à toi!
> You're going on holiday? Excellent. It's time you thought about yourself a bit.

> *Enfin* quelqu'un de compétent qui sait de quoi il parle!
> At last someone competent who knows what he's talking about.

> Je *n'aime pas la façon dont* vous organisez ces réunions.
> I don't like the way in which you organize these meetings.

> Je *ne comprends pas comment* il a pu faire une chose pareille!
> I don't understand how he could do such a thing.

> *Cela* me *déplaît que* tu traînes dehors jusqu'à des heures impossibles.
> I don't like you hanging around outside till all hours.

V
Argumentation

63 Agreeing and disagreeing

63.1 Agreeing

(a) There are many different ways of indicating that you agree with somebody or something. Here are some ways of saying that you agree totally with a statement:

Bien sûr!	**Oui, c'est ça!**
C'est sûr!	**Absolument!**
Exactement!	**Tout à fait!**
Vous avez (*or* tu as) raison!	**C'est vrai!**

The following examples were used in an exchange in the French National Assembly (5.4.94), but they could equally have occurred in informal conversation:

M. M. BERSON	**Ce sont bien les députés [. . .] qui ont refusé tous les amendements que nous avions déposés [. . .]**
M. J-P. BRARD	***Oui!***
M. M. BERSON	**[. . .] En un an, le gouvernement a commis beaucoup d'erreurs.**
M. J. DRAY	***C'est vrai!***
M. M. BERSON	But it was the deputies (in the National Assembly) who rejected all the amendments we'd proposed . . .
M. J-P. BRARD	Yes.
M. M. BERSON	In one year the government has made many mistakes.
M. J. DRAY	That's right.

Frequently, the forms are combined:

> **Oui, d'accord.**
> **Voilà, exactement.**
> **T'as raison, c'est ça.** (informal)

(b) If you want to be a little more formal when you are talking, once again you have a choice of expressions, which are equally appropriate in writing. In response to a statement or suggestion such as:

> **Elle croit que les aiguilleurs du ciel accepteront les nouvelles conditions d'emploi.**
> She thinks the air traffic controllers will accept the new conditions of work.

you can say or write:

> Je *suis entièrement d'accord* avec elle *sur* ce point/ce qu'elle vient de dire.
> I agree with her totally about that/with what she has just said.

and responding with a question to the same statement:

> Les syndicats *seront-ils*, cette fois, *d'accord* avec le gouvernement?
> Will the unions agree with the government this time?

(c) Here are some other ways of agreeing with a statement or suggestion. Remember: you need to know not just the verbs and verb phrases, but also the constructions that follow them.

Elle *partage notre avis sur* qch	She shares our opinion on . . .
Vous *avez raison de* + infinitive	You are right to . . .
Nous *convenons que* + indicative	We agree that . . .
Je *suis d'avis que* + indicative	I think that . . .
Elle *le soutient sur* qch	She supports him on . . .
Il *a exprimé son soutien à* qn	He has expressed his support for . . .
Nous *avons accepté* qch	We have accepted . . .
Ils *ont donné leur accord à* qch	They agree that . . .

(d) Note the following example in which the speaker expresses an opinion with **je suis d'avis que**, but it becomes agreement because of the addition of **comme vous**.

> *Comme vous, je suis d'avis qu'*il faut signer la Charte sociale européenne.
> I agree we must sign the Social Charter.

(e) Sometimes, to distance themselves from what someone says, the French use an impersonal phrase (see **46**).

> *Il est juste de* dénoncer les injustices du monde moderne.
> It is right to condemn the injustices of the modern world.

> *Il est vrai que* le monde moderne est plein d'injustices.
> It is true that today's world is full of injustices.

(f) Agreeing to do something:

> Les syndicats *accepteront d'*intervenir cette fois.
> The unions will agree to intervene this time.

63.2 Disagreeing

(a) Spontaneous and total disagreement with a statement can be expressed (as in agreement) through the use of an exclamation such as:

(Mais) non!	C'est faux!
Absolument pas!	Certainement pas!

Various nuances are conveyed in what follows the exclamation, for example there is a clear protest in:

Mais non, je n'ai jamais dit ça!
No! I never said that!

(b) When full disagreement with a proposal is expressed, a number of idiomatic expressions can be used:

Statement: **Il faut supprimer toutes les prestations sociales.**
We must end social security benefits.

Responses: **Certainement pas!**
Certainly not!
C'est hors de question!
Out of the question.
Vous plaisantez!
You must be joking!

(c) For disagreement followed by a statement of what is disagreed with, the verbs and verb phrases previously identified in 63.1 can simply be made negative:

Pourquoi *n'êtes-vous pas d'accord* avec moi *sur ce point*?
Why don't you agree with me about this?

Quant à ce nouveau projet de loi, il est évident que l'opposition *ne partage pas l'opinion* du gouvernement.
As far as the new bill is concerned, it is clear that the opposition does not share the government's views.

Positive expressions can also be used, for example verb + noun:

Prenez l'habitude de *contester* systématiquement *mon analyse* et vous développerez votre esprit critique. (see 25.3, 44.2)
Get into the habit of automatically disagreeing with my analysis and you will develop your critical faculties.

(d) In order to state clearly what is being disagreed with, it is often necessary to refer back to or repeat a statement or proposal:

Je *diffère* de M. Lambert *qui*, lui, *estime que* nous devrions ajourner cette réunion. (see 15.1)
I do not agree with M. Lambert who thinks that we should adjourn the meeting.

Le public *n'accepte pas l'idée selon laquelle* il faut de plus en plus avoir recours à des services privés. (see 15.5)
The public does not accept that we will have to move increasingly towards private sector services.

Le dernier orateur *a réfuté tout ce qui avait été dit* avant lui.
(see 15.11.1, 31)
The last speaker rejected everything that had been said.

(e) You can also refer back to the person/organization that has made the statement or proposal (see 67f):

Contrairement à M. Pasqua, je ne crois pas qu'il soit nécessaire ou même souhaitable d'emprisonner tous les jeunes délinquants.
Contrary to the view of M. Pasqua I do not believe it is necessary or even desirable to put every young offender in prison.

A la différence des autres pays européens , le Royaume-Uni *a rejeté* la
Charte sociale.
Unlike other countries in Europe the UK has rejected the Social
Charter.

(f) Disagreement can also be expressed using a noun (as subject of the verb) or an
impersonal form + infinitive:

● disagreement with a statement

> Vos *explications sont dépourvues de toute vraisemblance* et ne peuvent
> pas être retenues par le Conseil de discipline. (see **41**)
> Your explanations are quite improbable and cannot be accepted by the
> disciplinary board.

> *A mon avis, il est inadmissible de s'adresser en ces termes* à un
> professeur. (see **46**)
> In my opinion, it is unacceptable to talk in such a way to a teacher.

(In the previous example, note the use of **à mon avis** to reinforce the expression of
disagreement as a personal opinion.)

● disagreement with a proposal

> Pour l'instant, *il n'est pas envisageable de satisfaire* les
> consommateurs en ouvrant les supermarchés le dimanche. (see **46**)
> For the time being we simply cannot consider keeping customers happy
> by opening supermarkets on Sundays.

> *La décision de fermer* indéfiniment les locaux scolaires après
> l'apparition de quelques cas de méningite *paraît inacceptable.*
> (see **45.6**)
> The decision to close the schools indefinitely following the outbreak of
> meningitis seems unacceptable.

And note the following example taken from a debate in the European Parliament in
which members object to the views of JM. Le Pen:

> [. . .] C'est pourquoi, Monsieur le Président, Mesdames et
> Messieurs, je serai contre cette proposition, en soulignant
> qu'encore une fois elle est établie par un consensus sournois qui
> ne s'est exprimé par aucun courrier. Nous n'avons pas été invités
> à faire partie de . . . (Exclamation: *Ce n'est pas vrai!*) . . . c'est
> absolument vrai, je suis le président de ce groupe, j'ai tout ignoré
> de cette initiative.
>
> > (*Journal Officiel des Communautés Européennes*:
> > Débat du Parlement européen – Séance du 15.2.90)
>
> That's why, Mr Chairman, Ladies and Gentlemen, I will vote against
> the proposal, and I stress that once again a decision was taken
> behind my back and it was not put in writing. We were not asked to
> participate . . . (That is not true!) . . . it is absolutely true, I am the
> chairman of the group and I knew nothing about what was going
> on. (see **63.1**)

(g) Note the following range of negative responses – from informal spoken to formal written examples:

Situation:	**Une marchandise défectueuse vous a été livrée. Vous demandez réparation aux frais de la Société. La secrétaire vous annonce au téléphone que vous devez participer aux frais.**
	Faulty goods have been delivered to you. You ask for compensation from the company. The secretary telephones to say you must contribute.
Responses:	*Certainement pas! Vous plaisantez ou quoi?* **Passez-moi le directeur.** (spoken, informal)
	Certainly not! Are you joking? Put me on to the manager.
	Je ne suis pas d'accord pour payer **alors que je n'en suis pas responsable.** (spoken/written, informal/formal)
	I cannot agree to pay since I am not responsible (for this).
	Ecoutez, *je regrette mais je ne peux pas accepter* **étant donné que** . . . (spoken, formal) (see **42.1**)
	Look, I regret that I cannot agree because . . .
	La proposition de la direction selon laquelle je devrais assumer une partie des frais *ne peut être retenue* . . . (written, formal) (see **47.9**)
	The management's suggestion that I should meet part of the cost is unacceptable . . .

63.3 Agreeing to differ

When both sides of an argument have been expressed and no compromise reached, the participants might simply agree to differ before breaking off. Statements of agreement to differ often use personal pronouns, sometimes combined with idiomatic expressions such as **rester sur ses positions** or **avoir des idées bien arrêtées/des points de vue divergents**:

> **Chacun de nous** *reste sur ses positions*: **vous avez votre opinion, moi la mienne.** (see **8.1, 14.2**)
> We are each sure/convinced we are right: you have your views and I have mine.
>
> **Soit,** *vous,* **vous prenez à gauche,** *nous* **à droite et nous verrons bien quelle équipe arrivera en premier au sommet.** (see **14.2**)
> Right. You go on the left. We'll go on the right and we'll see which team gets to the top first.

In the second example, note how the second **nous** is different from the first one in that it includes everyone: **vous + nous** representing the two teams.

64

Asserting and confirming

64.1

Asserting

(a) There are many direct ways for someone to assert something in speech. When people wish to declare/state/assert something, they simply utter whatever it is they want to declare/state/assert. Occasionally, however, the function is made more explicit in the utterance itself, as in the following examples:

> **En tant que président de l'association, je *déclare* la conférence ouverte.**
> As President/Chairman of the Association, I declare the conference open.

> **Vous devrez *certifier sur l'honneur* l'exactitude des informations contenues dans ce document.**
> You must swear on your honour that the information contained in the document is accurate.

> **Les condamnés qui ont enfin été libérés *proclamaient* leur innocence depuis de nombreuses années.** (see **26.1.1**)
> The men who have finally been released had been proclaiming their innocence for many years.

(b) The previous examples involve the structure verb + noun and all of them contain a statement of an official nature. The passive form of the verb, or the structure noun + past participle can also be used in such a context:

> **Le discours sur le rôle des femmes dans la société *sera-t-il prononcé par* le Ministre de la condition féminine?** (see **41**)
> Will the speech on the role of women in society be given by the Minister for Women's Affairs?

> **Les journaux ne parlent que des *déclarations faites* hier, lors de la conférence de presse à Paris.** (see **42.1**)
> The papers are full of the declaration/statements made yesterday at the press conference in Paris.

(c) In a detailed report of an exchange, such as the following example from a police report, statements are introduced by a colon and transcribed between inverted commas:

> **14h35 – Le suspect déclare: 'J'ai passé la soirée du 2 novembre au cinéma.'**
> 14.35 The suspect stated: I spent the evening of the 2nd of November at the cinema.

Remember that the rules governing indirect speech (see **51**) have to be taken into account in other instances:

> **Le suspect *déclare avoir passé* la soirée au cinéma.**
> The suspect stated he had spent the evening at the cinema.

An example of minutes taken at a meeting:

> **Le comptable *a affirmé que* la situation financière de la société était satisfaisante.**
> The accountant confirmed that the financial situation of the company was satisfactory.

(d) In speech, it is not unusual to state your intention to make an assertion:

> **Laissez-moi parler, je *voudrais dire* quelque chose.** (see **33.1.3**)
> Allow me to speak, I want to say something.

> **Si vous le permettez et au nom de tous mes collègues, je *dirai* ceci:**
> If you will allow me, and on behalf of all my colleagues, I will say this . . .

64.2   Confirming

Usually, an arrangement, or a statement, is made and then confirmed.

(a) Confirmation of an arrangement:

> **A la suite de notre conversation téléphonique du 3.10.2003, *veuillez confirmer* ma réservation par retour du courrier.**
> Further to our telephone conversation of 3.10.2003, please confirm my reservation by return.

> **Il devrait être arrivé maintenant, il *a bien pris* le train à 8h00 comme prévu.**
> He should have arrived now. He *did* take the 8 o'clock train as planned.

(b) Confirmation of a statement:

> **Depuis notre bulletin de la matinée, les autorités maritimes *ont attesté* la présence de 950 personnes à bord du ferry au moment de l'accident.**
> Since our morning bulletin/announcement, the maritime authorities have confirmed that 950 people were on board the ferry at the time of the accident.

> **Mesdames et messieurs les jurés, notez bien que selon le témoignage de son épouse, l'accusé se trouvait en effet à son domicile ce soir-là, et que les voisins *confirment* également ses déclarations quant aux déplacements de la journée.**
> Ladies and gentlemen of the jury, please note that according to the evidence of his wife, the accused was in fact at home that night, and the neighbours also confirm his statement concerning his movements during the day.

(c) So, in fact, assertion often precedes confirmation, and confirmation can be achieved through the use of verbs such as **corroborer, confirmer, vérifier, attester** and through the use of adverbs such as **bien, en effet, effectivement**. Confirmation can be implied when specific 'negative' verbs are used with negative adverbs, as in **ne pas démentir, ne pas nier**:

> **Interrogé lors d'une conférence de presse tenue ce matin, l'athlète français *n'a pas démenti* les allégations faites contre lui dans les journaux sportifs.**
> Questioned at a press conference this morning, the French athlete did not deny the allegations made against him in the sports papers.

(d) A statement can also be confirmed through repetition, as in the following exchange:

> **On peut vous joindre à quel numéro? Au 447 2239 poste 357.**
> **Je répète: *447 2239 poste 357.***
> We can contact you at what number? 447 2239 Ext. 357. I'll repeat that: 447 2239 Ext. 357.

65   Admitting and conceding

65.1   Admitting

Admission is a mild form of agreement in the sense that it is assumed, despite initial reluctance, that a person has come round to the opinions of his/her interlocutor upon reflection. For example, one might say **c'est vrai, certain, exact, évident, incontestable,** but the intonation will be different from that of similar expressions listed in 63.1a and 63.1b: when you are admitting something a note of doubt will probably be added to the words.

(a) In most cases, admission is explicitly recognized through using one of the following verbs: (**en**) **convenir, reconnaître, admettre** . . .

> **Vous avez raison, j'*en conviens.***
> You are right, I (have to) admit/agree.

(b) So, a person may admit or agree to a statement or an idea in a discussion.

The same verbs can be used to admit mistakes or failures:

> **Il est temps que la communauté internationale *reconnaisse ses erreurs* en matière de protection de l'environnement.**
> It is high time (that) the international community admitted its errors concerning the protection of the environment.

> **La directrice de l'établissement devra *admettre*, devant le Conseil de parents d'élèves, *que* cet interne a été accusé à tort.**
> The headmistress will have to admit to the Parents' Association that the accusations made against the boarder were wrong.

65.2   Conceding

(a) Within the framework of argumentation, admitting is in fact often conceding, that is, agreeing in part with the interlocutor's point of view in order to disagree afterwards –

in other words going some of his/her way before taking a different path. A concession, therefore, can be identified in relation to what follows, and the general structure involved has three distinct stages:

1   The *concession* itself, which can be introduced by a verbal form such as **je dois l'admettre, si vous voulez, je vous concède ce point, je vous accorde que** 'I have to admit, if you like, I'll accept that point, I agree with you that', by an adverb such as **certes, en effet, effectivement, soit** 'that's true, yes indeed', by an impersonal form such as **il est vrai/exact/certain que** 'it is true that'.

2   The *transition* through a cohesive device marking opposition (see **73d**): **mais, n'empêche que, cependant, reconnaissez-le, cela dit, il n'en reste pas moins vrai que, en revanche, vous concéderez bien que, admettez tout de même que** 'but, nevertheless, yet, you must admit that, having said that, it is nonetheless true that, on the other hand, you will admit that, you have to admit nevertheless that'.

3   The *disagreement*, that is, the expression of a different point of view (see **63.2c, 63.2d**) which is, of course, open to concession on the part of the interlocutor.

(b) Concession is important in a debating or negotiating situation, in order to have civilized exchanges and to send the ball back into the interlocutor's court. Note the three stages in the following examples:

> *Je reconnais qu'* il y a beaucoup de circulation à cette heure-ci, *mais tout de même*, cela fait une semaine que vous arrivez en retard tous les matins, *ça ne peut plus durer.*
> I admit that there is heavy traffic at this time of day, but (nevertheless) you have been late every morning this week. That/This can't go on.

> *Certes*, il y a des cas d'utilisateurs de drogues dures qui sont aussi consommateurs de drogues douces. *Cela dit, reconnaissez-le*, on *n'a jamais prouvé que* l'usage de cannabis conduisait automatiquement à l'usage d'héroïne.
> Certainly, there are people who use both soft and hard drugs. Having said this, you must admit that it has never been proved that the use of cannabis automatically led to the use of heroin.

> **En effet,** *nous admettons tous que* la livraison correspondant au bon n° 235B a été effectuée avec trois jours de retard. *En revanche*, les marchandises étaient en parfait état au moment de l'expédition et par conséquent *nous ne pouvons vous verser* qu'une partie du montant exigé en dommages et intérêts.
> We admit that the delivery of order No. 235B was in fact three days late. However, the goods were in perfect condition when they were despatched. We will/can therefore pay only part of the amount you are seeking.

Correcting and protesting

These functions are used when the speaker wants to correct a statement previously made by himself/herself or by previous speakers – perhaps because of accuracy. It is also used in relation to texts or documents which require to be amended.

(a) If a speaker realizes that incorrect information has been conveyed, then apologies are often in order (see **56.1**):

> Attendez, *excusez-moi, je reprends. Ce que je voulais dire*, c'est qu'il y a 3 millions de chômeurs inscrits mais 5 millions de sans-emploi d'après les estimations.
> Wait a moment, I'm sorry, I'll start again. What I meant was that there are 3 million registered unemployed but 5 million out of work according to estimates. (and not the contrary as previously stated, for example)

(b) There is a tendency, when we are correcting, to deny the wrong statement or definition first, and then introduce the corrected one. This involves negative structures + **mais**. The following example is a kind of protest, in a case of misunderstanding:

> Attention, vous m'avez mal comprise, *je n'ai pas dit qu*'il ne fallait pas accorder de congés de paternité *mais que* l'on ne pouvait pas se le permettre pour le moment.
> Careful, you have misunderstood me. I did not say that paternity leave should not be granted, but that it could not be afforded for the time being.

Note how the conjunction **que** has to be repeated after **mais** to introduce the second clause. The next example involves clarification of a definition:

> Je ne sais pas si j'ai été très clair, quand je dis Europe, *j'entends non pas* la CE (Communauté européenne) *mais* la grande Europe, y compris toutes les nouvelles nations existant aujourd'hui.
> I don't know if I've made myself very clear. When I say Europe I don't mean the EC (European Community) but a wider Europe including all the new (emerging) countries/nations.

(c) In most cases, the speaker will announce his/her intention to rephrase or to clarify a statement that he/she has made by using one or a combination of the following expressions:

> **Permettez-moi d'apporter une précision:**
> Allow me to add a point:

> **Ce que je voulais dire, c'est ceci:**
> What I meant was this:

> **Je devrais peut-être m'exprimer autrement:**
> Perhaps I should express myself differently:

> **Je m'explique:**
> Let me explain:

> **En d'autres termes, . . . :**
> In other words, . . . :

(d) Many corrective statements are introduced by **j'aurais dû** + infinitive (see **33.1**):

> **En évoquant les problèmes de la femme, *j'aurais dû* préciser que je voulais parler de la femme active.** (see **43.1**)
> When I raised the problems of women, I should have made it clear that I was referring to working women.

(e) Similar expressions can of course be used when correcting someone else. In this case, there may first be an expression of disbelief or disagreement such as **vraiment?** 'really?', **d'après mes renseignements** 'as far as I am aware', **ce n'est pas le cas** 'that's not the case', followed by a negative structure + **mais**:

> ***Non*, vous *faites erreur; en réalité*, l'inflation *n'a pas atteint* 3% *mais* 2% cette année-là.**
> No, you're wrong. Inflation did not, in fact, reach 3% but 2% that year.

(f) Sometimes, you may wish to correct other people, not because you think that they are totally wrong but because you want to go further, and build on what they have said. You will be correcting very directly if you use an imperative form, such as **précisons** 'to be specific/let's be specific' or **disons plutôt que** 'or rather', or **je** + verb in the conditional as in **j'irais même plus loin/jusqu'à dire que** 'I would go further/as far as to say', and much less direct, of course, if you use an impersonal form or **on**:

> ***On pourrait même aller plus loin et préciser que* cela s'applique aussi à tous les autres pays du monde.**
> One could go even further and say that this/that is also true of all other countries.

(g) In previous examples, the object of the correction was refuted first and then corrected or replaced through using structures such as **non pas . . . mais**. In the following example, the object is not refuted but included and extended with **non seulement . . . mais aussi**:

> **J'ajouterais que ce phénomène existe *non seulement* en France *mais également* dans toute l'Europe.**
> I would add that this phenomenon exists not only in France but also in the rest of/throughout Europe.

(h) There are many instances of documents or texts being corrected with addenda, amendments or simply because successive versions undergo a revision process. When dealing with written documents such as statutes or laws, absolute accuracy and attention to detail are essential. The following examples are drawn from debates on Articles at the French National Assembly:

> **Par l'amendement n° 2, je propose de *rédiger* l'article 1er de la façon suivante:**
> In Amendment No. 2, I propose that Article 1 should read as follows:

> **Vous nous proposez, quant à vous, *la rédaction* suivante à l'article 2:**
> You propose the following wording in Article 2:

(i) Amendments have to be submitted in writing by MPs and usually involve infinitives:

> **M. Béteille, rapporteur, a présenté *un amendement*, n° 3, *rédigé* comme suit: '*supprimer* les sept premiers alinéas de l'article 2'.**
> M. Béteille, the rapporteur, has tabled an amendment, No. 3, which reads as follows: delete the first seven paragraphs of Article 2.

> **Après l'article 3, *insérer* l'article suivant:**
> After Article 3, insert the following Article:

These are examples of correction where something is taken out of or added to the initial document. When the existing text is *modified*, then both the original and the new proposed texts have to be inserted in inverted commas:

> **. . . il convient de lire: 'l'Institut d'Alsace-Moselle' et *non* 'd'Alsace'.**
> . . . for 'Alsace', read 'the Alsace-Moselle Institute'.

> **Dans le premier alinéa de l'article 2, *substituer* aux mots: 'les enfants à charge', les mots: 'les enfants nés des différentes unions'.**
> In the 1st paragraph of Article 2 replace 'dependent children' with 'children of different relationships'.

(j) The following expressions are also possible:

> ***Remplacer* X *par* Y.**
> For X substitute Y.

> ***Lire* Y *à la place/au lieu de* X.**
> For X read Y.

67   Contradicting and criticizing

Contradicting someone or contradicting a statement is adopting the opposite view. In that sense, it is like an extreme form of disagreement and is the opposite of confirming.

(a) The simplest and most direct expression of contradiction is **non** as a reply to a positive statement and **si** to a negative statement – here reinforced by **au contraire**:

> **Tu n'as pas le choix! – Mais *si, au contraire.* (see 47.7.2)**
> You have no choice! – But I do!

(b) In argumentation, for example in a debate or discussion, you can contradict by telling your interlocutor directly that his/her views are wrong:

> **Vous vous trompez. *or* Vous êtes dans l'erreur.**
> You're wrong/mistaken.

> **Vos arguments sont inadmissibles.**
> Your arguments are unacceptable.

(c) Alternatively, you can use **je** with various verbal forms which state that you are contradicting something. You can make it clearly and firmly your own personal conviction:

> ***Je rejette catégoriquement* ces arguments fallacieux.**
> I categorically reject these unfounded/fallacious arguments.

> *Je m'élève tout particulièrement contre* la dernière théorie avancée.
> I am particularly opposed to the last theory that was put forward.

In the previous two examples, note how adverbs can play an important role in contradiction.

(d) You can also use impersonal forms beginning with **il** or **ce**, to refer to the statement you want to contradict, as in the following example (see **12.2c**, **12.2d**):

> **Vous prétendez que la pauvreté a disparu en France,** *or il* **n'en est** *rien/mais c'est tout à fait faux.*
> You claim that poverty has been eradicated in France, but that is utterly wrong.

Note how the opposition (see **73d**) is introduced by cohesive devices **or** 'now' and **mais**, and also how **rien** and **tout à fait** contribute to the categorical nature of the opposition in this function. This is also true of **aucun** and **tout** in the following examples:

> *Rien n'est* **moins sûr!** (see **47.8**)
> Nothing could be further from the truth!

> **La réalité est** *tout* **autre!** (see **11.1c**)
> That is quite untrue!

> **Il** *n'y* **a** *aucune* **raison de le croire!** (see **47.8**)
> There is absolutely no reason to believe it!

(e) Having made it clear that you totally disagree with your interlocutor, you would then probably go on to explain/prove the contrary. When you state your intention to do this, imperative forms or **je vais** + infinitive are useful:

> *Laissez-moi* **vous** *démontrer* **le contraire.** (see **44.2**)
> Let me demonstrate the opposite.

> **Je** *vais* **vous le** *prouver.* (see **25.3.2**)
> I shall prove it to you.

(f) In order to emphasize the opposition, you might start the sentence with a clause introduced by **contrairement à** 'contrary to', **à la différence de** 'unlike' . . . (see **63.2e**):

> *Contrairement à* **ce que vous insinuez, je n'ai pas triché.** (see **15.11**)
> Contrary to what you are suggesting/implying, I did not cheat.

(g) In exposition, when denial is expressed, the verb **démentir** 'to deny' and its related forms can be used:

> **La famille royale** *a* **formellement** *démenti* **la rumeur selon laquelle la reine était sur le point d'abdiquer.** (see **15.5**)
> The royal family has formally denied the rumour that the queen was about to abdicate.

> **Le témoignage de l'automobiliste reste** *sans démenti.*
> The driver's evidence remains unchallenged.

68 **Suggesting and persuading**

Suggesting is used to recommend a particular course of action or line of thought to someone else. Therefore, it is perhaps similar to a first or mild stage of persuasion. It is used to recommend that someone does, or does not, do something. You may also want to influence other people, so that they come round to your idea/belief or so that they follow the right course of action and/or reject the wrong one. Examples of context where there *is* an attempt to influence people so that they believe, think or do something are legal pleas, evangelistic activities or debates. In such instances, one often attempts to persuade through the presentation of valid arguments. This is achieved in many different ways – and with many different grammatical forms, some of which are illustrated in 68.4.

68.1 **Suggesting**

(a) A number of verbs can be used: **recommander, suggérer, conseiller, proposer** followed by either **à qn de faire qch** or **que qn fasse** (subjunctive) **qch**:

> **Si les conditions changent durant la nuit, les forces de police** *recommanderont aux automobilistes d'équiper* **leurs véhicules de pneus-neige.** (see 33.1.1)
> If the conditions change during the night, the police will recommend that drivers put snow tyres on their cars.

> **Quand j'ai appelé le cabinet ce matin, votre secrétaire** *a suggéré que je prenne* **rendez-vous directement avec vous.** (see 39.2.1)
> When I called the office this morning, your secretary suggested I make an appointment to see you personally.

(b) The same verbs can be used with a little adjustment to the structure:

> **Vu la force du vent, je** *te conseille de ne pas sortir* **ta planche à voile aujourd'hui.** (see 42.1, 47.8)
> Because of the high wind, I suggest you don't go windsurfing today.

> **Le conseil municipal** *a recommandé que* **le public** *n'ait plus* **accès gratuitement aux musées de la ville.** (see 39.2.1)
> The municipal council has suggested/recommended that the public should no longer have free entry to museums and galleries.

In this negative sense, the function is often used to warn someone *against* something, through verbs such as: **déconseiller à qn de faire qch, déconseiller qch à qn, mettre qn en garde contre qch, avertir qn de ne pas faire qch**:

> *Il est* **fortement** *déconseillé aux techniciens de se tenir* **dans la zone de déchargement sans vêtements de protection.** (see 46)
> Technical staff must not enter the unloading area without protective clothing.

> *Avertissez-le de ne pas oublier* **de faire sa demande de visa avant d'entreprendre ce voyage.** (see 14.3b, 47.8)
> Remind/Warn him not to forget to apply for a visa before leaving on the journey.

(c) In speech, the fact that you intend to make a suggestion is often announced as a form of politeness, so as not to create the impression of giving an order, with expressions such as **permettez-moi, puis-je**:

> *Permettez-moi de vous suggérer* un plan d'action.
> May I suggest a plan of action?

> *Puis-je faire* une proposition?
> May I make a proposal?

> *J'ai une idée à proposer:*
> I have a suggestion to make:

(d) The conditional tense (also a form of politeness) (see **33.1.3**) is often used, sometimes in combination with **peut-être**:

> *Peut-être serait-il bon de* **soumettre cette question au vote, étant donné qu'un consensus ne semble pas pouvoir être atteint?**
> (see **42.1, 46**)
> Would it not be a good idea to put the question to the vote since there seems to be no possibility of reaching a consensus?

> **Puisqu'ils ne veulent rien savoir à la mairie,** *tu pourrais peut-être t'adresser* **à la préfecture?**
> Since the (local) council doesn't want to know, maybe you could ask at the Préfecture (Regional Council).

(e) In the previous example, it is the interrogative form (achieved through intonation) which helps to perform the function of suggestion. Other examples of this use of the interrogative, including negative forms, are the following:

> *Que dirais-tu de passer* **à la maison ce soir vers 8h00?**
> Would you like to come round tonight about eight?

> *Ne conviendrait-il pas de rajouter* **ce point à l'ordre du jour?** (see **46.2**)
> Would it not be a good idea to add this to the agenda?

(f) Suggestions can also be made through the use of impersonal verb phrases, in particular **il faut/il faudrait** + infinitive *or* + **que** + subjunctive (see **46.2**):

> **Le directeur du personnel pense qu'***il faudrait que* **les ouvriers** *soient tenus* **au courant de la nouvelle réglementation sur les conditions de travail.**
> The personnel manager thinks the work force should be kept informed of the new regulations on working conditions.

68.2 Persuading someone to think the way you do

(a) This can be achieved using verbs such as **persuader/convaincre qn de** + noun:

> **Il s'agit de** *convaincre les autorités de l'intérêt* **de ce projet.** (see **46.2**)
> It is a matter of persuading/convincing the authorities of the importance of the project.

or using the following, in complex sentences: **persuader/convaincre qn que** + indicative, **faire admettre/reconnaître à qn que** + indicative, **faire changer d'avis/d'idée à qn**:

L'avocat de la défense tentera de *convaincre les jurés que* le meurtre *était* non prémédité.
The defending counsel will try to convince the jury that the murder was not premeditated.

Il est difficile de *faire admettre aux adolescents que* leurs parents *ont* autrefois *connu* les mêmes difficultés. (see **45.3**)
It is difficult to convince young people that their parents had the same problems.

Leurs arguments ont été *si convaincants qu'ils m'ont fait changer d'avis.* (see **45.3**)
Their arguments were so convincing/persuasive that they made me change my mind/convinced me.

(b) Other verb constructions which are similar in terms of meaning are also available, for example **démontrer/prouver par A + B à qn que**. **Faire croire qch à qn** is in a slightly different league as it implies that the person aimed at is somehow being tricked into believing something:

Le gouvernement *nous fait croire qu'il y a* moins de chômeurs en manipulant les statistiques. (see **45.3**)
By manipulating the figures, the government would have us believe that there are fewer unemployed.

(c) You may want to state that you *are* persuaded, using passive expressions with **avoir** and **être**:

Ce témoignage *m'avait convaincue*: il était innocent, *j'en avais* désormais *la conviction.* (see **12.6b**)
The/This evidence persuaded me: he was innocent, I was (totally) convinced of it from that moment/point.

J'avoue que je *suis* désormais *persuadée que* les pratiques de ce fournisseur sont honnêtes.
I admit that I am now convinced that this supplier's business dealings are in order.

These expressions, and others such as **j'en mettrais ma main au feu** 'I'd swear to it' or **j'en donnerais ma tête à couper** 'I'd put my head on the block' can also be used to express certainty (see **71.1**).

(d) The verb **croire en/à** 'to believe, be convinced', can be used to express persuasion:

Depuis qu'il va au catéchisme, cet enfant *croit en* Dieu comme il *croit au* Père Noël.
Since he was taught his catechism, the child believes in God like he believes in Santa Claus.

Vu les résultats obtenus, de plus en plus de gens *croiront aux* vertus de l'homéopathie. (see **42.1**)
Because of its positive results, more and more people will believe in homeopathy.

Persuading someone to do/not to do something

(a) To persuade someone to do something, you can again use verbs such as **persuader/ convaincre qn de faire qch, amener/décider qn à faire qch**:

> La tâche du conseiller d'orientation consistera à *persuader cet élève de poursuivre* ses études.
> The job of the careers adviser will be to persuade this pupil to continue his/her studies.

> J'ai eu un mal fou à *le décider à venir* avec nous. (see **14.4a**)
> I've had terrible trouble persuading him to come with us.

(b) However, if you want to get someone to renounce a particular course of action, you can use one of the following: **dissuader qn de faire qch, déconseiller à qn de faire qch, persuader/convaincre qn de ne pas faire qch, détourner qn de qch**:

> Les délégués syndicaux arriveront-ils à *dissuader les grévistes d'occuper* les locaux? (see **52c**)
> Will the union representatives manage to persuade the strikers not to occupy the buildings?

> Le médecin a réussi à *le persuader de ne pas se faire opérer* pour le moment. (see **14.4, 47.8**)
> The doctor managed to persuade him not to have an operation for the time being.

> Dites ce que vous voulez, vous n'arriverez pas à *me détourner de cette entreprise.* (see **15.11, 44.2**)
> Say what you want, you'll never put me off (this).

Other ways of persuading and dissuading

These are numerous and varied but there seems to be an overall tendency to insist on or emphasize the arguments put forward to persuade or dissuade.

(a) by introducing the argument with verbs such as **savoir** 'to know', **voir** 'to see', **ignorer** 'to be ignorant of', **croire** 'to believe, think':

> Vous *voyez bien* que c'est *la seule* solution possible.
> You can see it's the only possible solution.

> Vous *n'ignorez quand même pas* que *toutes les autres* solutions envisagées ont été appliquées sans succès.
> You know very well that every other solution has been tried without success.

Note how **la seule** and **toutes les autres** as well as the adverbs **bien** and **quand même** contribute to reinforcing the appeal to common sense contained in the two examples.

(b) by using (rhetorical) questions, which can be positive:

> *Crois-tu vraiment* qu'en écrivant une lettre d'insultes tu seras pris au sérieux?
> Do you really believe that by writing a rude letter you will be taken seriously?

or negative:

> *Ne pensez-vous pas que* si les hommes étaient moins stupides, il y
> aurait moins de guerres?
> Don't you think that if men were not so stupid, there would be fewer
> wars?

> La *vraie* justice, *ne consisterait-elle pas* plutôt à présumer de leur
> innocence (et non pas de leur culpabilité)?
> Should (true) justice not consist of presuming someone innocent rather
> than guilty?

Again, note how **vraiment** and **vraie** reinforce the statement, and how in the second
example the initial position of **la vraie justice** creates maximum impact.

(c) by using specific structures to demonstrate that a particular course of action X is
either the right one (persuasion) or the wrong one (dissuasion):

to persuade someone to do X	to dissuade someone from doing X
en faisant X, tu obtiens . . .	en faisant X, tu risques de . . .
or si tu fais X, tu obtiens . . .	*or* si tu fais X, tu risques de . . .
en ne faisant pas X, tu risques de . . .	en ne faisant pas X, tu obtiens . . .
or si tu ne fais pas X, tu risques de . . .	*or* si tu ne fais pas X, tu obtiens . . .

> *En refusant* de te présenter au poste de police, *tu attires* les soupçons
> sur toi.
> If you refuse to go to the police station, you will (just) make them
> suspicious of you.

> *Si vous commandez* 1 000 bouteilles ou davantage, *nous vous
> accorderons* une remise de 15%.
> If you order 1,000 bottles or more, we will give you a 15%
> discount.

This process, which establishes relations of cause/effect, threat/reward, disadvantage/
benefits, is central to negotiating. The 'paired' structures involved express an essential
link between the two arguments:

> *Tu devrais* te présenter au poste de police, *sinon tu risques d'*attirer
> les soupçons sur toi.
> You should go to the police station, otherwise you run the risk of
> making/may make them suspect you.

> *Nous vous accorderons* une remise de 15%, *à condition que vous
> commandiez* 1 000 bouteilles ou plus.
> We will give you a 15% discount provided you order 1,000 bottles or
> more.

Other useful paired structures which establish a link between two clauses include **ce
n'est pas parce que . . . que, ce n'est pas en . . . que, tu devrais . . . auquel cas tu
pourras, tu as tout intérêt à . . . et tu obtiendras:**

> *Ce n'est pas en* restant chez toi à broyer du noir *que* tu te sortiras de cette dépression.
> It won't be by staying at home brooding that you'll get out of that depression.

> A ce prix, *vous avez tout intérêt à* en acheter deux, *et vous doublez* la durée d'utilisation.
> At that price you would do well to buy two of them, and you'll double the time you can use them.

(d) by using the imperative in very direct – and usually spoken – statements (see **44.2**):

> Oh si! Allez, *viens* avec nous, *tu ne le regretteras pas*!
> Oh yes, come on, come with us. You won't regret it!

> *Soyez* raisonnable, *laissez-moi* vous aider, *vous ne vous en tirerez pas autrement.*
> Be reasonable and let me help you. You won't manage otherwise.

Other imperatives commonly used include **sache/sachez que, écoute-moi, croyez-moi**. Note that the first person plural imperative is also used, usually as an exclamation: **voyons! allons! soyons sérieux!** (see **44.2.1**) and its English equivalent would come from a range of expressions such as 'There we are!, Let's go!, Be serious!'.

(e) by using expressions in apposition; a wide range of short phrases such as **je t'assure**, including the imperatives given above, can be used – and sometimes combined – to bring about a particular course of action:

> Encore une fois, *je te le répète*, tu n'as pas le choix, c'est la seule solution!
> I tell you once again, you have no choice, it's the only solution/way.

> *Croyez-moi, je vous en prie*, c'est la seule solution, vous verrez!
> Believe me, please, it's the only way, you'll see!

(f) by using the conditional tense – offering advice and a measure of persuasion – reinforced by an expression of personal opinion, which you can use when you know that your interlocutor respects your opinion:

> *Je crois que vous devriez* vraiment réfléchir avant de vous lancer dans cette affaire qui présente de nombreux risques. (see **15.1, 39.5**)
> I think you really should give the matter some thought before getting involved in this/the business because it's very risky.

> *A mon avis, tu ferais bien d'*intenter un procès pour dommages et intérêts avant qu'il ne soit trop tard. (see **39.2.2**)
> In my opinion, you'd be right to start proceedings for compensation before it's too late.

69 Expressing volition

When using this function you may definitely want (to do) something (see **69.1**), state your intention or wish (see **69.2**) or ask what someone else intends or wants (see **69.3**). When you want someone else to do something, then it usually becomes a request (see **69.4**), which in turn generates a particular response (see **69.5**). Volition also deals with the deliberate or spontaneous nature of an action (see **69.6**) and finally, you may, of course, state what you do not want (see **69.7**).

69.1   **Verbs expressing volition**

Verbs are frequently used to express volition: e.g. **vouloir, désirer, aimer, souhaiter, décider**. They may be followed by:

(a) a noun (direct object of a transitive verb):

> **Je *veux ton bonheur* et rien d'autre.**
> All I want is your happiness.

> **Les peuples du monde *désirent la paix.***
> People all over the world want peace.

(b) one, or two, infinitives (with or without a preposition) (see **45.2, 45.5, 45.5.1**):

> **Le directeur de l'établissement a annoncé qu'il *voulait voir augmenter* les effectifs d'ici l'an prochain.**
> The head of the company has announced that he wants to see staffing levels increased by next year.

> **Pas d'interruption pendant un quart d'heure, s'il vous plaît; je *souhaite être* seul avec ma cliente.**
> No interruptions for fifteen minutes please. I want to be alone with my client.

> **Ma fille *a décidé d'étudier* l'italien à l'université.**
> My daughter has decided to study/read Italian at university.

(c) **que** + subjunctive (see **39.2.1**):

> **Nous *voulons que* cette soirée *soit réussie.***
> We want this evening to be a success.

> **Ils *avaient* toujours *désiré que* leur fils *fasse* carrière dans la marine.**
> They had always wanted their son to make his career in the navy.

(d) In the conditional tense the same verbs, or verb phrases, can be used to express a wish (see **33.1.3**):

> **J'*aimerais changer* d'emploi avant la fin de l'année.**
> I'd like to change my job before the end of the year.

> **Le comité d'organisation *souhaiterait être informé* des résultats de cette étude.**
> The organizing committee would like to be informed of the results of the study.

Note that any verb in the conditional followed by **bien** indicates a wish. When spoken, the intonation would often be interrogative, as in 'I'd like to do this . . . (what do you think?)':

Puisqu'il nous reste un peu de temps, j'*irais bien voir* cette exposition.
Since we've got a little time left, I'd like to have a look at the exhibition.

Je *téléphonerais bien* aux renseignements pour avoir le numéro.
I'd be happy to phone directory enquiries to get the number.

(e) Some nouns or noun phrases can also be used – as subjects or complements:

La volonté du peuple est que règne la paix.
The people want peace.

Les pouvoirs ont pris *la résolution d'entreprendre* une campagne de protection de l'environnement.
The government has decided to embark on a campaign for the protection of the environment.

Si seulement je pouvais prendre des vacances, *j'ai envie de* mer et *de* soleil.
If only I could take a holiday: I want some sea and sunshine.

Note how the previous example combines expressions of wishing, one emphatic (**si seulement je pouvais**) and one much milder (**j'ai envie de**) which is given as a reason for the first one.

(f) Some verb phrases such as **je tiens à ce que** + subjunctive 'I insist', or adverbs such as **bien, résolument, absolument** can be used, or combined to express strong will:

Je tiens absolument à ce qu'ils sachent que nous sommes bien arrivés.
(see **39.2.1**)
I'm absolutely determined that they (should) know we have arrived.

Cette fois, il *est bien résolu* à la renvoyer.
This time he is determined to dismiss her.

69.2 Wishing and intending

When the wish to do something is expressed as an intention, a number of verbs and verb phrases are available.

(a) Verbs and verb phrases such as **prévoir, envisager, se proposer, avoir l'intention, former le projet** all followed by **de** + infinitive, and **songer à** + infinitive (see **45.5.1**):

J'*ai prévu de partir* tôt alors soyez prêts à 6h00.
I intend to leave early so be ready at six.

La direction *envisage de licencier* une partie du personnel.
The management intends to make some staff redundant.

(b) Some verbs such as **compter/penser, aller**, and sometimes **devoir**, require no preposition before the infinitive (see **45.2**):

Elle *pensait arriver* avant midi mais c'est impossible en raison de la grève des trains. (see **6.3b**)
Her intention was to arrive before noon, but that's impossible because of the rail strike.

En guise de conclusion, je *vais* vous *faire part de* mes impressions sur les différentes séances de travail tenues pendant le séminaire. (see **42.1**)
To conclude, I shall give you my impressions of the various workshops held during the seminar.

Il *devait* m'*accompagner* mais de toute évidence, il a changé d'avis.
He was to come with me but clearly he has changed his mind.

(c) Nouns or noun phrases, in various positions in the sentence, can also be used: **dans l'intention, le/son but est** followed by **de** + infinitive (see **45.6**):

Je suppose qu'il m'a convoquée *dans l'intention de* me *féliciter.*
I assume he has sent for me to congratulate me.

Son but est de redresser la situation financière de la société avant la fin de l'exercice.
His aim is to straighten out the company's financial situation before the end of the fiscal year.

69.3 **Asking what someone intends**

In order to ask what someone intends or wants, you can simply resort to questions (see **52**). The forms used depend on how specific the options provided by the question are.

(a) In the case of totally open choice, **que? qu'est-ce que? quoi?** can be used (see **16.1–16.3**):

Que désirez-vous?
What do you want?

Qu'est-ce que je peux faire pour vous?
What can I do for you?

Vous avez l'intention de faire *quoi* après le cinéma?
What are you going to do after the cinema?

(b) When the options are 'yes' or 'no', the focus is on the verb:

Comptez-vous venir à la réception ce soir?
Do you intend to come to the reception this evening?

Vous prendrez bien un verre?
Will you have something to drink?

(c) When the options fall within a specific and restricted range, interrogative adjectives + nouns or interrogative pronouns are usually used:

Quel fromage désirez-vous? (see **16.4.2**)
Which cheese would you like?

Parmi toutes ces écharpes, *laquelle* te plairait? (see **16.4.1**)
Which of all of these scarves would you like?

(d) When there are specific options, the interrogative adjectives and pronouns are frequently combined with structures such as **ou** or **soit . . . soit**:

> *Lesquelles* **voulez-vous, les Golden *ou* les Reinette?** (see **16.4.1**)
> Which would you prefer, the Golden Delicious or the Reinettes?

> *Quelle table* **préférez-vous? Vous pouvez vous installer *soit* en terrasse, *soit* à l'intérieur.** (see **16.4.2**)
> Which table would you prefer? You can sit on the terrace, or inside.

(e) All the examples above are direct questions which may or may not involve an inversion of the verb. (see **51c, 52**) Questions can also be indirect and again, the structures vary depending on how specific the options are:

> **J'*aimerais bien savoir ce que* tu comptes faire dans la vie!** (see **51b**)
> I'd like to know what kind of career you intend to follow!

> **Le plombier *voudrait savoir si* nous voulons qu'il commence les travaux demain.** (see **39.2.1**)
> The plumber wanted to know if we want him to start (the) work tomorrow.

> **Les partis politiques *se demandent quelles sont les mesures* souhaitées par l'opinion en matière de sécurité.** (see **16.4.2, 42.1**)
> The political parties are wondering what security measures the public wants.

> **Aide-moi! Je *ne sais pas laquelle des deux* je devrais choisir!** (see **16.4.1**)
> Help me! I don't know which of the two to choose!

69.4 Asking someone for something

(a) When you request something from someone else, you can, of course, use some of the verbs and verb phrases identified in 69.1 – with the appropriate personal pronoun.

> *Je veux que vous soyez prêts* **à partir à 8h00 et *j'aimerais que vous passiez* me prendre tout de suite après.** (see **39.2.1**)
> I want you to be ready to leave at eight, and I'd like you to come and pick me up right away.

(b) In the previous example, note how the use of the conditional tense 'softens' the request. This tense is often used to ask someone (politely) to do something – sometimes in interrogative forms for even more indirect requests (see **33.1.3**):

> *Est-ce que tu pourrais* **me *rejoindre* au Bar de la Place après la séance?**
> Could you meet me in the Bar de la Place after the meeting?

> *Ça vous ennuierait de me prêter* **votre voiture demain matin? La mienne est en panne.**
> Could you possibly lend me your car tomorrow morning? Mine has broken down.

Note the use of **si** in an alternative form of the previous example:

> *Ça m'arrangerait* **beaucoup *si vous me prêtiez* votre voiture demain matin.** (see **33.1.1**)
> It would help me a lot if you could lend me your car tomorrow morning.

(c) The conditional is used for a more formal request – in commercial correspondence – in the following example:

> **Auriez-vous l'amabilité de me faire savoir quels sont vos tarifs et conditions pour cet article?**
> Please let me have your prices and terms for that item.

(d) Naturally, for a more categorical request, you can use the imperative (see **44.2**):

> **Prends mon porte-monnaie et ramène-moi deux baguettes (s'il te plaît).**
> Take my purse and get me two baguettes (please).

(e) The imperative **veuillez** + infinitive or the expression **je vous prie de** + infinitive can be used to introduce requests, for example to make enquiries or place orders in commercial correspondence:

> **Veuillez m'envoyer les deux derniers numéros de votre publication.** (see **44.1**)
> Please send *me* the last (latest) two issues of your publication.

> **Je vous prie de me faire parvenir la commande avant le 30 mars.**
> Please send me the order before 30th March.

(f) As demonstrated in the previous example, set expressions used in correspondence are often followed by one, or several, verbs in the infinitive, and particular attention has to be given to pronouns and their place in the clause (see **14.3**):

> **Nous vous serions reconnaissants de bien vouloir nous confirmer l'heure d'arrivée de votre délégation à l'aéroport.**
> We would be grateful if you will confirm the time of arrival of your delegation at the airport.

> **Je vous serais obligée de me répondre par retour du courrier.** (see **4.4**)
> I would appreciate it if you will reply by return.

Other similar phrases include: **je vous saurais gré, veuillez avoir l'obligeance**, both followed by **de (bien vouloir) faire.**

(g) For more pressing or insistent requests, the appropriate verbs (+ infinitive or subjunctive) and (sometimes) adverbs can be used:

> **Je compte sur vous pour venir dimanche.**
> I am counting on you to come on Sunday.

> **Tu dois insister auprès de la gendarmerie pour que tes papiers te soient rendus immédiatement.** (see **39.2.2**)
> You must insist that the police return your papers to you immediately.

> **Vos professeurs souhaitent instamment que vous vous présentiez à cet examen.** (see **39.2.1**)
> Your teachers insist that you sit the exam.

69.5   **Expressing (un)willingness to act upon request**

The simplest expression of this is, of course, to use **oui** or **non** but in many cases, in particular when negative, the response is qualified.

(a) Short positive answers include: **Oui, d'accord!** 'Yes, of course', **Pas de problème!** 'No problem!', **C'est comme si c'était fait!** 'Take it as done!' (see **63**).

(b) Negative answers often include some sort of justification such as: **Je ne peux pas . . .** 'I simply can't . . .', **C'est impossible . . .** 'It's impossible . . .' (see **63**):

> **Malheureusement, *c'est impossible*, nos stocks sont épuisés.**
> Unfortunately, it's out of the question, we have run out of stock.

(c) A fuller response to a request can be given using the future tense (see **25.2**):

> ***Pas de problème*, je te *donnerai un coup de main* pour ta terrasse.**
> No problem, I'll give you a hand with the terrace.

> **Sachez que *nous ne livrerons pas* les ordinateurs que vous avez commandés (car notre dernière facture n'a pas encore été réglée).** (see **68.4d**)
> We are unable to deliver the computers you ordered (because our last invoice has not yet been paid).

or verbs, in particular **vouloir, pouvoir** + infinitive or **accepter de, refuser de** + infinitive:

> **Oui, les bénévoles de notre organisation *veulent bien assurer* l'animation dans votre club du troisième âge.** (see **45.2**)
> Yes, the helpers in our organization are happy/willing to organize the entertainment in your old folks' club.

> **La direction *a refusé d'accorder* aux vendeurs l'augmentation qu'ils demandaient.** (see **15.2, 45.5.1**)
> The management has refused the pay rise the shop assistants were seeking.

or other verb phrases of the type **être** + adjective *or* past participle + **à** + infinitive (see **45.6**):

> **Le tribunal *est* (tout) *prêt à* vous *accorder* la remise de peine dont vous avez fait la demande.** (see **15.8**)
> The court is ready/prepared to agree to your request for remission.

> **Non, (vu l'état dans lequel vous avez mis l'appartement,) nous *ne sommes pas disposés à renouveler* votre contrat de location.** (see **15.5, 42.1**)
> No, (because of the state the flat has been left in,) we are not prepared to renew your lease.

(d) There are also more indirect ways of accepting or refusing to act upon a request, with impersonal forms:

Aucun problème pour samedi, *il nous est possible de livrer* même les week-ends. (see **46**)
No problem for Saturday, we can deliver even at the weekend.

J'suis désolée, moi et Jean, *on* (ne) *pourra pas venir* à tes quarante ans. (informal) (see **11.8**)
Sorry, me and John, we can't come to your fortieth birthday bash.

In the previous example, note the colloquial 'abuse' of **on**, used in fact instead of **nous**.

Deliberate or non-deliberate actions

A number of terms and expressions convey the idea that something was done on purpose, or not. When it is a controversial issue, the statements often include **c'est/ce n'est pas . . . (que de** + infinitive):

(a) with a noun:

Non, je n'ai pas voulu ça, *c'était* un accident! (see **6.3b**)
No, I didn't want that to happen, it was an accident!

C'était bien son intention *que de t'obliger* à partir. (see **6.3b**)
He intended to force you to leave.

Note that with nouns such as **volonté** or **intention**, the more formal **tel** can also be used:

Je vois que vous êtes surpris de constater que *telle* était sa *volonté.* (see **11.10a**)
I see you're surprised that that was what he wanted.

(b) with an adjective:

Si je vous ai offensé, croyez bien que *ce n'était pas intentionnel.* *C'était* même tout à fait *involontaire.* (see **6.3b**)
If I have offended you, believe me I did not mean to. It was completely unintentional.

(c) A number of verb phrases are also available, sometimes reinforced by adverbs or idioms:

Je t'assure qu'ils *ne l'ont pas fait exprès.*
I assure you they did not do it deliberately.

Au contraire, je dirais qu'ils *ont agi volontairement* et *en toute connaissance de cause.*
On the contrary, I would say that they acted deliberately (*or* it was deliberate) and they knew exactly what they were doing.

(d) The notion of volition is, of course, central to the field of criminal law which provides numerous examples of use of the relevant terms, and in particular of structures involving the pair **avec, sans** + noun such as **intention, préméditation**:

Mesdames et messieurs les jurés, je vous rappelle qu'il s'agit d'un crime prémédité, mais *sans intention* de tuer. (see **42.1, 46.2**)
Ladies and gentlemen of the jury, I remind you that this was a premeditated crime, but (that) there was no intention to kill.

69.7   **Saying what you do not want**

Finally, volition is also concerned with expressing what a person does not want. Most of the examples given in previous sections could, of course, be made negative, and **69.5** deals with what a person does not want to do.

(a) However, taking an earlier example, note the difference, because of the shift of the negative in the sentence, between:

> Ma fille *n'a pas décidé* d'étudier l'italien à l'université. (see **47.8**)
> My daughter has not made up her mind to study Italian at university.

and

> Ma fille a décidé *de ne pas étudier* l'italien à l'université. (see **47.8**)
> My daughter has decided not to study Italian at university.

In the first case, she has not yet made up her mind whereas in the latter, she is definitely not going to study Italian. So the difference lies in the degree of determination about what will/might actually occur and the location of the negative. Note the difference in the following pair:

> Je *ne souhaite pas* qu'il vienne. (see **39.2.1, 47.8**)
> I do not want him to come.

> Je souhaite qu'il *ne vienne pas.*
> I hope he will not come.

(b) When the expression of volition in the first clause is positive, the subject has more control and makes a more deliberate stance on what he/she wants or intends:

> Le ministre *a l'intention de* ne pas démissionner. (he definitely intends not to) (see **47.8**)
> The minister intends not to resign.

> Le ministre *n'a pas l'intention de* démissionner. (at this stage)
> The minister does not intend to resign.

Such pairs could be identified for most expressions of volition although there are some exceptions where only one structure is desirable:

> Je *préférerais* que vous *ne soyez pas* trop en retard ce soir. (see **39.2.1**)
> I would rather you were not too late tonight.

(c) When both clauses have the same subject, the verb in the negative clause is followed by an infinitive:

> Nous *n'envisageons pas d'augmenter* le capital social pour le moment.
> We do not intend to increase share capital for the time being.

When there are two clauses with two different subjects, the negative verb is usually followed by **que** + subjunctive:

> Les chômeurs *ne souhaitent pas qu'on* leur *fasse* la charité.
> The unemployed do not want handouts.

(d) However, sometimes there are alternative structures, in particular with verbs such as **vouloir, savoir**:

Je ne veux pas que tu échoues **au baccalauréat./***Je ne veux pas te voir échouer* **au baccalauréat.** (see **39.2.1, 39.5**)
I don't want you to fail your bac (school-leaving certificate exam).

Ses parents n'ont pas envie qu'elle se perde **dans cette grande ville./***Ses parents n'ont pas envie de la savoir perdue* **dans cette grande ville.**
Her parents don't want her to get lost in that huge city.

(e) Adjectives or adverbs can be used to vary the degree of emphasis:

Les grévistes n'ont pas la *moindre* **intention d'annuler leur manifestation.** (see **10.12c, 45.6**)
The strikers have no intention/haven't the least intention of calling off their demonstration.

Croyez-moi, je n'avais *absolument* **pas l'intention de vous blesser.** (see **45.6**)
Believe me, I had absolutely no intention of hurting you.

Expressing permission and obligation

It is appropriate to look at expressing permission and obligation together as these functions entail giving (see **70.1**) or denying rights (see **70.2**) and imposing (see **70.3**) or exempting from duties (see **70.4**). You will see how, sometimes, these sub-functions overlap.

Permission

(a) Permission or rights can be granted using verb phrases such as **accorder, donner +**
la permission, l'autorisation, le droit de . . . à qn:

On *a accordé le droit de vote aux Françaises* **après la deuxième guerre mondiale.**
French women were given the vote after the Second World War.

Mes parents *m'ont donné l'autorisation de sortir* **jusqu'à minuit.**
My parents have given me permission to be out until midnight.

(b) Verbs expressing permission can also be used: e.g. **permettre à qn de faire qch,**
autoriser qn à faire qch, permettre/autoriser que qn fasse (subjunctive) **qch:**

Le proviseur *a autorisé que* **les cours** *soient annulés* **pour** *permettre*
aux élèves d'assister **à une pièce de théâtre.** (see **39.2.1**)
The headmaster has given permission for classes to be cancelled to allow pupils to go to see a play.

(c) When negative, all of the above structures are used to deny permission or right:

Le chef de rayon *n'autorise pas les vendeurs à s'asseoir* **et** *ne permet*
pas qu'ils prennent **plus de cinq minutes de pause.** (see **39.2.1**)
The department supervisor will not allow the shop assistants to sit down or take more than five minutes' break.

(d) The verb **pouvoir** also plays an important role, for example, when asking for permission:

> *Puis-je fumer?* – **Oui, *vous pouvez*, mais dans le coin fumeurs.**
> May I smoke? – Yes, you may, but in the smoking area.

An alternative would be:

> **Vous permettez que je fume?** (see **39.2.1**)
> May I smoke?

(e) There are numerous phrases combining **avoir** or **être** with a noun to express nuances of entitlement or permission to do something. Here are a few with **droit** (+ **à** + noun, + **de** + verb) as the noun:

> **Si je m'inscris dans cette filière de troisième cycle, *aurai-je droit à une bourse?*** (see **33.1.1**)
> If I register for this postgraduate course, will I be entitled to a grant?

> **En France, les femmes attendant des jumeaux *sont en droit de prendre* des congés maternité supplémentaires.** (see **43.1**)
> In France women expecting twins are entitled to additional maternity leave.

> **Tu *n'as pas le droit de me juger*!**
> You have no right to criticize me!

Droit is also central to many noun phrases, particularly in the legal field: e.g. **droit de grève**, 'right to strike', **droit de passage**, 'right of way', **droit de poursuite**, 'right of action', **droit de recours**, 'right of appeal', **droits d'auteurs** 'royalties'.

(f) Impersonal verbs or **on** can also be used to grant or deny permission in a more indirect way:

> ***Il est permis de consulter* un dictionnaire pendant l'examen.** (see **46**)
> Dictionaries are allowed in exams.

> ***Est-ce qu'on a le droit de poser* des questions?** (see **11.8**)
> Are we allowed to ask questions?

<h2>70.2 Prohibition</h2>

(a) Verbs expressing prohibition include **interdire, défendre à qn de faire qch, empêcher qn de faire qch**, and **interdire, défendre, empêcher que qn fasse** (subjunctive) **qch**.

(b) These are sometimes reinforced by adverbs:

> **Je *vous interdis formellement de me parler* sur ce ton!**
> I categorically forbid you to speak to me in that tone of voice.

> **La règle de l'ordre *défendait absolument que les moines se parlent pendant* les repas.** (see **39.2.1, 40.2.3**)
> The rule of the Order totally forbade the monks to speak during meals.

Verbs expressing prohibition have corresponding impersonal forms, followed by infinitives, and sometimes used with pronouns:

Il est interdit de sortir de l'enceinte du bâtiment avant que la sonnerie n'ait retenti. (see 39.2.2, 46.2)
It is forbidden to leave the grounds before the bell has rung.

Comme *il m'est défendu de vous parler*, je vous envoie ce mot en secret. (see 42)
Since I am forbidden to speak to you, I am sending you this note in secret.

(c) The passive form **être** + past participle is usually used in the negative, on notices, for example:

Les chiens *ne sont pas admis* dans le magasin. (see 41.2)
Dogs are not allowed in the shop.

Les chèques *ne sont pas acceptés.* (see 41.2)
Cheques are not accepted.

(d) Prohibitive notices can be even more direct and simply feature a noun (without an article) + infinitive or adjective:

Défense de stationner	No parking
Interdiction d'afficher	No posters
Pelouse interdite	Keep off the grass
Alcool prohibé	No alcohol

or both forms can be combined:

Propriété privée, défense d'entrer.
Private property, keep out.

NOTE | Other ways of prohibiting an action include negative forms of the expressions given in **70.1, 70.3**.

70.3 | **Obligation**

(a) A number of verbs and verb phrases are available to express obligation, for example **obliger, forcer, contraindre qn à faire qch, mettre qn dans l'obligation/en demeure de faire qch** and some verbs of volition + subjunctive (see 39.2.1) which are used when a duty is imposed on someone:

Les accidents toujours plus nombreux dus à l'excès d'alcool *contraignent les autorités à multiplier* les mesures de répression. (see 45.5.1)
The growing number of accidents caused by drink is forcing the government to introduce additional restrictive measures.

La facture ayant été expédiée il y a six mois, *nous vous mettons en demeure de nous régler* dans les huit jours.
The invoice was sent six months ago so we request that you settle the bill within a week.

La loi *exige que vous consultiez* un conseiller juridique indépendant. (see 39.2.1)
The law demands that you consult an independent legal adviser.

(b) **Etre** + past participle, in the structure **être tenu/forcé/contraint/obligé de faire qch,** can be used to show that a person has, or does not have, to do something (see **41.2**):

> **Le contrat stipule que nous ne sommes pas responsables et par conséquent** *nous ne sommes pas tenus de vous dédommager.*
> The contract states that we are not responsible and are not therefore obliged to pay (you) compensation.

> **Rapporte-le puisqu'il y a un trou: la vendeuse** *sera obligée de te l'échanger.* (see **14.3b, 14.4**)
> Take it back because there's a hole in it: the assistant will have to change it for you.

In the first of these two examples, note how the obligation – or absence of it – stems from a contract: **le contrat stipule que.** . . . This is often the case because any code, dogma, legal text, etc. creates a number of obligations and consequently is often referred to with expressions in apposition such as **selon le règlement, d'après les statuts, conformément à l'article 10, (vous êtes tenu de . . .):**

> **D'après les statuts de notre réseau régional, les nouveaux membres** *sont tenus de soumettre* **leur demande d'adhésion à l'organisation nationale dans les deux ans qui suivent leur inscription.** (see **4.4, 15.1**)
> In accordance with the regulations of our regional network, new members have to apply for membership of the national organization within the two years following their registration.

(c) The verb or noun **devoir** + infinitive *or* + **de** + infinitive is central to this function and features in several expressions such as **se devoir de, il est de mon devoir de, se faire un devoir de:**

> **Pour obtenir votre carte de séjour, vous** *devrez remplir* **ces deux formulaires avec soin.**
> To obtain your residence permit you must complete these two forms carefully.

> **Un bon chef d'équipe** *se doit* **parfois** *d'être* **autoritaire.**
> It is the duty of a good team leader to be authoritarian/show his authority at times.

Devoir + noun is used when something is owed to somebody:

> **Tu te souviens que** *tu me dois de l'argent*? (see **4**)
> You remember you owe me some money?

> **Beaucoup de gens pensent que les enfants** *doivent le respect à leurs parents.* (see **21, 22.3.1**)
> Many people think that children owe their parents some respect.

(d) **Avoir à** + infinitive also conveys obligation, with or without a complement:

> **Dites à votre patron que** *j'ai à lui parler.* (see **44.1**)
> Tell your boss that I have something to say to him.

> Les étudiants de première année *ont plusieurs feuilles d'inscription à remplir.* (see 11.3, 45.6)
> First-year students have to fill in several registration forms.

(e) Impersonal verbs can also be used, in particular **il faut** with a noun:

> Pour vous inscrire, *il me faut un extrait d'acte de naissance et deux photos.* (see 46.2)
> To complete your registration I need a copy of your birth certificate and two photographs.

or alternatively followed by an infinitive (same subject in both clauses) or **que** + subjunctive:

> Pour poser sa candidature, *il faut envoyer* un CV. (see 46.2)
> You have to send a CV when you submit an application.

> *Il faut* absolument *que tu sois rentrée* pour 10h00 car nous partirons aussitôt. (see 39.2.1, 46.2)
> You must be back at ten because we're leaving on the dot.

Other impersonal verbs include **il est indispensable/nécessaire/obligatoire de** + infinitive (same subject in both clauses) or **que** + subjunctive (see **46.2**).

(f) When used in the negative, the above expressions do not usually convey the absence of obligation but rather the obligation *not* to do something:

> *Vous ne devez pas toucher* cette porte, elle vient d'être peinte. (see 24.3)
> You must not touch this door. It has just been painted. (*not* You do not have to touch . . .)

> *Il ne faut pas ouvrir* les paquets avant Noël. (see 46.2)
> You must not open the parcels before Christmas.

and compare

> *Tu n'as pas à remplir* ce formulaire (mais celui-là). (see 45.5.1)
> You don't have to fill in this form (but that one).

with **ne pas avoir qch à** + infinitive:

> *Tu n'as pas de formulaire à remplir.*
> You don't have a form to fill in.

(g) The verb **pouvoir** can also convey obligation, in particular when combined with **ne . . . que**:

> Il a tellement insisté que finalement, ses parents *n'ont pu que s'incliner.*
> He insisted (on it) so much that finally his parents had to agree.

> A mon avis, *tu ne peux pas faire autrement que d'accepter* cette offre.
> In my opinion, you can't do anything but accept the offer.

(h) There are various ways of ordering someone to do something (obligation) or not to do something (prohibition) (see **44.2–44.2.2**):

- by using an imperative for a very direct order or instruction:

Présentez armes!	Present arms!
Tenez votre droite.	Keep to the right.
Attachez vos ceintures.	Fasten your seatbelts.
N'entrez pas!	Don't go in!
Ne *refais* jamais ça!	Never do that again!
Va-t'en!/*Vas*-y! (see **14.3b, 44**)	Clear off!/Get on with it!

- by using the future tense:

> **Puisque vous êtes si insolents, *vous irez* voir la directrice et lui *remettrez* cette note de ma part.**
> Since you are so insolent, you will go to the headmistress and give her this note from me.

> ***Tu ne tueras point.***
> Thou shalt not kill.

- the order or instruction can be given more politely with **veuillez** or a passive form:

> ***Veuillez attacher* vos ceintures et *éteindre* vos cigarettes.**
> Please fasten your seat belts and put out your cigarettes.

> **Les passagers *sont priés de ne pas fumer* pendant toute la durée du vol.** (see **41**)
> Passengers are asked not to smoke during the flight.

- instructions on notices or recipes, for example, are usually given in infinitives (see **45.1.1**):

> ***Sonner* avant d'entrer.**
> Ring before entering.

> ***Assaisonner* et *servir* immédiatement.**
> Add seasoning and serve immediately.

- or nouns + adjectives or past participles:

> ***Port* du casque *obligatoire* (dans la zone de déchargement).**
> Hard hats must be worn (in the unloading area).

> ***Tenue de soirée exigée.***
> Dress formal.

70.4 Exemption

(a) A number of verbs and verb phrases are available to denote that someone does not have to do something, e.g. **dispenser de** + infinitive:

> **Cet entretien vous *dispense de venir* à la réunion d'information où les mêmes renseignements seront communiqués.** (see **15.9**)
> This conversation means that you do not need to come to the information session which will deal with the same information.

(b) Passive forms are used frequently:

> *Il a été exempté de* **service militaire pour des raisons médicales.**
> (see **41.1.1**)
> He has been exempted from military service for medical reasons.

(c) In the same context and to indicate that the obligation has been fulfilled, a Frenchman would indicate in his CV:

> *Dégagé des* **obligations militaires.** (see **42.1**)
> Military service completed.

(d) Other verbs include **décharger, épargner, exonérer, soustraire** and, of course, negative forms such as **ne pas être tenu/forcé/obligé/contraint/dans l'obligation + de faire qch**, including many variations with verbs such as **se sentir, se croire**:

> **Surtout,** *ne vous sentez pas obligé de faire* **ça pour moi!**
> Above all, don't feel obliged to do that for me!

> **Elle** *ne se croyait pas tenue de répondre* **à ses lettres puisqu'il ne lui rendait jamais ses appels téléphoniques.**
> She did not feel obliged to reply to his letters because he never returned her telephone calls.

(e) **Sans** + infinitives such as **avoir à** or **devoir** may also be used:

> **Les banques peuvent désormais opérer dans tous les pays de l'Union Européenne** *sans avoir à établir* **de filiales à l'extérieur de leur pays d'origine.** (see **45.5.1**)
> Banks can now operate in all the countries of the EU without having to establish branches outside their country of origin.

(f) Impersonal verbs, either positive or negative, can also be used (see **46, 46.2**):

> *Il est inutile d'écrire;* **nous vous enverrons automatiquement le dossier d'inscription.**
> You do not have to write; we shall automatically send you the registration form.

> **Il** *ne sera pas obligatoire d'assister* **à la réunion d'inauguration pour adhérer à l'association.**
> It is not essential to attend the inaugural meeting to become a member of the association.

(g) Impersonal forms introduced by **ce n'est pas** (see **6.3**) provide alternatives, with or without a complement:

> **Une pièce d'identité? – Non,** *ce ne sera pas nécessaire.*
> An identity card? – No, it won't be necessary.

> **Tu avais dit que tu le ferais mais** *ce n'est pas une obligation.* (see **51b**)
> You said you would do it but it's not compulsory.

> *Ce n'est* **tout de même** *pas à toi de prendre* **cette décision.**
> It's not up to you anyway to take the decision.

> **Exceptionnellement,** *ce n'est pas la peine de composter* **car les machines sont en panne.**
> There's no point in punching your ticket today – the machines have broken down.

(h) And **ne pas avoir besoin de** + infinitive can be used with any personal pronouns, including **on**:

> *On n'a pas besoin de couper* l'électricité si on ne s'absente qu'un week-end. (see **11.8, 33.1.1**)
> There is no need to switch off the electricity if we're only away for a weekend.

> Les médecins *n'ont même pas eu besoin de me prévenir*; j'ai couru à l'hôpital car je savais qu'il était au plus mal.
> The doctors did not even need to call me; I rushed to the hospital because I knew he was dying.

Note that some of these impersonal forms tend to be shortened in spoken exchanges:

> *Pas besoin de venir* me chercher, je prendrai un taxi.
> No need to pick me up; I'll take a taxi.

> *Inutile de m'expédier* le document, mon secrétaire passera le prendre cet après-midi.
> No point sending me the document, my secretary will come and get it this afternoon.

Reminder: in order to avoid ambiguity, any of the above (see **70.4a–70.4h**) are preferable to **ne pas devoir** + infinitive, **ne pas avoir à** + infinitive, **il ne faut pas que** + subjunctive to express exemption, unless the context makes it absolutely clear that it is *not* a case of obligation not to do something (see **70.3f**).

71 Expressing doubt and certainty

Doubt and certainty (see **71.1**) are at opposite ends of a continuum where possibility and probability (see **71.2**) as well as condition and hypothesis (see **71.3**) are also to be found. Many different grammatical forms are used to express all the nuances of meaning involved, some of which are reviewed in this section with occasional emphasis on specific contexts such as expression of reservation in debate or in an economic forecast.

71.1 Doubt and certainty

These may be expressed simply through the meaning of individual verb or noun phrases.

(a) Verbs such as **douter que** + subjunctive, **ne pas douter que** + indicative, **douter de** + noun, **ne pas douter de** + noun:

> Je *doute que* le colis *ait été livré* car il n'a été posté qu'hier matin. (see **39.2.1, 47.10**)
> I doubt that the parcel will have been delivered because it was only posted yesterday morning.

> Après avoir entendu ce témoignage, tu *ne douteras plus* une seconde *de son innocence*.
> Having heard this evidence you will no longer have any doubts about his/her innocence.

The meaning of the verbs used may allow you to convey specific nuances of doubt and certainty; for example **savoir** for expressing certainty or uncertainty of knowledge, **se demander** 'to wonder':

> Je *sais* (avec certitude) qu'il ne me laissera pas tomber.
> I know he will not let me down.

> Nous *ne savons pas* encore ce que nous réserve l'avenir. (see **15.11**)
> We do not know what the future holds for us.

> Je te parie que nos concurrents *se demandent* bien *ce que nous allons faire*, et surtout *si nous allons lancer* le nouveau produit avant l'été. (see **25.3.2**).
> I am sure our competitors are wondering what we are going to do and especially whether we are going to launch the new product before summer.

(b) Nouns: in the following examples with a noun subject, note the structure noun + verb + **quant à**:

> *Le doute persiste quant au* nombre exact de personnes à bord de l'appareil au moment de l'accident.
> Doubt remains as to the exact number of people aboard the plane at the time of the accident.

> *Le doute n'est plus permis quant à la* responsabilité du conducteur d'autobus dans cet accident.
> There is no doubt that the driver of the bus was responsible for the accident.

Nouns also occur in phrases such as **de toute évidence, en toute certitude, sans aucun doute, sans le moindre doute** used as adverbs or in apposition:

> *De toute évidence*, cette loi qui est approuvée par tous les partis sera promulguée dans les mois à venir. (see **41.2**)
> Obviously, the legislation which is approved by all the political parties will be promulgated in the next few months.

> Le projet de tunnel tenant compte des considérations écologiques sera *sans aucun doute* préféré à tout autre. (see **41.2, 43.1**)
> The tunnel project which takes ecological considerations into account will without any doubt be the one selected.

The same forms can be used to express certainty (if positive) or doubt (if negative), for example, verb phrases with **être** or **avoir**:

> *Es-tu sûr que* la porte de l'appartement est fermée à clef?
> Are you sure that the door of the flat is locked?

> Oui, *j'ai la certitude de l'avoir fermée à clef* avant de partir.
> Yes, I am certain I locked it before we left.

> Non, *je n'en suis pas certain*. (see **12.6b**)
> No, I'm not sure.

Je ne suis pas persuadé que Patrick *l'ait fermée à clef* avant de me les rendre. (see **39.2.1, 39.5**)
I'm not convinced Patrick locked it before giving me back the keys.

NOTE Expressions of certainty + **que** are followed by the indicative whereas expressions of doubt + **que** are followed by the subjunctive (see **39.2.1**).

(c) There are many impersonal forms available to express doubt or certainty:

● an adjective:

La police retrouvera-t-elle les marchandises volées?
Will the police find the stolen goods?

certainty	**C'est évident.** (see **6.3b**)
(without a complement)	Yes, they will.
certainty	**Il est certain qu'elle fera de son**
(with a complement)	**mieux.** (see **6.3b**)
doubt	They'll certainly do their best.
(without a complement)	**Ce serait étonnant.** (see **6.3b**)
doubt	It would be surprising (if they did).
(with a complement)	**Il est douteux qu'elle puisse tout**
	retrouver. (see **39.2.1**)
	It is doubtful that she'll get
	everything back.

● verb and noun phrases, in particular for expressing certainty:

D'après les journaux de ce matin, *il ne fait aucun doute que* la maîtresse du ministre *espionnait* à l'époque pour le compte des Russes. (see **4.4, 39.4**)
According to this morning's papers, there is no doubt that the minister's mistress was spying at the time for the Russians.

Les journaux ne nous apprennent rien, *c'était l'évidence même!*
(see **6.3b**)
The papers haven't told us anything, it was common knowledge!

D'accord, on la soupçonnait, mais désormais *c'est une certitude.*
(see **6.3b**)
Right, we suspected it, but now we know.

En tout cas, avec tout ça, *il va sans dire que* ses mémoires qui sont sur le point de paraître *se vendront* très bien. (see **41.3, 50.3**)
Anyway, with all this fuss, there is no doubt that her memoirs which are just about to come out will sell very well.

(d) Certainty or doubt can be expressed with terms such as **rien + ne**, **personne + ne**, **tout** used as subjects:

Personne ne peut nier l'existence de ces documents. (see **47.8**)
Nobody can deny the existence of these documents.

Rien ne prouve que ces documents *existent.* (see **47.8**)
There is nothing to prove that these documents exist.

Tout me porte à croire qu'il dit la vérité. (see **11.1**)
Everything leads me to believe that he is telling the truth.

(e) The conditional tense can be used to express uncertainty about a fact. It is, for example, very commonly used in press articles when a particular piece of information has not been verified (see **33.1.5**):

Selon les rumeurs, le banquier incriminé dans cette affaire de fraude *aurait* déjà *quitté* le pays. (see **42.1**)
Rumour has it that the banker involved in the fraud case has already left the country.

D'après des sources proches du ministre, il *serait sur le point de présenter* sa démission. (see **4.4, 50.3b**)
According to sources close to the minister, he is about to tender his resignation.

(f) You may wish to express reservation or doubts about another person's statement in a debating situation. In order to do so, you can use adverbs such as **vraiment?, pas forcément!, pas nécessairement!**:

Selon les statistiques, l'économie de la France est en bon état. *Vraiment?*
According to statistics, the French economy is in good health. Really?

or adjectives, such as **sceptique, perplexe**:

Vous dites qu'il n'y a que 8% de chômage dans cette région; j'avoue que je suis *sceptique*. (see **47.10**)
You say/claim that there is only 8% unemployment in this area; I have to say I find that hard to believe.

Vous me voyez *perplexe*; je ne suis pas convaincue que ce soit vrai.
You can see I'm confused; I'm not convinced that that's true.

or verbs such as **douter de**:

Vous prétendez que notre service n'a pas répondu à vos lettres mais, franchement, *j'en doute*. (see **12.6b**)
You claim/state/say that our department has not replied to your letters but, frankly, I doubt that/have my doubts about that.

and questions expressing reservation or doubt:

Etes-vous sûr que ces chiffres *soient* (*or sont*) **exacts?** (see **39.2.1**)
Are you sure these figures are accurate?

Croyez-vous vraiment *que* ce *soit* le cas? (see **39.2.1**)
Do you really believe that's true/this to be the case?

(g) In a debating situation, intention to express reservation is often introduced using polite openings such as **permettez-moi de** + infinitive (same subject in both clauses) or **je voudrais** + infinitive *or* **que** + subjunctive:

> *Permettez-moi d'émettre certaines réserves* quant à la validité de cet argument. (see 71.1b)
>
> Allow me to express certain reservations about the validity of their argument.

> *Je voudrais faire part au* premier orateur *de ma perplexité* à l'égard des statistiques qu'il a mentionnées. (see 15.2, 42.4)
>
> I would like to say to the first speaker that I have reservations about the statistics he gave/referred to.

or the conditional tense of verbs expressing reservation:

> **80% de participation aux prochaines élections?** *Cela m'étonnerait!*
>
> 80% turnout at the next elections? I'd be surprised!

> *J'en serais* bien *étonnée!* (see 12.6b)
>
> I'd be very surprised!/That would really surprise me!

> *Je n'en mettrais pas* ma *main au feu*, si j'étais vous! (see 33.1.1)
>
> I wouldn't count on it, if I were you!

or impersonal phrases referring *back* to what is in doubt using **ce que, ce qui, cela**:

> *Ce que* vous venez d'avancer *est problématique et discutable.* (see 15.11)
>
> What you have just said/The point you have just put forward is problematic and debatable.

> **Vous nous avez tracé une courbe parfaite mais** *cela ne reflète pas forcément la réalité.*
>
> You have sketched/drawn a perfect curve/picture for us, but it does not necessarily reflect reality.

or impersonal phrases referring *forward* to what is in doubt using **il semble** + adjective + **que** + subjunctive, **il y a lieu de** + verb expressing reservation:

> *Il semble très étonnant qu'*une si faible proportion de l'échantillon *ait répondu* à cette question. (see 39.2.1, 46.3)
>
> It is very surprising that such a low proportion of the people in the sample survey replied to the question.

> *Il y a lieu de s'interroger sur* la marge d'erreur tolérée dans les relevés de données que vous mentionnez. (see 15.2, 42.1, 46)
>
> There is reason to doubt the margin of error in the data you refer to.

71.2 Possibility and probability

These notions can be seen as representing two intermediate stages on a spectrum from doubt to certainty (see **71.1**).

(a) Some expressions can be used to express both with slight variations, e.g. **il y a des chances/une chance**. Note the different constructions which follow these impersonal phrases (see **34**):

Il y a des chances pour que le directeur des ventes *parte* en voyage d'étude la semaine prochaine. (possibility)
It is possible that the sales director will leave on a study tour next week.

Il y a de fortes chances qu'il prenne l'avion lundi. (probability)
It's likely that he will fly (out)/take the plane on Monday.

Il y a peu de chances de pouvoir le contacter avant son départ. (improbability)
There's not much chance of being able to contact him before he leaves.

Il n'y a aucune chance de terminer le rapport à temps pour le lui confier. (impossibility)
There's no possibility/chance of finishing the report in time to give it to him.

(b) **Peut-être** is very commonly used to express possibility:

● either on its own as a response:

Comptes-tu garder cette vieille armoire? – *Peut-être (bien),* **on verra.**
Are you going to keep this/that old cupboard/wardrobe? – Yes, maybe, we'll see.

Alternatives include **ça se peut, ça se pourrait** (both informal, spoken) (see **6.3d**), **(c'est) possible, (ce n'est) pas impossible** (see **6.3b**).

● or within a sentence and in various positions:

Peut-être est-elle déjà *partie.* (note the inversion)
Perhaps she has already gone/left.

Peut-être qu'elle voudra bien venir. (informal, spoken)
Perhaps she'd like to come.

Elle est *peut-être* déjà partie. (no inversion)
Perhaps she has already gone/left.

(c) The verb **pouvoir** is central to a number of expressions indicating possibility. It can be followed by an infinitive:

Un accident *peut arriver* à tout moment.
An accident could happen at any time.

Attention! Un train *peut* en *cacher* un autre. (see **12.6b**)
Warning! Another train may be following.

or used in an impersonal expression such as **il se peut que** + subjunctive (see **39.2.1**):

Il se peut que les rues *soient* très *encombrées* à cette heure-ci.
The streets may be full of traffic just now.

Il peut arriver que je sois en retard mais c'est vraiment très rare. (see **6.3b**)
I may be late from time to time but it's most unusual.

and **pouvoir** and the other expressions can be used in the conditional tense (see **33.1.5**):

Vite, allume le poste, les premiers coureurs *pourraient* déjà avoir franchi la ligne d'arrivée. (see 45)
Quick/Hurry up, put on the TV, the first runners may/might have crossed the finishing line already.

Vu les protestations, *il se pourrait que* le gouvernement *fasse* marche arrière. (see 42.1)
In view of the protests the government may do a U-turn.

Dans cette enquête, nous avons toujours recherché deux suspects, or *il pourrait s'agir* de la même personne!
During this investigation we have always been looking for two suspects, but it might be (just) one person!

(d) Finally, adjectives such as **possible, impossible, éventuel** occur in various contexts and can be used to express possibility and impossibility:

● in impersonal expressions:

Il n'est pas impossible qu'ils aillent en France pendant les vacances. (see 39.2.1, 46)
It's not impossible/It's possible that they'll go to France during the holidays.

Il m'est impossible de vous rencontrer aujourd'hui. (same subject in both clauses, so use **de** + infinitive)
I can't meet you today.

● in verb phrases, for example **rendre possible** 'to make possible':

Ce changement d'attitude de la part du gouvernement israélien *rend possible* une amélioration des relations diplomatiques entre les deux pays.
This change of attitude by the Israeli government will make possible an improvement in diplomatic relations between the two countries.

● or with nouns:

Malheureusement, vous devez envisager une *aggravation éventuelle* de la maladie de votre père au cours des mois à venir.
Regrettably, you will have to consider that your father's illness may possibly get worse in the coming months.

(e) The corresponding nouns, or adverbs, are also used:

Les événements survenus dans l'ex-Yougoslavie prouvent que la *possibilité d'*une guerre *ne peut jamais être* totalement exclue. (see 41.2, 42.1)
Events in the former Yugoslavia demonstrate that the possibility of (a) war can never be totally excluded.

Pour l'encadrement du tableau, je ferai *éventuellement* appel à un spécialiste.
I'll probably get an expert to frame the picture.

(f) Sometimes, the line between possibility and probability is easily crossed, for example simply by using an adverb of reinforcement such as **bien**:

> **Regarde le ciel! Il semble *bien* que le temps va changer.** (see **46.3**)
> Look at the sky! It looks like the weather's going to change.

Il se pourrait bien, il est bien possible que + subjunctive are two possible alternatives as well as **on dirait bien que** for more informal language:

> **Ça alors! *On dirait bien que* quelqu'un a essayé de forcer la porte!**
> Blow me! You'd think someone had tried to break down the door!

(g) Other adverbial forms, such as **sans doute, certainement**, may be used to express probability (*not* certainty). Note the inversion in the first example:

> ***Sans doute a-t-elle été obligée de quitter* cette pièce momentanément pour aller répondre au téléphone.** (see **25.3.2**)
> She must have left the room for a moment to answer the telephone.

> **Comme tu n'as pas encore réglé ta facture, ils vont *certainement* vouloir te faire payer des intérêts.** (see **25.3.2**, **45.3**)
> Since you haven't paid the bill yet, they'll probably want you to pay interest.

(h) And, of course, terms whose meaning suggests probability or improbability may be used, in various positions in a sentence, as impersonal expressions (see **46**):

> ***Il est* très *vraisemblable qu'*un nouveau secrétaire général *sera nommé* d'ici quelques jours.** (see **41, 50.4e**)
> It is very likely that a new general secretary will be appointed in a few days.

> ***Il est peu probable que* le directeur licencié *soit remplacé* avant janvier.** (see **41**)
> It is unlikely that the manager who has been made redundant will be replaced before January.

(i) Note that negative forms of these impersonal verbs have to be followed by a verb in the subjunctive and also that there is a tendency to use **peu** *or* **guère vraisemblable/ probable** rather than **invraisemblable/improbable**. However, the latter may be found in some cases:

> **C'est plus qu'*improbable*, c'est carrément impossible!**
> It's more than unlikely/improbable, it's frankly impossible!

Terms whose meaning suggests probability or improbability may also be used as adverbs:

> **Les négociations ont *vraisemblablement* échoué en raison de l'intransigeance des parties en présence.** (see **48.4**)
> The negotiations have probably broken down because of the intransigence of the (two) sides/parties (involved).

as adjectives:

> **La tension croissante qui se fait jour laisse augurer un échec *probable* des négociations.** (see **43.1, 45.4**)
> The increasing tension makes a breakdown in negotiations look likely.

as nouns:

> **Selon toute *probabilité*, le tunnel ne sera pas ouvert au public à la date prévue.**
> It is quite likely that the tunnel will not be open to the public on the date scheduled.

(j) Verbs play an important part in expressing probability, in particular the verb **devoir**:

> **Tiens, il n'y a plus d'échaffaudage, les ouvriers *ont dû le démonter* pendant le week-end!** (see **46.2**)
> Look! The scaffolding's gone. The workmen must have taken it down/ dismantled it during the weekend.

> **Notre représentant *devrait passer* vous voir avec les échantillons en début de semaine prochaine.** (see **50.4b**)
> Our representative should call on you with samples at the beginning of next week.

(k) Some verbs are used specifically to express the probability of a negative occurrence, for example, **risquer de** + infinitive or **craindre (fort) que/avoir (bien) peur que** + **ne** + subjunctive:

> **Les dépenses occasionnées par le congrès *risquent* fort *de déstabiliser* les comptes de l'organisation pour l'exercice en cours.** (see **42.1, 47.1.3**)
> The expenses incurred by the conference may/might well upset the organization's budget for the present financial year.

> ***Je crains qu'il ne soit* trop tard pour le cinéma car c'est samedi et *il y a de fortes chances pour que* ce *soit* déjà complet.** (see **39.2.1**)
> I'm afraid that it may be too late for the cinema because it's Saturday and it's quite likely that it's already full.

In the previous double example, note the insertion of **ne** in the first part of the sentence following **je crains que** (see **47.12**).

(l) In a previous example (see **71.2i**), the use of **laisser** + **augurer** expressing probability was highlighted:

> **La tension croissante qui se fait jour *laisse augurer* un échec *probable* des négociations.**

Similar combinations are available with **permet de** + infinitive or **est à** + infinitive (see **45.5.1**):

> **La baisse des taux d'intérêt *permet d'envisager* une reprise du marché (de l')immobilier.**
> The drop in interest rates suggests a recovery in the property market.

> **A la suite des pluies torrentielles de la nuit dernière, des inondations *sont à prévoir* dans certaines régions.**
> After last night's torrential rain, flooding is likely in some areas.

(m) Other verbs in the conditional tense may be used to express probability (see **33.1.5**):

> ***Je parierais qu'il ne viendra* pas.**
> I bet he won't come.

> *Cela m'étonnerait que* le problème de l'Irlande du Nord *puisse être*
> entièrement *résolu* d'ici la fin de l'année. (see **39.2.1, 41, 50.4e**)
> It would surprise me if the Northern Ireland problem can be fully
> resolved by the end of the year.

The conditional tense is often used for forecasting, as in the following examples
(economic forecast) from *Capital* (August 1994):

> **Après avoir reculé de 0,9% en 1993, le PIB (Produit Intérieur Brut)**
> ***devrait progresser* cette année de 1,8%, selon l'OCDE (Organisation**
> **de Coopération et de Développement Economiques). (see 45.1.3)**
> Having dropped 0.9% in 1993, the GDP (gross domestic product) should
> rise this year by 1.8%, according to the OECD (Organization for
> Economic Cooperation and Development).

> **Les exportations *seraient* le moteur auxiliaire de cette reprise. . . .**
> **Elles *progresseraient* de 4,3%. . . . Mais nos succès à l'étranger *seraient***
> **insuffisants. . . . Résultat: notre excédent commercial *diminuerait***
> **sensiblement en 1995.**
> The recovery will be export-led. . . . Exports should rise by 4.3%. . . . But
> our results abroad will not be sufficient. . . . Our balance of payments
> surplus will consequently suffer a considerable decline in 1995.

71.3 Condition and hypothesis

Although different in meaning, these two notions are close in terms of the structures
used. Broadly, when the realization of one fact (usually in the main clause) depends on
the realization of another (hypothesis or condition in the dependent clause), then we
have a hypothetical sentence.

(a) **Si** is commonly used in a complex sentence of this type (see **33.1.1**):

> *Si* le témoin *parle*, l'accusé *sera condamné*. (see **41**)
> If the witness talks, the accused will be found guilty.

> *Dis-le* tout de suite, *si* tu ne *veux* pas y aller.
> Say now, if you don't want to go.

The hypothesis can be set in the present, in the past, or, as in the following example,
in the future. Particular attention has to be paid to the use of tenses (see **33.1.1**):

> *Si* le grand-père *venait* à disparaître, les petits-enfants *hériteraient*
> d'une grosse fortune.
> If their grandfather were to die, the grandchildren would inherit a vast
> fortune.

Quand + appropriate tense (future or future perfect) is an alternative (see **30**):

> **Tu pourras sortir *quand tu auras terminé* ton travail.**
> You can go out/leave when you have finished your work. (note the
> English tense)

(b) In all the above examples with **si**, note that the condition/hypothesis may become
a reality. In the following cases, however, the implication is that it cannot be realized
(see **33.1.1**):

> *Si j'avais joué* ma combinaison ce jour-là, *je serais* riche aujourd'hui.
> If I had used my combination of numbers that day, I'd be rich now.

> *Si je n'avais pas freiné* à temps, *je l'aurais renversée!*
> If I hadn't braked in time, I would have knocked her down!

(c) The following example illustrates an abstract principle. In this case, structures of the type **supposons que/si . . . alors/dans ce cas** are often used (with the indicative):

> *Si* x + 2 *est* égal à 6, *alors* x = **4.**
> If x + 2 equals 6, then x = 4.

and note the hypothesis in the following example:

> *Supposons qu'il a pris* le train de 8h00, *dans ce cas* il arrivera à Nantes à 12h30.
> If he caught the 8 o'clock train, he will arrive in Nantes at 12.30.

(d) Other ways of expressing condition include:

● using clauses with the conditional tenses

> *Au cas où vous ne seriez pas satisfait de* ce produit, *veuillez nous le renvoyer* dans son emballage d'origine.
> If the item does not meet with your approval, please return it to us in the original packing.

> Cet ordinateur est muni d'une mémoire auxiliaire *dans l'hypothèse où* la mémoire disponible *serait insuffisante pour* une application spécifique. (see **41**)
> This computer has expandable capacity should the memory prove inadequate for specific applications.

Sometimes, the condition is implied rather than explicit, especially in spoken, or colloquial, language:

> Tu *l'aurais vue* leur crier après comme ça . . . une vraie demeurée!
> (*Si tu l'avais vue, tu l'aurais prise* comme moi pour une demeurée.)
> If you'd seen her shouting at them like that . . . a real half-wit!

> *J'aurais l'argent*, je te le *rendrais* tout de suite, crois-moi, mais je suis fauchée!
> If I had the money, I'd give it back to you right away, believe me, but I'm broke!

● using clauses with the subjunctive

> Ce logiciel est très simple à utiliser, *à condition que vous observiez* bien les premières consignes de manipulation. (see **39.2.2**)
> This software package is very easy to use, provided you follow the instructions at the beginning.

> La délégation arrivera à l'hôtel dans quelques minutes, *à moins que l'autobus n'ait pris* du retard. (note the insertion of **ne** (see **47.12**))
> (see **39.2.2**)
> The delegation will arrive at the hotel in a few minutes, unless the bus is late.

> Dieu te pardonnera, *pourvu que tu ailles* te confesser. (see **39.2.2**)
> God will forgive you, if you go to confession.

and less directly:

> *Que je vous trouve* (subjunctive) **encore à traîner dans le quartier, et j'appelle les flics!** (see **39.1**)
> If I find you hanging about in the area any more, I'll call the police!

- using clauses with the indicative

> **Tu devras envisager différentes possibilités pour l'été prochain,** *selon que tu auras obtenu* **ou non ton permis de conduire en juin.** (see **11.2, 30**)
> You'll have to think about the different possibilities for next summer, depending on whether or not you get your driving licence in June.

> **Le tarif est différent,** *suivant que vous faites* **votre réservation au comptoir ou par téléphone.**
> The rate is different according to whether you make your reservation at reception or over the telephone.

- using relative clauses or gerunds

> **Toute personne** *qui entrerait* **sans badge d'identification serait immédiatement repérée par la caméra.** (see **4.4, 15.1, 41**)
> Anyone entering (*or* who may/might enter) without identification would be picked up immediately by the camera.

> *En signant* **cette pétition il aurait prouvé qu'il est vraiment opposé au nucléaire.** (see **33.1.5, 43.1**)
> By signing/If he signed the petition he would have proved he really is against nuclear power.

- using phrases such as **à condition de** or **à moins de** followed by an infinitive (see **39.5**)

> **Vous pouvez tous venir prendre un verre chez moi** *à condition de ne pas faire* **trop de bruit car les enfants dorment.** (see **47.8**)
> You can all come and have a drink in my house provided you don't make too much noise because the children are asleep.

> **Ce problème scientifique est si complexe qu'**à moins de s'unir**, les équipes de recherche ne pourront jamais en découvrir la solution.** (see **12.6**)
> This scientific problem is so complicated that unless they work together the research teams will never (be able to) find the solution.

- using a complement of condition introduced by **en cas de, sans, avec,** etc.

> *En cas de panne,* **les véhicules s'immobilisent sur la bande d'arrêt d'urgence et l'équipe de mécaniciens intervient aussitôt.**
> If there is a breakdown the cars stop in the emergency lane and the mechanics get to work immediately.

> *Sans chaînes,* **vous n'avez aucun espoir de franchir le col.**
> Without wheel-chains you've no hope of getting through the pass.

- using forms where the condition is implied, for example imperatives or forms in apposition

> ***Demande-lui*, tu verras, il te donnera exactement la même réponse!**
> Ask him and you'll see, he'll give you exactly the same answer!

> ***Une fois débarrassés de leur dette*, les pays du tiers-monde pourraient enfin organiser leur propre développement.**
> If they were free of their debt, third world countries could at last organize their own development planning.

(e) Finally, it is interesting to look more closely at the verb **supposer** to see how different forms convey different nuances of meaning. **Supposer que** (or equivalent expressions) + indicative is used to make or to check an assumption. This is an alternative way of expressing probability (see **71.2**):

> **Il est maintenant 10h00, *je suppose que* le facteur *est* passé.**
> It's 10 o'clock. I suppose the postman has been.

> ***Je suppose que* tu *restes* dîner?**
> I suppose/assume you're staying to eat/for dinner?

> **Jacqueline Pernet, je *présume*? . . . Louis Legrand, enchanté.**
> Jacqueline Pernet, I presume? . . . Louis Legrand, delighted to meet you.

However, with **supposons que, en supposant que, à supposer que**, you can indicate a hypothesis and you use the subjunctive:

> ***Supposons que* des élections *aient* lieu en juin, quelles sont vos prédictions?** (see **39.2.2, 71.3c**)
> Suppose the elections take place/are held in June, what is your forecast on the result?

With **supposer** (or **croire**) + adjective, you can indicate an assumption:

> **Il est parti avec une autre alors qu'elle l'avait toujours *supposé fidèle*.**
> He has left with somebody else and she had always thought he was faithful (to her).

and with **supposer** + noun, you can express a condition:

> **Tout crime *suppose un coupable*.**
> If there's a crime there's a guilty person.

(f) To summarize, the following example from *Capital* (August 1994) contains several forms contained in this section under condition, certainty, probability and possibility:

> **La hausse des taux longs, *si elle persiste, viendra alourdir* le financement des déficits publics. *Si ces derniers se creusent (c'est fort probable* à l'approche des échéances électorales), les banques centrales *pourront difficilement continuer à réduire* les taux courts, *ce qui risque de freiner* la reprise.**
> If the rise in long-term interest rates persists, it will cause difficulties in the public sector borrowing requirement. If public spending increases (which is highly likely as the next election approaches), the central banks will find it difficult to reduce short-term interest rates, and this will slow down the recovery.

72 **Expressing logical relations**

Cause (see **72.1**, **72.2** and consequence (see **72.3**, **72.4**) are inseparable notions and both are often present, explicitly or implicitly, in the same sentence.

Particular emphasis can be given to either. In this section we will also see how, although distinct in meaning, aim (see **72.5**) can be fairly close to consequence in terms of means of expression.

72.1 **Cause – explicit**

The emphasis may be *explicitly* on cause through:

(a) The meaning of individual words, either nouns:

> *La raison de* **son échec est simple: elle n'a rien fait cette année.**
> The reason for her failure/she failed is simple: she has done nothing this year.

> **Cette circulaire ministérielle représente** *la cause de* **tous nos problèmes.**
> This government (ministerial) circular is at the root of all our problems.

or verbs expressing cause:

> **Le nouvel engouement pour l'opéra** *s'explique par* **la notoriété de Pavarotti pendant la coupe du monde de football.**
> The/This new craze for opera is because of Pavarotti's reputation during the World Cup (football) series.

or passive forms:

> **Le déséquilibre de la balance commerciale** *est causé par* (*or* **est dû à**) **un excès d'importations.** (see **41**)
> The deficit in the balance of trade is a result of excessive imports.

or adjectives:

> **D'après les experts, la recrudescence de certaines maladies serait** *imputable à* **la pollution atmosphérique.** (see **4.4**, **33.1.5**)
> According to the experts, the renewed outbreak of some diseases is due to air pollution.

(b) Prepositional phrases used with a noun (see **48.4**):

> **Les agriculteurs se plaignent** *à cause du mauvais temps.*
> Farmers are complaining about/because of the bad weather.

> **Les rendements agricoles ont augmenté** *grâce aux bonnes conditions météorologiques.*
> The harvests have improved as a result of favourable weather conditions.

Note that **à cause de** and **grâce à**, respectively, introduce a negative and positive cause or reason. **En raison de** is usually neutral and could therefore be used as an alternative to either.

When the cause is the absence of something, you can use **faute de**:

> *Faute d'autres moyens de transport*, **nous allons être obligés de faire du stop.**
> Because there is no other kind of transport, we are going to have to hitch-hike.

When the cause is connected to time or duration, use **sous l'effet de** or **à force de**:

> **La température devrait baisser** *sous l'effet de l'aspirine.*
> His/Her temperature should go down with (*or* because of) the aspirin.

> *A force de persévérance*, **il finira bien par décrocher son diplôme.** (see **45.5**)
> If he perseveres, he will get his diploma.

Single prepositions such as **de, par, à, pour** may also be used, with nouns:

> **Il est malade** *de chagrin.*
> He is sick with grief.

> **Cet homme a quitté son travail et sa famille** *par amour du* **voyage.**
> The man left his job and his family because of his love of travel.

or with infinitives:

> **Tu te ruines la santé** *à fumer* **autant!**
> You'll ruin your health if you smoke so much/with all that smoking.

> **Cet employé a été licencié** *pour avoir provoqué* **une bagarre dans les vestiaires.**
> The employee was sacked for causing a disturbance in the cloakroom/ changing room.

(c) Conjunctions:

For a straightforward explanation, you can use **parce que**:

> **N'est-il pas en situation d'échec** *parce que personne ne l'encourage?*
> Is he not underachieving because nobody is giving him any encouragement?

In order to state categorically (rather than explain), use **car**:

> **Le professeur ne viendra pas ce matin** *car il est malade.*
> The teacher won't be here this morning because he is ill.

NOTE A clause introduced by **car** is *never* used *first* in the complex sentence.

Puisque is emphatic as well as causal. In the following example, the cause is shown to be the decisive factor for the resignation and known both by you and the person you are speaking to.

> *Puisque vous ne voulez pas m'augmenter*, **je démissionne.**
> Since you will not increase my pay/salary, I am resigning.

Note that when there is more than one cause, **que** introduces the other causes:

> Les femmes vivent plus longtemps que les hommes *parce qu'elles se*
> *préoccupent* davantage de leur santé et *qu'elles sont* moins sujettes
> à certains accidents.
> Women live longer than men because they are more concerned about
> their health and (because) they are less prone to certain types of
> accident.

To express a logical connection between two facts, you can use **comme**:

> *Comme il refusait de manger*, sa mère a fait venir le médecin. (see
> **45.3, 45.5.1**)
> Because he was refusing to eat, his mother called the doctor.

and to reinforce a statement expressing cause, use **d'autant que** (see **49.9c**):

> Tu pourrais prendre froid, *d'autant que tu n'as presque rien* sur le
> dos!
> You'll catch cold, because you've hardly any clothes on!

When you want to cast some doubt on a given cause, you can use **sous prétexte que** +
indicative or **de** + infinitive:

> Bon nombre d'étudiants n'étaient pas en cours ce matin, *sous*
> *prétexte que* les routes *sont enneigées*. (see **22.3, 22.3.1**)
> A lot of students were not in class this morning, supposedly because of
> the snow on the roads.

When speaking and/or for emphasis, **si . . . c'est que** or **c'est . . . que** may be used:

> *S'ils ne sont pas* encore là, *c'est qu'ils ont raté* l'autobus.
> If they're not here/there yet, it's because they've missed the bus.

> *C'est à cause de lui que tu pleures?*
> Are you crying because of him?

> J'espère que *ce n'est pas parce que nous arrivons que vous partez!*
> I hope it's not because we're arriving that you're leaving!

When the cause is denied, **non que** or **ce n'est pas que** may be used with the
subjunctive. This is a particularly useful device in argumentation:

> Je ne suis pas d'accord avec vous, *non que* vos chiffres *soient* inexacts,
> mais parce que votre interprétation me paraît fausse.
> I don't agree with you, not because your figures/statistics are inaccurate,
> but because your interpretation of them seems wrong to me.

(d) Adverbs such as **en effet** or **tant**:

Use **en effet** to emphasize your point:

> On peut dire que les jeunes représentent une catégorie vulnérable
> sur le marché du travail. *En effet*, comme l'indique ce tableau, leurs
> emplois sont souvent précaires.
> One can/could say young people are a vulnerable group in the labour
> market. Indeed, as this table indicates, they often work in casual
> jobs.

and **tant** to put emphasis on the cause:

> **Il fait le vide autour de lui *tant il est agressif.***
> He alienates everyone, he's so abrasive!

Cause – implicit

Cause may be conveyed *implicitly* in various ways:

(a) in apposition:

> ***En voyant* tout ce sang, la passante s'est évanouie.** (see **42.3, 43**)
> When she saw all the blood the passer-by fainted.

> ***Découragés par* des méthodes policières violentes, les jeunes adhérents du parti ne pouvaient plus se mobiliser.** (see **42.1**)
> Repelled by the violent methods of the police, young party supporters withdrew their support.

> ***Crevé comme tu l'es*, tu ne pourras jamais rouler de nuit.** (see **42.1**)
> You're so exhausted you'll never be able to drive at night.

> ***Furieux devant* un tel déploiement de CRS (Compagnie Républicaine de Sécurité), les manifestants ont commencé à jeter des pierres dans leur direction.**
> Outraged by the sheer numbers of CRS (riot police) the demonstrators began to stone them.

(b) in separate clauses:

> **La voiture *étant tombée en panne* à l'entrée du village, nous avons dû faire le reste du chemin à pied.** (see **43.1**)
> Because the car broke down as we were entering the village we had to go the rest of the way on foot.

> **Les voitures, *qui menacent la vie urbaine*, doivent être éliminées du centre de Paris.** (see **15.1**)
> Cars, which are threatening (the quality of life in) the city, must be banned from the centre of Paris.

> **Je refuse d'adopter une proposition *qui n'a aucun sens*.** (see **15.1, 47.8**)
> I refuse to adopt a meaningless proposal.

(c) Sometimes, in particular when speaking, the causal relation might be simply suggested by context, intonation or, when writing, by punctuation:

> **Il ne va pas venir aujourd'hui, il est malade.**
> He is not coming today, he is ill.

and in a newspaper report:

> **Tempête en Bretagne: cinq pêcheurs portés disparus.**
> Storm in Brittany: five fishermen reported lost.

If you consider the first of the two examples, the man's absence (the context) would be the cause of this explanation. By adding appropriate intonation (indicating pleasure, sadness, regret, indifference . . .) to the second clause **il est malade**, and an appropriate Gallic shrug, you can convey the cause, and what you think about it.

Consequence – explicit

When the emphasis is *explicitly* on consequence:

(a) If you want to indicate in a neutral way the logical result of a fact or an action, use clauses introduced by **si bien que** or **de sorte que**:

> **C'est un cercle vicieux: les jeunes sans domicile n'ont par définition pas d'adresse *si bien qu'on ne leur confie pas* d'emploi.**
> It's vicious circle: if young people are homeless they have no address so they can't get a job. (consequence)

> **Les colis ont été postés ce matin *de sorte qu'ils arriveront* en France avant Noël.** (see **39.2.2**)
> The parcels were posted this morning so they will arrive in France before Christmas. (result)

(b) In order to stress the importance of the consequence, you may use **au point que** (see **39.2.2**):

> **La maladie l'a défigurée, *au point qu'elle en est devenue* méconnaissable.**
> The disease disfigured her to such an extent that she is unrecognizable.

or structures such as **tant de, si, tant, tellement . . . que** with nouns (see **21**):

> ***Tant d'années ont passé* depuis l'accident *que je ne m'en rappelle plus* la date exacte.**
> It's so long since the accident that I can't remember the exact date any more.

or with adjectives or adverbs (see **10.10**):

> **Ce conflit est *si complexe* et dure *depuis si longtemps qu'il semble* que personne ne trouvera de solution.**
> The conflict is so complex and has gone on for so long that it looks lilke no-one will find a solution to it.

or with verbs:

> **Votre fils *a tellement progressé* depuis l'an dernier *qu'il se retrouve* en tête de classe.**
> Your son has made so much progress since last year that he is at the top of the class.

In a sense, such double structures put emphasis on both cause and consequence:

> **Le gouvernement *est tellement corrompu*** (cause) ***qu'il n'inspire plus* confiance à quiconque.** (consequence)
> The government is so corrupt that it no longer inspires confidence in anyone.

Note that you have to use the subjunctive when the sentence is negative or interrogative:

> *Il n'est tout de même pas si tard que vous deviez* **déjà partir!**
> But it's not so late that you have to leave (already).

> **Leur fils** *a-t-il* **vraiment** *tant de* **travail** *qu'il ne puisse même pas* **leur rendre visite à Noël?**
> Has their son really so much work that he can't visit them at Christmas?

(c) Prepositions such as **pour** and **à** may also be used to express consequence. **Pour** may be combined with adverbs such as **trop** or **assez** in constructions such as

> **trop/assez** + adjective + **pour** + infinitive
> **trop/assez** + adjective + **pour que** + subjunctive

or with impersonal verbs such as

> **il suffit de** + infinitive (*or* noun) + **pour** + infinitive (*or* **pour que** + subjunctive)
> **il faut que** + subjunctive + **pour** + infinitive (*or* **pour que** + subjunctive)

> **Mes collègues sont** *assez jaloux pour avoir essayé* **de me faire licencier.**
> My colleagues are jealous enough to have tried to have me sacked.

> **Certains pensent que cet écrivain affiche** *trop d'excentricité pour qu'on le prenne* **au sérieux.** (see **39.2.2**)
> Some people think that this/the writer is too eccentric to be taken seriously.

> **Il** *suffit* **d'un bon café** *pour se redonner* **du tonus.**
> A good coffee is enough to get your energy back.

> **Il** *faut* **toujours** *graisser* **le moule** *pour que le gâteau n'attache pas.*
> Always grease the tin so that the cake does not stick.

A and **au point de** are also followed by an infinitive:

> **Je vais vous annoncer une nouvelle** *à vous couper* **le souffle!**
> I'm going to announce some news which will take your breath away.

> **Les chômeurs de longue durée peuvent être déprimés** *au point de ne plus faire* **le moindre effort pour trouver du travail.** (see **47.8**)
> The long-term unemployed can be so depressed that they will not make any effort to find work.

(d) Conjunctions or adverbs may also be used to express consequence. Some always *introduce* the clause containing the consequence, for example **c'est pourquoi, aussi, d'où**, while others can *move* within the sentence, for example **donc, par conséquent, en conséquence, ainsi, dès lors**:

> **Les ouvriers ont saccagé l'usine;** *c'est pourquoi* **ils ont été licenciés.** (see **41.1.1**)
> The workers vandalized the factory; that's why they have been sacked.

> **Notre VRP (Voyageur Représentant Placier) parcourt une région de fortes chaleurs estivales. *Aussi* avons-nous muni son véhicule de fonction d'un système de climatisation.**
> Our representative covers an area/region which can become very hot in summer. So, we have installed air-conditioning in his company car.

> **Vous m'avez remboursé, je retire *donc* ma plainte. *or* Vous m'avez remboursé *et donc* je retire ma plainte.**
> You have repaid me so I'm withdrawing my complaint.

> **La délégation japonaise a eu un empêchement de dernière minute. *En conséquence*, nous prions tous les services concernés d'annuler les réservations et autres arrangements initialement prévus pour la journée de demain.** (see 2.3)
> The Japanese delegation were delayed at the last minute. Therefore, we are asking all the departments concerned to cancel bookings/ reservations and other arrangements originally made for tomorrow.

> **Mesdames et messieurs les jurés, vous avez désormais entendu tous les témoins ayant exposé leur version des faits.** (see 50.1) **Vous disposez *ainsi* de toutes les informations nécessaires à vos délibérations.**
> Ladies and gentlemen of the jury, you have now heard all the witnesses (give their version of the events). You therefore have all the information necessary to help you reach a verdict.

> **Les forces de police ont toléré, voire participé au trafic d'ivoire. *Dès lors*, on ne peut s'étonner que des troupeaux entiers d'éléphants aient été décimés dans cette région.** (see 39.2.1, 41.1.1)
> The police have turned a blind eye to, and have even participated in, the ivory trade. So, it is no surprise that entire herds of elephants have been destroyed in the area.

Note the various nuances: **c'est pourquoi**, **aussi** (with inversion of the verb), **donc**, **dès lors** stress the undeniable logic of the consequence, **en conséquence** is often used in a formal administrative context, and **ainsi** can allow you to sum up and draw a conclusion from an argument.

(e) Like cause, consequence may be conveyed simply through the meaning of individual nouns:

> **Les *effets de la récession* se font particulièrement sentir dans certains secteurs.** (see 40.2, 45.3)
> The effects of the recession are being felt particularly in certain sectors.

> **Tu ne te rends pas compte des *conséquences de tes actes*!**
> You aren't aware of the consequence of your actions.

or verbs:

> **Les crues *ont entraîné* d'énormes problèmes aux Etats-Unis.** (see 4.2)
> The flooding has caused enormous problems in the USA.

L'utilisation croissante des matières plastiques *se traduit par* **une dégradation de l'environnement.** (see **41**)
Increasing use of plastics has led to/resulted in damage to the environment.

Consequence – implicit

(a) Just as in the case of cause, sometimes there is no explicit cohesive device between two independent clauses. Consequence is *implied* by context, intonation or punctuation (see **72.2c**):

> **Vous êtes rentrés tout à l'heure avec des chaussures pleines de boue, la moquette est couverte de taches!**
> You came in a few moments ago with your shoes covered in mud, and the carpet is covered in marks.

Note the use of the pronoun **en** in the following example. It refers back to the cause in the clause containing the consequence:

> **Cet exercice est beaucoup trop compliqué, j'***en* **perds mon latin.**
> (see **12.6c**)
> This exercise is much too difficult, I can't make head or tail of it.

(b) In some cases, in particular when speaking, **et** is used but the context indicates that there is in fact a cause/consequence relation:

> **J'ai senti que quelqu'un me suivait** *et* **je me suis mise à courir.**
> I sensed someone was following me and I began to run.

(c) Relative clauses may also be used:

> **Le camion a heurté la voiture** *qui a fait deux tonneaux* **avant de s'immobiliser.** (see **15.1, 39.5**)
> The lorry hit the car which somersaulted twice before it came to a halt.

Aim

(a) The same conjunctions (see **72.3a**) may be used to express both consequence and aim. For instance, in the following example there is not enough context to indicate whether the result was intended (aim) or not (consequence):

> **Il s'est mal conduit** *de sorte que* **ses voisins** *ne viennent plus* **le voir.**
> He behaved badly to stop his neighbours coming to see him. (aim)
> *or* He behaved badly so his neighbours don't come to see him any more. (consequence)

If aim is intended, **viennent** is subjunctive. If it is consequence that is meant, **viennent** is in fact the present indicative (see **39.2.2**). In the following example, the distinction is clearer:

> **J'entretiens ma voiture** *de sorte qu'elle soit* **encore en bon état dans dix ans.** (aim)
> I look after my car so that it will still be in good condition in ten years' time.

> **J'entretiens ma voiture** *de sorte qu'elle est* **encore en bon état (malgré son âge).** (consequence)
> I look after my car so that it is still in good condition (despite its age).

Similarly, **pour que** can introduce an aim (**pour que** is *always* followed by the subjunctive so the distinction between aim and consequence is often clear only because of context):

> **Cette école impose l'uniforme** *pour que* **les élèves** *soient* **tous sur un pied d'égalité.**
> The school insists on uniforms so that the pupils are all equal. (aim)

and compare:

> **Tu es maintenant assez grand** *pour que* **je te** *fasse* **certaines confidences sur ma vie.**
> You are adult/old enough now for me to tell you some of my secrets.

If in doubt about difference between aim and consequence, try adding the emphatic **c'est . . . que**. If it works, it is aim, if not, it is consequence. Let us test this with the previous examples:

> *C'est pour que* **les élèves** *soient* **tous sur un pied d'égalité** *que* **cette école impose l'uniforme.** (This makes sense, it works: so = aim) It's to make all the pupils equal that the school insists on uniforms.

> *C'est pour que* **je te** *fasse* **certaines confidences sur ma vie** *que* **tu es maintenant assez grand.** (This does not make sense, it does not work so the original statement expressed is not an aim but a consequence)

Sometimes, in particular after an imperative, **pour que** is abbreviated to **que**:

> **Tourne un peu,** *que* **je** *voie* **la coupe de ce mainteau.**
> Turn round a bit so that I can see the cut of this coat.

Other conjunctions will allow you to express the notion of an objective to be *reached*, for example **afin que, de façon que** + subjunctive . . . (see **39.2.2**):

> **J'ai convoqué tout le personnel ce matin** *afin que* **le calendrier de l'année à venir** *puisse* **être établi.**
> I've called all the staff together this morning so that the planning/ schedule for the year can be organized.

> **Il faudrait raccourcir le voile** *de façon qu'il ne tombe pas* **plus bas que la taille de votre robe.**
> You'd/I'd have to shorten the veil so that it doesn't fall below the waist of your dress.

or what you aim to *avoid*, for example **de peur que, de crainte que** + **ne** + subjunctive (see **39.2.2**):

> **Cette femme a caché l'existence de son enfant** *de peur que* **les services sociaux** *ne* **lui en** *retirent* **la garde.**
> The woman concealed her child's existence to avoid the social services taking him/her away from her.

> Le PDG (Président-Directeur Général) veut former lui-même son jeune collaborateur *de crainte qu'il ne soit pas* à la hauteur des nouvelles responsabilités qui lui incombent.
> The chairman/managing director wants to train his young assistant himself to ensure he is up to his new responsibilities. (in case he is not up to them)

Be careful to distinguish between the expletive **ne** following **de peur que** (in the first example above) (see **47.12**) and the negation **ne . . . pas** (in the second one).

(b) Prepositions may also be used when you are aiming at something, with nouns:

> Cette promotion, tu la veux *pour la gloire* ou *pour l'argent*?
> Do you want this promotion for the prestige or the money?

> De nombreux ménages font des économies *en vue d'une escapade estivale*. (see **4.2**)
> Many families save up for a summer jaunt.

or infinitives:

> *Afin d'éviter* à l'avenir ces problèmes de cash-flow, nous devrons exiger de nos clients qu'ils règlent leurs factures rapidement. (see **39.2.1, 39.5**)
> To avoid cash-flow problems in future, we must request that our customers settle their invoices quickly.

> Elle prend des cours du soir *dans l'intention de passer* un concours le mois prochain.
> She is taking evening classes in order to sit an exam next month.

or when you are aiming at *avoiding* something:

> Il s'est levé à 5h00 du matin *de peur d'être* en retard à son entretien. (see **39.5**)
> He got up at five in the morning because he was scared he might be late for his interview.

> *Par crainte des incendies*, les propriétaires désireux de louer des chambres d'étudiants doivent installer des détecteurs de fumée. (see **39.5**)
> Because of increased fire risk, householders wishing to rent rooms to students must install smoke detectors.

(c) A relative clause will allow you to be more specific about the aim. In the following example note the use of the subjunctive casting doubt on the existence of the office in question (see **39.3**):

> Pour établir notre siège dans cette ville, nous sommes à la recherche d'un bureau *qui soit* assez proche du centre.
> To set up our headquarters in this city, we are looking for an office near the centre.

(d) Finally, you may express aim through the meaning of nouns and noun phrases:

> Les starlettes déambulaient sur la Croisette *dans le but/à seule fin de
> se faire remarquer* par les cinéastes. (see **39.5**)
> Starlets wandered along the Croisette (in order) to be noticed by
> directors.

or verbs and verb phrases:

> C'est un artiste provocateur qui *cherche à faire réagir* son public.
> He's a provocative performer in that he tries to make the audience
> react.

or a combination of verbs and nouns:

> Grâce à d'habiles manœuvres dans l'entreprise, il a pu *atteindre* les
> *objectifs* qu'il *visait*. (see **15.2, 48.4**)
> By clever/skilled manœuvring in the company he managed to achieve
> his aims.

73 Expressing opposition

Naturally, opposition is related to disagreement (see **63.2**), concession (see **65.2**),
protest (see **66**), lack of volition (see **69.5**) and prohibition (see **70.2**). However, it is
appropriate to bring together in this section some of the many forms which allow
you to express the absence of logical relations (see **72**) and to associate independent
facts set against one another. Although there are explicit ways of associating opposing
ideas – especially through the use of concessive forms such as **bien que** 'although', **si**
'although', **qui que** 'whoever' – opposing or contrasting ideas are very often linked by
apposition, or by implication.

(a) Prepositions such as **malgré, avec, sans** may be used with nouns:

> Le bâtiment a été partiellement détruit par l'incendie *malgré
> l'intervention* rapide des pompiers.
> The building was partially destroyed by fire despite the swift
> intervention of the firemen.

> *En dépit du succès* obtenu par la Communauté, toutes les réalisations
> espérées au moment de sa fondation n'ont pas été concrétisées.
> (see **41.2, 42.1**)
> In spite of the success of the Community, not all of the results envisaged
> when it was created have been achieved.

In some cases, for example with **avec** or **sans**, opposition is less explicit:

> *Avec son air innocent*, elle est capable des actes les plus
> diaboliques.
> Despite her innocent appearance, she is capable of the most diabolical
> actions.

When reality is different from what might have been expected, you can use **au lieu de**
or **loin de** if the emphasis is on what did *not* take place. These prepositional phrases are
followed by infinitives:

> *Contre toute attente*, le chauffeur s'est engagé dans une ruelle *au lieu de prendre* l'artère principale.
> Contrary to all expectations, the driver went down a small street instead of taking the main road.

> *Loin d'apaiser* le débat, les propos de l'évêque ont provoqué un tollé général.
> Instead of calming the discussion, the bishop's words provoked general uproar.

Note the reinforcement of opposition in the first example by the use of **contre toute attente** (see **73c**).

(b) If you wish to say that part of something is excluded from the whole, use **sauf, excepté, à part, si ce n'est, hormis . . .**, and **sinon** following a negative clause:

> *Tous les cours, sauf un*, sont assurés le matin.
> All the classes except one take place in the morning.

> *Tous les cours* sont assurés le matin, *excepté l'anglais* qui a lieu le même jour à 18h00.
> All the classes take place in the morning, except English which is at 6 p.m. on the same day.

> *Aucun* livre *ne* les *intéresse, sinon* les bandes dessinées.
> They are not interested in any books except comics/comic strips.

(c) Clauses may be introduced by or contain adverbs, or adverbial phrases such as **au contraire, par contre** – usually referring back to a previous statement/ sentence:

> La France semble être très favorable à l'Union Economique et Monétaire; le Royaume-Uni, *au contraire*, ne cache pas sa réticence.
> France seems to be very much in favour of Economic and Monetary Union; the UK, on the other hand, is clearly reluctant.

> Une dépression très active arrive sur le nord. *Par contre*, l'anticyclone des Açores continuera à protéger le bassin méditerranéen.
> (see **45.5.1**)
> A deep depression is approaching northern areas. But the anticyclone over the Azores will ensure calm weather over the Mediterranean.

NOTE **Contre** features in many set phrases, e.g. **nager à contre courant** 'to swim against the current', **être contre nature** 'to be unnatural', without a definite article (see **4.4**).

The following are examples where opposition is suggested rather than expressed in the use of **en vain, finalement** . . . (emphasized by **c'est . . . que** in the second example):

> Les médecins *ont tenté en vain* (*or ont vainement tenté*) de le ranimer.
> (see **45.5.1**)
> The doctors have tried without success to revive him.

Berlusconi avait annoncé qu'il viendrait tête haute; *c'est finalement*
profil bas *qu'***il s'est présenté devant les juges.** (see 31, 40.2)
Berlusconi had announced that he would come with his head held high;
in the end he kept a low profile in front of the judges.

Note how the adjective **seul** implies a contrast in the following example:

**L'ensemble de la CEI (Communauté des Etats Indépendants) sera
sous la pluie.** *Seules* **Moscou et St Pétersbourg auront le plaisir de
quelques éclaircies.**
Rain will affect most of the CIS (the former USSR). Moscow and St
Petersburg will have some sunny spells.

(d) Cohesive devices such as **mais, néanmoins, quand même, pourtant, n'en . . . pas
moins**, are very useful for expressing opposition. They also refer back to a previous
sentence or clause, or to an expression in apposition (see **65.2**). Note that two of the
devices occur in the first example:

Il neigera sur l'ensemble de l'Ecosse *mais* **le soleil fera** *néanmoins* **son
apparition sur la partie est du pays.**
There will be snow throughout Scotland but with some sunny spells in
the east (of the country).

Appelés à manifester, les Milanais sont *pourtant* **venus moins
nombreux que les journalistes.**
The Milanese had been called on to demonstrate publicly but there were
fewer demonstrators than journalists.

Acculé à la faillite, il *n'en est pas moins décidé* **à acquérir une
deuxième entreprise.**
Despite his bankruptcy, he was determined to acquire another
business.

(e) Clauses may be introduced by conjunctions such as **alors que** or **tandis que** to
express opposition and simultaneity, with the indicative:

Alors que **des millions d'emplois** *se perdaient* **encore dans la première
moitié des années 80, des millions d'emplois nouveaux** *ont* **depuis
lors** *été créés.* (see 26.1, 41)
Millions of jobs were still being lost in the early 1980s; subsequently
millions of new jobs have been created.

L'aile droite du parti socialiste *soutient* **la proposition** *tandis que*
l'extrême gauche la *dénonce* **avec vigueur.**
The right wing of the socialist party is backing the proposal whereas it is
being condemned strongly by the far left.

and by conjunctions such as **bien que, quoique, malgré que** 'although', with the
subjunctive (see **39.2.2**):

Bien qu'il soit **de nature essentiellement économique, le programme
de mesures prend en compte la protection de l'environnement et du
consommateur.**
Although it is essentially an economic plan, the measures take into
account environmental and consumer protection.

Si is frequently used to express opposition (here reinforced by **immanquablement**) or concession. It does not introduce a condition in the following example and, therefore, is not restricted to the sequence of tenses used for expressing conditions:

> *Si* **les problèmes de Bernard Tapie ne touchent pas directement les socialistes, ils vont *immanquablement* affaiblir l'électorat de gauche.** (see 25.3.2)
> Although Bernard Tapie's problems do not affect the socialists directly, they will inevitably weaken the socialist vote.

And there are conjunctions such as **quand bien même, même si** 'even if' with the conditional in the main clause:

> *Quand bien même* **il m'offrirait la lune, je ne *l'épouserais* pas.**
> Even if he offered me the moon, I wouldn't marry him.

> *Même si* **les forces de l'ONU (Organisation des Nations Unies) intervenaient rapidement, tous les civils ne *pourraient* pas être sauvés du massacre.**
> Even if the UN forces were to intervene quickly, not all the civilians could be rescued from the massacre.

(f) Sometimes emphasis is placed on particular elements in the sentence expressing opposition, for example, on the noun. Note the wide range of concessive constructions such as **quel que** (adjective) 'whatever', **quelque** (adjective) + noun + **que** 'whatever', **quelque . . . que, aussi . . . que, tout . . . que, si . . . que** 'however' (adverb) + subjunctive which imply opposition (see **39.2.2**), and focus on an element in the sentence – in the following examples on nouns:

> *Quels que soient les exercices donnés*, **cet élève refuse de les faire.**
> Whatever exercises are set, this pupil refuses to do them.

> *Quelques avertissements que l'on communique* (subjunctive), **il y a toujours des gens qui skient hors-piste et s'exposent aux risques d'avalanche.** (see 11.11a)
> Whatever warnings are given, there are always people who ski off-piste and expose themselves to the risk of avalanche.

and in the following examples on past participles and adjectives, and in the last one on an adverb:

> *Quelque déterminées qu'elles soient*, **ces deux étudiantes n'obtiendront pas d'être inscrites dans le même groupe de travaux dirigés.** (see 11.11b)
> However determined they are, these two students won't succeed in getting into the same tutorial group.

Note that in this case **quelque** is an adverb, and is therefore invariable, whereas in the previous example **quelques (avertissements)** is an adjective. An alternative way of saying the same thing would be:

> *Aussi déterminées qu'elles soient*, **ces deux étudiantes n'obtiendront pas d'être inscrites dans le même groupe de travaux dirigés.**

Similarly, note in the following example how **tout** can be adverb (**tout chrétiens**) or adjective (**toutes pieuses**) (see **11.1**), with the indicative:

> *Tout chrétiens qu'ils sont*, ils ne font preuve d'aucune compassion et *toutes pieuses qu'elles paraissent*, la générosité leur est inconnue.
> However Christian they may be, they show no compassion, and however pious they seem, they do not know the meaning of generosity.

Finally, an example with **si** 'despite the fact that, however', focusing on an adverb:

> *Si mal qu'il lise*, le Conseil de classe a décidé de l'autoriser à passer dans la classe supérieure.
> Despite the fact that he is not a good reader, the staff meeting has decided to allow him to proceed to the next year.

(g) Concessive relative pronouns **qui que** 'whoever', **où que** 'wherever', **quoi que** 'whatever', with the subjunctive, can be used (see **39.2.2**):

> *Qui que ce soit*, je ne suis pas là!
> Whoever it is, I'm not here!

> *Où que vous vous cachiez*, vous ne m'échapperez pas.
> Wherever you hide, you won't get away from me.

> Ils ne seront pas d'accord, *quoi que tu dises*.
> They won't agree, whatever you say.

And sometimes opposition is *implicit* in relative clauses (with the indicative):

> Imaginez-vous que ce texte, *qui comporte plusieurs erreurs*, a été sélectionné pour l'épreuve de français! (see **15.1, 41.1**)
> Can you imagine, this text, which has several errors in it, has been chosen for the French exam!

(h) Of course, there are other implicit ways of expressing opposition; for example, by using apposition or simply in the meaning of verb phrases:

> *Tu peux dire tout ce que tu voudras*, je ne changerai pas d'avis. (see **15.11.1**)
> You can say anything you want, I won't change my mind.

> *On a beau placer* des poubelles sur les parkings, les gens continuent à jeter leurs ordures n'importe où. (see **11.13c, 45.5**)
> Even though there are litter bins in car parks, people will continue to throw their rubbish any old place.

or through the use of different parts of the verb such as the imperative or the conditional tense – especially when speaking (see also **72.2, 72.4**):

> *Crie* si ça te défoule, je ne te donnerai pas ce livre!
> Make as much noise as you like, I won't give you the book!

> On me *donnerait* tout l'or du monde que ça ne changerait rien à ma décision!
> Even if they gave me all the money in the world, I wouldn't change my mind.

(i) Finally, it is well worth noting the use of antithesis, which is often used for stylistic reasons in literature, and exploited fully in advertising because it allows you to express everything and its opposite. Examples of these short sharp symmetrical formulae or slogans abound in advertising:

Minimir, *miniprix* mais il fait le *maximum.* (washing powder)
Minimir (= Persil, Daz), miniprice maxijob!

Un petit clic vaut mieux qu'*un grand choc*! (safety belt)
A little click is better than a big bang!/Clunk-click: every trip!

74   Structuring

Whether you want to give a presentation, make a speech, send a memo, write an essay/
a report or intervene in a meeting, what you say or write will have more impact if it is
structured. Broadly, you will need an introduction, a middle section and a conclusion.
In this section, you will find a number of useful forms under three headings: Beginning
(introduction) (see **74.1**); Continuing (middle section) (see **74.2**); Ending (conclusion)
(see **74.3**).

74.1   Beginning

(a) The very beginning

Before getting to the topic itself, it is advisable to use polite formulae, especially when
you take the floor (in front of your classmates or in any formal spoken context),
sometimes emphasised by **c'est . . . que**:

> *C'est un grand plaisir que* de vous présenter aujourd'hui mon exposé
> sur l'enseignement supérieur en Belgique.
> It is a great pleasure for me to give a paper today on higher education in
> Belgium.

> *C'est* pour moi *un grand honneur que* de pouvoir m'adresser à un
> public d'éminents experts.
> It is a great honour for me to be able to address an audience of eminent
> experts.

Alternatively, you can use **je/nous** + verb phrase *or* verb + infinitive:

> *Je suis* très *heureux de pouvoir prononcer l'allocution de bienvenue*
> dans un cadre aussi magnifique. (same subject in both clauses so use
> **de** + infinitive)
> I am very pleased to be able to give the welcoming address in such
> magnificent surroundings.

> *Nous apprécions d'avoir été invités à présenter* les résultats de nos
> recherches à d'autres étudiants. (see 41.2)
> We are pleased to have been invited to present our research findings to
> fellow students.

At the very beginning, it is quite usual to refer *back* to an event/a fact. Noun phrases
may be used in this case:

> *En réponse à* votre lettre du 2 janvier, nous sommes heureux de vous
> soumettre une offre pour les articles suivants:
> In reply to your letter of 2 January, we are pleased to make you an
> offer for the following articles:

> *A l'occasion de* ce 21ème congrès de l'Organisation, je souhaite la bienvenue aux membres présents parmi nous pour la première fois.
> On the occasion of this 21st conference of the Organisation, I extend a (warm) welcome to those members who are with us for the first time.

(b) Introducing the topic

In writing a letter, a report or an essay, the topic may simply be announced with a noun followed by a colon:

> *Objet:* **demande d'offre** (in commercial correspondence)
> Re: request for quotation

> *Motif:* **organisation des équipes de nuit** (in a report)
> Re: night shift schedule/roster

> *Sujet:* **pour ou contre les OGM** (in an essay)
> Topic: for or against GMOs

The topic may also be contained in the title or introductory sentence, after phrases such as **au sujet de, à propos de, sur, concernant, relatif à** . . .

> **Rapport du contremaître** *au sujet de* **l'accident survenu le 13 mars à Evry sur le chantier n° 2.** (see **42.1**)
> Foreman's report on the accident at construction site 2 at Evry on 13 March.

> **Proposition de résolution des députés Ernst de la Graete et autres, au nom du groupe des Verts au Parlement européen,** *sur* **la cohésion économique et sociale.**
> Motion for a resolution tabled by MEPs Ernst de la Graete and others, on behalf of the Green Group in the European Parliament, on social and economic cohesion.

> *Mémoire de Maîtrise relatif à* **la politique des transports urbains à Genève.**
> Final year dissertation on urban transport policy in Geneva.

In verb phrases, you should use the conditional tense (see **33.1.3**):

> *Je voudrais* **parler de la contraception.**
> I should like to speak about contraception.

> *J'aimerais* **aborder le thème de l'éducation pré-scolaire.**
> I should like to tackle the subject of pre-school education.

or in a relative clause following the topic:

> **Telle est la question** *à laquelle je voudrais* **répondre.** (see **15.6**)
> That is the question I should like to answer.

> **Voilà** *ce dont je voudrais* **vous entretenir.** (see **15.8**)
> That is what I would like to talk to you about.

For a more direct or powerful introduction, use the present or future tense:

> **Je *tiens à* évoquer le problème suivant:**
> I wish to raise the following matter:

> **Dans mon exposé, je *traiterai* la question de l'autonomie des régions.**
> In my presentation, I shall deal with the question of regional autonomy.

A noun + relative clause may precede the topic:

> **La question qui nous intéresse concerne le développement des autoroutes de l'information.** (see 15.1)
> The question which interests us is the development of information superhighways.

> **Le thème qui me préoccupe a trait au rôle des femmes dans les sociétés actuelles.** (see 15.1)
> My concern today is the role of women in contemporary society.

> **Le problème que nous allons analyser porte sur le recyclage des déchets nucléaires.** (see 15.2)
> The problem we are going to analyse concerns the recycling of nuclear waste.

(c) Announcing an outline

The future tense is often used to introduce the outline of a text:

> **Je traiterai la question en trois points: premièrement . . . , deuxièmement . . .** (see 47.1)
> I shall deal with the question in three parts: first . . . , second . . .

In the following example, note the use of the future tense, followed by **avant que + ne** + subjunctive or **avant de** + infinitive (see 39.5) to present the outline of a dissertation:

> **C'est pourquoi un premier chapitre *rappellera* les grandes étapes de la décentralisation en France *avant que* le deuxième *ne traite* plus en détail des dispositions du nouveau projet de loi sur la décentralisation. Par ailleurs, *il nous faudra* insister au chapitre III sur les incidences de la nouvelle législation pour les collectivités territoriales de la ville de Tours *avant d'aborder* enfin au chapitre IV les craintes et espoirs qu'elle suscite au niveau de la commune, du département et de la région.**
> Thus the first chapter will review the main stages of decentralisation in France, and the second will look in more detail at the provisions of the new bill on decentralisation. Then, we will focus in the third chapter on the implications of the new legislation for regional and local authorities in Tours. Finally, in the fourth chapter we will deal with the hopes and fears which it is giving rise to at the level of the *commune*, the *département*, and the region.

In the following spoken interventions, the speech is introduced by **je voudrais . . .** , and followed by some of the numerous cohesive devices available for presenting an outline: **d'une part . . . d'autre part, durant la première partie, dans un deuxième temps:**

> **Madame la Présidente, mes chères collègues, *je voudrais*
> essentiellement dans mon intervention aborder deux aspects du
> programme législatif et je le ferai brièvement. *D'une part* l'énergie et
> *d'autre part* la recherche et ses implications en matière de politique
> industrielle.**
> Madam President, colleagues, I should like to concentrate in my
> presentation on two aspects of the legislative programme and I shall do
> so briefly. First of all, energy, and second, research and its implications in
> terms of industrial policy.

> ***Je voudrais*** **si vous le permettez, diviser cet exposé en deux temps
> séparés par une pause. *Durant la première partie,* j'aborderai la
> question de la mondialisation et de ses définitions. *Dans un
> deuxième temps,* j'évoquerai les arguments employé par les
> défenseurs et les détracteurs de la mondialisation.**
> I should like to divide my talk into two parts with a break in between.
> In the first part, I shall deal with the issue of globalisation and its
> definitions. In the second I will review the arguments put forward by
> those who support or those who oppose globalisation.

When breaking down an outline into its various components, corresponding, for
example to the various sections or chapters of an essay or a dissertation, the following
forms may occur:

Noun (relating to the section or chapter) + verb announcing the topic:

> ***La seconde partie porte, elle, sur*** **les politiques d'emploi.** (see **14.2d**)
> The second part deals with employment policies.

> ***Le chapitre 7 vise à*** **situer la place de la politique de l'emploi dans
> les enjeux de la dernière décennie.**
> Chapter 7 aims to situate employment policy among the major issues of
> the last decade.

Once the topic is announced, subsequent sentences are frequently introduced by **c'est**
which is often followed by a relative clause:

> ***C'est*** **le thème des deux derniers chapitres.**
> This is the topic of the final two chapters.

> ***C'est*** **de tout cela *dont il est question* dans la première partie de ce
> document.**
> That is the subject matter of the first part of this document.

> ***C'est l'objet*** **des deux premières parties de cette dissertation *que de*
> répondre à ces questions.**
> The purpose of the first two sections of this essay is to answer these
> questions.

Adverb + **il faut** or **il convient de** + infinitive may also be used:

> ***Ensuite, il faut rappeler*** **les principaux obstacles au développement
> dans ces régions. Enfin, *il convient de s'interroger* sur les moyens à
> déployer pour y faire face.**
> Then we shall touch on the main obstacles to development in those
> regions. Finally, we should examine the means to tackle these obstacles.

Finally, it is worth noting the use of punctuation (especially the use of brackets) when giving the outline of a longer text:

> **Les chapitres correspondent chacun à un mode de transport et ont été ordonnés selon les taux de fréquentation. Les réseaux de tramway (chapitre 2) et d'autobus (chapitre 3) connaissent un déclin relatif. En revanche, les secteurs du chemin de fer (chapitre 4) et de l'automobile (chapitre 5) se portent plutôt bien. Les conséquences de ces évolutions sont analysées en termes d'impact sur l'environnement (chapitre 6) et sur la santé des usagers (chapitre 7).**
> Each chapter deals with an individual mode of transport and these are arranged in terms of their frequency of use. Tram (chapter 2) and bus (chapter 3) networks are in relative decline, whereas rail (chapter 4) and car (chapter 5) transport are doing quite well. An analysis is carried out of the impact of these trends both on the environment (chapter 6) and on the state of health of those using these forms of transport (chapter 7).

74.2   **Continuing**

(a) Adverbs are often used to indicate a transition, that is, a move from one topic or idea to another. Adverbs of opposition (see **73c–73d**), for example, may introduce the second part of a for-and-against type of argumentation:

> **Pour toutes ces raisons, la réduction du temps de travail apparaît comme la solution du chômage. *Cependant*, il importe aussi d'en évoquer les inconvénients.**
> For all of these reasons, a reduction in working hours seems to be the solution to the problem of unemployment. However, it is just as important to consider the disadvantages (of such a policy).

Adverbs and adverbial phrases may introduce the various points which contribute to argumentation within the text:

> **Il faut fournir aux femmes qui travaillent des structures adéquates pour la garde de leurs enfants, *d'abord* parce qu'elles ont comme tout citoyen le droit de travailler, *en second lieu* parce qu'il y a une demande importante de main d'œuvre qualifiée. *D'ailleurs* dans certains des secteurs concernés, les femmes nouvellement qualifiées sont plus nombreuses que leurs homologues masculins; *et d'un autre côté*, parce que leurs performances au travail sont meilleures lorsqu'elles jouissent d'une sécurité d'esprit par rapport à leurs enfants.**
> We must provide working women with adequate structures (assistance) in caring for their children; first because, like every member of society, they have a right to work, and second because there is a substantial demand for a qualified labour force. Moreover, in certain of the sectors in question there is a greater number of recently qualified women than men; also, their performance is better when they have peace of mind with regard to their children's welfare.

(b) Impersonal verbs followed by expressions indicating that the discussion is to continue are useful means of structuring what you want to say or write (see **46**):

Il y a un *autre problème à résoudre avant de clore* les débats:
There is another problem to be resolved before the discussion ends:

Il faut maintenant *aborder le premier point* de l'ordre du jour:
We must now turn to the first item on the agenda:

Il convient d'évoquer un deuxième aspect de ce programme qui pourrait nous être utile.
It is appropriate at this point to raise another aspect of the programme which might be useful to us.

(c) **Pour** + infinitive may also be used, for example, to introduce a response:

Pour répondre à votre question, je ferai deux remarques:
In answer to your question, I shall make two comments:

or to return to a point, perhaps after a digression:

Pour en revenir au problème qui nous préoccupe, je voudrais proposer la solution suivante:
To return to the problem under discussion, I should like to propose the following solution:

(d) Finally, first person plural imperatives are often used to change the subject (see **44.2**):

Si vous le voulez bien, *passons au* point suivant car le temps passe.
If you have no objection, let us turn to the following point because time is pressing.

Vous avez évoqué vos qualifications; *venons-en* maintenant *à* votre expérience professionnelle.
You have discussed your qualifications; can we turn now to your professional experience.

or to return to the point:

Excusez-moi de cette interruption . . . maintenant, *revenons à nos moutons.*
I apologize for interrupting . . . now, could we return to the matter in hand.

Cette remarque sur les immigrés est intéressante mais *ne perdons pas de vue notre sujet* qui est la population active dans son ensemble.
That comment on immigrants is interesting, but let's not lose sight of our topic – the working population as a whole.

74.3 Ending

(a) When concluding a speech or a written text, it is often necessary – indeed advisable – to sum up the main points covered. In order to announce your intention to do so, you may ask direct questions:

Quelle vue d'ensemble peut-on maintenant dégager de la structure de l'Union Européenne et de son ordre juridique?
What then is the general conclusion concerning the structure of the European Union and its legal system(s)?

In conclusions, direct questions are also used to open up the debate and suggest further points to be explored:

> **Le revenu minimum d'insertion. *Quelle va être son efficacité?***
> Income support? How effective will it be?

> **Dans les cinquante ans qui viennent, la pression à l'émigration du Sud va être extrêmement forte:** *est-ce une menace ou une chance à saisir?* **Les deux à la fois probablement.**
> During the next fifty years, emigration pressure from the South will be immense: does this pose a threat or is it an opportunity? Probably both.

(b) It is not uncommon to find a noun followed by a colon. In the following example, **certitudes . . .:** is used to indicate a summing up of the various points in the conclusion:

> **Deux certitudes pour la population française au siècle prochain: elle sera plus âgée et sa part dans la population mondiale sera réduite.**
> Two facts about population (trends) in France in the next century: the number of elderly people will be greater, and in terms of numbers it will form a smaller proportion of the world population.

(c) The conditional tense is often used in the conclusion:

> **Plutôt que de l'emploi, il *faudrait*, on l'a vu tout au long de ce livre, parler des emplois.**
> As we have seen throughout the book it would be better to talk of jobs rather than employment.

and sometimes the conditional is used in combination with structures referring back to preceding argumentation, for example, **dans ces conditions, pour ces motifs:**

> ***Dans ces ces conditions*, il *conviendrait*/il *y aurait lieu* d'entamer des poursuites contre le transporteur des marchandises.**
> In the circumstances, it would be appropriate/there are grounds for taking legal action against the carrier.

The impersonal form **il serait** (or equivalent) + adjectives such as **opportun, utile, nécessaire, indispensable, souhaitable de** + infinitive is also useful here, in particular for making recommendations:

> **Pour toutes ces raisons, *il serait opportun de* ne pas *porter* jugement trop hâtif sur la question.**
> For all of these reasons it would be advisable not to pass too hasty a judgment on the matter.

(d) In a written report, you can use dashes, with noun phrases or infinitives, in order to recap and/or make recommendations as clearly as possible:

> **Cet accident met en évidence la nécessité:**
> **– *d'un effort de* sensibilisation aux risques du personnel employé**
> **– *d'une révision des* consignes de sécurité**
> **– *d'un contrôle* accru *du* personnel au moment du relèvement des équipes.**

Note the changes when changing from noun phrases to infinitives:

> Cet accident met en évidence la nécessité:
> – *de* mieux *sensibiliser* le personnel employé aux risques
> – *de réviser* les consignes de sécurité
> – *de* mieux *contrôler* le personnel au moment du relèvement des équipes.

> The English equivalent would probably use infinitives:
> The accident highlights the need to
> – improve safety-consciousness among personnel
> – keep safety instructions up-to-date
> – improve supervision of personnel during shift changeovers.

The following is another example of the use of dashes to structure the information:

> Ainsi, sans porter l'affaire devant un service de contentieux, et compte tenu
> – *d'une part de la* qualité des services de M. Dupuis
> – *d'autre part du* cas social présenté par la famille dont il assurait la subsistance
> il semblerait équitable de donner une suite favorable à la demande de la famille.
> So, to avoid legal proceedings, and taking into account
> – the quality of service given by M. Dupuis
> – and the case made by the family, for whose welfare he was responsible
> it would seem fair to give a sympathetic hearing to the family's request.

(e) Naturally, when drawing conclusions, you will often have recourse to adverbs expressing consequence (see **72.3d**):

> La politique de l'emploi est *ainsi* nécessairement plurielle et mixte.
> Le plus urgent est *donc* de nous préparer à cette évolution, d'aménager notre société et ses rapports avec le monde extérieur en fonction de cette nouvelle donne démographique.
> Employment policy is therefore necessarily pluralistic.
> Preparation for these changes is urgently needed, and we must adapt our society and its relations with the outside world in terms of this new demographic order.

But you may also want to dismiss *wrong* conclusions with structures such as **non pas que** + subjunctive (see **39.2.2**):

> Mais c'est bien sûr du côté de la fécondité que se joue le jeu essentiel.
> *Non pas qu'il faille* craindre de voir vieillir la pyramide des âges ou les populations du Nord perdre du poids par rapport à celles du Sud, mais simplement pour que la population française continue d'exister.
> But the crucial matter is of course the fertility rate. Our concern should not be that there is a higher proportion of elderly people nor that there is a decline in the Northern populations relative to the South, but simply that the population of France should continue to exist.

> Cela *ne veut pas* dire *pour autant qu'il faille* se désintéresser de l'évolution des variables démographiques.
>
> That does not mean however that we can ignore demographic changes.

(f) The meaning of individual words and phrases may of course indicate that they are part of a concluding remark:

- **en** + noun or noun phrase: **en résumé, en définitive, en fin de compte, en somme, en guise de conclusion** . . .
- **pour** + infinitive: **pour en finir/en terminer/conclure** . . .
- specific verbs in the future tense: **terminer** . . .

> Je *terminerai* en disant que nous courons au désastre si nous n'agissons pas rapidement.
>
> I will conclude by saying that we are courting disaster if we do not act quickly.

And there are various devices, such as the framing structure **c'est . . . que**, or the use of phrases in apposition, available to focus on the conclusion:

> Et *c'est* sur ce terrain – la capacité à mobiliser le potentiel humain d'un pays – *que* se jouera inévitablement la bataille mondiale de la compétitivité.
>
> And it is here on this ground – the ability of a country to mobilize its human resources – that global competition will be fought.

> *Enfin*, et *ce sera* ma *conclusion*, il est évident que ces problèmes ne sont pas près de disparaître.
>
> Finally, and this will be my conclusion, it is obvious that these problems are not about to disappear.

(g) At the *very* end, punctuation or direct questions (see **74.3a**) may be used for 'finishing effect':

> A ce jeu, la majorité des Français pourraient bien se retrouver floués . . .
>
> In this, the majority of French people could well find themselves to be the losers . . .

> Ne conviendrait-il pas d'inverser le propos et d'essayer de savoir pourquoi les couples aujourd'hui font encore des enfants afin de comprendre ce qui peut les motiver à en faire encore demain?
>
> Would it not be better to look at the matter the other way round and try to establish why couples today continue to have children in order to understand what will motivate them to have children in the future?

And in speech, thanking is often in order, in particular with **remercier de** + infinitive or noun:

> Je vous *remercie d'avoir répondu à* mes questions.
>
> Thank you for answering my questions.

Nous *remercions* **le public** *de sa participation* **active.**
We would like to thank everyone present for their active participation.

Merci de votre attention.
Thank you for your attention.

Enfin! Merci!

VI
The sounds of French

Sections 75–8 contain guidelines on the sounds of French: vowels, semi-vowels and consonants. The international phonetic alphabet, in square brackets, is used to represent the sounds, each of which is followed by examples for practice. Sections 79–81 contain guidelines on the use of accents, liaison and elision. Dictionaries, such as the *Collins Robert French Dictionary* (2002) and the *Oxford Hachette French Dictionary* (2001) describe sounds using these conventions.

75 Vowels

[i]	ph*y*s*i*que, *il*, s*i*	[o]	le n*ô*tre, *au*x, *eau*
[e]	*et*, donn*er*, *été*, j'*ai*	[u]	t*ou*t, p*ou*rtant, geno*u*
[ɛ]	m*ai*s, p*è*re, f*ê*te, fais*ai*t	[y]	r*u*e, voul*u*, pl*u*s
[a]	p*a*rt, p*a*tte, pl*a*t	[ø]	bl*eu*, d*eu*x, cr*eu*se
[ɑ]	p*â*te, p*a*sse, b*a*s	[œ]	n*eu*f, pr*eu*ve, imm*eu*ble
[ɔ]	f*o*rt, n*o*tre, d*o*nner	[ə]	l*e*, pr*e*mier, d*e*

76 Nasal vowels

[ã]	*an*, c*en*t, t*em*ps	[ɔ̃]	s*on*, r*on*de, *om*bre
[ɛ̃]	v*in*, m*ain*, pl*ein*	[œ̃]	*un*, h*um*ble, br*un*

77 Semi-vowels/semi-consonants

[w]	*ou*i, n*oi*r, n*ou*er	[j]	p*i*ed, a*il*, fam*ill*e
[ɥ]	p*ui*ts, l*ui*, m*u*et		

78 Consonants

[b]	*b*on, ro*b*e, ru*b*an	[ʒ]	*j*e, *g*ilet, *g*êne
[d]	*d*ur, *d*eman*d*e, ai*d*e	[k]	*qu*i, sa*c*, *c*orps, ar*ch*éologue
[f]	*ph*rase, a*ff*aire, *f*raude		

[g]	*g*ant, se*c*ond, ba*gue*			
[l]	seu*l*, *l*ent, e*ll*e	[t]	*th*éâ*t*re, vi*t*e, pa*tt*e
[m]	fe*mm*e, *m*on, da*m*e	[v]	*v*ous, rê*v*e, *v*i*v*re
[n]	*n*i, auto*mn*e, to*nn*e	[z]	*z*éro, di*s*ons, di*x*ième
[p]	sou*p*e, *p*our, o*b*tenir			
[ʀ]	*r*ouge, Pa*r*is, di*r*e	[ʃ]	*ch*at, ar*ch*itecte, lâ*ch*e
[s]	le*ç*on, di*x*, *s*e, *c*e, na*t*ion	[ɲ]	a*gn*eau, vi*gn*e, pei*gn*e

---

The letters k, w, h

The letters **k** and **w** occur only in imported words: **k**ilo, **w**agon. The letter **h** is not pronounced, but a distinction is made between a mute **h**, as in **h**omme [ɔm] in which **h** is treated as a vowel, and an aspirate **h**, as in **h**aricot [aʀiko] in which **h** is treated as a consonant. This important distinction has implications for liaison and elision (see **80** and **81**).

---

79 Accents, cedilla, diaeresis

79.1 There are three accents in French: the acute (**accent aigu**), the grave (**accent grave**), and the circumflex (**accent circonflexe**).

79.2 The acute ´ is used only over an *é* as in *é*té, *é*cole. Often, it indicates that an 's' may occur in the English equivalent: *é*chapper 'escape'.

79.3 The grave ` is used over **è**, **à** and also **ù** in the word **où** 'where'. The grave may indicate that the letter **è** is in a stressed syllable: **j'espère**, 'I hope', **elles regardèrent** 'they looked at', **poète** 'poet', **manège** 'merry-go-round'. Over an **à** or **ù** the grave is used to distinguish different words: **à** (preposition), **a** (verb); **là** (adverb), **la** (definite article or pronoun); **où** (adverb or pronoun), **ou** (conjunction). It is also used in **çà et là** 'here and there', **voilà** 'there it is', **au delà de** 'beyond', **déjà** 'already'.

79.4 The circumflex ˆ can be used over any vowel: **â**me 'soul', **frêle** 'frail', **fraîche** 'fresh', **prôner** 'to advocate', **dûment** 'duly'. It may indicate that the vowel is long: **extrême** 'extreme', **grâce** 'grace'. Often it indicates the disappearance of an 's': **maître** 'master', **pâte** 'paste'. It may indicate a contraction from a Latin source word: **âme** (*anima*) 'soul', **sûr** (*securus*) 'sure, safe'. It may be used to distinguish different words: **dû** (past participle – masculine singular only – of **devoir**), **du** (partitive article), **crû** (past participle of **croître**), **cru** (past participle of **croire**). Note that the circumflex over **î** replaces the dot: **croître** 'to grow', **vînmes** 'came'.

79.5 The cedilla (**cédille**) **ç** shows that **c** is pronounced [s] before **a**, **o**, **u**: **commençâmes** [kɔmɑ̃sɑːm] 'began', **garçon** [gaʀsɔ̃] 'boy', **déçu** [desy] 'disappointed'. Compare these with the following three words where there is no cedilla: *ca*pable [kapabl] 'capable', *c*ommencer [kɔmɑ̃se] 'begin', *cu*be [kyb] 'cube'. The cedilla is never used before **e** or **i**.

79.6 The diaeresis (**tréma**), used over **ë**, **ï**, **ü** indicates that the vowel must be given full and separate pronunciation: **Noël** [nɔɛl] 'Christmas', **astéroïde** [asteʀɔid] 'asteroid'. The feminine form of adjectives ending in **-gu** (**aigu** 'sharp', **ambigu** 'ambiguous') has a diaeresis: **aiguë** to indicate that the ending should be pronounced like the masculine form: **aigu, aiguë** [egy]. Without the diaeresis the last two letters of the feminine form would be silent, as in **fatigue** [fatig] 'fatigue', **intrigue** [ɛ̃tʀig] 'intrigue'. The diaeresis replaces the dot over an **i**: **haïr** 'to hate'.

80   Liaison

80.1   Liaison is the linking of words to facilitate pronunciation. It occurs when a word begins with a vowel or a mute **h**. The final consonant of the preceding word – not normally pronounced in French – *is* pronounced and may be slightly modified in its new function of easing pronunciation: **elle est allée** [ɛlɛtale] 'she has gone'. Liaison is used only where words are closely linked in meaning and the words are spoken as a unit. It is therefore likely to occur between a pronoun and verb, adjective and noun, article and noun.

Some examples: **les enfants** [lezɑ̃fɑ̃] 'the children', **trois hommes** [tʀwazɔm] 'three men', **beaux arts** [bozaʀ] 'arts', **grand amour** [gʀɑ̃tamuʀ] 'great love', **long escalier** [lɔ̃kɛscalje] 'long staircase', **allez-vous-en** [alevuzɑ̃] 'go away'.

80.2   **Aucun, bien, combien, en, on, rien** keep their nasal sound: **on aime** [ɔ̃nɛm] 'we like', **un homme** (ɛ̃nɔm] 'a man'. But, in other cases, the final nasal **n** is pronounced as an ordinary **n**: **bon enfant** [bɔnɑ̃fɑ̃] 'good little child', **ancien élève** [ɑ̃sjɛnelɛv] 'former pupil'. Note that the nasal vowel is also pronounced as an ordinary vowel in such cases.

80.3   There is usually no liaison with an aspirate **h**: **un homard** [ɛ̃ɔmaʀ] 'a lobster', **les haricots** [leaʀiko] 'haricot beans'.

80.4   Some exceptions: there is no liaison in **vous et elle** [vueɛl] 'you and she', or in **mais oui** [mɛwi] 'yes', or in certain numbers: **les onze** [leɔ̃z] '11', **les huit** [leɥit] '8', **cent un** [sɑ̃ɛ̃] '101', **quatre-vingt-un** [katʀəvɛ̃ɛ̃] '81', and note **il est onze heures** [ilɛɔ̃zœʀ] 'it's 11 o'clock', **dix-huit** [dizɥit] '18'.

81   Elision

81.1   In written French **e** or **a** are elided, or dropped, before a word beginning with a vowel or a mute **h**, and are replaced by an apostrophe: **e** is dropped from the pronouns **je, me, te, se** and the article or pronoun **le**, and from **ce, de, ne, que**; **a** is dropped from the article or pronoun **la**.

Some examples: **j'écoute** 'I am listening', **il m'aime** 'he loves me', **va-t'en** 'go away', **il s'habille** 'he is getting dressed', **c'est moi** 'it's me', **l'homme** 'the man', **la nuit d'avant** 'the night before', **elles n'entendent jamais** 'they never hear', **la femme qu'il adore** 'the woman he loves', **l'habitude** 'the habit', **l'amie** 'the friend'. Note the exception **le onze** '11'.

81.2   The **e** is also dropped from **lorsque, puisque** and **quoique** before **il(s), elle(s), en, on, un(e)**: **lorsqu'on lui écrit** 'when we write to him/her', **quoiqu'elle y aille souvent**

'although she goes there often'. It is also dropped from **jusque** before **a, au, en, ici, où** and **alors: jusqu'ici** 'until now', **jusqu'à quelle heure** 'until when'.

81.3 There is no elision when **je, ce, le, la** follow a verb:

Aurai-*je* assez de temps pour le faire?	Will I have enough time to do it?
Est-*ce* important de le faire?	Is it important to do it?
Offrez-*le* à la dame!	Offer it to the lady.
Descendez-*la* (la valise) avant de sortir!	Bring it down before you go out.

81.4 The **i** of **si** is dropped in **s'il(s)** only: *s'il* **est là** 'if he is here', *s'ils* **nous voient** 'if they see us'.

81.5 Other words where elision occurs: **quelqu'un** 'someone', **presqu'île** 'peninsula'.

Verb tables

The following tables contain a selection of verbs from the four main conjugations (**-er, -ir, -re** and **-oir** infinitives) and some of the irregular verbs in frequent use. The principal parts of the verb included are: the present infinitive, the participles, the present, future, imperfect, past historic, perfect and conditional tenses, the imperatives, and the present tense of the subjunctive. The six parts of each of the tenses correspond to the first, second and third persons singular (**je, tu, il/elle/on**) and plural (**nous, vous, ils/elles**). The reflexive verb **s'asseoir** is given with its reflexive pronouns, and both the positive and negative forms of its imperative are included. The first and third persons of the imperfect subjunctive and the first person singular of the perfect and pluperfect subjunctive are given.

Guidelines on the formation of simple tenses are given in sections 24.2, 25, 26, 27.1, and for the formation of compound tenses, refer to the guidelines on the auxiliary verbs **avoir** (see **28.1**) and **être** (see **28.2**). Remember, once you know the simple tenses of **avoir** and **être** and the past participle of the verb you want to use, you can form any of the compound tenses. The perfect infinitive is formed by using the present infinitive of the auxiliary verb and the past participle (see **45**).

Three important points to remember:

1 Most French verbs are regular. They conform to the guidelines on formation of tenses. Nevertheless, irregular verbs are in frequent use and verb tables are provided so that students have easy access to a checklist. Most of the irregular verbs are in groups too: when you know **mettre**, for example, you also know its compounds, and knowing what happens with verbs ending in **-indre** (see **craindre**, for example, in the verb tables), means that you have all the verbs with infinitives ending in **-indre** at your fingertips.

2 Formation of the third person singular of the interrogative – and its negative forms – for all forms ending in a vowel: remember you *must* add -t- before **il**, **elle** and **on**, or use **est-ce que?**

A-t-il donné?	Has he given?	**N'a-t-elle pas écrit?**	Hasn't she written?
Va-t-on?	Are we/you/they going?	**Ne parle-t-il plus?**	Doesn't he speak any more?
Chante-t-elle?	Is she singing?	**Ne va-t-elle pas?**	Isn't she going?
Finira-t-il?	Will he finish?	**Ne répondra-t-on jamais?**	Won't we ever reply?

or

Est-ce qu'il donne?   **Est-ce qu'il ne donne pas?**

If the verb doesn't end in a vowel, then the interrogative is formed in the usual way: **prend-il?, n'aurait-elle pas?, reçoit-on?** The only exception to this is **vaincre** 'to conquer' and its more useful compound **convaincre** 'to convince': **convainc-t-il/elle/ on?**

3 There are various ways of asking questions with the first person singular. You can simply make a statement and add the intonation of a question, or you can start your question with **Est-ce que?, Qu'est-ce que?, Que?, Où?**. . . . But it is possible with a very few verbs to use inversion with **je: ai-je, dis-je?, dois-je?, sais-je?, suis-je?, vais-je?,** and note the interrogative form for **pouvoir: puis-je?**

4 For formation of the future perfect, conditional perfect, pluperfect and past anterior tenses, see **28.1, 28.2**.

INFINITIVE & PARTICIPLES	INDICATIVE			
	Present	Future	Imperfect	Past historic
avoir 'have'	ai	aurai	avais	eus
ayant, eu	as	auras	avais	eus
	a	aura	avait	eut
	avons	aurons	avions	eûmes
	avez	aurez	aviez	eûtes
	ont	auront	avaient	eurent
être 'be'	suis	serai	étais	fus
étant, été	es	seras	étais	fus
	est	sera	était	fut
	sommes	serons	étions	fûmes
	êtes	serez	étiez	fûtes
	sont	seront	étaient	furent
aller 'go'	vais	irai	allais	allai
allant, allé	vas	iras	allais	allas
	va	ira	allait	alla
	allons	irons	allions	allâmes
	allez	irez	alliez	allâtes
	vont	iront	allaient	allèrent
appeler 'call'	appelle	appellerai	appelais	appelai
appelant, appelé	appelles	appelleras	appelais	appelas
	appelle	appellera	appelait	appela
	appelons	appellerons	appelions	appelâmes
	appelez	appellerez	appeliez	appelâtes
	appellent	appelleront	appelaient	appelèrent
s'asseoir 'sit'	m'assieds	m'assiérai	m'asseyais	m'assis
s'asseyant, assis	t'assieds	t'assiéras	t'asseyais	t'assis
	s'assied	s'assiéra	s'asseyait	s'assit
	nous asseyons	nous assiérons	nous asseyions	nous assîmes
	vous asseyez	vous assiérez	vous asseyiez	vous assîtes
	s'asseyent	s'assiéront	s'asseyaient	s'assirent
boire 'drink'	bois	boirai	buvais	bus
buvant, bu	bois	boiras	buvais	bus
	boit	boira	buvait	but
	buvons	boirons	buvions	bûmes
	buvez	boirez	buviez	bûtes
	boivent	boiront	buvaient	burent
commencer 'begin'	commence	commencerai	commençais	commençai
commençant, commencé	commences	commenceras	commençais	commenças
	commence	commencera	commençait	commença
	commençons	commencerons	commencions	commençâme
	commencez	commencerez	commenciez	commençâtes
	commencent	commenceront	commençaient	commencèren

	CONDITIONAL	IMPERATIVE	SUBJUNCTIVE	
erfect			**Present**	
i eu	aurais	aie	aie	**Imperfect**
s eu	aurais	ayons	aies	eusse, eût
eu	aurait	ayez	ait	**Perfect**
vons eu	aurions		ayons	aie eu
vez eu	auriez		ayez	**Pluperfect**
nt eu	auraient		aient	eusse eu
i été	serais	sois	sois	**Imperfect**
s été	serais	soyons	sois	fusse, fût
été	serait	soyez	soit	**Perfect**
vons été	serions		soyons	aie été
vez été	seriez		soyez	**Pluperfect**
nt été	seraient		soient	eusse été
uis allé(e)	irais	va	aille	**Imperfect**
s allé(e)	irais	allons	ailles	allasse, allât
st allé(e)	irait	allez	aille	**Perfect**
ommes allé(e)s	irions		allions	sois allé(e)
tes allé(e)(s)	iriez		alliez	**Pluperfect**
ont allé(e)s	iraient		aillent	fusse allé(e)
i appelé	appellerais	appelle	appelle	**Imperfect**
s appelé	appellerais	appelons	appelles	appelasse, appelât
appelé	appellerait	appelez	appelle	**Perfect**
vons appelé	appellerions		appelions	aie appelé
vez appelé	appelleriez		appeliez	**Pluperfect**
nt appelé	appelleraient		appellent	eusse appelé
ne suis assis(e)	m'assiérais	assieds-toi	m'asseye	**Imperfect**
'es assis(e)	t'assiérais	asseyons-nous	t'asseyes	m'assisse, s'assît
'est assis(e)	s'assiérait	asseyez-vous	s'asseye	**Perfect**
ous sommes assis(es)	nous assiérions	ne t'assieds pas	nous asseyions	me sois assis(e)
ous êtes assis(e)/(es)	vous assiériez	ne nous asseyons pas	vous asseyiez	**Pluperfect**
e sont assis(es)	s'assiéraient	ne vous asseyez pas	s'asseyent	me fusse assis(e)
i bu	boirais	bois	boive	**Imperfect**
s bu	boirais	buvons	boives	busse, bût
bu	boirait	buvez	boive	**Perfect**
vons bu	boirions		buvions	aie bu
vez bu	boiriez		buviez	**Pluperfect**
nt bu	boiraient		boivent	eusse bu
i commencé	commencerais	commence	commence	**Imperfect**
s commencé	commencerais	commençons	commences	commençasse,
commencé	commencerait	commencez	commence	commençât
vons commencé	commencerions		commencions	**Perfect**
vez commencé	commenceriez		commenciez	aie commencé
ont commencé	commenceraient		commencent	**Pluperfect**
				eusse commencé

INFINITIVE & PARTICIPLES	INDICATIVE			
	Present	Future	Imperfect	Past historic
conduire 'lead' conduisant, conduit	conduis conduis conduit conduisons conduisez conduisent	conduirai conduiras conduira conduirons conduirez conduiront	conduisais conduisais conduisait conduisions conduisiez conduisaient	conduisis conduisis conduisit conduisîmes conduisîtes conduisirent
connaître 'know' connaissant, connu	connais connais connaît connaissons connaissez connaissent	connaîtrai connaîtras connaîtra connaîtrons connaîtrez connaîtront	connaissais connaissais connaissait connaissions connaissiez connaissaient	connus connus connut connûmes connûtes connurent
construire 'build' construisant, construit	construis construis construit construisons construisez construisent	construirai construiras construira construirons construirez construiront	construisais construisais construisait construisions construisiez construisaient	construisis construisis construisit construisîmes construisîtes construisirent
courir 'run' courant, couru	cours cours court courons courez courent	courrai courras courra courrons courrez courront	courais courais courait courions couriez couraient	courus courus courut courûmes courûtes coururent
craindre 'fear' craignant, craint	crains crains craint craignons craignez craignent	craindrai craindras craindra craindrons craindrez craindront	craignais craignais craignait craignions craigniez craignaient	craignis craignis craignit craignîmes craignîtes craignirent
croire 'believe' croyant, cru	crois crois croit croyons croyez croient	croirai croiras croira croirons croirez croiront	croyais croyais croyait croyions croyiez croyaient	crus crus crut crûmes crûtes crurent
devoir 'have to, owe' devant, dû (due, dus, dues)	dois dois doit devons devez doivent	devrai devras devra devrons devrez devront	devais devais devait devions deviez devaient	dus dus dut dûmes dûtes durent
dire 'say, tell' disant, dit	dis dis dit disons dites disent	dirai diras dira dirons direz diront	disais disais disait disions disiez disaient	dis dis dit dîmes dîtes dirent

	CONDITIONAL	IMPERATIVE	SUBJUNCTIVE	
Perfect			Present	
ai conduit	conduirais	conduis	conduise	**Imperfect**
as conduit	conduirais	conduisons	conduises	conduisisse, conduisît
a conduit	conduirait	conduisez	conduise	**Perfect**
avons conduit	conduirions		conduisions	aie conduit
avez conduit	conduiriez		conduisiez	**Pluperfect**
ont conduit	conduiraient		conduisent	eusse conduit
ai connu	connaîtrais	connais	connaisse	**Imperfect**
as connu	connaîtrais	connaissons	connaisses	connusse, connût
a connu	connaîtrait	connaissez	connaisse	**Perfect**
avons connu	connaîtrions		connaissions	aie connu
avez connu	connaîtriez		connaissiez	**Pluperfect**
ont connu	connaîtraient		connaissent	eusse connu
ai construit	construirais	construis	construise	**Imperfect**
as construit	construirais	construisons	construises	construisisse, construisît
a construit	construirait	construisez	construise	**Perfect**
avons construit	construirions		construisions	aie construit
avez construit	construiriez		construisiez	**Pluperfect**
ont construit	construiraient		construisent	eusse construit
ai couru	courrais	cours	coure	**Imperfect**
as couru	courrais	courons	coures	courusse, courût
a couru	courrait	courez	coure	**Perfect**
avons couru	courrions		courions	aie couru
avez couru	courriez		couriez	**Pluperfect**
ont couru	courraient		courent	eusse couru
ai craint	craindrais	crains	craigne	**Imperfect**
as craint	craindrais	craignons	craignes	craignisse, craignît
a craint	craindrait	craignez	craigne	**Perfect**
avons craint	craindrions		craignions	aie craint
avez craint	craindriez		craigniez	**Pluperfect**
ont craint	craindraient		craignent	eusse craint
ai cru	croirais	crois	croie	**Imperfect**
as cru	croirais	croyons	croies	crusse, crût
a cru	croirait	croyez	croie	**Perfect**
avons cru	croirions		croyions	aie cru
avez cru	croiriez		croyiez	**Pluperfect**
ont cru	croiraient		croient	eusse cru
ai dû	devrais	dois	doive	**Imperfect**
as dû	devrais	devons	doives	dusse, dût
a dû	devrait	devez	doive	**Perfect**
avons dû	devrions		devions	aie dû
avez dû	devriez		deviez	**Pluperfect**
ont dû	devraient		doivent	eusse dû
ai dit	dirais	dis	dise	**Imperfect**
as dit	dirais	disons	dises	disse, dît
a dit	dirait	dites	dise	**Perfect**
avons dit	dirions		disions	aie dit
avez dit	diriez		disiez	**Pluperfect**
ont dit	diraient		disent	eusse dit

INFINITIVE & PARTICIPLES	INDICATIVE			
	Present	**Future**	**Imperfect**	**Past historic**
dormir 'sleep' dormant, dormi	dors	dormirai	dormais	dormis
	dors	dormiras	dormais	dormis
	dort	dormira	dormait	dormit
	dormons	dormirons	dormions	dormîmes
	dormez	dormirez	dormiez	dormîtes
	dorment	dormiront	dormaient	dormirent
écrire 'write' écrivant, écrit	écris	écrirai	écrivais	écrivis
	écris	écriras	écrivais	écrivis
	écrit	écrira	écrivait	écrivit
	écrivons	écrirons	écrivions	écrivîmes
	écrivez	écrirez	écriviez	écrivîtes
	écrivent	écriront	écrivaient	écrivirent
envoyer 'send' envoyant, envoyé	envoie	enverrai	envoyais	envoyai
	envoies	enverras	envoyais	envoyas
	envoie	enverra	envoyait	envoya
	envoyons	enverrons	envoyions	envoyâmes
	envoyez	enverrez	envoyiez	envoyâtes
	envoient	enverront	envoyaient	envoyèrent
espérer 'hope' espérant, espéré	espère	espérerai	espérais	espérai
	espères	espéreras	espérais	espéras
	espère	espérera	espérait	espéra
	espérons	espérerons	espérions	espérâmes
	espérez	espérerez	espériez	espérâtes
	espèrent	espéreront	espéraient	espérèrent
essayer 'try' essayant, essayé	essaye	essayerai	essayais	essayai
	essayes	essayeras	essayais	essayas
	essaye	essayera	essayait	essaya
	essayons	essayerons	essayions	essayâmes
	essayez	essayerez	essayiez	essayâtes
	essayent	essayeront	essayaient	essayèrent
faire 'do, make' faisant, fait	fais	ferai	faisais	fis
	fais	feras	faisais	fis
	fait	fera	faisait	fit
	faisons	ferons	faisions	fîmes
	faites	ferez	faisiez	fîtes
	font	feront	faisaient	firent
falloir 'must' fallu	il faut	il faudra	fallait	il fallut
fermer 'shut' fermant, fermé	ferme	fermerai	fermais	fermai
	fermes	fermeras	fermais	fermas
	ferme	fermera	fermait	ferma
	fermons	fermerons	fermions	fermâmes
	fermez	fermerez	fermiez	fermâtes
	ferment	fermeront	fermaient	fermèrent

	CONDITIONAL	IMPERATIVE	SUBJUNCTIVE	
Perfect			Present	
ai dormi	dormirais	dors	dorme	**Imperfect**
as dormi	dormirais	dormons	dormes	dormisse, dormît
a dormi	dormirait	dormez	dorme	**Perfect**
avons dormi	dormirions		dormions	aie dormi
avez dormi	dormiriez		dormiez	**Pluperfect**
ont dormi	dormiraient		dorment	eusse dormi
ai écrit	écrirais	écris	écrive	**Imperfect**
as écrit	écrirais	écrivons	écrives	écrivisse, écrivît
a écrit	écrirait	écrivez	écrive	**Perfect**
avons écrit	écririons		écrivions	aie écrit
avez écrit	écririez		écriviez	**Pluperfect**
ont écrit	écriraient		écrivent	eusse écrit
ai envoyé	enverrais	envoie	envoie	**Imperfect**
as envoyé	enverrais	envoyons	envoies	envoyasse, envoyât
a envoyé	enverrait	envoyez	envoie	**Perfect**
avons envoyé	enverrions		envoyions	aie envoyé
avez envoyé	enverriez		envoyiez	**Pluperfect**
ont envoyé	enverraient		envoient	eusse envoyé
ai espéré	espérerais	espère	espère	**Imperfect**
as espéré	espérerais	espérons	espères	espérasse, espérât
a espéré	espérerait	espérez	espère	**Perfect**
avons espéré	espérerions		espérions	aie espéré
avez espéré	espéreriez		espériez	**Pluperfect**
ont espéré	espéreraient		espèrent	eusse espéré
ai essayé	essayerais	essaye	essaye	**Imperfect**
as essayé	essayerais	essayons	essayes	essayasse, essayât
a essayé	essayerait	essayez	essaye	**Perfect**
avons essayé	essayerions		essayions	aie essayé
avez essayé	essayeriez		essayiez	**Pluperfect**
ont essayé	essayeraient		essayent	eusse essayé
ai fait	ferais	fais	fasse	**Imperfect**
as fait	ferais	faisons	fasses	fisse, fît
a fait	ferait	faites	fasse	**Perfect**
avons fait	ferions		fassions	aie fait
avez fait	feriez		fassiez	**Pluperfect**
ont fait	feraient		fassent	eusse fait
il a fallu	il faudrait		il faille	**Imperfect**
				il fallût
				Perfect
				il ait fallu
				Pluperfect
				il eût fallu
ai fermé	fermerais	ferme	ferme	**Imperfect**
as fermé	fermerais	fermons	fermes	fermasse, fermât
a fermé	fermerait	fermez	ferme	**Perfect**
avons fermé	fermerions		fermions	aie fermé
avez fermé	fermeriez		fermiez	**Pluperfect**
ont fermé	fermeraient		ferment	eusse fermé

VERB TABLES

INFINITIVE & PARTICIPLES	INDICATIVE			
	Present	Future	Imperfect	Past historic
fournir 'provide' fournissant, fourni	fournis fournis fournit fournissons fournissez fournissent	fournirai fourniras fournira fournirons fournirez fourniront	fournissais fournissais fournissait fournissions fournissiez fournissaient	fournis fournis fournit fournîmes fournîtes fournirent
lire 'read' lisant, lu	lis lis lit lisons lisez lisent	lirai liras lira lirons lirez liront	lisais lisais lisait lisions lisiez lisaient	lus lus lut lûmes lûtes lurent
manger 'eat' mangeant, mangé	mange manges mange mangeons mangez mangent	mangerai mangeras mangera mangerons mangerez mangeront	mangeais mangeais mangeait mangions mangiez mangeaient	mangeai mangeas mangea mangeâmes mangeâtes mangèrent
mettre 'put' mettant, mis	mets mets met mettons mettez mettent	mettrai mettras mettra mettrons mettrez mettront	mettais mettais mettait mettions mettiez mettaient	mis mis mit mîmes mîtes mirent
ouvrir 'open' ouvrant, ouvert	ouvre ouvres ouvre ouvrons ouvrez ouvrent	ouvrirai ouvriras ouvrira ouvrirons ouvrirez ouvriront	ouvrais ouvrais ouvrait ouvrions ouvriez ouvraient	ouvris ouvris ouvrit ouvrîmes ouvrîtes ouvrirent
paraître 'appear' paraissant, paru	parais parais paraît paraissons paraissez paraissent	paraîtrai paraîtras paraîtra paraîtrons paraîtrez paraîtront	paraissais paraissais paraissait paraissions paraissiez paraissaient	parus parus parut parûmes parûtes parurent
partir 'leave' partant, parti	pars pars part partons partez partent	partirai partiras partira partirons partirez partiront	partais partais partait partions partiez partaient	partis partis partit partîmes partîtes partirent
perdre 'lose' perdant, perdu	perds perds perd perdons perdez perdent	perdrai perdras perdra perdrons perdrez perdront	perdais perdais perdait perdions perdiez perdaient	perdis perdis perdit perdîmes perdîtes perdirent

	CONDITIONAL	IMPERATIVE	SUBJUNCTIVE	
Perfect			**Present**	
ai fourni	fournirais	fournis	fournisse	**Imperfect**
as fourni	fournirais	fournissons	fournisses	fournisse, fournît
a fourni	fournirait	fournissez	fournisse	**Perfect**
avons fourni	fournirions		fournissions	aie fourni
avez fourni	fourniriez		fournissiez	**Pluperfect**
ont fourni	fourniraient		fournissent	eusse fourni
ai lu	lirais	lis	lise	**Imperfect**
as lu	lirais	lisons	lises	lusse, lût
a lu	lirait	lisez	lise	**Perfect**
avons lu	lirions		lisions	aie lu
avez lu	liriez		lisiez	**Pluperfect**
ont lu	liraient		lisent	eusse lu
ai mangé	mangerais	mange	mange	**Imperfect**
as mangé	mangerais	mangeons	manges	mangeasse, mangeât
a mangé	mangerait	mangez	mange	**Perfect**
avons mangé	mangerions		mangions	aie mangé
avez mangé	mangeriez		mangiez	**Pluperfect**
ont mangé	mangeraient		mangent	eusse mangé
ai mis	mettrais	mets	mette	**Imperfect**
as mis	mettrais	mettons	mettes	misse, mît
a mis	mettrait	mettez	mette	**Perfect**
avons mis	mettrions		mettions	aie mis
avez mis	mettriez		mettiez	**Pluperfect**
ont mis	mettraient		mettent	eusse mis
ai ouvert	ouvrirais	ouvre	ouvre	**Imperfect**
as ouvert	ouvrirais	ouvrons	ouvres	ouvrisse, ouvrît
a ouvert	ouvrirait	ouvrez	ouvre	**Perfect**
avons ouvert	ouvririons		ouvrions	aie ouvert
avez ouvert	ouvririez		ouvriez	**Pluperfect**
ont ouvert	ouvriraient		ouvrent	eusse ouvert
ai paru	paraîtrais	parais	paraisse	**Imperfect**
as paru	paraîtrais	paraissons	paraisses	parusse, parût
a paru	paraîtrait	paraissez	paraisse	**Perfect**
avons paru	paraîtrions		paraissions	aie paru
avez paru	paraîtriez		paraissiez	**Pluperfect**
ont paru	paraîtraient		paraissent	eusse paru
suis parti(e)	partirais	pars	parte	**Imperfect**
es parti(e)	partirais	partons	partes	partisse, partît
est parti(e)	partirait	partez	parte	**Perfect**
sommes parti(e)s	partirions		partions	sois parti(e)
êtes parti(e)(s)	partiriez		partiez	**Pluperfect**
sont parti(e)s	partiraient		partent	fusse parti(e)
ai perdu	perdrais	perds	perde	**Imperfect**
as perdu	perdrais	perdons	perdes	perdisse, perdît
a perdu	perdrait	perdez	perde	**Perfect**
avons perdu	perdrions		perdions	aie perdu
avez perdu	perdriez		perdiez	**Pluperfect**
ont perdu	perdraient		perdent	eusse perdu

INFINITIVE & PARTICIPLES	INDICATIVE			
	Present	Future	Imperfect	Past historic
plaire 'please' plaisant, plu	plais plais plaît plaisons plaisez plaisent	plairai plairas plaira plairons plairez plairont	plaisais plaisais plaisait plaisions plaisiez plaisaient	plus plus plut plûmes plûtes plurent
pleuvoir 'rain' pleuvant, plu	il pleut	il pleuvra	il pleuvait	il plut
pouvoir 'can, be able' pouvant, pu	peux, puis peux peut pouvons pouvez peuvent	pourrai pourras pourra pourrons pourrez pourront	pouvais pouvais pouvait pouvions pouviez pouvaient	pus pus put pûmes pûtes purent
prendre 'take' prenant, pris	prends prends prend prenons prenez prennent	prendrai prendras prendra prendrons prendrez prendront	prenais prenais prenait prenions preniez prenaient	pris pris prit prîmes prîtes prirent
recevoir 'receive' recevant, reçu	reçois reçois reçoit recevons recevez reçoivent	recevrai recevras recevra recevrons recevrez recevront	recevais recevais recevait recevions receviez recevaient	reçus reçus reçut reçûmes reçûtes reçurent
rendre 'give back' rendant, rendu	rends rends rend rendons rendez rendent	rendrai rendras rendra rendrons rendrez rendront	rendais rendais rendait rendions rendiez rendaient	rendis rendis rendit rendîmes rendîtes rendirent
répondre 'reply' répondant, répondu	réponds réponds répond répondons répondez répondent	répondrai répondras répondra répondrons répondrez répondront	répondais répondais répondait répondions répondiez répondaient	répondis répondis répondit répondîmes répondîtes répondirent
savoir 'know' sachant, su	sais sais sait savons savez savent	saurai sauras saura saurons saurez sauront	savais savais savait savions saviez savaient	sus sus sut sûmes sûtes surent

	CONDITIONAL	IMPERATIVE	SUBJUNCTIVE	
Perfect			**Present**	
ai plu	plairais	plais	plaise	**Imperfect**
as plu	plairais	plaisons	plaises	plusse, plût
a plu	plairait	plaisez	plaise	**Perfect**
avons plu	plairions		plaisions	aie plu
avez plu	plairiez		plaisiez	**Pluperfect**
ont plu	plairaient		plaisent	eusse plu
il a plu	il pleuvrait		il pleuve	**Imperfect**
				il plût
				Perfect
				il ait plu
				Pluperfect
				il eût plu
ai pu	pourrais		puisse	**Imperfect**
as pu	pourrais		puisses	pusse, pût
a pu	pourrait		puisse	**Perfect**
avons pu	pourrions		puissions	aie pu
avez pu	pourriez		puissiez	**Pluperfect**
ont pu	pourraient		puissent	eusse pu
ai pris	prendrais	prends	prenne	**Imperfect**
as pris	prendrais	prenons	prennes	prisse, prît
a pris	prendrait	prenez	prenne	**Perfect**
avons pris	prendrions		prenions	aie pris
avez pris	prendriez		preniez	**Pluperfect**
ont pris	prendraient		prennent	eusse pris
ai reçu	recevrais	reçois	reçoive	**Imperfect**
as reçu	recevrais	recevons	reçoives	reçusse, reçût
a reçu	recevrait	recevez	reçoive	**Perfect**
avons reçu	recevrions		recevions	aie reçu
avez reçu	recevriez		receviez	**Pluperfect**
ont reçu	recevraient		reçoivent	eusse reçu
ai rendu	rendrais	rends	rende	**Imperfect**
as rendu	rendrais	rendons	rendes	rendisse, rendît
a rendu	rendrait	rendez	rende	**Perfect**
avons rendu	rendrions		rendions	aie rendu
avez rendu	rendriez		rendiez	**Pluperfect**
ont rendu	rendraient		rendent	eusse rendu
ai répondu	répondrais	réponds	réponde	**Imperfect**
as répondu	répondrais	répondons	répondes	répondisse, répondît
a répondu	répondrait	répondez	réponde	**Perfect**
avons répondu	répondrions		répondions	aie répondu
avez répondu	répondriez		répondiez	**Pluperfect**
ont répondu	répondraient		répondent	eusse répondu
ai su	saurais	sache	sache	**Imperfect**
as su	saurais	sachons	saches	susse, sût
a su	saurait	sachez	sache	**Perfect**
avons su	saurions		sachions	aie su
avez su	sauriez		sachiez	**Pluperfect**
ont su	sauraient		sachent	eusse su

INFINITIVE & PARTICIPLES	INDICATIVE			
	Present	Future	Imperfect	Past historic
suivre 'follow' suivant, suivi	suis suis suit suivons suivez suivent	suivrai suivras suivra suivrons suivrez suivront	suivais suivais suivait suivions suiviez suivaient	suivis suivis suivit suivîmes suivîtes suivirent
tenir 'hold' tenant, tenu	tiens tiens tient tenons tenez tiennent	tiendrai tiendras tiendra tiendrons tiendrez tiendront	tenais tenais tenait tenions teniez tenaient	tins tins tint tînmes tîntes tinrent
venir 'come' venant, venu	viens viens vient venons venez viennent	viendrai viendras viendra viendrons viendrez viendront	venais venais venait venions veniez venaient	vins vins vint vînmes vîntes vinrent
vivre 'live' vivant, vécu	vis vis vit vivons vivez vivent	vivrai vivras vivra vivrons vivrez vivront	vivais vivais vivait vivions viviez vivaient	vécus vécus vécut vécûmes vécûtes vécurent
voir 'see' voyant, vu	vois vois voit voyons voyez voient	verrai verras verra verrons verrez verront	voyais voyais voyait voyions voyiez voyaient	vis vis vit vîmes vîtes virent
vouloir 'want, wish' voulant, voulu	veux veux veut voulons voulez veulent	voudrai voudras voudra voudront voudrez voudront	voulais voulais voulait voulions vouliez voulaient	voulus voulus voulut voulûmes voulûtes voulurent

	CONDITIONAL	IMPERATIVE	SUBJUNCTIVE	
Perfect			**Present**	
ai suivi	suivrais	suis	suive	**Imperfect**
as suivi	suivrais	suivons	suives	suivisse, suivît
a suivi	suivrait	suivez	suive	**Perfect**
avons suivi	suivrions		suivions	aie suivi
avez suivi	suivriez		suiviez	**Pluperfect**
ont suivi	suivraient		suivent	eusse suivi
ai tenu	tiendrais	tiens	tienne	**Imperfect**
as tenu	tiendrais	tenons	tiennes	tinsse, tînt
a tenu	tiendrait	tenez	tienne	**Perfect**
avons tenu	tiendrions		tenions	aie tenu
avez tenu	tiendriez		teniez	**Pluperfect**
ont tenu	tiendraient		tiennent	eusse tenu
suis venu(e)	viendrais	viens	vienne	**Imperfect**
es venu(e)	viendrais	venons	viennes	vinsse, vînt
est venu(e)	viendrait	venez	vienne	**Perfect**
sommes venue(e)s	viendrions		venions	sois venu(e)
êtes venu(e)(s)	viendriez		veniez	**Pluperfect**
sont venu(e)s	viendraient		viennent	fusse venu(e)
ai vécu	vivrais	vis	vive	**Imperfect**
as vécu	vivrais	vivons	vives	vécusse, vécût
a vécu	vivrait	vivez	vive	**Perfect**
avons vécu	vivrions		vivions	aie vécu
avez vécu	vivriez		viviez	**Pluperfect**
ont vécu	vivraient		vivent	eusse vécu
ai vu	verrais	vois	voie	**Imperfect**
as vu	verrais	voyons	voies	visse, vît
a vu	verrait	voyez	voie	**Perfect**
avons vu	verrions		voyions	aie vu
avez vu	verriez		voyiez	**Pluperfect**
ont vu	verraient		voient	eusse vu
ai voulu	voudrais	veuille	veuille	**Imperfect**
as voulu	voudrais	veuillons	veuilles	voulusse, voulût
a voulu	voudrait	veuillez	veuille	**Perfect**
avons voulu	voudrions		voulions	aie voulu
avez voulu	voudriez		vouliez	**Pluperfect**
ont voulu	voudraient		veuillent	eusse voulu

Index of grammar structures and functions

References are to sections. Sections from 49 onwards refer to functions. Where items are followed by several references, these are generally ranked in terms of numbers of examples of the item in a section. In some cases, specific functions have been identified – in addition to a list of references – in order to indicate the range of functions for which a grammar structure may be used.

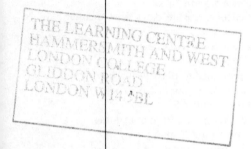